QBASIC COMMANDS QUICK REFERENCE

Shift F1	Help	ALT F	File menu
F3	Repeat last find	ALT E	Edit menu
F4	Output screen	ALT V	View menu
F5	Run	ALT S	Search menu
F6	Change window	ALT R	Run menu
F8	Step	ALT H	Help menu

BASICA AND GWBASIC COMMANDS QUICK REFERENCE

Note: Anything between <   > is required.
Anything between [   ] is optional.

Command	Parameters	What Happens
AUTO[line],[inc]	line = starting line number inc = value added to successive line numbers	Generates program line numbers automatically so you don't have to.
CLS	None	Clears the active screen and places the OK prompt in upper left corner.
DELETE[ln1],[–ln2]	ln1 = Beginning line number ln2 = Ending line number Period indicates the current line number.	Will remove the specified range of line numbers.
EDIT<line>	line = Line number to be edited	Use for editing a specific line, brings up the line and places cursor under first digit of the line number.
FILES["file"]	file = File specification to be displayed	Displays all files matching the file specification. If file specification is omitted, will display all files in current directory.
KILL<"file">	file = File specification of files(s) to be erased	Erases all files matching the given file specification.
LIST[ln1],[–ln2]	ln1 = Beginning line number ln2 = Ending line number	Will display the specified range of given line numbers.

Command	Parameters	What Happens
LLIST[ln1],[–ln2]	ln1 = Beginning line number ln2 = Ending line number	Transfers the specified range of line numbers to the printer. Having only a period prints the current line number.
LOAD<“file”>,[R]	file = File name of BASIC program R = Runs program after loading	Causes the BASIC program stored in specified file name to be loaded. The R option will run it after loading.
NAME<“old”>, AS<“new”>	“old” = Current disk file name of BASIC program “new” = New disk file name of BASIC program	Changes the file name of the BASIC program.
NEW	None	Deletes the BASIC program currently in memory.
RENUM[new#], [,[old#]][,inc#]]	new# = First line number of new line numbering sequence old# = Old line number to start new numbering sequence inc# = Difference between successive line numbers in new sequence	Renumbers a specified range of line numbers in the BASIC program. Default values are 10 for old beginning line number of new squence;current line number to start renumbering and 10 for the difference in successive line numbers of new sequence.
RUN[line]	line = Line number where program will start to run	Runs (executes) the current BASIC program from the specified line number. Default value if first line number of program.
RUN<“file”>[,R]	“file” = File name of BASIC program	Loads and runs the BASIC program specified by “file.” The R option keeps all data files open.
SAVE<“file”>[,A]	“file” = File name BASIC program is to be saved to	Saves the BASIC program to the disk in the active or specified drive. The A option saves the program as a text file (ASCII format).
SHELL	None	Allows you to go into DOS while still saving your current BASIC program in memory. Type EXIT to leave DOS and return to your BASIC program.
SYSTEM	None	Leaves BASIC and returns you to DOS.

Structured BASIC Applied to Technology

Fourth Edition

TOM ADAMSON

KENNETH C. MANSFIELD JR.
Broome Community College

JAMES L. ANTONAKOS
Broome Community College

Prentice Hall
Upper Saddle River, New Jersey   *Columbus, Ohio*

To my sisters, Cindy and Yvonne.

Kenneth C. Mansfield Jr.

To my memories of learning BASIC with my friends.

James L. Antonakos

Library of Congress Cataloging-in-Publication Data

Adamson, Thomas A.
Structured BASIC applied to technology / Tom Adamson, Kenneth C. Mansfield, James L. Antonakos. — 4th ed.
p. cm.
Includes index.
ISBN 0-13-081139-4
1. BASIC (Computer program language) 2. Structured programming. 3. Technology—Data processing. I. Mansfield, Kenneth C. II. Antonakos, James L. III. Title.
QA76.73.B3A33 2000
005.265—dc21 98-50032
CIP

Publisher: Charles E. Stewart, Jr.
Production Editor: Alexandrina Benedicto Wolf
Production Supervision: Custom Editorial Productions, Inc.
Cover Designer and Coordinator: Karrie Converse-Jones
Production Manager: Deidra M. Schwartz
Marketing Manager: Ben Leonard

This book was set in Times Roman by Custom Editorial Productions, Inc., and was printed and bound by R. R. Donnelley & Sons Company. The cover was printed by Phoenix Color Corp.

Printed in the United States of America

10 9 8 7 6 5 4 3 2 1

ISBN: 0-13-081139-4

Prentice-Hall International (UK) Limited, *London*
Prentice-Hall of Australia Pty. Limited, *Sydney*
Prentice-Hall Canada Inc., *Toronto*
Prentice-Hall Hispanoamericana, S. A., *Mexico*
Prentice-Hall of India Private Limited, *New Delhi*
Prentice-Hall of Japan, Inc., *Tokyo*
Prentice-Hall (Singapore) Pte. Ltd., *Singapore*
Editora Prentice-Hall do Brasil, Ltda., *Rio de Janeiro*

Preface

Introduction

The material in this text is appropriate for an introductory programming course in structured programming using the BASIC language. BASIC is an acronym for Beginner's All-purpose Symbolic Instruction Code; thus, students are introduced to the concept of structured programming. No prior programming experience is needed or assumed. This text is designed for technologically oriented programs at community colleges, trade and technical schools, and four-year engineering technology programs.

This text is suited to the introductory programming course because

- Each new concept is presented in the context of a required structure using the BASIC programming language.
- BASIC is an easily learned language, and is used to teach the beginning student good programming habits required by higher-level languages such as C/C++.
- Programming is presented within a consistent program structure and uses top-down design.
- The BASIC used in this text will work on any personal computer.
- All examples and problems are presented in the context of technical applications. Each area of technology is clearly defined to stimulate student interest.
- The simplest possible examples are used to illustrate new concepts. This approach prevents students from getting "bogged down" in complex mathematical or technical details that may distract them from learning the programming material.
- Practical technical applications are presented so that the student sees programming as another important tool for the solution, analysis, and design of technical problems.

Chapter Topics

Chapter 1 familiarizes students with the personal computer, showing them how to format and handle floppy disks and boot the computer. The concept of language levels is discussed.

Chapter 2 demonstrates the methods used to create a working BASIC program.

Chapter 3 illustrates how to develop structured BASIC programs. Flowcharting, subroutines, and the WHILE-WEND loop are also presented.

Chapter 4 shows how to perform mathematical calculations in BASIC. Order of operations is discussed, and comparisons using the IF-THEN statements are introduced.

Chapter 5 describes the use of branch blocks. The concept of controlling program execution through choices is illustrated.

Chapter 6 provides additional details of loop blocks. The FOR-NEXT loop is described, and nested loops are examined.

Chapter 7 demonstrates how numerical arrays are utilized in a BASIC program. Several applications are presented to illustrate this powerful data structure.

Chapter 8 shows the various string operations that are allowed by BASIC.

Chapter 9 covers the details of the BASIC graphic system. The algebra of rectangular coordinate systems is presented, along with functions to draw lines, circles, and other graphical shapes.

Chapter 10 illustrates various ways of using data files in a program. Examples of reading, writing, and processing data files are provided.

Changes and Additions for the Fourth Edition

A number of changes and additions were made to this edition.

- A section on Troubleshooting Techniques has been added to every chapter, providing useful tips and techniques for the beginning programmer.
- Situational examples have been added to introduce each chapter. Each features Ken Koder, a fictitious employee (recently graduated) working at RWA Software, a fictitious software company. The examples expose the student to real-life, on-the-job experiences as a programmer.
- A section on the Waveform Viewer Project, a book-long programming example that continually builds on new concepts, has been added to Chapters 3 to 10.
- Appendix B introduces the student to Visual BASIC programming. Enough material is presented in this new appendix to allow the students to do their programs in Visual BASIC, if so required.
- Chapters 3 and 4 have been swapped so that Structured Programming is covered first.
- Many new questions and examples have been added.

The Companion Disk

A disk containing all the BASIC programs presented in the book is included. The files are stored in separate directories related to their specific chapters. The disk contains an executable file called README.COM that explains the disk contents in detail.

Acknowledgments

We would like to thank our editor, Charles Stewart, and his assistant, Jennifer Stagman, for all their help while we were revising this book. We would also like to thank the many students and instructors who used the third edition. In addition, we would like to thank our copyeditor, Cindy Lanning, and especially Todd Tedesco, who managed the book through production.

Kenneth C. Mansfield Jr.
mansfield_k@sunybroome.edu
http://www.sunybroome.edu/~mansfield_k

James L. Antonakos
antonakos_j@sunybroome.edu
http://www.sunybroome.edu/~antonakos_j

Contents

1 Getting Started

Ken Koder, a recent graduate, was in the middle of a job interview with a local software company, RWA Software, Inc. He was applying for an entry-level position as a programmer.

Don, the senior technician at RWA Software, asked Ken, "What do you know about the personal computer?"

Ken replied, "I used them at school for most of my courses. I'm familiar with DOS and Windows, I know how to work with floppies and hard drives, and I can install new hardware and software without too much difficulty."

Ken took a sip of water and continued. "One of my instructors had our class build a computer from individual parts. It took a few classes to install all the hardware and plug in the cables. Then we partitioned and formatted the hard drive, installed a CD-ROM driver, and loaded Windows 95. It's a really nice machine."

Don was impressed. "It doesn't look like you will need any help getting started."

Objectives

After reading this chapter, you should be able to

1. Describe the major parts of a computer and their purpose.
2. Explain what a computer language is and why there are different computer languages.
3. Define structured programming and explain how such programming is important in business or technical fields.
4. Safely handle, label, and write-protect floppy disks.
5. Know the storage capabilities of computer disks.
6. Know how to set up and turn on a personal computer.
7. Perform a cold boot and a warm boot.

8. Set the system date and time.
9. Format a floppy disk and create a system disk.

Introduction

This chapter provides a short introduction to the personal computer environment. You will learn how to *boot* the personal computer, format disks, and understand the meaning of such terms as byte, DOS, and CPU. It is necessary to have a good working knowledge of the personal computer, since the BASIC programs we will be writing will be executed on the personal computer. It is important to fully understand the material presented in this chapter so that you are able to spend your time on BASIC programming instead of wondering what to do with a floppy disk.

1.1 How to Use This Text

Chapter Organization

Each chapter, with the exception of this introductory chapter, is organized as follows. Each is divided into small sections, with a review at the end of each section. At the end of each chapter, there are

1. *Troubleshooting techniques* that provide details of commonly encountered real-world programming situations.
2. *Interactive exercises* to try with your computer. They are usually short, and informative.
3. *Self-test* questions that pertain to a sample computer program. These are usually designed to assist you in practicing program "debugging."
4. *Study questions,* selected in different areas of technology, to reinforce new programming concepts presented in the chapter. You will find most of these questions to be practical as well as stimulating.

It is recommended that you first read the material in each section, then try the section review, then check your answers at the end of the book. This strategy identifies problem areas you may have and prevents you from reading new material until you have a good understanding of "old" material.

The **interactive exercises** help introduce you to structured BASIC. Don't do these exercises unless you are within three feet of your computer, as these exercises are intended for interaction!

It's a good idea to do the **self-test** as soon as you have completed reading the chapter. These tests are carefully designed to point out key features presented in the chapter. Using the test while the material is still fresh in your mind makes it fun. It also helps you retain the information longer.

Ideally, you should select the **study questions** from an area of your interest. This method may not always be possible in a classroom environment. However, you should find many questions with applications that you can use and apply to other courses or to your own needs.

Conclusion

This section does not contain a Section Review. Read on to begin learning how the personal computer operates.

1.2 How the Computer Works

This section introduces the main elements of a computer. Because microcomputers are so popular, they will be discussed here. Hopefully, the components are similar to the ones you will be using with this text.

Hardware

Computer **hardware** consists of the computer and all the physical components attached to it. Figure 1.1 shows the major elements of computer hardware: the computer itself, which

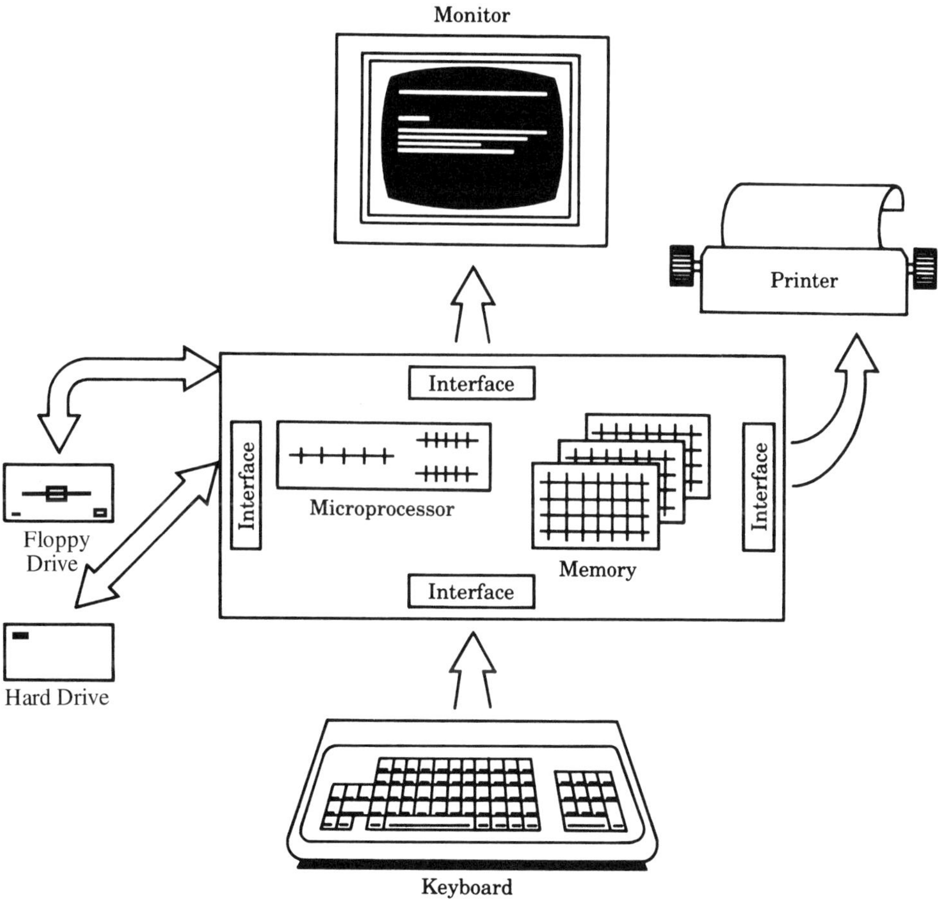

Figure 1.1 Computer Hardware

includes the **processor** and **memory;** and the **peripheral devices,** which are the **monitor** (the screen), the **keyboard** (lets you put information into the computer), the **disk drive** (where you can save your information and get information from others); and the **printer** (where you get a "hard copy"). These peripheral devices are connected to the computer through special circuits called **interfaces.**

Software

The computer **software** is a list of instructions, called a **program,** that the computer processor will perform. One kind of software is stored in the computer's **Read-Only Memory (ROM).** These programs are installed inside the computer at the factory, and you, the computer operator, cannot change them. For this reason, they are called **firmware** or **system software** programs. These programs are necessary in order to instruct the processor how to read the keyboard, how to display items on the screen, and how to operate the printer.

Applications Software

Applications software consists of instructions (programs) that are brought into the main memory from a peripheral device such as the disk drive to allow you to perform specialized tasks with the computer. These programs allow the computer to act as a word processor, spelling checker, video game, or one of many other applications.

The Processor

The **processor** for a microcomputer consists of an **integrated circuit.** This part is sometimes referred to as a **chip.** The chips shown in Figure 1.2 are called **microprocessors** because they are so small. But don't let the size fool you. These microprocessors are very fast and powerful.

The microprocessor interacts with memory and performs a series of instructions such as arithmetic and logic operations. All processors have a limited number of instructions. What makes them appear so powerful is their ability to perform these instructions quickly (millions each second).

Main Memory

The **main memory** is the region inside the computer where the processor stores information (programs and data). This memory is called **RAM,** which stands for **Random Access read-write Memory.** This definition means that, unlike ROM (where information can only be read), new information can be entered into RAM as well as read from it. Another difference is that when the computer is turned off, everything inside RAM is forgotten. So if you have information you want to save for later use, you must store what is in RAM, using the disk drive or printer, before you finish using the computer.

Disk Operating Systems

A **disk operating system (DOS)** is a program that can be loaded into the computer (usually through the disk drive) that allows you to easily work with the disk drive system. This

Figure 1.2 Typical Microprocessor Chips (Courtesy Intel Corporation)

program contains instructions to the processor on how to copy information from one disk to another, transfer information to other devices, and many other useful functions. It enables you to give a simple command, such as COPY, and have the information contained on one disk automatically copied to another. Figure 1.3 shows some of the functions performed by a disk operating system.

The Disk

The **disk** is where your BASIC programs and data will be stored. Section 1.5 of this chapter will go into much more detailed information about DOS and computer disks. As you will see, it is important to learn about some of the basic DOS commands, as well as how to care for and use computer disks. This information will be helpful to you as you begin to develop your programming skills in BASIC. Sections 1.6 and 1.7 of this chapter will give you more of the details of DOS.

Conclusion

This section introduced you to computer hardware and software. No matter what computer system you will be using, these basic concepts will apply. Test your new knowledge in the following Section Review.

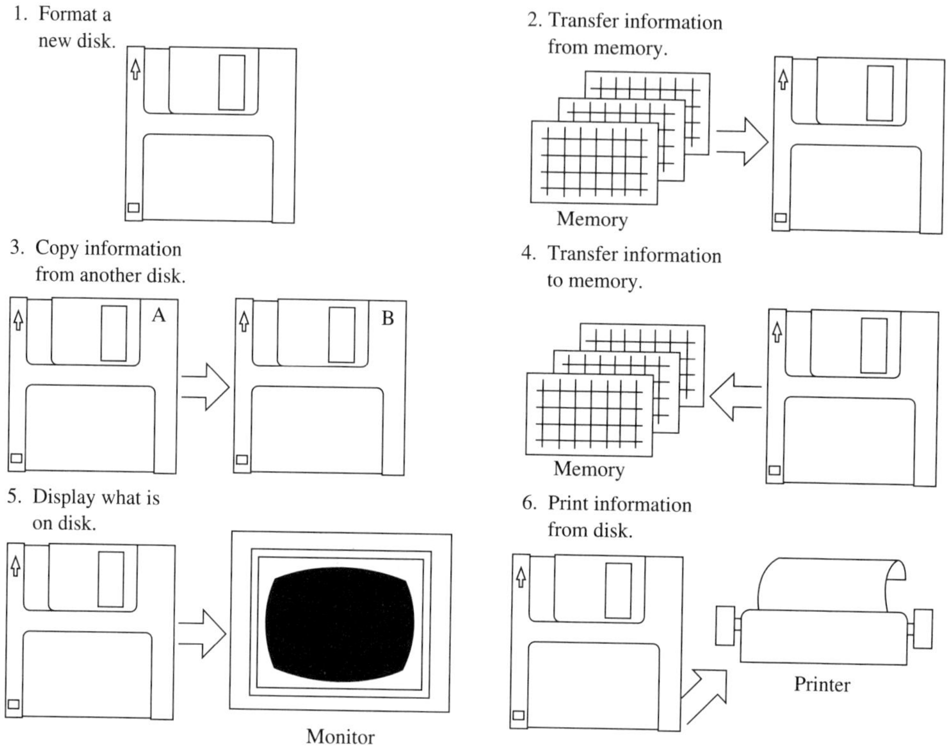

Figure 1.3 Some Functions of a Disk Operating System

1.2 Section Review

1. Describe the major parts of a computer system.
2. How do you explain the difference between hardware and software?
3. List some examples of a peripheral device.
4. Explain the purpose of application software.
5. State the difference between RAM and ROM.
6. Describe the purpose of a disk operating system.
7. State the functions that can be performed by DOS.

1.3 Computer Languages

What the Computer Understands

All computers understand only two things: **ON** and **OFF.** These ONs and OFFs are fed into the computer using a 1 for an ON and a 0 for an OFF. As an example, the sequence

```
01000011
```

is an **instruction** to the microprocessor used inside the PC that causes the microprocessor to perform addition. The instruction is written in the **binary number system.** Each 1 or 0 (on/off) is called a *bit.* Instructions are composed of unique groups of 8-bit chunks called *bytes.* The bytes for each instruction must be entered into the computer's memory before the program can be executed. This process is easy for the computer to understand, but it requires a great deal of training and practice for people. In the "old days," this is how a computer was programmed. To program a computer this way required time and patience, and is rarely done today. Instead, computer languages such as BASIC are used. These languages contain easy-to-follow instructions called statements, such as

```
BX = BX + 1
```

Computer Language

A **computer language** can be defined as a set of **characters** that form symbols and the rules for using these symbols so that the programmer and the computer can communicate. Remember that the microprocessor inside your computer understands only one computer language, the language of **1s** and **0s.** The 1/0 pattern for each instruction the microprocessor can perform is called a **machine language.** Since this is the most fundamental language understood by the computer, it is called a **low-level language.**

What People Understand

Rather than using a machine language of 1s and 0s, it would be easier to give instructions and get answers back using symbols that we already understand. The easiest set of characters that we can use is the English alphabet. It would be very easy to program if you could give an instruction to the computer such as

> Figure out my income tax for me and let me know when you're finished so I can tell you where to mail it.

Although computers can't quite yet follow those instructions, a program can be written in words that people easily understand. When the computer is programmed using symbols and letters that the operator can read, this computer language is called a **high-level language.** The language presented in this text, BASIC, is a high-level language.

Figure 1.4 illustrates the different levels of computer languages.

Language Levels

Any language that is higher in level than machine language requires a program to convert that language into machine language. For example, the next level above the 1s and 0s understood by the microprocessor is the **hexadecimal number system,** a number system containing 16 symbols: the digits 0–9 and the letters A–F. Using the hexadecimal number system, the instruction

```
01000011
```

could be entered into the computer as

```
43
```

—two keystrokes instead of eight!

Programming a computer this way is still called machine-language programming by many programmers. However, it is very difficult to write complete programs in machine language. It is easier to enter a BASIC statement, such as

```
BX = BX + 1
```

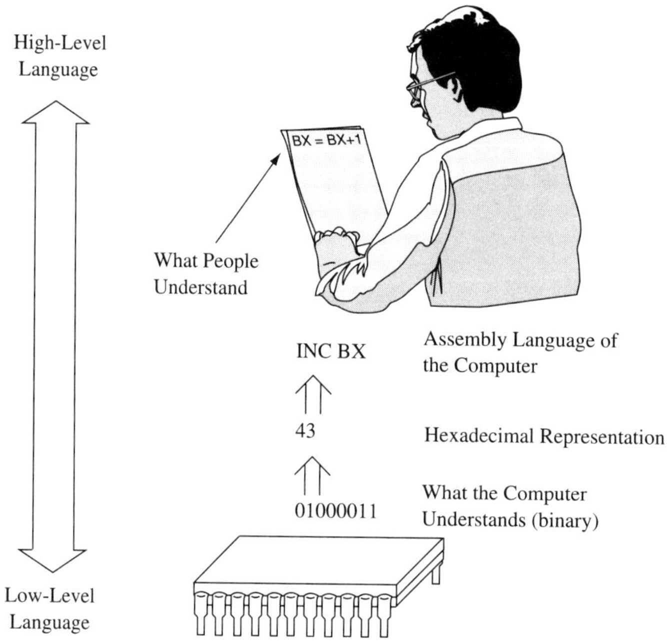

Figure 1.4 Different Levels of Computer Languages

than to try and remember the correct machine language to enter. For this reason, a special program called a **BASIC interpreter** is used to automatically convert the high-level BASIC language into the low-level machine language understood by the microprocessor. The BASIC interpreter looks at each BASIC statement and converts it into the machine language required by the microprocessor. Luckily, most desktop computers come with a BASIC interpreter. If you want to program the computer in another language, such as C or Pascal, you'll need to purchase a special program called a **compiler,** which will convert the C or Pascal statements into the 1s and 0s that the microprocessor understands. The main difference between an interpreter and a compiler is that the interpreter is used every time the program is executed, whereas the compiler is used only once, to create an *executable* machine-language program. The compiler creates an entirely new program containing only machine language. The BASIC interpreter must determine the correct machine language for every BASIC statement each time the program is executed. It is for this reason that compiled programs run much faster than interpreted programs.

The action of an interpreter is illustrated in Figure 1.5.

BASICA, GWBASIC, and QBASIC are three examples of interpreted BASIC. A package called Visual BASIC is capable of creating executable machine-language programs, and thus performs the actions of a compiler. Appendix B provides more information on Visual BASIC.

There are many different programming languages available. Table 1.1 lists some of the more common languages and their particular strengths.

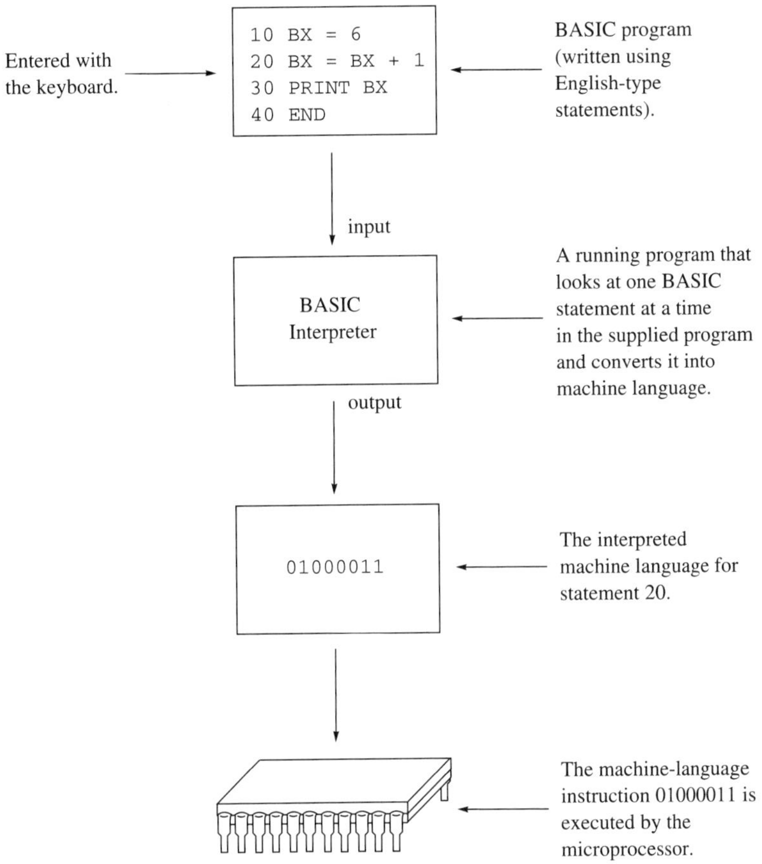

Figure 1.5 Action of an Interpreter

Table 1.1 Some Programming Languages and Their Advantages

Programming Language	Reason for Use
APL	(A Programming Language) A very powerful language for scientific work.
Assembly language	A low-level programming language that allows direct control of the microprocessor.
BASIC	Easy to learn.
COBOL	(Common Business-Oriented Language) For business-oriented programming.
LOGO	A simple programming language originally designed to teach children how to use computers.
Pascal	Teaches good programming habits.
FORTRAN	(Formula Translation) To solve mathematical formulas.
C/C++	More control over computer than other high-level languages, and built-in machine-language interface.

Conclusion

Some fundamental concepts about computer languages were presented in this section. The study of these languages is the major discipline of **computer science.** Your task will be to use structured BASIC in a manner that assists you in using and developing your technical knowledge, with an added advantage—you will be well prepared for the study of other structured languages, the type preferred by science and industry.

Test your understanding of this section by trying the following Section Review.

1.3 Section Review

1. Explain what is meant by a computer language.
2. Describe the two things that computers "understand."
3. State the name of the computer language that is used by the microprocessor in your computer.
4. Explain what is meant by language levels concerning computer languages.
5. Describe the function of an interpreter as applied to computers.
6. What is meant by a BASIC interpreter?
7. What must your computer have before it can use any high-level language?
8. Give the names of some of the most commonly used high-level languages and the reasons for their use.
9. What is the main difference between an interpreter and a compiler?

1.4 Structured Programming

Structured Versus Unstructured Programming

One of the measures of a "good" computer program is that it can be read and understood by anyone, even nonprogrammers. For example, read Program 1.1.

No one doubts what this program will do. You can even see exactly where the program is going to do what it is supposed to do. Compare that program with Program 1.2.

Program 1.1

```
100 REM Resistor Tolerance Program
110 REM
120 REM This program computes the maximum and minimum values of a resistor.
130 REM The program user must enter the values of the resistor and the
140 REM percent tolerance.
150 REM
160 REM The program will then compute and display the maximum and minimum
170 REM allowable values for the resistor.
180 REM
190 REM Variables Used:
200 REM
210 REM R  = Value of the resistor
220 REM T  = Tolerance of the resistor in percent
230 REM RM = Maximum value of the resistor
240 REM RS = Minimum value of the resistor
250 REM
```

```
300 REM Get value of resistor from program user
310 INPUT "What is the resistor value ==> "; R
320 INPUT "What is the tolerance in percent ==> "; T
330 REM End of this block
340 REM
400 REM Calculate the maximum and minimum resistance values
410 LET RM = R + (T * R) / 100: REM Compute maximum value
420 LET RS = R - (T * R) / 100: REM Compute minimum value
430 REM End of this block
440 REM
500 REM Display answers
510 PRINT "The maximum value of the resistor is "; RM; " Ohms."
520 PRINT "The minimum value of the resistor is "; RS; " Ohms."
530 REM End of this block
540 REM
600 REM End of program
610 END
```

Program 1.2

```
10 REM Input the values
20 PRINT "Value of: "
30 GOTO 100
40 RT = R1 + R2
50 GOTO 130
100 INPUT "R1";R1
110 INPUT "R2";R2
120 GOTO 40
130 PRINT RT
```

Obviously, the second program is neither easy to read nor to understand. If you know some BASIC programming, you probably figured out that the second program is simply adding two numbers and displaying the answer. If you didn't figure this out, don't worry. If you've never programmed before, you're not expected to know what it does.

Program 1.1 is an example of **structured programming.** Program 1.2 is an example of **unstructured programming.** Both programs are written in the programming language called BASIC, and the computer will have no trouble running either of the programs. A structured program is created so that it's easier for people to work with.

The Structured Program

Note that Program 1.1 explains exactly what the program is going to do. It explains the purpose of each of the variables, and breaks the program into small, paragraph-like sections. The start of each section describes what is to be accomplished. You are told when a section ends, what each computation accomplishes, and when the program ends. This is a form of structured programming that's easy for anyone to follow. You may not know the coding of the language itself (such as what REM means or why each line starts with a number), but you don't need to know anything about the programming language to understand what the program is doing and where in the program the doing gets done!

The Unstructured Program

Program 1.2 is typical of most programs written in BASIC. The program is difficult to follow, which means that it will be difficult to modify, correct, or expand on. This kind of programming is not professional, is unworkable with more involved programs, and is frowned upon by potential employers. Hence the reason for structured BASIC, and the reason for this text.

Advantages and Disadvantages of Structured Programming

The main disadvantage of structured programming for those who have been programming in their own style is that old habits die hard. If you've never programmed before, structured programming will not have major disadvantages for you.

In the past, **computer memory** was relatively expensive and limited, and it thus paid to conserve computer memory space by making programs as brief as possible. Today, when even pocket computers have more memory than many of the older, larger machines, there is no longer the necessity to be brief in programming. There is, however, the necessity to be clear in programming and to develop good programming habits that result in a completed program that is easy to understand, easy to modify, and easy to correct. That is the purpose of this book.

When you complete this text, you will be proficient in creating programs using structured BASIC, and you will be able to apply what you have learned to any structured language such as C or Pascal.

Conclusion

This section contrasted structured and unstructured programming. You will learn much more about this as well as the power of BASIC as a programming language. Test your new skills in the following Section Review.

1.4 Section Review

1. What is one measure of a good computer program?
2. Explain the main points of structured BASIC.
3. Describe the main differences between structured BASIC and unstructured BASIC.
4. What are the advantages of unstructured BASIC?
5. What are the disadvantages of structured BASIC?

1.5 Disk Details

Discussion

As a beginning student, you need to know some of the fundamentals of the computers you will be working with. You need to know this regardless of what programming language you will be using. First, you should know some more details about your computer system.

The Computer System

Figure 1.6 shows the major parts of a typical microcomputer system, similar to the kind you will be using when you begin programming in BASIC.

The main unit contains all the essential electrical circuits that make up the microcomputer. The keyboard acts as one of the main *input devices,* while the monitor acts as one of the main *output devices.* An input device allows information to be placed into the computer, whereas an output device allows information to be copied from the computer (such as copying information to the monitor screen).

Another very important input device is the disk drive. This versatile part of the computer not only can place information into the computer, it also can copy information from the computer. Since you will be using the disk drives quite often in the process of learning BASIC, you should know something about them. Many computers now come with internal CD-ROM drives and sound cards. The sound card connects to a set of stereo speakers and to the CD-ROM, allowing you to play musical CDs on your system.

Disk Drives

Four kinds of disk drives are used in microcomputers. These are

1. The hard disk drive (also called *fixed* disk)
2. The 5¼-inch floppy disk drive
3. The 3½-inch floppy disk drive
4. The CD-ROM drive

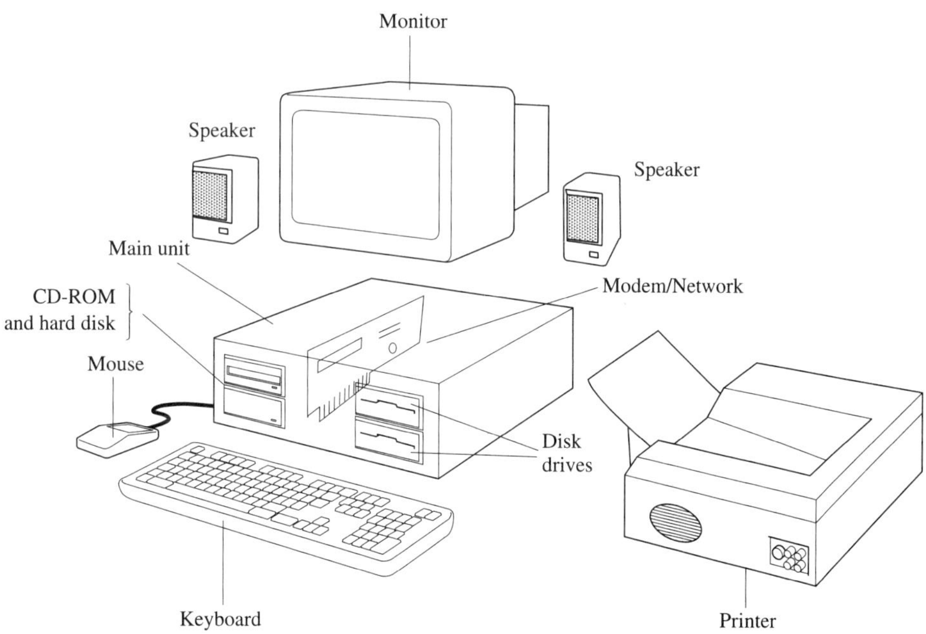

Figure 1.6 Major Parts of a Basic Microcomputer System

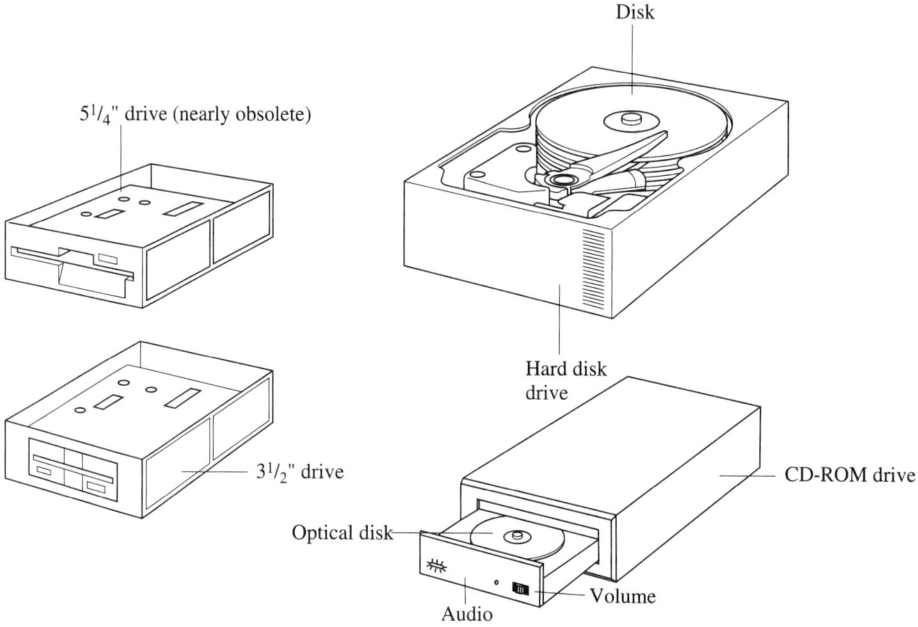

Figure 1.7 Four Types of Disk Drives

Figure 1.7 illustrates each of these different disk drives.

The location of the hard disk drive is inside the main unit of the microcomputer. The hard disk itself is not physically accessible to the computer user. (As a user, you cannot remove or insert a new hard disk; the same one always stays there.) The other three types of disk drives are also usually housed in the main unit of the microcomputer, but the user may freely insert and remove the disks used by them.

Many systems use a single hard disk drive and one or more floppy disk drives. To distinguish one disk drive from the other, they are named after the letters of the English alphabet. The hard disk drive is normally referred to as the C: drive. It is conventional to place a colon after the drive letter; doing this makes it clear that you are talking about a disk drive for the computer. You will find other important reasons for doing this, so it's a good habit to get into right away.

If one floppy disk drive is used, it is called the A: drive, and if a second floppy disk drive is used, it is called the B: drive.

Floppy Disks

Figure 1.8 shows the two most popular types of floppy disks: the 5¼-inch and the 3½-inch. Figure 1.9 shows how a 3½-inch disk is constructed.

Surprisingly, you will find that the smaller, 3½-inch floppy can generally store more information than its larger, 5¼-inch counterpart. The 3½-inch disk can store more information in a smaller physical space because the quality of its magnetic surface is higher.

You must take a few important precautions when handling floppy disks. These precautions are illustrated in Figure 1.10.

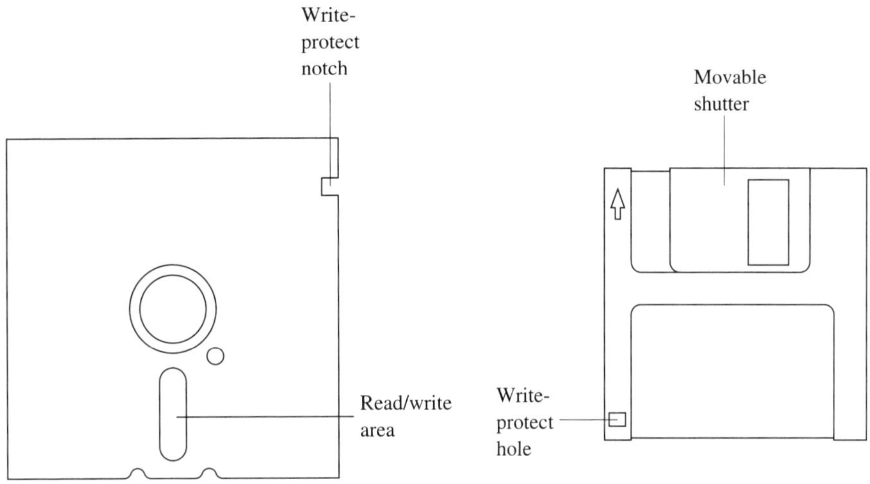

(a) $5^1/_4$" floppy disk (b) $3^1/_2$" floppy disk

Figure 1.8 Two of the Most Popular Types of Floppy Disks

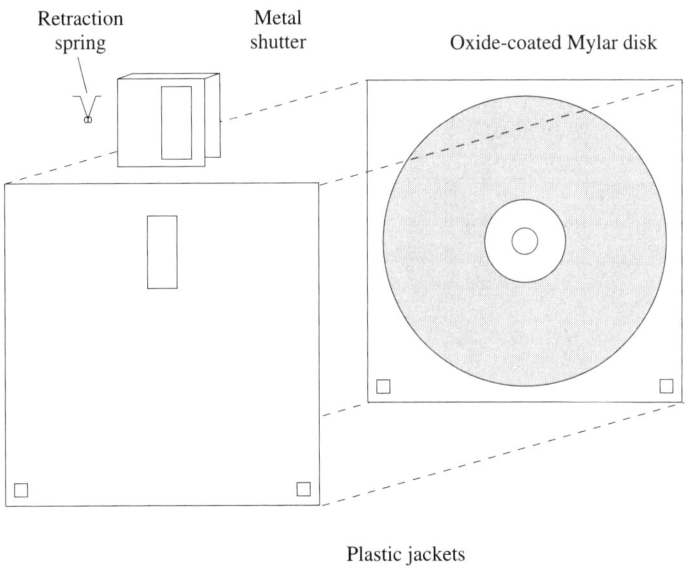

Figure 1.9 Construction of a 3½-inch Floppy Disk

Labeling Floppy Disks

It's important for you to know what is contained on floppy disks. There is a correct way to label disks. Special labels are made for both 5¼- and 3½-inch disks. These labels are designed to stick to the surface of each disk type. Figure 1.11 illustrates how to apply labels to each.

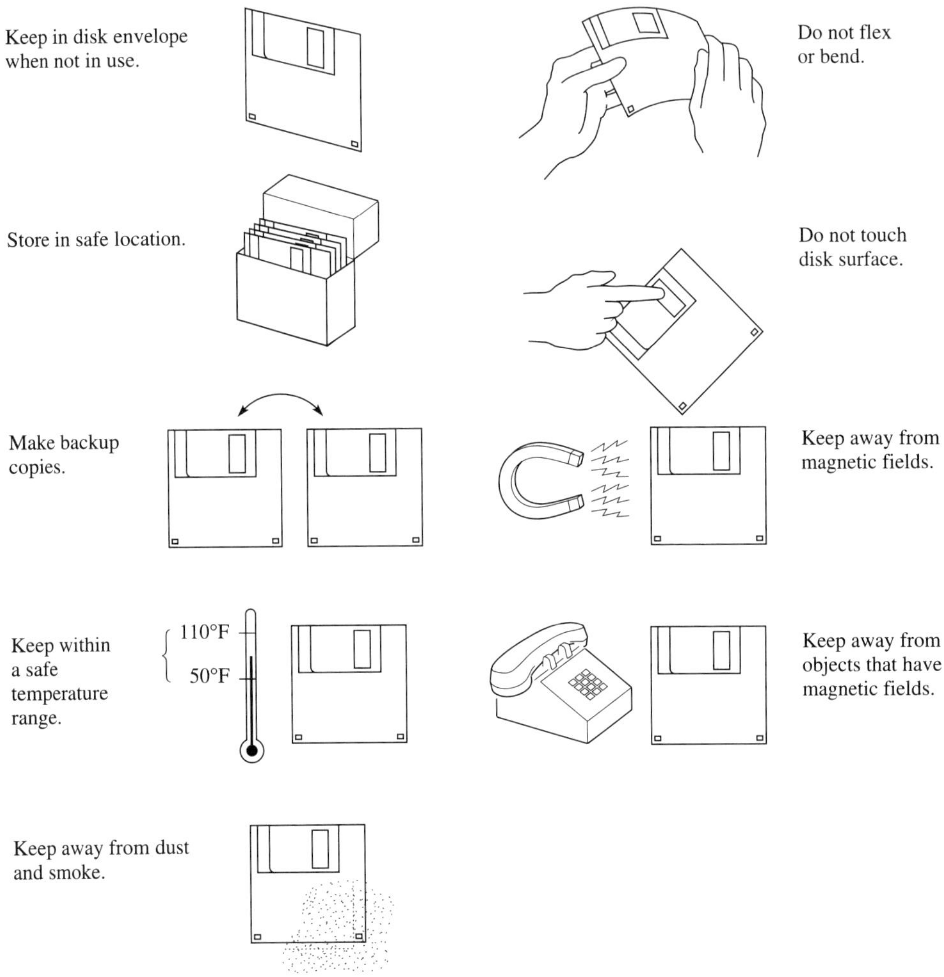

Figure 1.10 Precautions for Handling Floppy Disks

You should use labels made especially for this purpose. The labels are made so that they will not stick in a disk drive when you remove a disk. The adhesive on the label back is also made not to damage the disk surface.

Figure 1.12 shows the correct method for writing information on the disk labels.

Write-Protecting the Disks

Information placed on a floppy disk can sometimes replace existing information on the disk. To ensure that this does not happen, you can write-protect the disk. Write-protecting a disk also ensures that you do not accidentally erase information from the disk when it is being used in the system. Figure 1.13 illustrates how to write-protect both types of floppy disks.

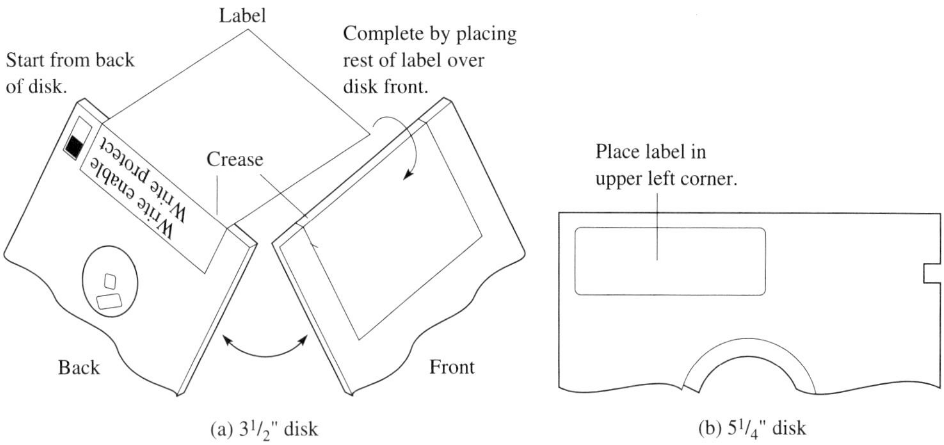

Figure 1.11 Applying Labels to Floppy Disks

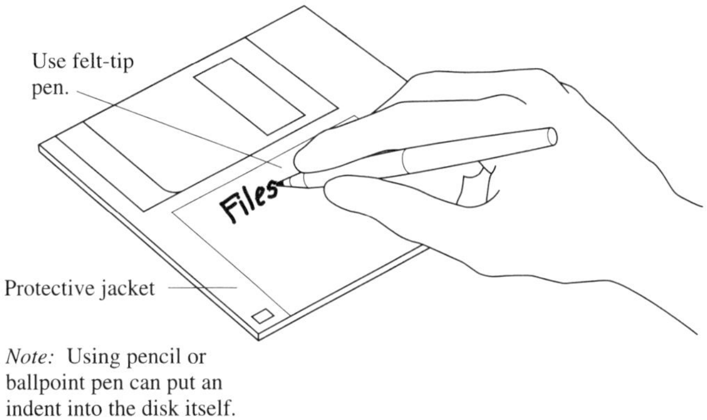

Figure 1.12 Writing Information on the Disk Labels

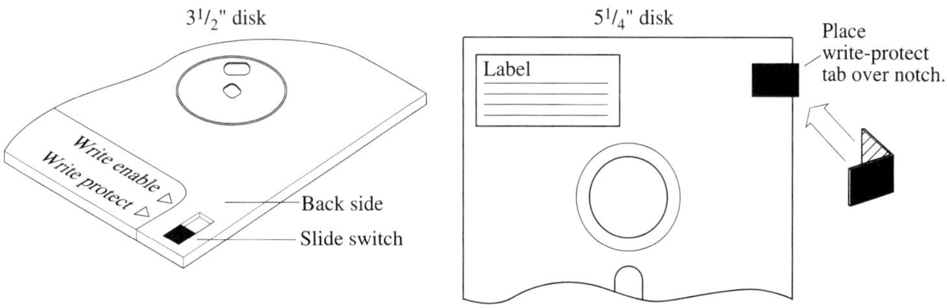

Figure 1.13 Write-Protecting the Floppy Disks

Storage Capabilities

The 5¼- and 3½-inch floppy disks have different storage capacities, as shown in Table 1.2.

A byte consists of 8 bits; a bit is the most fundamental element of computer information. The bit represents either a 1 (an electrical ON condition) or a 0 (an electrical OFF condition).

Effectively, everything gets stored on the disk as little magnetic 1s and 0s. This idea is shown in Figure 1.14.

A disk that is capable of storing 184,320 bytes is theoretically capable of storing 184,320 characters (such as letters of the alphabet). However, you will see that other information must also be placed on the disk. Just to give you some idea, a single-spaced, typed page contains about 4,000 characters, including all the spaces and punctuation marks.

The storage capacity of all disk drives is not the same. A disk drive that is capable of reading and writing only a 368,640-byte disk will also work with a lower density 184,320-byte disk, but not with the higher density 1,228,800-byte disk.

Table 1.2 Storage Capacities of Floppy Disks

Disk Type	Storage Capacity
5¼-inch	
Double-density, single-sided	184,320 bytes
Double-density, double-sided	368,640 bytes
Quad-density, double-sided	1,228,800 bytes
3½-inch	
720K disk, double-density	737,280 bytes
1.4MB disk, high-density	1,474,560 bytes

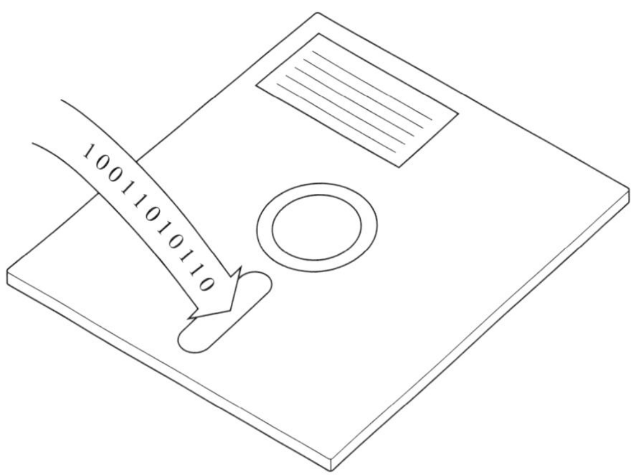

Figure 1.14 Concept of How Information Is Stored on a Disk

The obvious advantage of the larger capacity disks is that they store more information. The disadvantage is that these disks cost more, as do their corresponding disk drives.

Conclusion

This section gave you an important introduction to the various types of disk drives and disks you will be using as you learn to program in BASIC. You saw the various types of drives available, as well as different kinds of disks you may use with them. You were also shown how to care for and label your disks. Check your understanding of this section by trying the following Section Review.

1.5 Section Review

1. Name two input devices for the computer.
2. Name two output devices for the computer.
3. What is the main difference between a hard drive and a floppy disk drive?
4. What are the names of the drives of a computer with a hard drive and two floppy disk drives?
5. Generally speaking, which size of floppy disk can hold the most information: the 5¼-inch or the 3½-inch disk?

1.6 Introduction to DOS

What Is DOS?

As previously stated, DOS stands for **D**isk **O**perating **S**ystem. DOS is system software that contains instructions for your computer so it can interface not only with the disk drives but also with the monitor and the printer. It also acts as an aid to help application programs work with your computer.

There are two main manufacturers of DOS for IBM computers. One is PC-DOS, the other is MS-DOS. PC-DOS is from IBM, whereas MS-DOS is from Microsoft Corporation. For all practical purposes, both kinds of DOS are the same.

Figure 1.15 shows the relationship between DOS, your computer, and application programs.

DOS Numbering System

DOS has been improved many times over the years. Each version of DOS is followed by a numbering system consisting of two numbers separated by a decimal point, as shown below:

```
[MAJOR REVISION].[MINOR REVISION]
```

The first version of DOS appeared in 1981 and was called DOS 1.0. Table 1.3 lists the different versions of MS-DOS and some of the reasons for the changes. The version of DOS your computer is using can be displayed using the VER command.

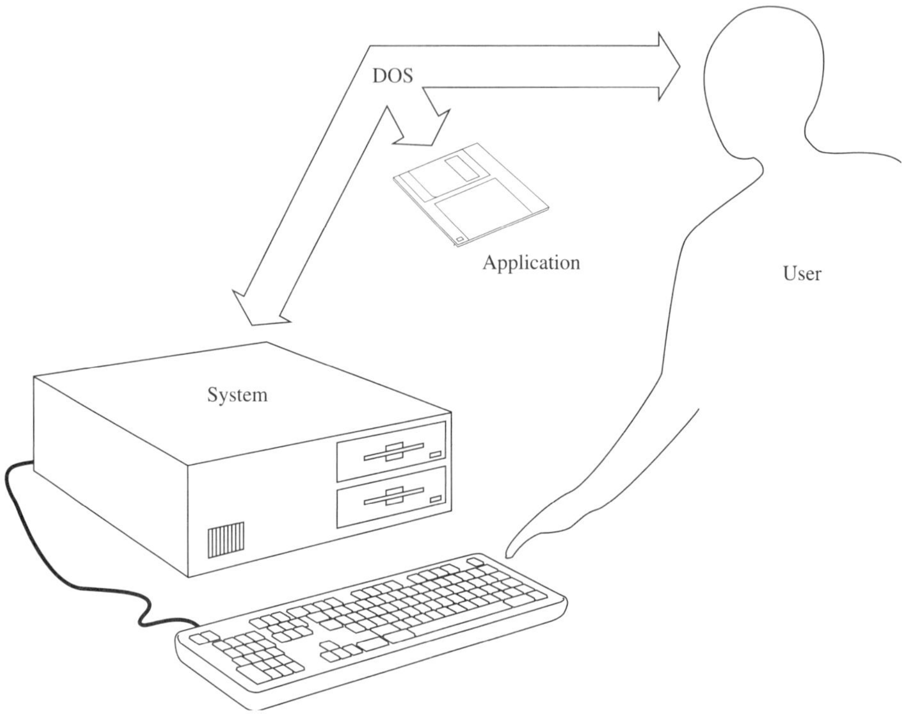

Figure 1.15 Relationship Between DOS and Other Parts of the System

Table 1.3 MS-DOS Versions and Reasons It Has Changed

Version	Year	Reason
1.0	1981	First DOS
1.25	1982	Allowed use of double-sided disks
2.0	1983	Made subdirectories possible
2.01	1983	Allowed use of international symbols
2.11	1983	Fixed errors in DOS 2.01
2.25	1983	Allowed more characters
3.0	1984	1.2MB and larger hard disk
3.1	1984	Allowed networking of PCs
3.2	1986	3½-inch floppy disk
3.3	1987	IBM PS/2 line of computers
4.0	1989	Use of menus to operate
5.0	1991	Computer memory management, new editor
6.0/6.2	1993	Disk compression, custom boot sequence, virus detection
6.22	1994	New compression technique

How DOS Gets into Your Computer

Figure 1.16 shows the two major ways DOS gets into your computer.

As shown in the figure, DOS can be automatically loaded into the computer from the hard disk when you first turn on the computer. Your computer already has a small program built into it at the factory called the basic input/output system, abbreviated BIOS. The BIOS causes the computer to look first in your floppy disk drive to see whether a disk is there that contains DOS. If there is, it will load the DOS into itself. This is called *booting* because it is like "picking yourself up by your bootstraps." In this process, the computer gets more instructions from DOS on how to get more DOS into the computer system.

If the floppy disk in your drive does not contain DOS, the computer looks at the hard drive (C: drive) for DOS. If there is no DOS in the hard drive (or no hard drive), then some computers will come up in BASIC programming mode. Others simply ask for a different disk.

How the Computer Is Set Up

Before you can operate your computer, you should know how it is "set up"—that is, how it is connected to all its different parts. As a student taking a first course in BASIC programming, you will not really need to set up the computer yourself, but you should have a general idea of what a computer setup looks like. Figure 1.17 shows the typical cable

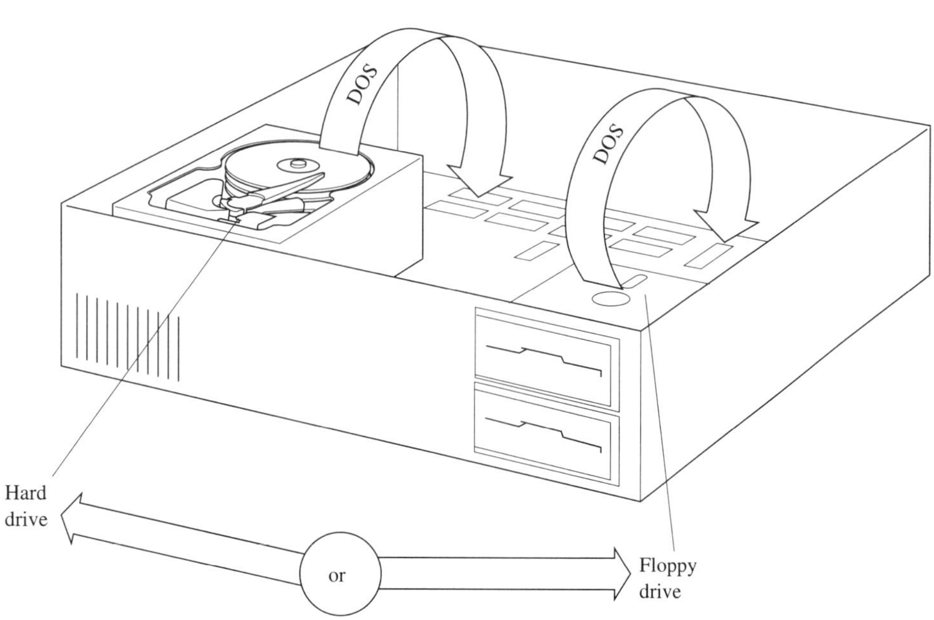

Figure 1.16 Getting DOS into Your Computer

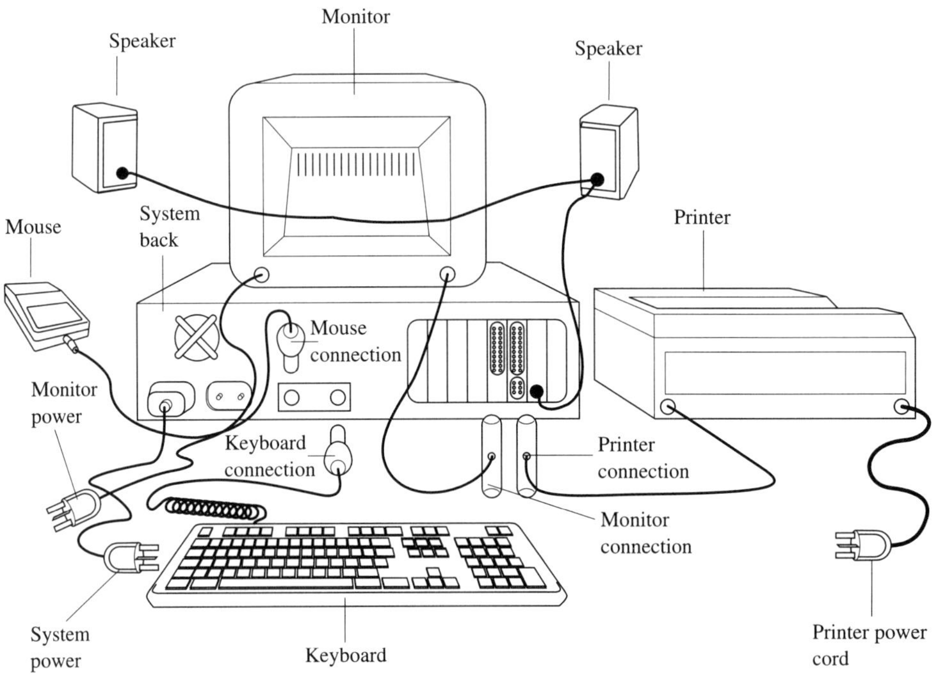

Figure 1.17 Typical IBM PC Cabling

connections for an IBM PC. The actual setup used by the computers you will be programming with may differ somewhat from what is shown in the figure.

Turning on Your System

Figure 1.18 shows a typical turn-on sequence for a microcomputer. Yours may differ slightly, but the general concepts are the same.

Conclusion

In this section you learned some important information about DOS, you learned how DOS gets into your computer, and you learned about the DOS numbering system. You also saw how a typical computer system is connected as well as a typical computer turn-on sequence. Check your understanding of this section by trying the following Section Review.

1.6 Section Review

1. What is the difference between MS-DOS and PC-DOS?
2. What version of DOS is your computer using?
3. From where does the term *booting* originate?
4. Where is the term *booting* used?
5. How does DOS normally get into the computer?

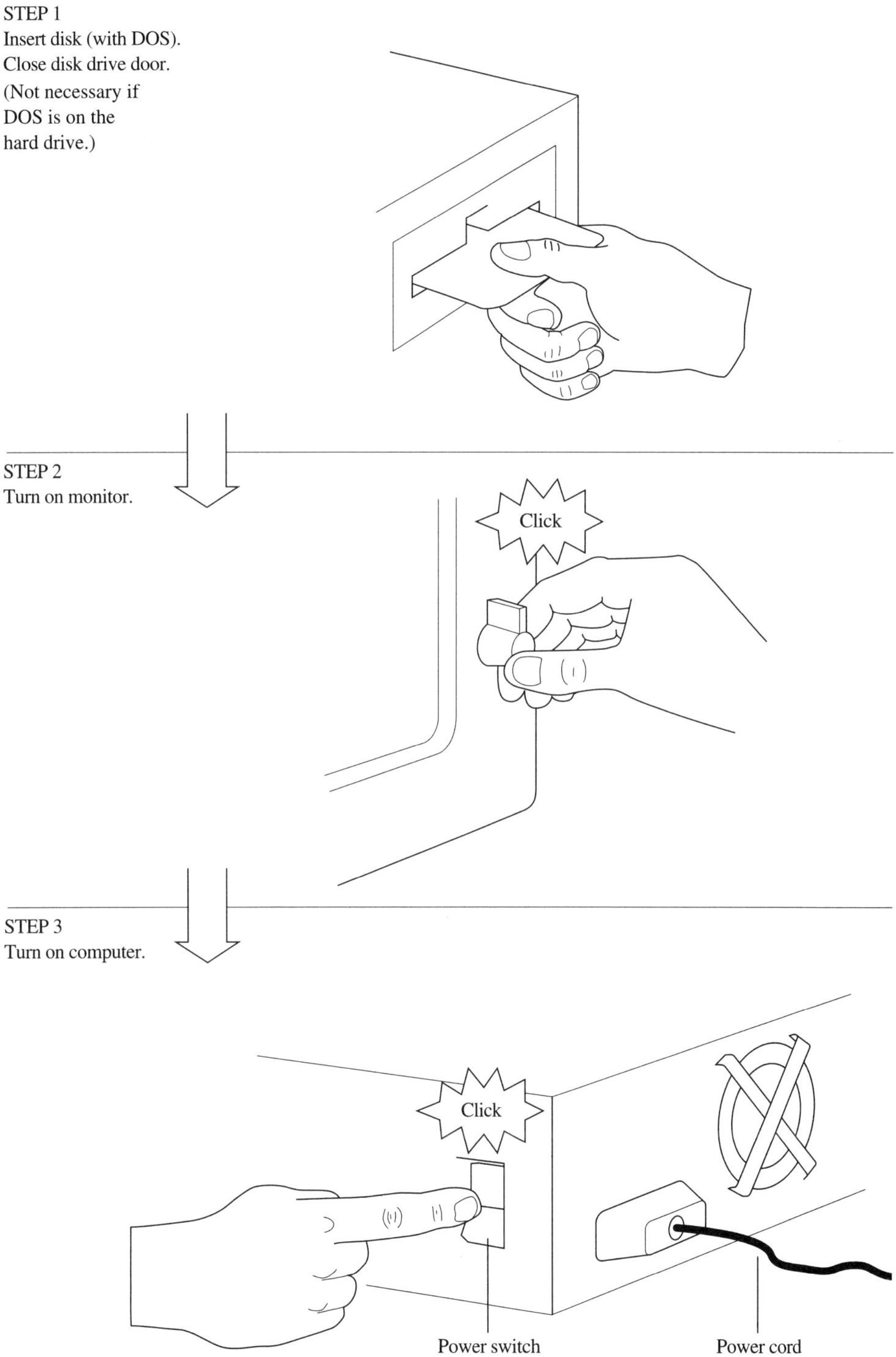

Figure 1.18 Typical Computer Turn-On Sequence

1.7 Getting Started with DOS

Booting Methods

In the last section, you learned the meaning of booting. In this section you will learn how to boot your computer (load it with DOS). There are basically two methods of booting your computer. One method is to place a floppy disk containing DOS into drive A: and turn on the power to your system. When you turn on the computer, it will go through the sequences shown in Figure 1.19.

The other method of getting DOS into your computer is to have a hard disk inside your computer and a copy of DOS on that disk.

Setting Date and Time

Once DOS is loaded into your computer, you will see the message shown in Figure 1.20.

Some computers have a system clock that is contained on a separate board and is maintained by a small battery—much the same as your digital watch. When this is available, the date and time are put in automatically. DOS itself cannot remember the date. The message shown in Figure 1.20 asks you to put the correct date into the computer. An important rule to remember when working with DOS is to always make sure your computer shows the correct date. The reason for this will be obvious shortly.

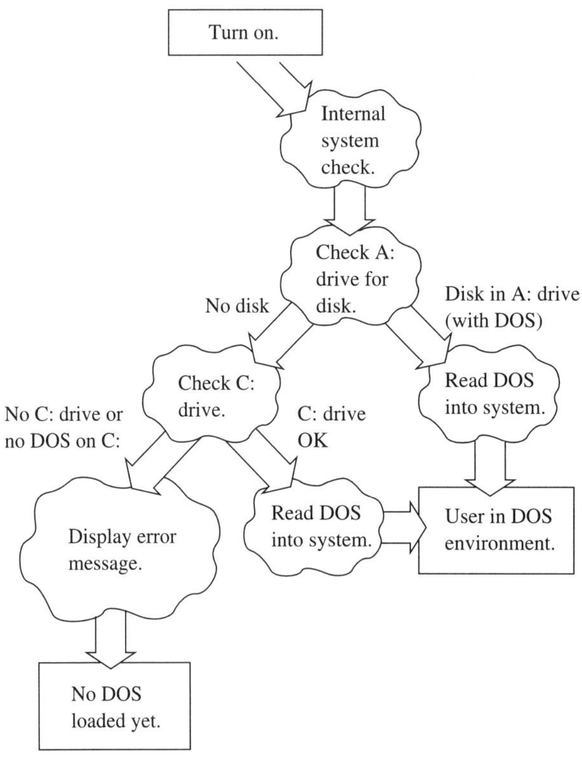

Figure 1.19 Computer Turn-On Sequence

```
Current date is Fri 5-7-99
Enter new date (mm-dd-yy):
```

Figure 1.20 First DOS Message

To enter the date, use punctuation to create any one of the following formats:

```
mm-dd-yy
mm/dd/yy
mm.dd.yy
```

where mm is the month number (1 through 12), dd is the day number (1 through 31), and yy is the last two digits of the year (00 through 99).

After correctly entering the date, press the ENTER key. To correct a mistake, simply use the BACKSPACE key to delete the incorrect input and start over again.

After you enter the date, DOS asks for the correct time, as shown in Figure 1.21. The format for entering time is

```
HH:MM:SS:hh
```

where HH is the hour (expressed in military time; e.g., 1:00 P.M. is written as 13:00), MM the minutes, SS the seconds, and hh the hundredth second. You need enter only the hour and minute, then press RETURN. For example, if it is 3:15 P.M., you enter

```
15:15
```

When you press the ENTER key, you are returning control of the computer to the computer. Newer versions of DOS allow an "a" or "p" to be placed at the end of the time input to specify A.M. or P.M.

DOS Prompt

After entering the correct date and time, you see a message similar to the one shown in Figure 1.22.

You will see the DOS prompt, such as

```
A>
```

The A means that disk drive A: is active. The greater-than sign (>) is the symbol DOS uses to mean that the control of the computer has been turned over to you and that you are in the DOS environment. DOS is waiting for you to enter a command.

```
Current time is 04:12:28.25
Enter new time:
```

Figure 1.21 Second DOS Message

```
Microsoft (R) MS-DOS (R) Version 6.2
(C) Copyright Microsoft Corp 1981-93.

A>
```

Figure 1.22 DOS Message and Prompt

Remember, a colon after the DOS prompt is used to emphasize a disk drive. To change the DOS prompt—that is, to make a different disk drive active—simply type the drive letter followed by the colon, as in

```
B: <ENTER>     Note: <ENTER> means press the ENTER key.
```

Assuming that you have a second floppy disk drive, this will cause drive B: to become the active drive, and the DOS prompt will change to B:. Similarly, typing C: will change the active drive to the C: drive.

Changing the Date and Time

Table 1.4 shows two DOS commands for changing the date and the time.

Figure 1.23 shows the action of these two DOS commands.

Resetting the Computer

Resetting the computer is the process of restarting DOS in its initial state. Doing this automatically clears out your BASIC programs in memory. There are two methods of doing this. One is called a *cold boot,* the other is a *warm boot.* To do a cold boot if there is no

Table 1.4 DOS DATE and TIME Commands

Command	Action
DATE	Allows you to change the date.
TIME	Allows you to change the time.

```
Current date is Fri 5-7-99
Enter new date (mm-dd-yy):
```

(a) Date

```
Current time is 14:27:36.14
Enter new time:
```

(b) Time

Figure 1.23 Action of DATE and TIME Commands

hard drive or DOS on the hard drive, place the DOS disk in drive A:, turn the system off, wait a few seconds, and then turn the system back on. To do the other method, a warm boot, start with the system already on and press the CTRL, ALT, and DEL keys on your keyboard all at the same time.

Formatting a Disk

When you buy a new floppy disk, it has no software on it. The manufacturer of the disk has no way of knowing what brand of computer you will be using. You must **format** the disk before you can use it on your system. Formatting does the following things to your disk:

- Erases any and all programs that may be on the disk.
- Places invisible (to you) tracks on the disk to get it ready to receive other programs.
- Puts some of its own programs on the disk for use by DOS.

Note that if you format a disk that already has programs on it, you will lose all of those programs, *forever!*

The basic DOS command for formatting a disk is

```
FORMAT [d:]
```

where [d:] is the drive that contains the disk you want to format. You must have the DOS disk in the active drive. The reason for this is that the FORMAT program is contained on the DOS disk. When you issue the FORMAT command, the computer looks for a disk in the active drive and then looks for the DOS FORMAT program on that disk. If it doesn't find these, you get an error message and the process does not continue. If you have a hard drive with DOS on it and the computer has been properly set up, the FORMAT program is taken from the hard drive automatically when you ask for it.

Figure 1.24 shows the process of formatting a disk in drive A:.

For a computer with a hard drive that contains DOS, simply place the disk to be formatted in the A: drive and use the format command FORMAT A:. Then follow the instructions shown on the monitor. Never, never format the hard drive (the C: drive). If you do, you will remove all the information from the hard drive. If you do this with a school computer, formatting the C: drive will also deprive other students of using the programs (including DOS) placed on this drive. Remember, *don't format the C: drive!*

DOS offers you many different options to use when formatting a disk. For example, if you want DOS to make your newly formatted disk bootable, you must enter the following:

```
FORMAT A: /S
```

The /S extension tells DOS to place certain programs on your disk (including DOS) so that the newly formatted disk can now be used to boot your system.

Conclusion

In this section you learned about different booting methods as well as how to set the date and time. You read some important information about the DOS prompt and about what it means, as well as some specific commands for formatting the disk. Check your understanding of this section by trying the following Section Review.

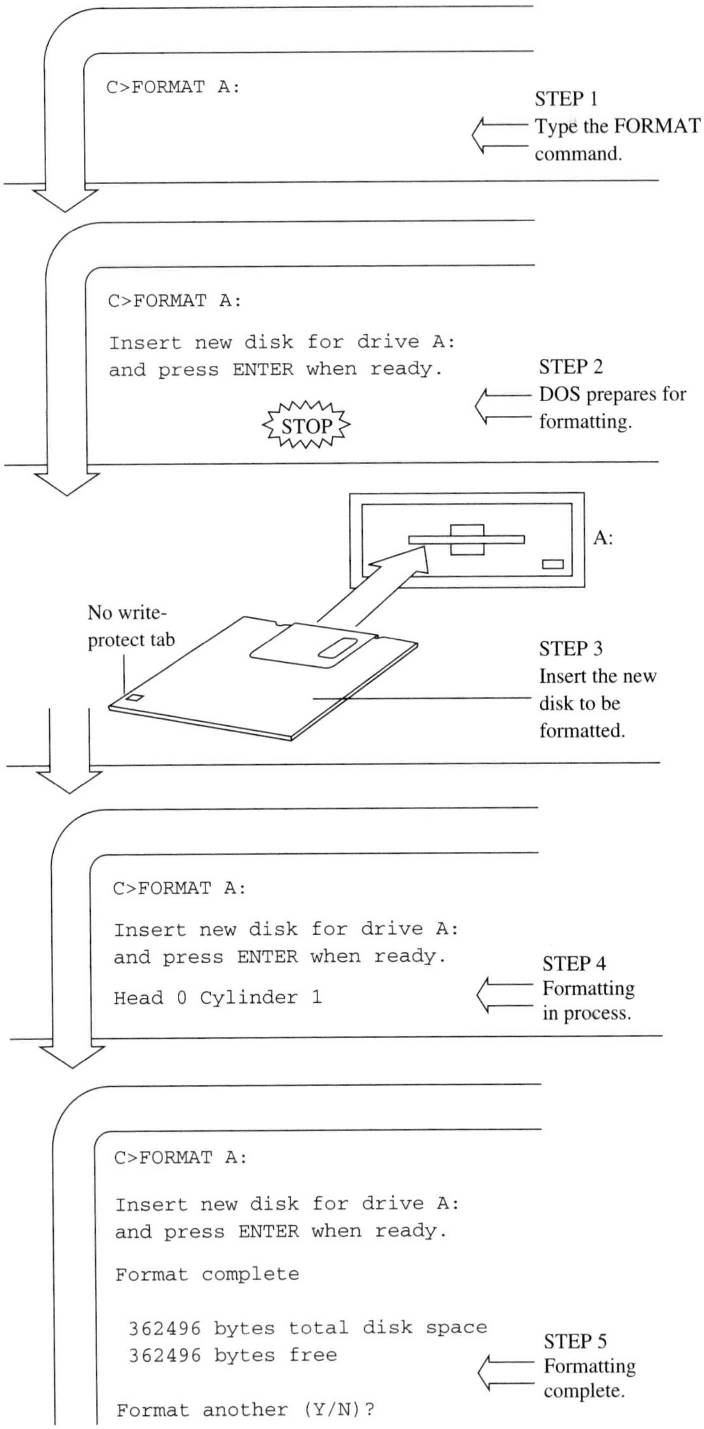

Figure 1.24 Formatting a Disk in Drive A:

1.7 **Section Review**

1. What is the purpose of the DOS DATE command?
2. What is the purpose of the DOS TIME command?
   This lxkgj
3. What does the DOS prompt A> mean?
4. What are the two methods of resetting the computer? What are they called?
5. How do you make your formatted disk bootable?

1.8 Troubleshooting Techniques

Everyone needs to know how to work with a computer. The more you use one, the more prepared you will be to face the problems that all users face at some time or another. For example, the most important thing you can do for yourself as a new BASIC programmer is to learn how to make backup copies of all of your important files. You do not want to be in the position of not having a backup file when a disaster occurs.

Keep in mind, even when you do have backup files, many other potential problems can be encountered. What do you do when one of your floppy disks cannot be read? Throw it away? The best course of action may be to try the disk in another disk drive if one is available because the alignment of the read/write heads in each disk drive may be a little different. You must be creative when dealing with any computer problems.

Conclusion

Check your understanding of this material by trying the following Section Review.

1.8 **Section Review**

1. What is one of the most important things you can do for yourself as a new BASIC programmer?
2. Describe the best course of action to take when a floppy disk cannot be read.

Interactive Exercises

DIRECTIONS

These exercises require that you have access to a computer that supports BASIC. They are provided to give you valuable experience and immediate feedback on what the concepts and commands introduced in this chapter will do.

Exercises

1. Find the brightness control on your monitor. What happens when you turn the brightness control fully counterclockwise? What happens when you turn it fully clockwise? About where do you place it for the most comfortable viewing? (***Note:*** You need to adjust this to produce the least amount of eye-strain. Proper adjustment requires sharp characters with the darkest possible background.)

2. Find the contrast control on your monitor. What happens when you turn the contrast control fully counterclockwise? What happens when you turn it fully clockwise? Where do you place it for the most comfortable viewing (meaning the least eye-strain)?
3. How many floppy disk drives does your computer have?
4. What size are these drives (3½-inch or 5¼-inch)?
5. Are these drives high- or low-density? How did you determine this?
6. Does your computer system have a hard drive?
7. If your system has a hard drive, does it contain the DOS that is loaded into the computer? How did you determine this?
8. Using one of your own floppy disks that is compatible with your computer system, format the disk so that it is now a DOS system disk. How did you do this? If you are not sure how to do this, ask for assistance.
9. Once your disk is formatted, try doing a cold boot using your disk in the A: drive. Observe whether the system is now booted from your disk and not the C: drive. If you are not sure how to determine this, ask for assistance.

Self-Test

DIRECTIONS

Program 1.3 was developed for construction technology. The information in the program could be used in the design of heating/cooling systems or in the design of a total structure. It is used to calculate the volume of a room. Answer the following questions by referring to this program.

Program 1.3

```
100 REM Room Volume Program
110 REM
120 REM Developed by:  A. Good Programmer
130 REM
140 REM This program computes the volume of a room.  The program
150 REM user must enter the values of the length, width and height.
160 REM
170 REM Variables Used:
180 REM
190 REM        L = Length of room
200 REM        W = Width of room
210 REM        H = Height of room
220 REM        V = Volume of room
230 REM
300 REM Explain program to the user
310 PRINT "This program will compute the volume of a room."
320 PRINT
330 PRINT "Simply enter the value of the room length, width and height"
340 PRINT "and I'll do the rest."
350 REM End of block
360 REM
400 REM Get the values from the user
410 PRINT "Enter the length of the room: "
420 INPUT L
430 REM
440 PRINT "Enter the width of the room: "
450 INPUT W
```

```
460 REM
470 PRINT "Enter the height of the room: "
480 INPUT H
490 REM End of block
500 REM
600 REM Do computations
610 LET V = L * W * H
620 REM End of block
630 REM
700 REM Display answers
710 PRINT
720 PRINT "The volume of the room is "; V; " units."
730 REM End of block
740 REM
800 REM End of program
810 END
```

Questions

1. Describe what Program 1.3 does.
2. In what order does Program 1.3 perform its functions?
3. List the variables that are used in the program and state the purpose of each.
4. Which line number displays the answer?
5. What is different about the INPUT statements in this program compared to Program 1.1?

Study Questions

Answer the Following Questions as Indicated

True/False

Mark the following questions with a T to indicate TRUE or an F for FALSE.

_____ 1. To do the Interactive Exercises section of each chapter, you must have access to a computer.

_____ 2. The computer **hardware** consists of the computer itself and all its physical components.

_____ 3. Computer software can be thought of as a list of instructions that the computer processor performs.

_____ 4. New information can be entered into ROM memory.

_____ 5. When the computer is turned off, all information in RAM memory is lost.

_____ 6. Machine language consists of groups of 0s and 1s.

Multiple Choice

Answer the following questions by circling the best answer.

7. DOS stands for
   a. Disk Operations and Savings.
   b. Disk Operating System.
   c. Disk Opening and Saving.
   d. None of the above is correct.
8. The purpose of DOS is to
   a. Help transfer information from the disk to memory.
   b. Run programs.

   c. Control the printer.
   d. All of the above are correct.
9. The set of characters that form symbols and the rules for using these symbols so that the programmer and computer can communicate is called a(n)
   a. Software package.
   b. DOS.
   c. Language.
   d. Interpreter.
10. The higher the level of a programming language, the easier it is for
   a. A user to read and understand.
   b. A computer to execute commands directly.
   c. The system to operate efficiently.
   d. All of the above are correct.
11. The function of a program called the **interpreter** is to
   a. Reduce the level of the programming language so that it can be understood by the microprocessor.
   b. Increase the level of the programming language so that it can be understood by the programmer.
   c. Take the place of DOS when the system is being programmed.
   d. Help the monitor, disk drives, and printer function during programming.
12. When a brand-new disk is first used, it should be
   a. Formatted.
   b. Labeled with a meaningful label.
   c. Used to boot the computer.
   d. Both a and b.

Matching

Match the DOS commands on the left to the correct action(s) stated on the right.

13. FORMAT
14. TIME
15. DATE
16. FORMAT /S
17. DOS

a. This is *not* a DOS command.
b. Creates a system disk.
c. Prepares a disk for system use.
d. Allows the system date to be changed.
e. Allows the system time to be changed.
f. None of these.

Fill in the Blank

Fill in the following blanks with the correct answer(s).

18. A program that is easy to read and understand is the goal of a(n) ____________ program.
19. When the computer is first turned on, a(n) ____________ boot is performed.
20. When you ____________ a disk, all the existing information on it is lost.
21. The hard drive is normally referred to as the ____________ drive.
22. A byte consists of ____________ bits.

Program Design

Use Program 1.1 as a guide in solving the following programming problems.

23. Write a BASIC program that converts a Celsius input temperature into Fahrenheit and then displays the new temperature.
24. Write a BASIC program to convert a distance of 15 meters into the equivalent number of feet.
25. Write a BASIC program that computes the speed of a car in miles/hour when the user supplies the distance traveled by the car and the time spent traveling.

2 Using the Computer

Ken Koder sat back in his chair on the first day on the job, thinking about how great it was to work at RWA Software. He had just returned from being introduced to each of the other employees. Everyone was very friendly toward him.

Don, the senior technician, walked through the office toward Ken's desk, carrying a box. He put it on the corner of Ken's desk and said, "Ken, here are the BASIC manuals for the system you will be working on. Start looking these over and I will be back later to tell you about your first assignment."

Ken opened the box and removed all the materials. He was surprised by the amount of information provided with the software. As he leafed through one of the manuals, he took special note about some of the memory features he was unfamiliar with. He thought to himself, "I hope I get to work on this sort of stuff." He continued looking at all of the manuals until Don reappeared.

"How about some lunch, Ken?" Don asked.

Ken replied, "Sure, all of this reading makes me hungry!"

Don noticed how neat and orderly Ken's desk was, even with all of the manuals spread out. Don continued, "When we get back, I'll show you the system."

Objectives

After reading this chapter, you should be able to

1. Back up your programs.
2. Remember important information concerning DOS files.
3. Perform the steps necessary to begin entering a BASIC program.
4. Understand the difference between a BASIC command and a BASIC statement.

5. Edit your BASIC program using various methods.
6. Save your BASIC program to the disk.
7. Get your BASIC program from the disk.
8. See what is on your disk.
9. Rename programs stored on the disk.
10. Remove programs stored on the disk.
11. Print your BASIC program.
12. Renumber program lines.
13. Save selected parts of your program to the disk.
14. Merge two BASIC programs.
15. Get into and out of DOS from BASIC.

Introduction

This chapter presents many of the foundation skills you need before you can begin programming efficiently in BASIC. You will learn how to interact with your BASIC program and the rest of the computer environment, including the floppy disk and the printer. You will also see the powerful editing features available in the BASIC environment. Learn this material well. It will help make learning BASIC more of an enjoyment and less of a chore.

2.1 Working with Your Disks

Backing up Your Disk

At times you will find it necessary to make backup copies of programs on a disk. Remember that purchased software is copyrighted and the legal owner of the software is usually allowed to make one backup copy to keep in case the original gets damaged. It is illegal to make copies of software to avoid or reduce the purchase price without express written permission of the software manufacturer.

To make a copy of a disk on a dual-drive system, follow the procedure shown in Figure 2.1.

To copy a disk on a single-drive system, the user is asked repeatedly to switch the disk in the drive from source to target and back again until the copying is complete.

The DOS DISKCOPY command is for the purpose of making backup copies of original disks. You should not use original disks on a daily basis; instead, you should run your programs from the backup copies.

Internal and External DOS Commands

When you boot DOS into your system, many commands are placed within your computer, including DATE and TIME. This means that when you enter the command DATE, your computer, through its internal DOS, will immediately respond to this command. Because DOS has placed this command inside your computer (and it will stay there until you turn your computer off), it is called an internal DOS command. What this means is that you do not need the DOS disk in any of your disk drives to use an internal command.

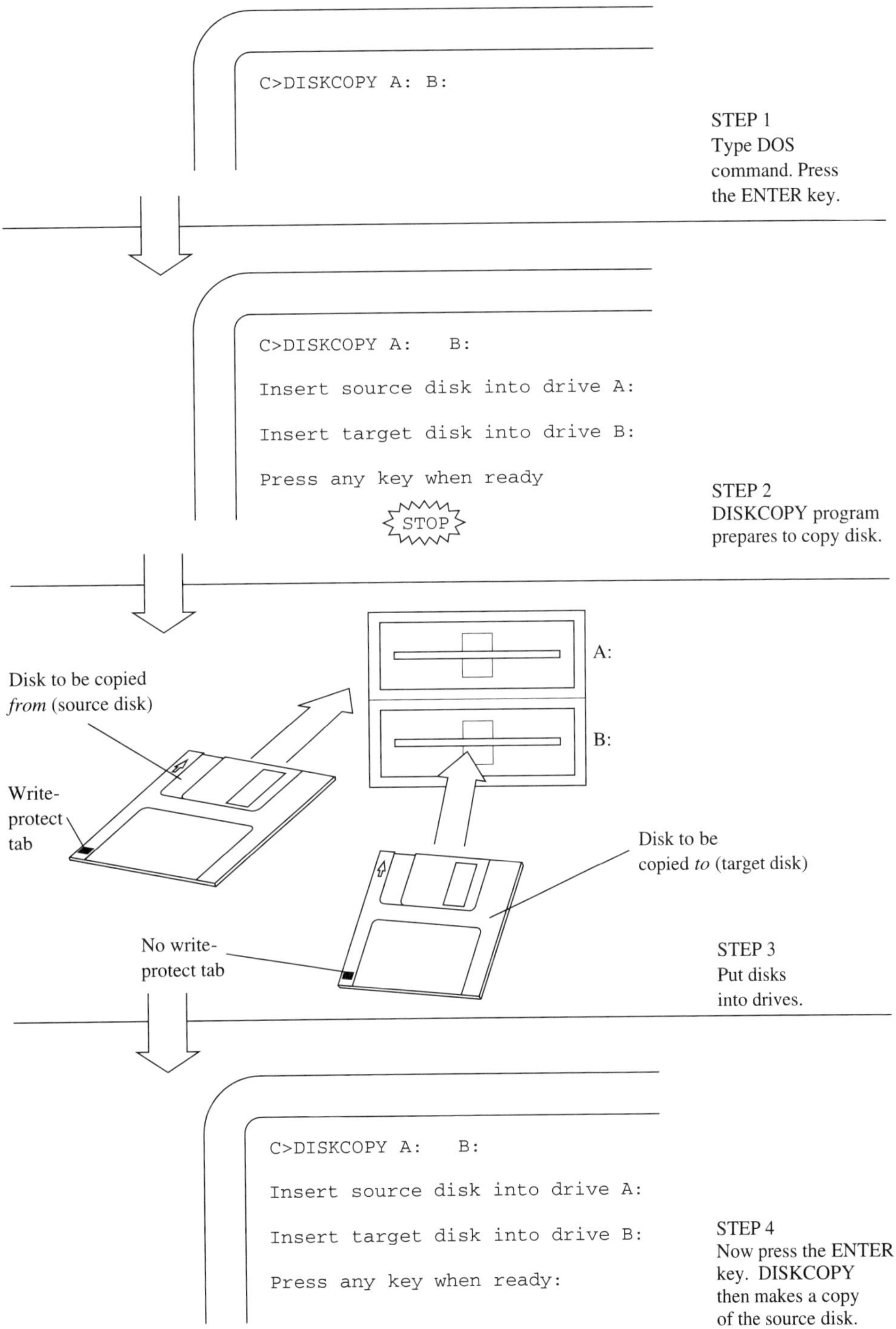

Figure 2.1 Copying a Disk on a Dual-Drive System

The FORMAT command is not an internal DOS command. This command is stored as a separate DOS program (FORMAT.COM) on the DOS disk, not inside your computer. As a result, the FORMAT command is called an external command. What this means is that the DOS disk must be in one of your disk drives (or contained on your C: drive) for the command to be executed.

The external DOS command programs (such as FORMAT.COM) are located in the \DOS directory on the hard drive.

What Are DOS Files?

The reason for having a disk is to store programs. When you store information on a disk, DOS places this information in what is called a file. You can think of computer disks as being like filing cabinets into which you would place information. You will learn how to change the contents of disk files, give them names, change their names, transfer them to other places within the computer system (other disks, to the printer or monitor), or erase them completely.

To begin, you should know how DOS names a file. Every DOS file has a name. The DOS file name consists of two important parts: the file name and the extension, as in

```
FILENAME.EXT
```

The following rules apply when choosing file names:

`FILENAME` = Must contain from one to eight characters, starting with a number or letter of the alphabet and then any letter or number, including the symbols ("{ }__-!@#%^&) but no blanks!
`EXT` = Optional, but may contain up to three characters, numbers, or symbols, as allowed in FILENAME.

The following are all legal DOS file names:

```
COMMAND.COM
PLAYIT.EXE
DO_12
WOW.!!!
FILE.05
12345.678
```

The file names that follow are not legal DOS file names and would not be accepted by DOS:

`TOOMANYLETTERS` = More than eight characters.
`.WOW` = No FILENAME, just an extension.
`BIG.EXTENSION` = More than three letters in the extension.

DOS has some special file names that it reserves for its own special use. These are

```
AUX    COM1     COM2    COM3    COM4
CON    CLOCK$   LPT1    LPT2    LPT3
NUL    PRN
```

File Extensions Used by DOS

Table 2.1 lists the file extension naming conventions used by DOS.

In addition, special programs, such as many business application programs, use their own special extensions. Consult the application program to know what these are.

Displaying DOS Files

DOS places files on your disk in a list called a *directory.* You can display the disk directory on the computer monitor to see the files contained on your disk. The command for displaying the list of file names is

```
DIR
```

This command causes DOS to list the disk files on the active drive, as shown in Figure 2.2. Note that in the figure the volume name of the disk is given at the top of the screen. It also states what drive the disk is in, then a list of the files, and at the bottom displays a summary of how many files are on the drive and how many bytes are left on the disk.

Each file is displayed as follows:

```
FILENAME.EXTENSION   SIZE      DATE      TIME
```

For example:

```
NIBBLES.BAS          24,103    04-09-91 5:00a
```

You see the name of the file with its optional extension. This is followed by the size of the file, in bytes.

Table 2.1 DOS File Extensions

Extension	DOS Meaning
.COM	DOS commands or programs you can directly execute. To execute the program, simply enter the file name of the program (without the .COM extension), press ENTER, and the program will be loaded into your computer and will begin running. Application programs may have this extension.
.BAS	Files containing programs in BASIC.
.BAT	DOS batch files. A way of storing several DOS commands in a file and having them done automatically just by entering the name of the file.
.DAT	Data files used by programs.
.CPI	Code page information, which contains foreign character sets.
.EXE	DOS-executable programs. To execute the program, simply enter the file name of the program (without the .EXE extension), press ENTER, and the program will be loaded into your computer and will begin running. Some application programs may have this extension.
.SYS	For installing device drivers. These are programs that allow DOS to communicate with hardware devices attached to your computer, such as the keyboard, printer, and monitor.
.TXT	Files used for word processing.

Note: The main difference between the .COM and .EXE extensions is how the program uses memory when loaded into the computer.

```
Volume in drive C is SUPERSTUFF
Volume Serial Number is 1037-11D2
Directory of C:\

DOS          <DIR>              03-18-95   8:23p
68000        <DIR>              03-18-95   8:28p
68PROJ       <DIR>              03-18-95   8:26p
CALCS        <DIR>              03-18-95   8:26p
CSTUFF       <DIR>              03-18-95   8:28p
TD386        <DIR>              03-18-95   8:26p
WP           <DIR>              03-18-95   8:26p
WPST         <DIR>              03-18-95   8:26p
ZIPS         <DIR>              12-27-94  10:39a
CHESS    ZIP          225,763   03-18-95  11:06a
D2H      SCR              914   03-09-93   7:28a
EDITDIR  SCR              815   04-09-93   6:54a
MORT     BAS              570   04-05-94   7:20p
MPAY     BAS              177   07-18-92  12:32p
NIBBLES  BAS           24,103   04-09-91   5:00a
PKPAK    EXE           21,720   08-02-88  12:00a
PKUNPAK  EXE           15,112   08-02-88  12:00a
PKXARC   COM           12,242   07-21-90   2:03a
       18 file(s)            301,416 bytes
                         664,716,800 bytes free
```

Figure 2.2 A Sample Directory Listing

The date and time shown in the last two columns of the listing in Figure 2.2 tell you when the file was created or last modified. This is why it is so important to correctly set the date and the time in your computer.

To clear the screen on your monitor, use the internal DOS command:

```
CLS
```

Your computer screen will be cleared, and the DOS prompt will appear at the top left corner of the monitor screen.

You can use the DIR command in several ways. Sometimes there are so many files on the disk that they will simply scroll up to the top of the screen until the last file is displayed at the bottom of the screen. This may cause some of the beginning files not to be seen on the monitor. To prevent this, you can use the DOS DIR modifier:

```
DIR/P
```

The /P stands for Pause and causes the displaying of files not to proceed once the screen is full. You may then press any key on the keyboard to see the rest of the files. Another way to stop the files from scrolling off the screen is by pressing the CTRL key at the same time you press the S key (for Stop/Start). Press the same keys again to allow scrolling to continue.

```
Volume in drive D is SUPERSTUFF
Volume Serial Number is 1037-11D2
Directory of C:\TD386

[.]            [..]           DPMI16BI.OVL   DPMILOAD.EXE   DPMIMEM.DLL
RTASM.BAK      RTASMA.BAT     TASM.EXE       TD.ZIP         TD386.EXE
TDCONFIG.TD    TDDEBUG.386    TDDEV.EXE      TDH386.SYS     TDHELP.TDH
TDINST.EXE     TDMAP.EXE      TDMEM.EXE      TDNMI.COM      TDREMOTE.EXE
TDRF.EXE       TDSTRIP.EXE    TDUMP.EXE      TLINK.CFG      TLINK.EXE
LAB10A.ASM     CH1            1.O            1.E            LAB11A.ASM
LAB12A.ASM     LAB13B.ASM     TOC6811        W.BAT          TOC6811.BK!
3866.ASM       3866.MAP       3866.EXE       3866.LST       3866.OBJ
3866.BAK       RTASM.BAT      0386.ASM       0386.OBJ       0386.LST
0386.MAP       0386.MAP       0386.EXE       WOLF3D.ASC     TD.EXE
Y.OBJ          Y.ASM          Y.MAP          Y.EXE          WOLFCODE.DAT
[X]            CHKLIST.MS
     57 file(s)     2,456,649 bytes
                  664,708,608 bytes free
```

Figure 2.3 Results of the DIR/W Command

Another useful modifier is

```
DIR/W
```

Think of the /W as standing for Wide. The results of issuing this command are shown in Figure 2.3.

As shown in Figure 2.3, the DIR/W command allows the display of more files at the same time. What is lost here is the individual file size and creation/modification date.

Conclusion

In this section you saw how to make a backup copy of your disk. You saw the structure of a DOS directory file and learned how DOS names files. You learned various ways to display the files on your disk drive. Check your understanding of this section by trying the following Section Review.

2.1 **Section Review**

1. Why is it necessary to make backup copies of a disk?
2. State the difference between an internal DOS command and an external DOS command.
3. What is a DOS file?
4. Give the rules for a DOS file name.
5. Give the rules for a DOS file extension.
6. What is a DOS directory?
7. What DOS command is used to display a list of files stored on a disk?

2.2 Getting Started with BASIC

Introduction

You now have enough information about your computer and DOS to get started programming in BASIC. The computer system you are using may differ somewhat from what has been presented up to this point. However, what is important is that the concepts are the same for all systems. Remember, one thing you can count on in the field of programming and computers is that they do change. Change is a given in this field. However, what changes the most are the specifics of exactly how something is done (for example, saving a program on a long-term storage device such as a disk). What doesn't change as fast is the concept of what is to be done, such as the concept of having programs kept in some kind of long-term storage media (for now, floppy and hard disks are used for this purpose).

As you will discover in this section, you need to develop two major skills to program in BASIC (or any other programming language for that matter). The first major skill is how to use the computer system you will be using for programming, and the second is knowing the rules of the programming language you will be using.

What You Need to Know

Figure 2.4 illustrates what it takes to write a working program in the BASIC programming language.

There are four main areas involved in the BASIC programming process:

1. Beginning a new program.
2. Using the program.
3. Modifying an existing program.
4. Saving the program.

It is assumed that a working copy of BASICA, GWBASIC, or QBASIC is available on your computer.

This section shows you how to accomplish the first area, beginning a new BASIC program.

Getting Ready

Before beginning a new BASIC program, you need your own formatted disk on which to save your programs. This is called your BASIC DATA disk. It should have a label that contains the following information:

BASIC DATA DISK[1]
[YOUR NAME]
[INSTRUCTOR'S NAME]
[DATE OF LABEL]

Experienced programmers always make a backup copy of their programs. This is done by using a second formatted disk that contains a copy of all the programs contained on the BASIC DATA disk. *Experienced* programmers do this because they have had plenty of experience losing programs on their BASIC DATA disk (or simply losing the

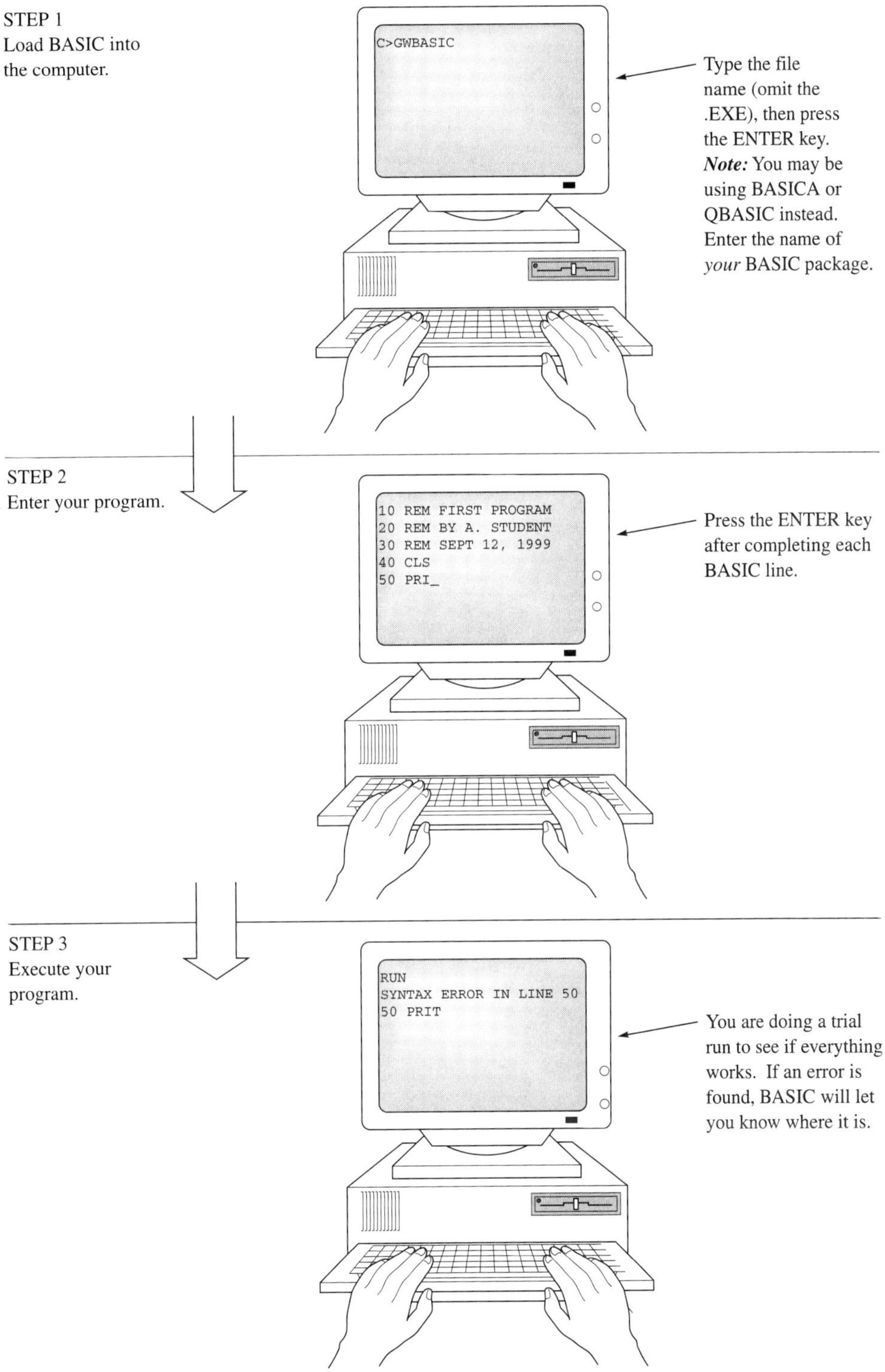

Figure 2.4 The BASIC Programming Process

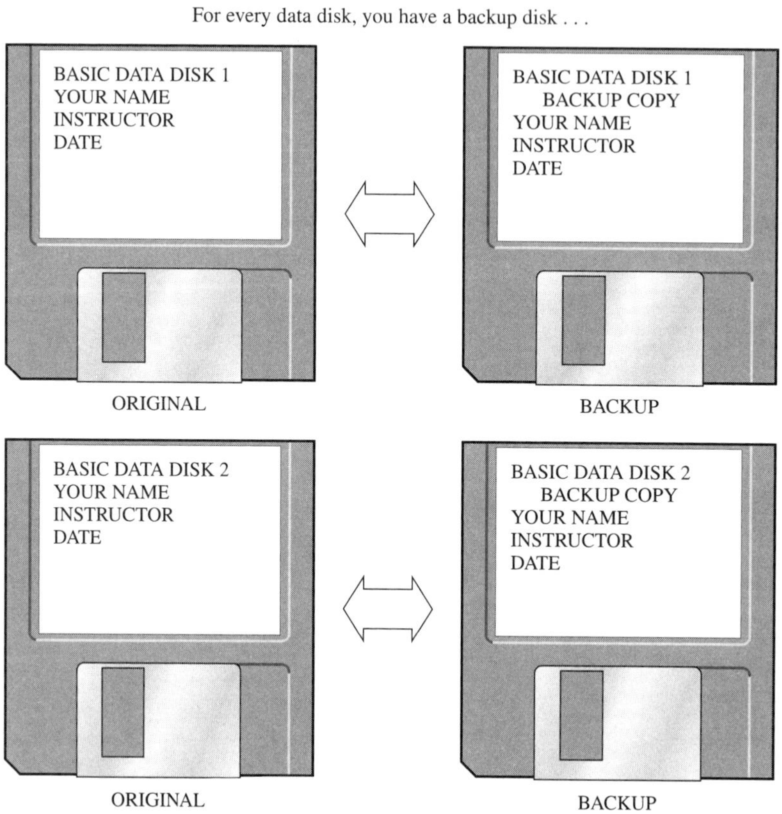

Figure 2.5 Getting Your Data Disks Ready

entire disk). So if you want to save yourself much frustration, have a backup disk on which you can save a copy of all your programs from your BASIC DATA disk. The label of your backup disk should contain the following information:

BASIC DATA DISK[1]
backup COPY
[YOUR NAME]
[INSTRUCTOR'S NAME]
[DATE OF LABEL]

As you progress in your programming, you may have more than one BASIC DATA disk (with its backup copy). Thus, your first BASIC DATA disk should be labeled "BASIC DATA DISK 1," the second, "BASIC DATA DISK 2," and so on. Be sure to do the same with the corresponding backup disk label. This idea is shown in Figure 2.5.

Beginning a New Program

To begin a BASIC program on a system with a hard drive (where the hard drive contains DOS and BASIC), follow the procedure in Table 2.2.

Table 2.2 Starting a New BASIC Program

Step	Procedure	Comments
1	Place your BASIC DATA disk into drive A:	Make sure this disk has been formatted and is properly labeled.
2	Now change the active drive to the A: drive. Do this by typing A: <ENTER>	Doing this will make the active drive the A: drive and will make it easier for you to access it from the BASIC editor.
3	At the A> prompt, type: BASICA or GWBASIC or QBASIC	Check with your instructor if you are not certain how to get the BASIC interpreter loaded from the C: drive.
4	You are now in the BASIC editor and ready to enter a BASIC program.	Be sure that your backup disk is ready and available.

Conclusion

You are now ready to enter your first BASIC program. Because you haven't learned any BASIC yet, the program you enter will be very simple. In the next section, you will see how to enter your first BASIC program. You will also be introduced to some of the important editing features so that you may make changes if you need to.

Check your understanding of this section by trying the following Section Review.

2.2 **Section Review**

1. State the four main areas involved in the BASIC programming process.
2. Give an example of the information that should be on your floppy disk label.
3. State the steps you must complete before beginning a new BASIC program.
4. What version of BASIC is available on your computer?

2.3 First BASIC Program

Introduction

In this section you will learn some of the fundamentals of the programming language called BASIC. The program will compute the area of a circle for a given radius. You will recall that the formula for the area of a circle is

$$AREA = \pi R^2$$

where AREA = The area of the circle in square units.
π = The constant pi, which is approximately equal to 3.14159.
R = The radius of the circle.

This is illustrated in Figure 2.6.

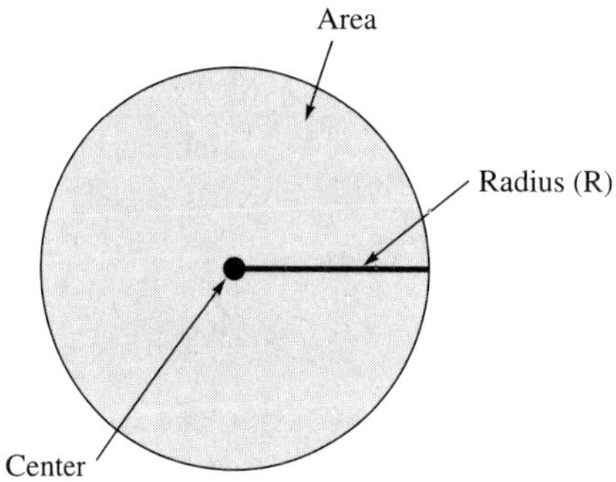

Figure 2.6 Computing Circle Area

BASIC Statement

A *statement* is an instruction to the computer to perform some action. A BASIC statement may have a maximum of 255 characters. Look at Program 2.1.

Program 2.1

```
10 REM Area of a Circle Program
20 LET PI = 3.14159
30 CLS
40 PRINT "This program finds the area of a circle."
50 PRINT "Enter the value of the radius and"
60 PRINT "the program will do the rest."
70 INPUT R
80 LET AREA = PI * R * R
90 PRINT "The area in square units is "; AREA
100 END
```

Program 2.1 will compute the area of a circle for a given radius. When the program is executed, the output on the monitor will appear as shown in Figure 2.7.

What the Program Does

As you can see from Figure 2.7, when the program is executed it clears the screen and tells the program user what the program will do and how it is to be used. Then the program waits for the user to enter a number that represents the radius of a circle for which the user wants to find the area. When the user enters the value of the radius and presses the ENTER key, the program computes the area of the circle and displays the result.

Look again at the program. You see that it consists of ten lines, each line beginning with a number. Each line contains a BASIC statement. This idea is illustrated in Figure 2.8.

In BASICA and GWBASIC, line numbers are required for each BASIC statement in the program. This helps the editor keep the program statements in order. The line number specified by the programmer tells the editor where the statement belongs in the program.

In QBASIC, line numbers are *not* required, but may be used if desired. The built-in editor available with QBASIC is called a **screen editor,** which does not require line

```
This program finds the area of a circle.
Enter the value of the radius and
the program will do the rest.
? 6
The area in square units is 113.0973
```

Figure 2.7 Output of Circle Area Program

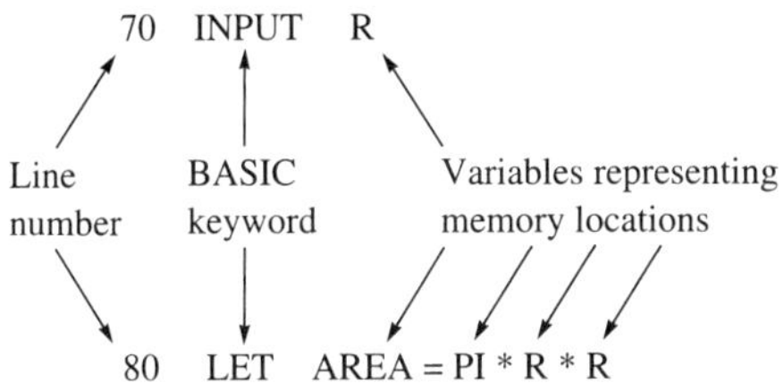

Figure 2.8 Typical BASIC Statement Structure

numbers to keep statements in order. Editing is performed by using the arrow keys (or mouse) to position the cursor at the location where a new statement will be inserted, or a current statement edited or deleted. In general, statements in QBASIC execute in the order that they appear on the screen.

BASIC Statement Definitions

Table 2.3 lists the definitions of each of the BASIC statements used in Program 2.1.

You will learn more details about these BASIC statements in later sections. The main purpose of the program presented here is to give you a program that you can use for practice using the BASIC system.

Conclusion

In this section you were introduced to the first BASIC program you will use to input and execute in your computer. You learned some important facts about such a program as well as the purpose of the BASIC statements used in the program.

Check your understanding of this section by trying the following Section Review.

2.3 Section Review

1. What is meant by a BASIC statement?
2. What must each BASIC statement have?
3. State the maximum number of characters that may appear in a single BASIC statement.
4. What is the purpose of the REM statement?
5. What is a screen editor?
6. Explain the difference between the PRINT statement and the INPUT statement.

Table 2.3 BASIC Statements in Program 2.1

BASIC Statement	What It Does	Use in the Program
REM	This is a remark. It does not cause the BASIC program to do anything.	The REM statement is used by the programmer for comments and notes within the program.
LET	This is the LET statement. It signifies the beginning of a computation or logic statement.	The LET statement sets the value of the *variable* PI to the value of 3.14159. Now, whenever PI is used in the program, it will have the value of 3.14159.
CLS	This statement clears the monitor screen and starts the cursor at the upper left corner of the monitor.	The CLS cleared the BASIC program itself from the screen. This was done to allow only the program output to appear.
PRINT	This statement causes the characters enclosed inside double quotes to be displayed (printed) on the monitor when the program is executed.	The PRINT statements cause the instructions to be displayed on the monitor as well as the results of the calculation.
INPUT	This statement causes the program to wait for the user to input a value and press the ENTER key.	The INPUT statement causes the program to display a question mark and wait for the user to input the value of the radius of the circle.
*	The asterisk ("*") indicates multiplication.	The * is used to indicate multiplication. In this case, it is used to calculate the area of a circle: AREA = πR^2 AREA = PI * R * R
LINE NUMBERS	Indicates the order in which each BASIC statement will be executed. Program execution goes from the lowest line number to the largest. Line numbers may be in the range from 0 to 65529.	The program starts with line 10 and continues sequentially to line 100. Usually BASIC line numbers are numbered in units of 10. This is done in case the program needs modification and a new statement is required between two existing ones.

2.4 Entering the BASIC Program

Introduction

In the last section you were introduced to your first BASIC program. You were shown the purpose of the BASIC statements used in the program that computed the area of a circle. In this section you will be shown how to enter this program, how to save it, and how to send a copy of it to the printer.

Table 2.4 BASIC Statements and Commands

Instruction Type	Meaning	Example
BASIC statement	Instructions placed inside the BASIC program to control the program during execution.	The PRINT statement that causes information to be displayed on the monitor screen when the program is executed.
BASIC command	Instructions used to perform some action on the BASIC program.	The SAVE command that causes the program to be saved to a disk.

BASIC Statements and Commands

To begin entering your program, all you need to do is start typing. There are actually two types of instructions you can give to your computer after you have started the BASIC interpreter. One type is called a BASIC **command;** the other is called a BASIC **statement.** Table 2.4 shows the difference.

Entering the Program

Once you are in the BASIC editor screen, you simply type in the program, pressing the ENTER key at the end of each program statement. Here again is Program 2.1 presented in the last section:

Program 2.1

```
10 REM Area of a Circle Program
20 LET PI = 3.14159
30 CLS
40 PRINT "This program finds the area of a circle."
50 PRINT "Enter the value of the radius and"
60 PRINT "the program will do the rest."
70 INPUT R
80 LET AREA = PI * R * R
90 PRINT "The area in square units is "; AREA
100 END
```

The BASIC editor screen for your system may appear as shown in Figure 2.9 or 2.10.

As shown in Figure 2.9, the numbers along the bottom of the screen indicate the function keys on your computer keyboard. Depending on the type of computer you have, these keys may be along the side of the keyboard or along the top row of the keyboard. These function keys offer shortcuts to many of the BASIC commands.

Figure 2.10 shows the structure of the QBASIC editing screen. Everything that the programmer needs to do is done from the editing screen. Across the top of the screen are single-word *pull-down menu* items. A pull-down menu contains a list of related actions that may be performed when selected. The contents of each pull-down menu are

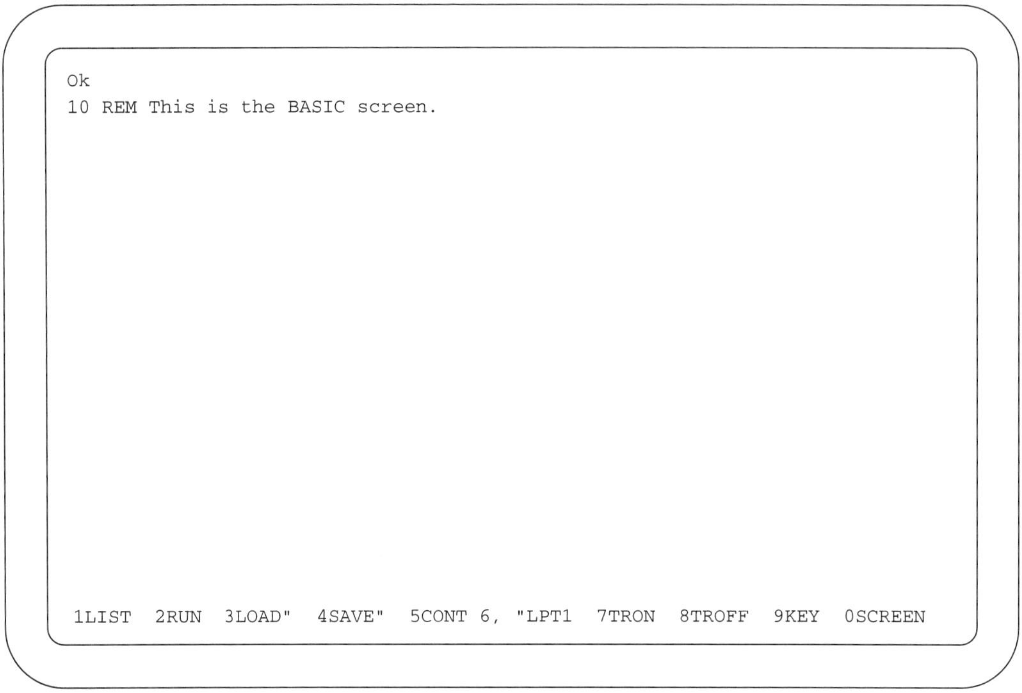

Figure 2.9 Typical Editor Screen for BASICA and GWBASIC

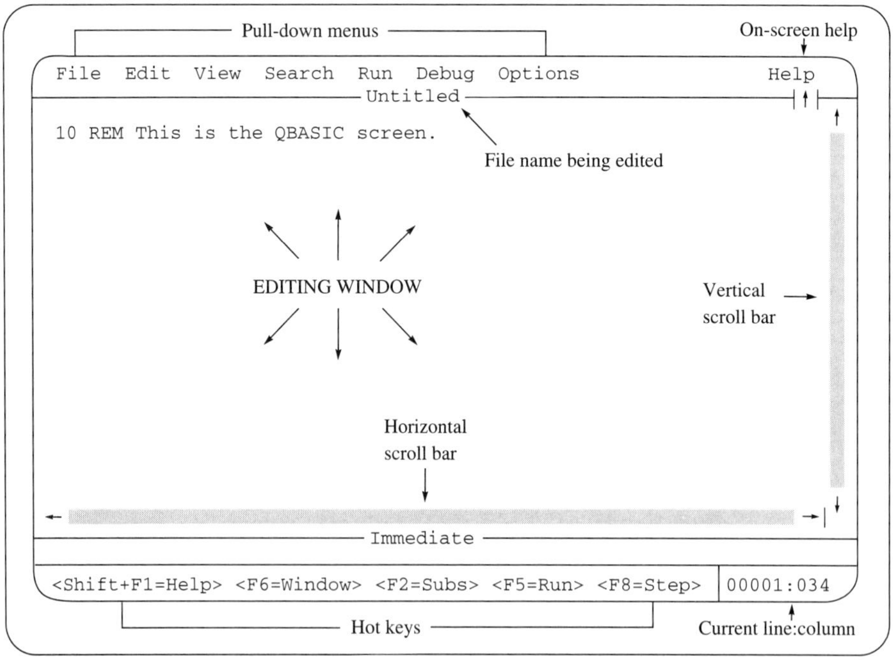

Figure 2.10 Typical Editor Screen for QBASIC

not displayed until the menu is selected. The programmer selects a pull-down menu by positioning the mouse over the menu name and clicking the left mouse button. The keyboard may also be used to select a menu by pressing the ALT key and then the highlighted letter within the menu name (such as ALT followed by F to select the File menu). Normally, the first letter of any menu item is the highlighted letter, although there are exceptions (such as the x in the Exit option found in the File menu). Once a menu is selected, its contents will appear on the screen. The mouse (or the arrow keys) can be used to choose an item from the menu. Pressing ESC on the keyboard closes the menu, with no action taken.

When entering a BASIC program, simply type each line one by one, pressing ENTER after each line. Recall that line numbers are not required in QBASIC but may be used to assist in readability. Program statements that run longer than 80 characters will cause the entire screen to scroll right. Programs with many statements in them will cause the screen to scroll up. The current line and column is always indicated in the lower right corner. Practice using the editor with Program 2.1. The BACKSPACE and DELETE keys may be used to correct typing errors. To get on-screen help, select the Index option from the Help menu and then press the first letter of the topic you need help with.

When you are finished with your editing session, use ALT, F, X to exit back to DOS.

Executing the Program

To execute the BASIC program just entered, type the BASIC command RUN and press the ENTER key (or select Start from QBASIC's Run menu). If there are no errors, the program will begin execution starting with the lowest line number and will continue until it reaches line number 70, where the INPUT causes the program to pause while waiting for user input. Then, when the user presses the ENTER key, the program will continue to line 100. Or, if there is an error in the program, program execution will halt and the following message will appear on the screen:

```
Syntax error in line (number)
```

where `number` = The line number containing the error.

As an example, suppose you incorrectly typed the BASIC statement PRINT in line number 40. It should read

```
40 PRINT "This program finds the area of a circle."
```

Instead you entered

```
40 PIRNT "This program finds the area of a circle."
```

When you tried to execute this program with the RUN command, you got the following message:

```
Syntax error in line 40
OK
40 PIRNT "This program finds the area of a circle."
```

Notice that the program line with the syntax error is also displayed for you. This is done so that you may easily make corrections on the line. QBASIC will also report a syntax error and highlight the portion of the statement that is incorrect.

You should note that the BASIC interpreter will catch errors that have to do directly with BASIC statements. It will not catch errors that are not in any way connected with any BASIC command. For example, what you enclose between the quotes in a PRINT statement is up to you; it will appear on the monitor exactly as you entered it. For example, suppose you entered line 40 as

```
40 PRINT "This program finds the area of a cycle."
```

Here the word "cycle" was entered instead of "circle." It is up to you, the programmer, to catch these kinds of programming errors. The next section will show you how to edit your BASIC program.

Looking at Your Program

The order in which you enter each BASIC statement in BASICA and GWBASIC makes no difference. What this means is that you could have entered line 80 first, then line 10, line 50, and so on for all 10 of the program lines in the example program. The editor places them into the proper order in memory. When you execute the program, it will always be executed beginning with the lowest line number, then progressing sequentially to the largest line number. In QBASIC you must enter statements in order, because line numbers are not used for placement, just reference.

To list your BASIC program, in BASICA or GWBASIC, you use the BASIC command:

```
LIST
```

When you list your program, it will be displayed (listed) sequentially from the lowest line number to the largest line number. The use of the LIST command is shown in Figure 2.11. The LIST command is required in BASICA and GWBASIC because the editor is not a screen editor. QBASIC does not have a LIST command.

```
This program finds the area of a circle.
Enter the value of the radius and
the program will do the rest.
? 6
The area in square units is 113.0973
Ok
LIST
10 REM Area of a Circle Program
20 LET PI = 3.14159
30 CLS
40 PRINT "This program finds the area of a circle."
50 PRINT "Enter the value of the radius and"
60 PRINT "the program will do the rest."
70 INPUT R
80 LET AREA = PI * R * R
90 PRINT "The area in square units is "; AREA
100 END
Ok
```

Figure 2.11 Using the LIST Command

Saving the Program

Right now, the program you just entered is in computer memory (in RAM). If you turned off the computer now, you would lose your program forever! BASIC will not automatically save the program to your floppy disk. You must do this yourself using the proper BASIC command. The BASICA or GWBASIC command for saving your BASIC program to the disk is

```
SAVE "filename"
```

where `filename` = The name of the DOS file for your program.

The file name of your program must obey all of the rules for DOS file names. If you want to SAVE the program under the file name of PROG1, for example, you would enter the BASIC command:

```
SAVE "PROG1"
```

In this example, an extension is not given. When an extension is not given, BASIC will automatically give the extension .BAS. In this case, the program would appear on the disk as

```
PROG1.BAS
```

The .BAS extension lets you know that it is a BASIC program.

Once you have completed the preceding steps, your program is saved to the active drive.

You may give your BASIC programs file extensions of your own. For example, you could have saved your BASIC program as

```
SAVE "PROG.1"
```

In this case, the program would be saved with the file name

```
PROG.1
```

In QBASIC, if you try to exit the editor without saving your BASIC program, a warning message will appear, and you will be given a chance to save your work. You must deliberately choose to lose your work, since QBASIC will always catch a file that has not been saved.

To save your program, use the Save option from the File menu. The Save option allows you to give the file a name before it is saved.

Backing up Your Program

To save the program to your backup disk, simply remove your first BASIC DATA DISK and replace it with your backup BASIC DATA DISK. Then enter the SAVE command again. Be sure to use the same name for the file. Once you have done this, replace the backup disk with your primary BASIC DATA DISK. The concept of doing this is illustrated in Figure 2.12.

If the A: drive is not the active drive, then the active drive is probably the C: drive and your program was saved there. If this is the case, indicate within the BASIC SAVE command that you want the program saved to the A: drive:

```
SAVE "A:PROG1"
```

This command will force the BASIC program to be saved on the disk in drive A:.

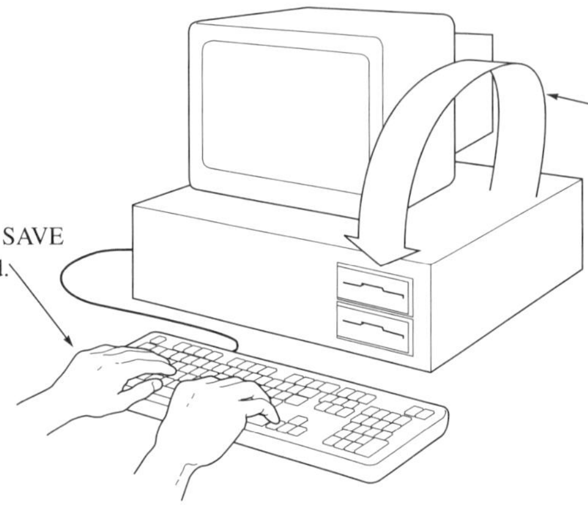

Figure 2.12 Saving the BASIC Program

Looking at Program Files

You can look at the files contained on your disk directly from the BASICA or GWBASIC editor screen. The BASIC command for doing this is

```
FILES
```

Assuming that you saved the program as PROG1, you will see the following displayed:

```
A:
PROG1.BAS
```

The display informs you that there is one file on the disk in drive A: and it is named PROG1.BAS. In QBASIC, use the Open option from the File menu to get a directory listing of the current directory on the active drive.

Erasing the Program from Memory

Suppose you are now ready to enter another BASIC program. Say you are satisfied with the one for finding the area of a circle that you just finished saving to your disk (and to the backup disk as well). Suppose you now want to write a BASIC program that will find the voltage across a resistor when the current and resistance are known. Before you can do this, you need to get rid of the program that is currently in the computer's memory (in RAM). One way to do this is to turn off the computer and start all over again; however, this is not the proper method. There is a command for clearing the computer memory of a BASICA or GWBASIC program. It is

```
NEW
```

The command **NEW** will cause the BASIC program currently in memory to be erased from there. The program will still appear on the monitor screen if the screen hasn't been cleared, but the program is no longer in that part of the computer's memory where it can be executed by the BASIC **RUN** command. To erase the program from the monitor screen, use the BASIC command:

```
CLS
```

With CLS used as a command, the monitor screen will be cleared of the BASIC program. If you try to list the program after entering the NEW command, nothing will be listed because the program will have been erased from memory. Figure 2.13 shows the actions of the BASIC **CLS,** NEW, and **LIST** commands.

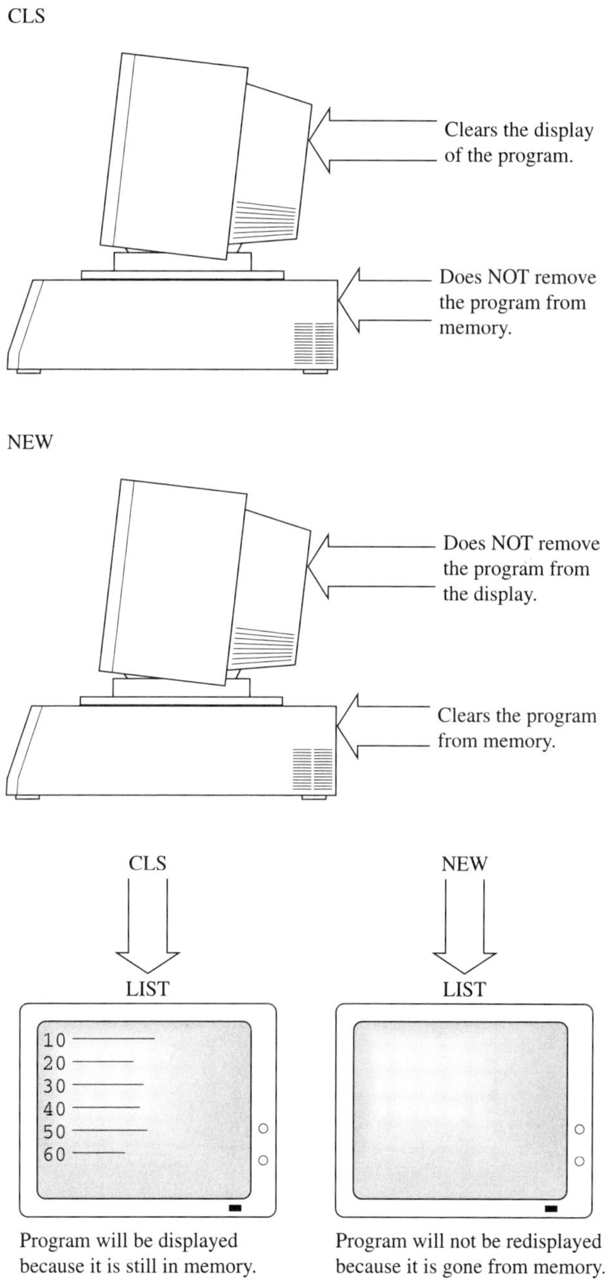

Figure 2.13 Actions of the CLS, NEW, and LIST Commands in BASICA or GWBASIC

In QBASIC, select the New option from the File menu to start a new program.

Remember, save your program to the disk before starting a new program. If you do not, your old program will be lost forever.

Printing Your BASIC Program

To send a copy of your BASICA or GWBASIC program to a printer (and to get what is called a **hard copy**), all you need to do is make sure a printer is connected to your computer, that the printer is on, and that it has an adequate supply of paper in it. Then enter the BASIC command:

```
LLIST
```

Your program will now be sent to the printer and printed out on paper. You may also print on the printer just what you see on the monitor screen. To do this, hold down the SHIFT key and at the same time press the Print Screen key. Whatever is currently on the monitor screen will now be printed to the printer. This concept is shown in Figure 2.14.

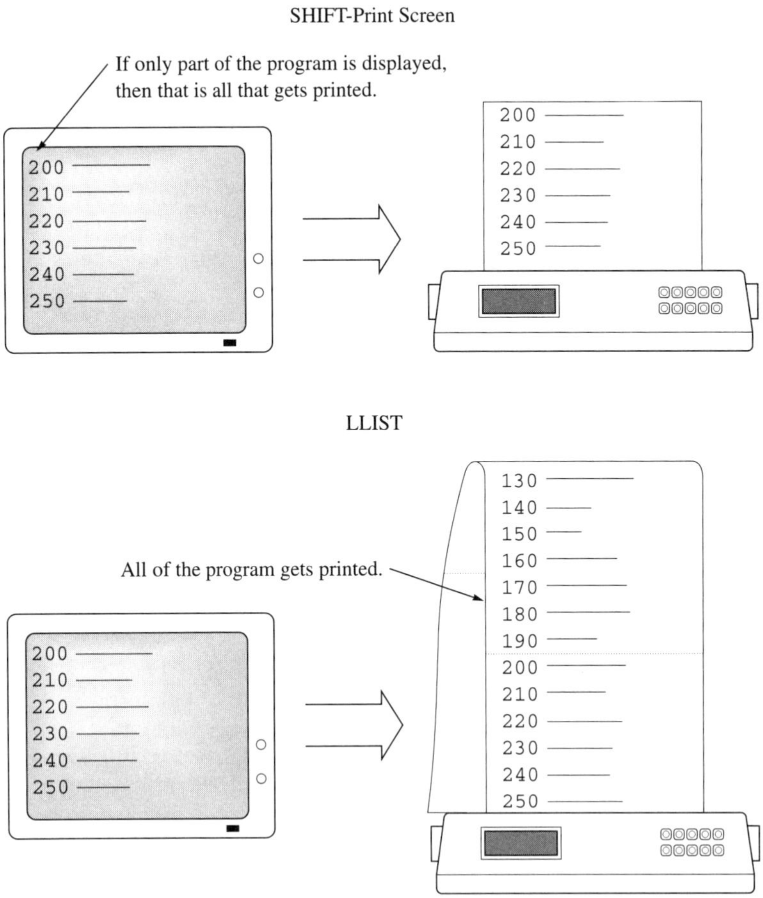

Figure 2.14 Using LLIST and SHIFT-Print Screen

As shown in Figure 2.14, you must use the LLIST command to print the entire program if the program has more lines than will fit on a single monitor screen. Otherwise, the SHIFT-Print Screen combination will print only that part of the program that is currently displayed on the monitor screen.

In QBASIC, select Print from the File menu. You will be given a choice of printing the entire program, the current screen, or selected text.

Conclusion

This section contains a lot of important information. You saw how to enter, execute, and save your BASIC program. You also saw how to prepare for a new BASIC program, and you saw the important relationship between what you see on the monitor screen, what is in the computer's memory, and what is on your data disk.

Check your understanding of this section by trying the following Section Review.

2.4 Section Review

1. State the difference between a BASIC statement and a BASIC command.
2. Give an example of when a BASIC instruction may be used as a command or as a statement.
3. Explain how a BASIC program is executed.
4. What is meant by syntax error?
5. Will all errors found in a BASIC program cause a syntax error? Explain.
6. What command do you use to view the entire BASIC program?
7. How do you cause a BASIC program to be copied to your floppy disk?
8. Explain what you need to do to see the names of the files on your floppy disk when programming a BASIC program.
9. State the purpose of the BASIC command NEW. When is this command normally used?
10. What are some of the key features of QBASIC?

2.5 Editing the BASIC Program

Introduction

In the last section you saw how to enter, save, and print your BASIC program. In this section you will learn how to edit it. We all make typing mistakes and sometimes programming mistakes. There are also times when you will want to modify your original program, perhaps to add graphic features or some other improvements. Knowing how to efficiently edit a program in any programming language will help make you a more efficient and successful programmer. It will also make programming a lot more fun.

Loading the BASIC Program

Now that you know how to save your BASIC program to your floppy disk, you need to know how to get the program back into the computer so that you can execute or modify your program anytime you want. Place your BASIC DATA DISK in the A: drive and start the BASIC interpreter. The BASICA or GWBASIC command for copying a BASIC program into the computer is

```
LOAD "filename"
```

where `filename` = The file name given to the BASIC program you want to copy into the computer's memory.

In QBASIC, choose the Open option from the File menu to select a program to load into memory.

Example of the LOAD Command

Some examples of using the BASIC LOAD command are shown in Table 2.5.

Note the use of the ,R option on the LOAD command to automatically run the BASICA or GWBASIC program after it is loaded.

BASIC Editing Features

Several basic editing features are available in the BASIC editor. These features are listed in Table 2.6.

As you can see from Table 2.6, many powerful editing features are available. The Interactive Exercises section of this chapter will give you an opportunity to practice using them. The best way to learn them is to force yourself to use them. The more you use them, the more natural they will become; if you do this enough you will get to the point where you don't even have to think about what to do, it will happen almost automatically. But this will come only through practice.

QBASIC contains an Edit menu that provides additional editing features beyond the simple editing that may be performed using BACKSPACE and DELETE. These features allow you to select an entire block of statements to copy, move, or delete. To perform any of these operations, the block must first be selected. This is done by holding down the SHIFT key while using the arrow keys to highlight the block of statements. Then, after the block is highlighted, the Edit menu is used to perform the desired operation.

Table 2.5 Examples of Using the LOAD Command

Example	What It Does
LOAD"PROG1"	Loads (copies) the BASIC program named PROG1.BAS from the disk in the active drive into computer memory.
LOAD"A:PROG1"	Loads (copies) the BASIC program named PROG1.BAS from the disk in the A: drive into computer memory.
LOAD"PROG.01"	Loads (copies) the BASIC program named PROG.01 from the disk in the active drive into computer memory.
LOAD"B:MYTHING.ONE"	Loads (copies) the BASIC program named MYTHING.ONE from the disk in the B: drive into computer memory.
LOAD"PROG1",R	Loads (copies) the BASIC program PROG1.BAS from the disk in the active drive and executes (runs) it once it is loaded into computer memory.
LOAD"A:THIS.PGM",R	Loads (copies) the BASIC program THIS.PGM from the disk in the A: drive and executes (runs) it once it is loaded into computer memory.

Table 2.6 BASICA and GWBASIC Editing Features

Feature	How It's Done
Add one or more characters to an existing line.	Using the arrow keys, move the cursor one character to the right of where the insertion is to take place. Then press the INSERT key (this places you in the insertion mode). Type the character(s) to be inserted and press the ENTER key when done. Press the Ins key again to get you out of the insertion mode.
Remove one or more characters in an existing line.	Using the arrow keys, move the cursor to the first character to be removed (deleted). Press the DELETE key for each character to be removed.
Change a character in an existing line.	Using the arrow keys, move the cursor to the character to be changed. Enter the new character and then press the ENTER key. ***Note:*** Be sure you are not in the insertion mode. If you are, simply press the INSERT key to get out of it.
Make a new program line in an existing program.	Type the program line, using a line number whose value is between that of the two existing program lines where the new line is to be. Press the ENTER key when finished.
Remove a program line from an existing program.	Type only the line number of the existing program line, then press the ENTER key.
Replace an existing program line with a new one.	Type the new program line using the same line number as the one to be replaced. When finished, press the ENTER key.
Make a copy of an existing program line so that there are two or more identical program lines, each with a different line number.	Using the arrow keys, move the cursor to the program line to be copied. Place the cursor over the line number and type the new line number. Press the ENTER key when finished. There will now be two identical lines, one with the original line number and the other with the new line number.
Renumber an existing program line.	Using the arrow keys, move the cursor to the new program line. Place the cursor over the line number and type the new line number. Press the ENTER key when done. Next, LIST the program and use the editing feature for removing the original program line.
Remove a series of existing program lines.	Enter the BASIC command DELETE followed by the numbers of the program lines to be removed, then press the ENTER key.

Renumbering Program Lines

The BASICA or GWBASIC editor allows you to renumber any of your program lines. This is a handy feature to have during program development and modification. The BASIC command for renumbering program lines is

```
RENUM[newnumber][,[oldnumber]],[increment]]
```

where `new number` = The first program line number in the new numbering sequence. If it is not specified, the default value is 10.

`old number` = The first program line in the sequence to be renumbered. If it is not specific, the default value will be the first program line of the existing program.

`increment` = The difference (increment) value between each line number of the new numbering sequence. If this is not specified, the value will be 10.

Note: All three parameters are optional.

Examples of Renumbering

Table 2.7 lists some examples of using the BASIC **RENUM** command.

As you gain experience in programming, you will see that the BASIC RENUM command is a powerful editing feature. This command will help you write large programs in which you may easily rearrange their sequence.

Since line numbers are not used by QBASIC, there is no RENUM command available.

Conclusion

This section presented some of the fundamental editing features available in the BASIC editor. Here you saw how to load an existing BASIC program into your computer. You were then introduced to many powerful editing features. These features included making changes in single program lines as well as in several program lines.

Check your understanding of this section by trying the following Section Review.

2.5 Section Review

1. State how you would copy a BASIC program from your floppy disk into computer memory.
2. Explain the action that will be taken by the BASIC command LOAD"B:MYBASIC.1".
3. What is the process you would use to add one or more characters to an existing BASIC statement?
4. How would you give an existing program line a new line number?
5. State how to remove a given program line from an existing BASIC program.
6. What is required before using the Edit menu in QBASIC?
7. Explain what the BASIC command RENUM does.

2.6 Editing Tips

Introduction

There are a few more editing features and disk concepts you should know before diving into BASIC programming. That is what the material in this section covers. Understanding and using the material presented in this section can help save you some programming frustration in the future.

In this section, you will learn what you should watch for when saving an edited program to your disk. You will also learn how to interface with DOS as well as some more important and powerful editing features.

Table 2.7 Examples of Using the RENUM Command

Example	**What It Does**
RENUM	Renumbers all the line numbers starting with the first line, from 10 on up, in increments of 10. Example: 5 REM First line. 8 REM Second line. 10 REM Third line. RENUM <ENTER> 10 REM First line. 20 REM Second line. 30 REM Third line.
RENUM 100	Renumbers all line numbers starting with the first line, from 100 on up, in increments of 10. Example: 5 REM First line. 8 REM Second line. 10 REM Third line. RENUM 100 <ENTER> 100 REM First line. 110 REM Second line. 120 REM Third line.
RENUM 100,8	Renumbers all line numbers, starting with line 8, from 100 on up, in increments of 10. Example: 5 REM First line. 8 REM Second line. 10 REM Third line. RENUM 100,8 <ENTER> 5 REM First line. 100 REM Second line. 110 REM Third line.
RENUM 100,,5	Renumbers all line numbers starting with the first line, from 100 on up, in increments of 5. Example: 10 REM First line. 20 REM Second line. 30 REM Third line. RENUM 100,,5 <ENTER> 100 REM First line. 105 REM Second line. 110 REM Third line.
RENUM,,5	Renumbers all line numbers starting with the first line, from 10 on up, in increments of 5. Example: 100 REM First line. 110 REM Second line. 120 REM Third line. RENUM,,5 <ENTER> 10 REM First line. 15 REM Second line. 20 REM Third line.

Saving the Edited Program

If you saved your BASIC program to your disk and later call it back into the computer—for instance, to make some improvements on it—and then save it back to the disk by the same file name, it will write over the original program.

If you save your BASIC program under another file name, the original program will not be lost. It's usually a good idea to do this because you may not be satisfied with the changes you have made. Having the original program to go back to can be a great time saver.

Erasing Your Program

There are times when you may want to remove one or more BASIC programs from your disk. Consider carefully whether you really want to do this, because once they are removed, you may consider them gone forever. (Under certain conditions there are special programs that can find an erased program on the disk, but don't count on its being able to get any program you have erased. Think first, erase last.)

The BASICA or GWBASIC command for removing a program from the disk is

```
KILL "filename"
```

where `filename` = The file name of the file to be removed (erased) from the disk, including the extension.

Remember, before using the KILL command, make sure you really want to get rid of the program in that file forever.

For example,

```
KILL "PROG1.BAS"
```

will remove (erase) the file PROG1.BAS from the disk in the active drive—forever! You cannot delete a file from within QBASIC. You must go to DOS to delete a file.

Automatic Features

The BASICA and GWBASIC editor has some automatic features that may make your programming easier. One of these is the command for automatically numbering your program lines as you write them. This command is as follows:

```
AUTO[linenum],[inc]
```

where `linenum` = The starting number.
`inc` = The incremental value of the line numbers to follow.

If no specifications are given in the AUTO command, then the default values are 10 and 10, meaning that the first program line number will be 10 and each succeeding line number will be in multiples of 10. The use of the AUTO command is shown in Figure 2.15.

Another automatic feature is the use of the function keys (the keys on your keyboard identified as F1, F2, F3, and so on). The bottom of the BASICA or GWBASIC editor screen displays these keys and gives you an idea of what they do. For example, the F1 key automatically invokes the LIST command, just as if you had typed the word LIST. It simply saves you from having to type the word. The F2 key automatically invokes the RUN command, again just as if you had typed it. QBASIC provides function key operations as well. These are often listed in the pull-down menus themselves. For example, to run a QBASIC program, use SHIFT-F5 (see Run menu).

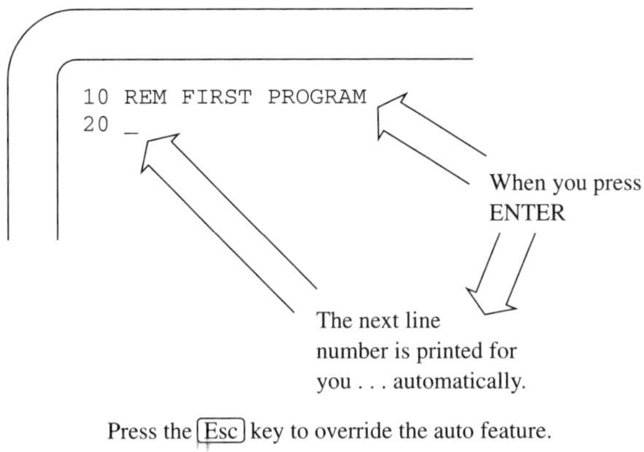

Figure 2.15 Example of the AUTO Command

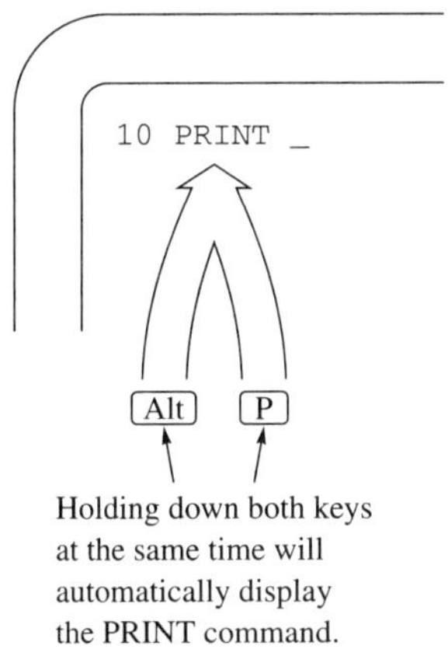

Figure 2.16 Automatically Entering a Command

A third automatic feature of the BASIC editor is that you can automatically enter an entire command by holding down the ALT key while at the same time pressing an appropriate alphabetical key. For example, ALT-P will cause PRINT to be displayed on the screen at the position of the cursor just as if you had typed this command. This concept is illustrated in Figure 2.16. Try other ALT-key combinations yourself with the letters B through Z. This feature is not available in QBASIC.

Deleting Selected Lines

During the development of a BASIC program, you may want to delete one or more programming lines from memory. There is a BASIC command for doing just that. The BASIC command for deleting one or more program lines from memory is

```
DELETE[line1][-line2]
```

where `line1` = The first program line to be deleted from memory.
`line2` = The last in the series of program lines to be deleted from memory.

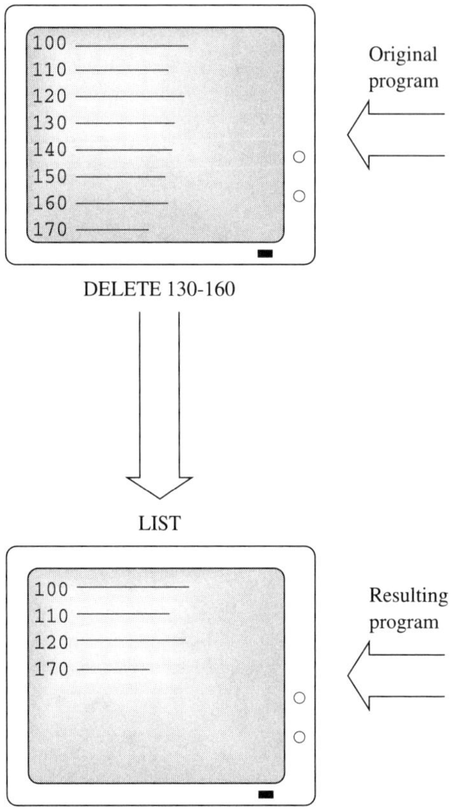

Figure 2.17 Deleting Selected Program Lines

For example:

```
DELETE 100
```

will cause line number 100 to be deleted from the program in memory, whereas

```
DELETE 100-500
```

will cause all of the program lines from 100 to and including 500 to be deleted from the program in memory. Figure 2.17 illustrates the process of deleting selected program lines from the program in memory. To delete one or more lines in QBASIC, position the cursor at the beginning of the first line, then hold the SHIFT key down while using the arrow keys to select the lines. Then press DELETE to delete the selected block.

Getting into DOS

There may be times that you are in the middle of programming and you need to get into the DOS environment so that you can use DOS commands to look at or manipulate special files. Of course, one way to do this is to first SAVE your BASIC program to the disk, get out of BASIC, and then work in the DOS environment. Doing that means that once you are finished in DOS, you must then get back into the BASIC environment and LOAD the program you were working on from the disk back into memory. There is a much easier way. BASIC provides a command for getting into the DOS environment while still saving the program you are working on in memory.

The BASIC command for getting into the DOS environment from the BASIC environment while keeping the program you were working on in memory is

```
SHELL
```

Figure 2.18 illustrates the use of the SHELL command.

As shown in Figure 2.18, to return to your BASIC environment and the program you were working on, simply type EXIT and you will leave the DOS environment. There is no shell capability in QBASIC.

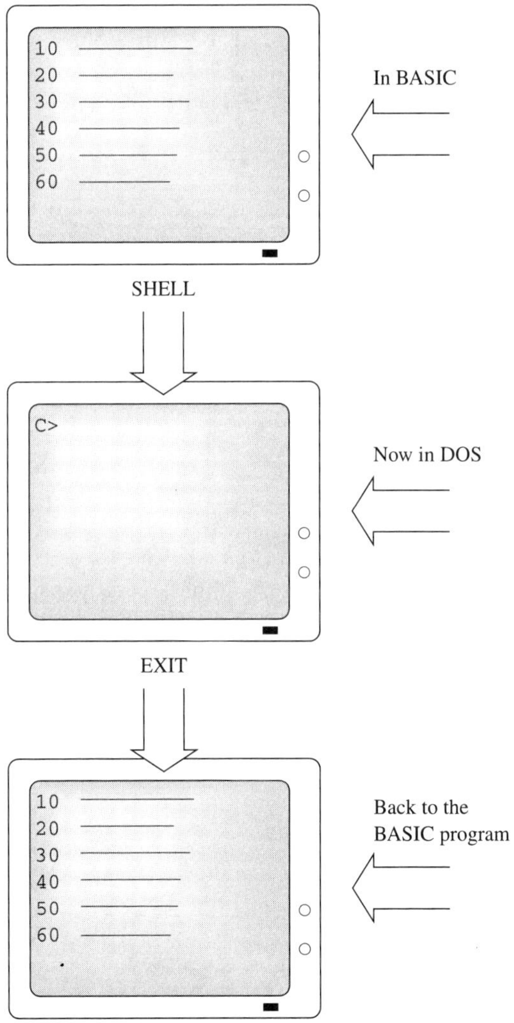

Figure 2.18 Use of the SHELL Command

Leaving the BASIC System

To leave BASIC and return to DOS (this may be required in some computer lab settings), use the command:

```
SYSTEM
```

When the SYSTEM command is used, you will permanently leave BASIC (which will also erase your program from memory) and return to DOS. To exit to DOS from QBASIC, select Exit from the File menu.

Conclusion

This section concludes many of the editing and program control features of BASIC. You now have enough information to begin writing BASIC programs with a minimum of the frustration experienced by most students who are beginning their study of their first programming language.

Check your understanding of this section by trying the following Section Review.

2.6 Section Review

1. What happens to the existing BASIC program on your floppy disk when you save another BASIC program on the same disk by the same file name?
2. What does the command KILL"MYSTUFF.05" do?
3. Does QBASIC allow you to delete a file?
4. How can you get into DOS from the BASIC editor without losing your BASIC program from memory? How do you get back into BASIC?
5. How do you leave BASIC to get permanently back to DOS?

2.7 Troubleshooting Techniques

It is common for a new BASIC programmer to make mistakes when entering code. Depending on the type of error, your BASIC system may actually display a message, reporting the error condition. Other types of errors, such as a typographical error, may be accepted by the system but cause the program to work improperly. Every programmer must develop the programming skills necessary to identify and resolve these types of errors. The more familiar you are with the system and software, the more likely the errors can be located and resolved quickly.

Conclusion

Check your understanding of this material by trying the following Section Review.

2.7 Section Review

1. Does BASIC report every type of error condition? Explain.
2. Why is it important to become familiar with both the system and software?
3. How can program errors be located and solved quickly?

Interactive Exercises

DIRECTIONS

These exercises require you to have access to a computer that supports BASIC. The exercises are provided to give you valuable experience and immediate feedback on what the concepts and commands introduced in this chapter will do. ***Note:*** You will need a blank floppy disk for these exercises.

Exercises

1. Label your blank floppy disk. State what you put on the label.
2. Boot up the computer.
3. Format your floppy disk. Explain how you did this.
4. Get into BASIC. How is this done on the computer you are using?
5. Enter Program 2.2, using the indicated line numbers:

Program 2.2

```
10 REM Another BASIC program
20 CLS
30 PRINT
40 PRINT "This program adds two numbers:"
50 PRINT
60 PRINT "Enter the first number:"
70 INPUT FIRST
80 PRINT "Enter the second number:"
90 INPUT SECOND
100 LET ANSWER = FIRST + SECOND
110 PRINT
120 PRINT "The sum is "; ANSWER
130 END
```

6. After you have entered Program 2.2, execute it. State how you executed this program.
7. Did you have any syntax errors when you first tried to execute the program? Explain. How did you correct the errors?
8. Now save the program to your floppy disk under the file name PROG1. Explain how you did this.
9. Verify that your program has been saved to the disk. State how you did this. Exactly what is the file name of the program now?
   Note: QBASIC users may skip steps 10–13.
10. Issue the command RENUM 100. Now LIST the program. What is different about your program now? Explain.
11. Make sure that your program has been saved to the disk. Then erase it from memory. How did you do this? Does your program still appear on the monitor screen? Explain.
12. What happens when you now try to LIST your program? Why does this happen?
13. Clear the program from the monitor screen. How did you do this?
14. Copy your program from the disk back into memory. State how you did this. How can you now tell that your program is back in memory?
15. Modify your program so that it will now multiply the two numbers instead of adding them. Explain how you did this.
16. Execute the modified program. Did you have any syntax errors? Explain.
17. Now save the modified program to your disk so that it does not overwrite your first program. Explain how you did this.
18. Without losing your BASIC program that is in memory, temporarily go to DOS. How did you do this? Is this possible using QBASIC?

19. While in DOS, do a directory listing of your disk. Which of the two BASIC programs is larger? Or are they the same size? How did you determine this?
20. Return from DOS to BASIC. State how you did this.
21. Return the computer to the condition it was in just before you loaded BASIC into it. How did you do this?

Self-Test

DIRECTIONS

For the following questions, refer to Program 1.3, presented in the self-test at the end of Chapter 1.

1. When the program is executed, will any of the REM statements be displayed?
2. State the line numbers in which each variable receives its value.
3. List all the different BASIC instructions used in this program.
4. What is the purpose of the PRINT statement used in line 320?
5. What does line 420 cause the program to do?

Study Questions

DIRECTIONS

The following questions apply to Program 2.3:

Program 2.3

```
100 REM Resistors in Parallel Program
110 REM
120 REM Developed by: R. A. Programmer
130 REM
140 REM This program will compute the total value of two resistors
150 REM in parallel.
160 REM
170 REM Variables Used:
180 REM
190 REM R1 = Value of the first resistor
200 REM R2 = Value of the second resistor
210 REM RT = Value of total resistance
220 REM
300 REM Explain program to user
310 CLS
320 PRINT
330 PRINT "This program will compute the total resistance of two resistors"
340 PRINT "in parallel.  You need only enter the value of each resistor"
350 PRINT "in ohms."
360 PRINT
370 REM
400 REM Get resistance values from user
410 INPUT "Value of R1 = "; R1
```

```
420 INPUT "Value of R2 = "; R2
430 REM
440 LET RT = R1 * R2 / (R1 + R2): REM Compute total resistance
450 REM
500 REM Display the answer
510 CLS
520 PRINT
530 PRINT "The total resistance of "; R1; " ohms in parallel"
540 PRINT "with "; R2; " ohms is "; RT; " ohms."
550 REM
600 REM End of program
610 END
```

Questions

1. State what the program will do.
2. What are the variables used in the program?
3. How many main sections does the program have? Name them.
4. Are there any errors in the program? If so, what are they?
5. Explain how you would copy the program to a printer.
6. Assume that you had just entered the program and saved it to your data disk. How would you now make a copy of your program to your backup disk?
7. What BASIC command would you use to clear this program from the screen? To clear it from memory? To remove it from the disk?
8. If you needed to go into DOS without clearing the program from memory, what would you do? How would you return to BASIC?
9. Insert the following statement into Program 2.3:

   ```
   545 CLS
   ```

   How does execution change?

Program Design

Use Program 2.3 as a guide in solving the following programming problems.

10. Write a BASIC program that calculates the area of a rectangle. The user must enter the length and width of the rectangle. Display the area in square units.
11. Write a BASIC program that converts inches to centimeters. The user must enter the number of inches. Display the equivalent number of centimeters, as follows:

    ```
    10 inches equals 25.4 centimeters.
    ```

12. Write a BASIC program that determines the length of the hypotenuse of a right triangle. The user must enter the length of the other two sides. Since you will need to find the square root of a number in this problem, use the following type of statement to do so:

    ```
    Y = X ^ 0.5
    ```

    Y will equal the square root of X.
13. Consider the coordinates of two points on an X–Y grid. Point A is located at (10,10) and point B is located at (40,30). To calculate the distance between these two points, the formula shown in Figure 2.19 is used. Write a BASIC program that implements the formula and displays the distance between points A and B.

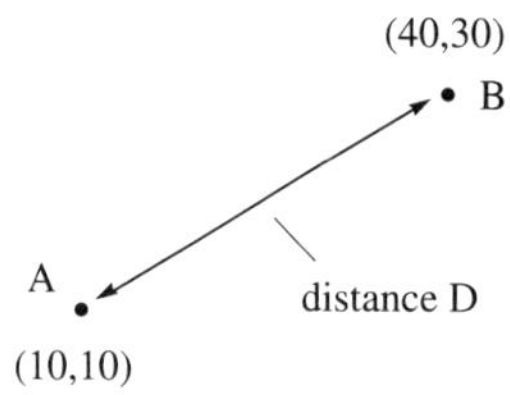

$$D = \sqrt{(40 - 10)^2 + (30 - 10)^2}$$

$$D = \sqrt{30^2 + 20^2}$$

$$D = \sqrt{900 + 400}$$

$$D = \sqrt{1300}$$

$$D = 36.06$$

Figure 2.19 For Question 13

14. Write a BASIC program that will compute a 6 percent sales tax on a purchase. The user must input the amount of the purchase. The program must display the purchase amount, the tax, and the total of the two.
15. Write a BASIC program that will generate a payroll stub when supplied with the hours worked and the rate per hour. Deductions are as follows: 10 percent for federal tax, 5 percent for state tax, 1.5 percent for local tax, $10 for union dues, and $50 for supplemental retirement. Display the gross pay (hours worked * rate), all deductions, and the resulting net pay.
16. Write a BASIC program that determines how many feet a photon of light travels in one nanosecond. The speed of light is 186,000 miles/second. There are 5280 feet in one mile.
17. Write a BASIC program that converts your weight from pounds into kilograms. There are 2.2046 pounds/kilogram.
18. Use BASIC to determine how long it takes a photon of light to travel from the Sun to the Earth. The distance travelled is approximately 93 million miles.

3 Structured Programming

Ken Koder received a call from Don, the senior technician. Don had just gotten out of an emergency meeting called by one of RWA's customers. The customer reported a problem with one of the programs that control part of the operations on his company's shop floor. Don said, "Ken, I have another assignment for you. Can you come to my office?"

"Of course!" Ken replied. "I'll be right there." Before leaving his desk he started a password-protected screen saver program to lock his workstation.

"What can I do for you?" Ken asked as he entered Don's office.

Don, looking very serious, said, "Ken, one of our best customers is having a problem with some BASIC code that RWA wrote several years ago. Put your current project on the back burner and start working on this one right away." Don gave Ken the details of the problem, along with a large computer printout containing all the code.

As Ken looked at the code, one of the first things he noticed was more than a few GOTO statements. He tried to follow the program logic but had a very difficult time. "What a mess, Don."

Don smiled and said, "That's called spaghetti programming, Ken."

"Who wrote this?" Ken asked.

Don responded, "A programmer no longer with RWA Software."

Ken spent the rest of the day and most of the evening working on the program. Eventually he found the source of the problem.

Objectives

After reading this chapter, you should be able to

1. Recognize a block structured program.
2. Develop a block structured program using BASIC.

3. Use top-down design in the design of a computer program for any computer language.
4. Understand the use of GOSUB and RETURN as they apply to structured BASIC.
5. Develop a structured BASIC program that contains a main programming block.
6. Recognize and use the fundamental symbols for flowcharting.
7. Develop an understanding of the use of flowcharting in structured BASIC programming.
8. Use the WHILE-WEND for program repeats.

Introduction

In this chapter you will learn how to develop program blocks using the BASIC programming language.

When you complete all of the exercises here, you will be able to recognize a **block structured** program in BASIC or in almost any other computer programming language. You will also learn about "top-down" design of a computer program. This is really the foundation chapter for this text, as it sets the stage for all the other structured languages you will study.

You will learn some new and powerful statements, including **GOSUB** and its companion **RETURN,** used to create the **programming blocks** found in structured BASIC.

Flowcharting is also presented in this chapter. You will learn about its place in structured programming. You will also see how to allow the program user to repeat the execution of the program.

3.1 Program Blocks

Introduction

The larger programs presented in the first two chapters of this text use a **block structure.** This was done because this is a book about structured programming. BASIC is not normally programmed in a structured format, as illustrated by the **unstructured** program in Program 3.1.

Program 3.1

```
10 REM Typical Program
20 REM
30 REM Developed by:
40 REM   Your Typical Programmer
50 REM
60 REM This program illustrates nothing more than a
70 REM typical unstructured BASIC program.
80 REM
90 REM Constants Used:
100 REM   None
110 REM
120 REM Variables Used:
```

```
130 REM   None
140 REM
150 REM Explain program to user
160 PRINT "This is a BASIC program that illustrates the"
170 PRINT "typical unstructured approach to writing a"
180 PRINT "program in BASIC."
190 PRINT "When the program is RUN the program user can't"
200 PRINT "tell that the program is unstructured; only the"
210 PRINT "programmer can."
220 PRINT "Hence a structured program in BASIC is useful"
230 PRINT "only to the programmer, the programmer's boss, the"
240 PRINT "programmer's teacher, those who need to modify or"
250 PRINT "change it and to those who are living with the programmer"
260 PRINT "while he/she is finding bugs in the program."
```

Blocking the BASIC Structure

You probably had no trouble following exactly what Program 3.1 would do. It simply prints a series of messages on the computer screen. So why structure it?

You should consider several points. First of all, the program structure looks boring. Every program line starts in the same place—that is, one space after the line number. The structure could be made more readable by using paragraphs. This would help to distinguish one part of the program from another. Second, more REM statements are necessary to describe the activity of the program. A little extra effort now will make the program easier to understand in the future.

Program 3.2 shows a simple way of making Program 3.1 a little more interesting.

Program 3.2

```
10 REM A Block Structured Program
20 REM
30 REM Developed by: A Block Programmer
40 REM
50 REM This program illustrates the most simple form
60 REM of a block structure for BASIC.
70 REM
80 REM Constants: none
90 REM
100 REM Variables: none
110 REM
200 REM First paragraph of program explanation
210 PRINT "This is a BASIC program that"
220 PRINT "illustrates a blocked approach"
230 PRINT "to writing a program in BASIC."
240 REM
300 REM Second paragraph of program explanation
310 PRINT "When the program is RUN the program"
320 PRINT "user can't tell that the program is"
```

```
330 PRINT "blocked; only the programmer can."
340 REM
400 REM Last paragraph of explanation
410 PRINT "Hence a blocked program in BASIC"
420 PRINT "is useful only to the programmer,"
430 PRINT "the programmer's boss, the programmer's"
440 PRINT "teacher, those who need to modify or"
450 PRINT "change it, and to those who are living"
460 PRINT "with the programmer while he/she is"
470 PRINT "finding bugs in the program."
480 REM
500 REM End of the program
510 END
```

Note the use of REM statements to separate the program into blocks. This causes the program to be divided into a paragraph or block structure.

Definition of Block Structure

Block structure means that the program will be constructed (programmed) so that it consists of a few groups of instructions rather than one continuous listing of instructions. This is the way the larger programs in Chapters 1 and 2 were presented.

The first block in each program is the **programmer's block.** In the programmer's block we provide information about the program, such as the name of the program, the name of the programmer, a brief description of the program, and a list of the variables and constants.

All other program blocks are defined by a REMark statement at the beginning of the block. This REMark statement contains some text to describe briefly what is being performed in the block. Then a block is terminated by a blank REMark statement at the end of the block. These are called the **block separators.** An example of a block separator used in Program 3.2 is

```
340 REM
400 REM Last paragraph of explanation
```

Notice line 340 is the end of a previous block and line 400 is the beginning of the next block. The body of each program block is identified in this way. This helps make identifying the program blocks easier.

The program body begins with a REMark statement and ends with a REMark statement. A typical example, from Program 3.2, is

```
110 REM
200 REM First paragraph of program explanation
210 PRINT "This is a BASIC program that"
220 PRINT "illustrates a blocked approach"
230 PRINT "to writing a program in BASIC."
240 REM
```

Some Important Rules

What is important in a structured BASIC program is that there is no jumping around using the GOTO statement. People can understand things a lot easier if they can follow logically from one step to another. Hence, you should always follow these important rules when doing block structured programming:

1. All blocks are entered from the top.
2. All blocks are exited from the bottom.
3. When the computer finishes one block, it goes on to another or it ENDs.

Can you design every computer program this way? Yes, you can, with absolutely no exceptions. There is no excuse for writing a program in BASIC that doesn't contain block structure.

Types of Blocks

No matter what programming language you use, there are only three types of blocks:

1. Action block.
2. Loop block.
3. Branch block.

What does each of these blocks do? An **action block** is the simplest kind of programming block. It is nothing more than a straight sequence of action statements (e.g., PRINT). A pure action block does not contain any decision-making or branching commands. A **loop block,** however, can cause the computer to repeat a part of the program, whereas a **branch block** gives the option of performing a different sequence of instructions. Program 3.2 used all action blocks.

The concepts of these three different kinds of blocks are shown in Figure 3.1.

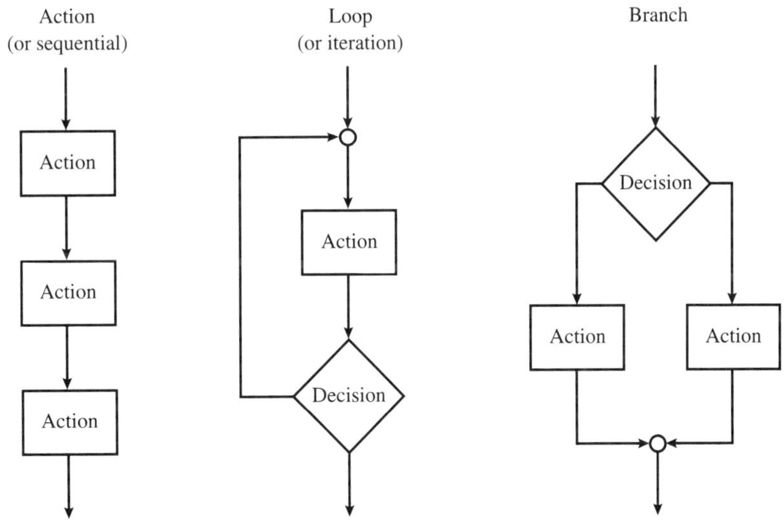

Figure 3.1 Concepts of the Three Types of Programming Blocks

Any computer program, no matter how complex, can be solved using action blocks, loop blocks, and branch blocks.

Conclusion

In this section we examined the idea of a block structured program. The remainder of the chapter is devoted to developing a programming style for structuring programs. Test what you have learned in this section by answering the questions in the following Section Review.

3.1 Section Review

1. Does a computer with a BASIC interpreter require structured programming to execute a BASIC program? Explain.
2. Define the term *block structure.*
3. State how each program block must begin.
4. Explain how program blocks are separated. Give an example.
5. Explain how the body of a program block is highlighted.
6. Name the three types of blocks.
7. State the purpose of the programmer's block.
8. State the purpose of each type of block.

3.2 Top-Down Design

Introduction

Top-down design is an approach used in designing a computer program. The opposite of top-down is bottom-up design.

Bottom-up design is used mostly by amateur programmers. It consists of entering program **code** first with the idea of getting the program to work as soon as possible. The resulting program generally goes little beyond the "satisfied my curiosity" or "Wow! Look what that does!" stage.

Top-down design is used by technical professional programmers who are developing the program for commercial purposes. The method consists of designing the program using the most general but complete terms first, then entering program code as the very last step in the programming process.

Top-down design can be explained in the following steps used for BASIC:

1. Start with the most generalized idea of what you want the program to do. Write this down in outline form.
2. Assign line numbers to each major block of the completed outline. Enter these by using no more than REMark or LET statements.
3. Develop and test each of the separate major program headings by entering program code.

The following example illustrates the process of top-down design.

An Example

Suppose you are working for a bank and need to write a program to compute the total value of an investment over a period of years by using the following formula:

$$\text{Accumulated Value} = \text{Amount Invested} * \text{Interest}^{\text{Years}}$$

The first step in writing a program in top-down design:

> Start with the most generalized idea of what you want the program to do. Write this down in outline form.
>
> Start out by stating the problem in writing, making note of all program variables:
>
> Compute the accumulated value of an investment. The program user will INPUT the *amount* to be invested, the *interest rate,* and the *number of years*. The program will display the accumulated value.

Next, write down in outline form the steps the program will follow. Here is a suggested outline:

I. Programmer's Block
   A. Program Name
   B. Developer Name
   C. Description of the Program
   D. Set All Constants
   E. Explain All Variables
II. Explain Program to the User
   A. Purpose of the Program
   B. What the User Has to Do
   C. Any Limitations of the Program
III. Get Values from the Program User
   A. Amount Invested
   B. Interest Rate
   C. Number of Years
IV. Compute the Accumulated Value
   A. Interest = 1 + (Interest Rate / 100)
   B. Accumulated Value = Amount Invested * $\text{Interest}^{\text{Years}}$
V. Display the Result

You could have another section of program statements to ask if the program is to be repeated. But do not worry about that now; you will learn the structured way to do that later.

So far, you have not used any BASIC statements, but you have developed a program. You could be using any programming language to implement the outline; all that is necessary now is the coding. The outline is the hardest part and requires the most thought. The coding is the easy part.

When you use structured programming techniques, you will find that the specific statements will change, but the organization of the program and the use of standard procedures you develop will create well-structured and logical programs in any computer language.

Assigning Line Numbers

The next step in the development of a BASIC program using top-down design is to assign blocks of line numbers to each major heading of the completed outline.

It is good practice to start the programmer's block at line 100. Start all other blocks of the program in multiples of 100 or 1000 depending on the size of the program you are writing.

100 I. Programmer's Block
- A. Program Name
- B. Developer Name
- C. Description of the Program
- D. Set All Constants
- E. Explain All Variables

1000 II. Explain Program to the User
- A. Purpose of the Program
- B. What the User Has to Do
- C. Any Limitations of the Program

2000 III. Get Values from the Program User
- A. Amount Invested
- B. Interest Rate
- C. Number of Years

3000 IV. Compute the Accumulated Value
- A. Interest = 1 + (Interest Rate / 100)
- B. Accumulated Value = Amount Invested * $\text{Interest}^{\text{Years}}$

4000 V. Display the Result

You have now assigned space to each major part of the program. You are now ready to enter the steps of your program into the computer by entering LET and REMark statements.

Programmer's Block

Here is the programmer's block created from the outline:

```
100 REM Future Value of an Investment Program
110 REM
120 REM Developed by: A. Good Programmer
130 REM
140 REM A program to compute the future value of an investment.
150 REM The program user must supply the Amount Invested, the
160 REM interest rate, and the number of years.
170 REM
180 REM Variables used:
190 REM   AMOUNT    = The dollars to invest
200 REM   RATE      = The yearly interest rate
210 REM   INTEREST  = The adjusted interest rate
220 REM   YEARS     = The total number of years invested
230 REM   TOTAL     = The accumulated value of the investment
240 REM
250 REM Constants used: None
260 REM
```

Next, do the same for the other parts of the completed outline.

Explain Program to the User

```
1000 REM Explain the program to the user
1010 PRINT "This program will compute the total accumulated"
1020 PRINT "value of an investment."
1030 PRINT
1040 PRINT "You must provide the total amount invested, the"
1050 PRINT "interest rate, and the number of years."
1060 PRINT
1070 REM
```

Get Values from the Program User

```
2000 REM Get values from program user
2010 INPUT "Enter amount invested ==> "; AMOUNT
2020 INPUT "Enter yearly interest rate ==> "; RATE
2030 INPUT "Enter number of years ==> "; YEARS
2040 REM
```

Compute the Accumulated Value

```
3000 REM Compute the total accumulated interest
3010 INTEREST = 1 + (RATE / 100)
3020 TOTAL = AMOUNT * INTEREST ^ YEARS
3030 REM
```

Display the Result

```
4000 REM Display the result on the screen.
4010 PRINT
4020 PRINT "The total accumulated value is $"; TOTAL
4030 PRINT
4040 PRINT "Thanks for using the program!"
```

The **outline blocks** (or **program stubs,** as they are sometimes called) are now complete.

Conclusion

You have now finished the beginning of a structured program using top-down design. After you save what you have on your disk, make a backup copy and a printout. Now you can develop each block separately, test it, and debug it if necessary. Each of the blocks can be thought of as a program stub.

You are now almost ready to implement the last step of top-down design using block structured BASIC.

> Develop and test each of the separate major program headings by entering program code.

Before you do this, one more important block, the block that gives the overall structure to the program, must be inserted into the program. This block is called the **main programming block,** but before you can use it, you must know how to use the GOSUB and RETURN statements. That's what the next section is all about. Test your understanding of this section by trying the following Section Review.

3.2 Section Review

1. Explain bottom-up design.
2. Explain top-down design.
3. State the three steps used in top-down design.
4. Name the five major sections in the example program in this section.
5. Explain what is meant by program stubs.
6. Name some of the advantages of using program stubs.

3.3 GOSUB and RETURN

Main Programming Block

The main programming block is the block that tells anyone, at a glance, exactly how the program is structured. It also ties the whole structure of the program together.

The main programming block always goes immediately after the programmer's block. Program 3.3 shows the main programming block for the future value program.

Program 3.3

```
500 REM Main programming block
510 GOSUB 1000:           REM Explain program to user
520 GOSUB 2000:           REM Get values from user
530 GOSUB 3000:           REM Compute future value
540 GOSUB 4000:           REM Display result
550 END
```

The GOSUB Statement

Even if you don't know what the BASIC statement GOSUB means, you or anyone else can see the exact structure of the program just by reading the main programming block in Program 3.3. It's obvious to everyone, programmer or not, exactly what the program will do.

What does the GOSUB statement do? It causes the program to go to a different part of the program—in this case, a specific program block. For example, line 510 tells the computer to go to the program block starting at line 1000. What is at line 1000? That's the beginning of the program block that explains the program to the user. The target of the GOSUB statement in this case is line 1000. This is illustrated in Figure 3.2.

Note that in the main program block, each GOSUB statement also contains a colon and a REMark statement. This is called the **companion remark.** The companion remark should contain the same information as the **target line.** For example, line 520

```
520 GOSUB 2000:REM Get values from user
```

has as its target line 2000, which you already programmed as

```
2000 REM Get values from user
```

Every GOSUB statement has as its target a line number that is a REMark statement that duplicates the companion remark used with the GOSUB.

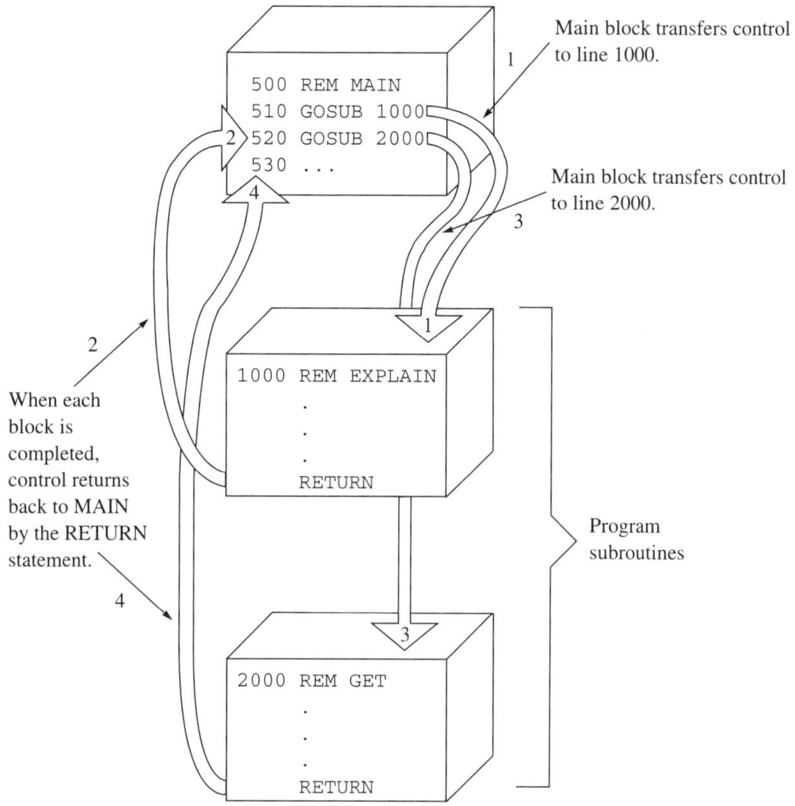

Figure 3.2 Action of the GOSUB and RETURN Statements

The RETURN Statement

Since the GOSUB statement will cause the program to go to the target and continue within the program block, the RETURN statement is used to get the program back to the main program block when the **target block** is completed.

The **RETURN** statement is used to return control back to the next line following the GOSUB statement. In this manner, the main programming block retains control of the structure and flow of control for the entire BASIC program.

You have now defined a group of **subroutines.** Each subroutine is defined as a program block. Your program will now consist of a few blocks of instructions rather than one long list of instructions.

Structuring a program in this manner causes the main programming block to have complete control of the program structure. If you need to change or modify the flow of the program, you simply change the main programming block and add, delete, or modify program block(s). You don't have to search through a continuous list of BASIC statements to modify a block structured program.

Since the main programming block controls the sequence of the program from start to finish, it must have as its last command the **END** statement. This is necessary to prevent the program from "falling through" into the next program block. If this happens, the main programming block will lose control of the program structure; therefore, every main programming block must end with the END statement.

Completing the Program

To complete the program, simply enter the correct BASIC coding. Program 3.4 shows the complete program for the future value program using structured BASIC programming techniques.

Program 3.4

```
100 REM Future Value of an Investment Program
110 REM
120 REM Developed by: A. Good Programmer
130 REM
140 REM A program to compute the future value of an investment.
150 REM The program user must supply the Amount Invested, the
160 REM interest rate, and the number of years.
170 REM
180 REM Variables used:
190 REM   AMOUNT   = The dollars to invest
200 REM   RATE     = The yearly interest rate
210 REM   INTEREST = The adjusted interest rate
220 REM   YEARS    = The total number of years invested
230 REM   TOTAL    = The total value of the investment
240 REM
250 REM Constants used: None
260 REM
500 REM Main program block
510 GOSUB 1000:          REM Explain program to user
520 GOSUB 2000:          REM Get values from user
530 GOSUB 3000:          REM Compute future value
540 GOSUB 4000:          REM Display result
550 END
1000 REM Explain the program to the user
1010 PRINT "This program will compute the future value"
1020 PRINT "of an investment."
1030 PRINT
1040 PRINT "You must provide the total amount invested, the"
1050 PRINT "interest rate, and the number of years."
1060 PRINT
1070 RETURN
1080 REM
2000 REM Get values from user
2010 INPUT "Enter amount invested      ==> "; AMOUNT
2020 INPUT "Enter yearly interest rate ==> "; RATE
2030 INPUT "Enter number of years      ==> "; YEARS
2040 RETURN
2050 REM
3000 REM Compute the future value of the investment
```

```
3010 INTEREST = 1 + (RATE / 100)
3020 TOTAL = AMOUNT * INTEREST ^ YEARS
3030 RETURN
3040 REM
4000 REM Display the result on the screen.
4010 PRINT
4020 PRINT "The total accumulated value is $"; TOTAL
4030 PRINT
4040 PRINT "Thanks for using the program!"
4050 RETURN
4060 REM
```

A sample execution of Program 3.4 is as follows:

```
This program will compute the future value
of an investment.

You must provide the total amount invested, the
interest rate, and the number of years.

Enter amount invested       ==> ? 1000
Enter yearly interest rate ==> ? 5
Enter number of years       ==> ? 2

The total accumulated value is $ 1102.5

Thanks for using the program!
```

Conclusion

Understanding how to design and structure a program is as important as understanding the syntax of the programming language. In the next section, you will be introduced to flowcharting and its use in structured BASIC. But first, check your understanding of this section by trying the following Section Review.

3.3 Section Review

1. State the purpose of the main programming block.
2. Explain what the BASIC statement GOSUB does.
3. Define the term *target line.*
4. Define the term *companion remark.*
5. State the relationship between the target line and the program block.
6. Explain the purpose of the RETURN statement in BASIC.
7. What must be the last command for each main programming block? Why?

3.4 Flowcharting

Introduction

Flowcharting is one of the classic ways of beginning the design of a new program. Many programming texts describe how programmers first write complete flowcharts and then start working on the actual program. You will find that very few practicing programmers actually do this. Flowcharting is now more of a textbook exercise for students than it is a requisite for designing computer programs. As such, flowcharting will be used in this text to help explain and illustrate explanations given in the text.

If you use the methods of top-down design presented earlier in this chapter, flowcharting is not needed for initial program development. You might wonder why you should even learn about flowcharting. This section will explore some of its useful features. But first, you should know some of the basic symbols used in flowcharting.

Flowchart Symbols

The flowchart symbols that will be used in this text are shown in Figure 3.3.

Process Operation. The flowchart symbol **process operation** represents an action block in structured BASIC. The **process block** could represent that part of the program that performs a calculation or sets the value of a constant. (Not included are operations that cause a program to skip program lines and branch to another part of the program, or operations that involve input or output.) For most technical programs, this flowchart symbol is the most common.

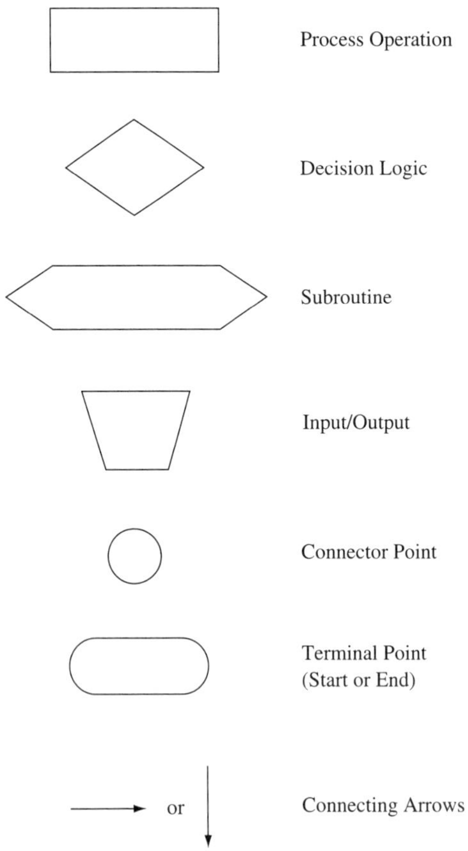

Figure 3.3 Flowchart Symbols

Decision Logic. The flowchart symbol that represents **decision logic** is equivalent to the **branch block** or the **loop block** in structured BASIC. It most commonly uses the **IF/THEN** statement. This flowchart symbol will be used to explain the branch and loop blocks in following chapters.

Subroutine. The flowchart symbol for the **subroutine** is implemented by the **GOSUB** command. The main programming block used in structured BASIC makes extensive use of this flowchart symbol.

Input/Output. The **input/output** flowchart symbol represents data that are received from a device external to the computer (such as the keyboard). It also represents the outputting of data to a device external to the computer such as the monitor, printer, or disk drive. Note that the disk drive unit can input information to the computer as well as get information from the computer. Thus, programming commands that interact with the disk drive always use this symbol.

Connector Point. The **connector point** symbol allows the flowchart to be constructed with a minimum amount of connecting lines. The application of this flowchart symbol will be illustrated later.

Terminal Point. The **terminal point** flowchart symbol is used to mark the start and end of a program. It will also be used in this text to mark the RETURN statement at the end of a program block.

Connecting Arrows. In flowcharting, the various symbols are connected by **connecting arrows.** Following the direction of the connecting arrows shows the structure of the program. Connecting arrows may be drawn in any direction, but usually they are drawn **vertically** or **horizontally.**

Flowcharting a Program

It is relatively easy to construct a flowchart from a block structured BASIC program. This is illustrated in Figure 3.4, using Program 3.4, Future Value.

Flowchart Analysis

Note how the main programming block is displayed using dotted lines. Also note that because the BASIC program is structured, it is easy to follow the flow of the program just by following the subroutines in the main programming block. In this way, each of the programming blocks is a simple appendage. This flowchart graphically illustrates the simplicity in reading and understanding the sequence of operations of a structured program. If you are interested in any of the programming details, you only need to look at that particular appendage for the given subroutine. It isn't necessary to read through many lines of flowcharting to discover the purpose or the structure of the program.

Advantages of Flowcharting

There are some advantages to flowcharting. One is that flowcharting gives a pictorial representation of the program. For some, this view may be useful in program analysis. As seen in Figure 3.4, a flowchart representation of a program may give you more of an insight into the program structure.

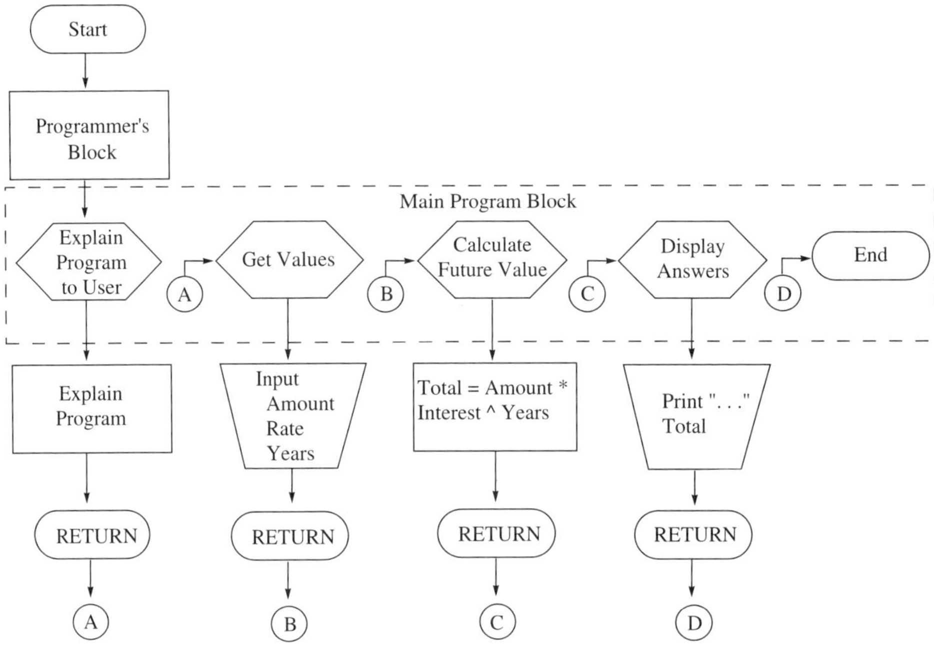

Figure 3.4 Flowchart of Future Value Program

Another advantage of flowcharting is that it is **computer language–independent.** A person need not know any programming language to follow the purpose and structure of the program. But, as you have seen, this is the same advantage structured BASIC offers.

Flowcharting is widely used in areas other than computer programming. Understanding how to use flowcharting now could be beneficial in other areas of interest.

Conclusion

Flowcharting will be used in this text as an aid in illustrating the action of different programming blocks. Flowcharts can be useful in explaining how a section of a program works; hence, they are popular in programming texts and in the documentation of many programs used in industry.

Flowcharting will not be used as a step in the initial design of a program; it will be used only for specific analysis and illustration of new concepts. Before going on, however, check your understanding by trying the following Section Review.

3.4 Section Review

1. State the main use of flowcharting as it applies to computer programming.
2. Identify each of the flowchart symbols shown in Figure 3.5.
3. Explain what is meant by a process block flowchart symbol. Give an example of a BASIC command that could be used for a process block.

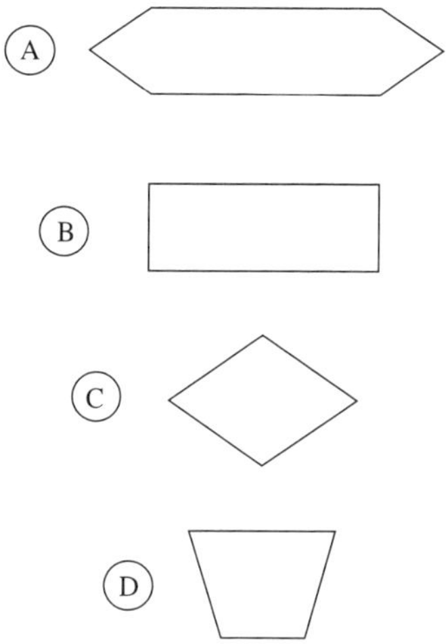

Figure 3.5 Flowchart Symbols for Section Review 3.4

4. State the use of a decision logic block flowchart symbol.
5. State what an input/output block flowchart symbol represents. Give an example.
6. Explain the purpose of a terminal point in flowcharting.

3.5 WHILE-WEND Loop

What Is a Loop?

You can think of a program **loop** as that part of a program that can repeat itself. A useful feature to have in a program is to give the program user the option of repeating the program automatically. Generally, this is done by displaying the following message at the end of a program:

```
Do you want to repeat the program (Y/N) => ?
```

This statement is requesting the user to enter a **Y** for yes or an **N** for no, depending upon whether or not the program is to be repeated. Figure 3.6 shows a flowchart example of this idea.

You will be happy to know that BASIC provides an easy way of implementing a repeat option for the program user.

The WHILE-WEND Structure

Figure 3.7 illustrates the concept of a BASIC WHILE-WEND loop.

From Figure 3.7 you can see that the **WHILE-WEND** structure actually consists of two parts: the WHILE and the WEND. In between these two parts is that part of the program you want repeated. The WHILE must be followed by some condition. As long as the condition following the WHILE part is true, then the program section between the WHILE and the WEND will be repeated.

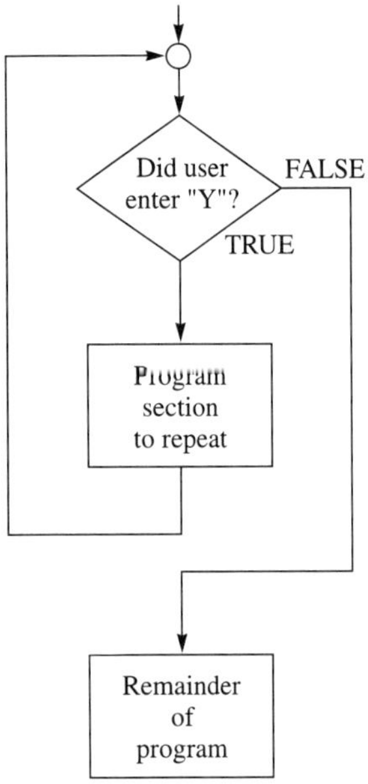

Figure 3.6 Flowchart of a Program Repeat Option

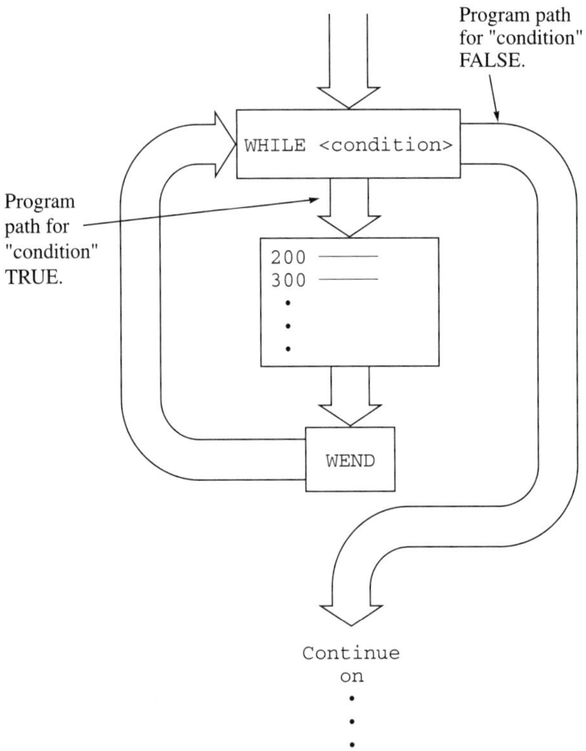

Figure 3.7 Concept of the WHILE-WEND Loop

A more formal definition of the WHILE-WEND command is

WHILE<condition>
:
[other BASIC statements]
:
WEND

where condition = Any legal BASIC expression that can have a TRUE or FALSE condition.

Note: You can have as many BASIC statements as you wish within the WHILE-WEND loop, up to the maximum number of statements acceptable to your system.

Programming Example

Program 3.5 illustrates the use of the BASIC WHILE-WEND loop to let the user repeat the program.

Program 3.5

```
10 GO$ = "Y":           REM Set initial value of GO$
20 WHILE GO$ = "Y"
30    GOSUB 100:        REM Explain program to user
40    GOSUB 200:        REM Body of program
50    GOSUB 300:        REM Ask for program repeat (update GO$)
60 WEND
70 END
100 REM Explain program to user
110 REM Body of block
120 RETURN
130 REM
200 REM Body of program
210 REM Program action statements go here
220 RETURN
230 REM
300 REM Ask for program repeat
310 CLS
320 PRINT
330 PRINT
340 INPUT "Do you want this program repeated (Y/N) =>"; GO$
350 RETURN
360 REM
```

The important part of Program 3.5, for the purposes of the WHILE-WEND loop, is the following segment:

```
10 GO$ = "Y":           REM Set initial value of GO$
20 WHILE GO$ = "Y"
30    GOSUB 100:        REM Explain program to user
40    GOSUB 200:        REM Body of program
50    GOSUB 300:        REM Ask for program repeat (update GO$)
60 WEND
70 END
```

Note that as long as GO$ is a "Y", line numbers 30, 40, and 50 will be executed. These lines are all GOSUB commands, and as such may contain a considerable amount of programming. The point is that the *main programmer's block* is kept simple and easy to read and still presents an overall view of the structure of the program. It is necessary to update GO$ at the end of each loop so that the condition is tested properly. This is done in the GOSUB 300 subroutine.

Start using the WHILE-WEND command in the programmer's blocks of your programs. It will give your programs a professional look while making your programs easier to use.

Conclusion

In this section you were introduced to the idea of making a program easily repeatable from the standpoint of the program user. Here you saw the WHILE-WEND statements. You were shown how these statements could be used to make your programs easily repeatable by the program user. Check your understanding of this section by trying the following Section Review.

3.5 Section Review

1. State what is meant by a *program loop*.
2. Explain how the two parts of the WHILE-WEND structure are used in a program.
3. In the WHILE-WEND structure, what determines whether the loop will be repeated?
4. Explain what will happen in the following program excerpt:

```
100 SELECTION$ = "B"
110 WHILE SELECTION$ = "A"
120       GOSUB 200
130       GOSUB 300
140       GOSUB 400: REM Update SELECTION$
150 WEND
160 END
```

3.6 The Waveform Viewer Project

This section begins a programming project that incorporates many of the topics that are covered in the remaining chapters. Every chapter will reveal another portion of the Waveform Viewer program.

The first step in tackling a large programming project is examining its *specification.* The specification for the Waveform Viewer is as follows:

The Waveform Viewer program accepts the name of a WAV file from the user. If the file exists, its contents are used to graphically display the associated analog waveform. A set of horizontal and vertical axes is also displayed. Figure 3.8 shows a sample screen shot of the Waveform Viewer output.

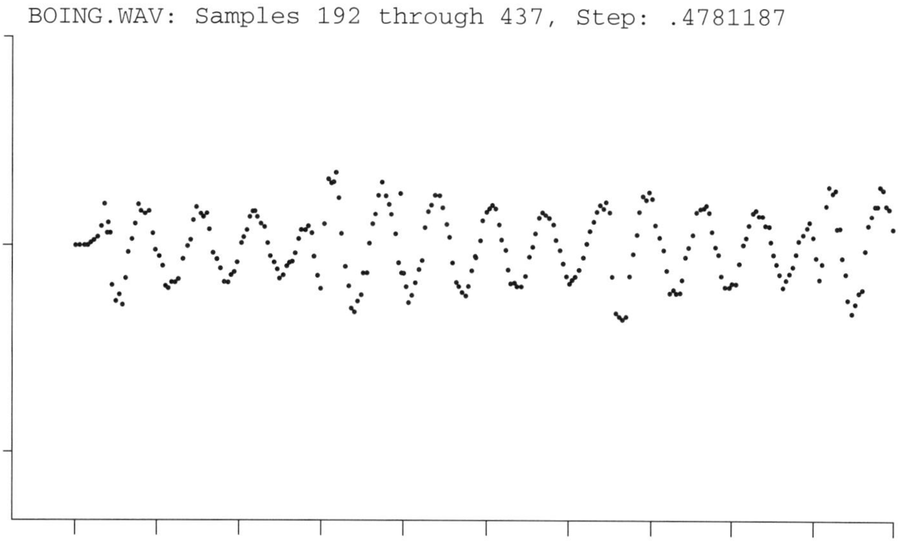

Figure 3.8 Sample Waveform Viewer Output

If the file does not exist an error message is displayed. WAV file restrictions are as follows:

- Only the first 8192 samples are displayed.
- Only mono channel, 8-bit PCM encoded WAV files are to be processed.

A zoom-in feature must provide the ability to move two on-screen pointers (to indicate the beginning and end of the zoom area) and redisplay the waveform. Zoom-out is not required.

Notice that the specification does not indicate how the Waveform Viewer should perform its job. The details of the program implementation are left to the programmer. Any questions concerning what the program should do must be answered by the details included within the specification. For example, the programmer may not be familiar with the format of a WAV file, but it is clear that only 8-bit mono-channel PCM encoded WAV files are allowed.

Conclusion

In the remaining chapters, we will see how the various components of the Waveform Viewer program are coded. For now, check your understanding of this material by trying the following Section Review.

3.6 Section Review

1. What is the purpose of a specification?
2. What information is left out of a specification?
3. What would the Waveform Viewer do with a WAV file that contains 20,000 samples?

3.7 Troubleshooting Techniques

Several examples in this chapter used the WHILE-WEND structure with a loop variable that was initialized to a specific value prior to entering the loop. For example, the code shown here requires that the XYZ variable equal zero before the WHILE-WEND loop is entered.

```
100 XYZ = 0
110 WHILE XYZ < 1
120     PRINT "Calling routine..."
130     GOSUB 500
140     XYZ = XYZ + 0.25
150 WEND
```

In general, it is not good programming practice to write code that does not contain an initialization section. There is no guarantee that the variables used in the program are initialized to the correct value by the BASIC system. This is why line 100 is required in the programming example.

Just as important as the initialization method is the manner in which the loop variable is adjusted. This helps prevent entering an *infinite loop*. Line 140 indicates how XYZ is adjusted. Eventually XYZ will be larger than 1 and the loop condition will become FALSE, terminating the loop.

Conclusion

Check your understanding of this material by trying the following Section Review.

3.7 Section Review

1. Why initialize a loop variable?
2. How many times is the GOSUB executed?

Interactive Exercises

DIRECTIONS

To complete these exercises you need to have access to a computer that uses BASIC. They are provided here to give you valuable experience and immediate feedback on what the concepts and commands introduced in this chapter will do.

Exercises

1. Develop a programmer's block of your own. Get your instructor to approve it.
2. Enter Program 3.6 and execute it.

Program 3.6

```
1000 REM Branch to line 2000
1010 GOSUB 2000
1020 REM Branch to line 3000
```

```
1030 GOSUB 3000
1040 REM Branch to line 4000
1050 GOSUB 4000
1060 REM
2000 REM Branch to line 2000
2010 PRINT "This is the first program block."
2020 REM End of block.
2030 REM
3000 REM Branch to line 3000
3010 PRINT "This is the second program block."
3020 REM End of block.
3030 REM
4000 REM Branch to line 4000
4010 PRINT "This is the third program block."
4020 REM End of block.
```

a. When Program 3.6 is executed, what is displayed on your monitor?
b. Were all four programming blocks executed (did they print messages on the screen)?
c. If all four programming blocks were executed, why did you get a syntax error during program execution?

3. Modify the program given in Exercise 2 so that it appears as shown in Program 3.7. Note the only changes are the substitution of RETURN statements at the end of each program block.

Program 3.7

```
1000 REM Branch to line 2000
1010 GOSUB 2000
1100 REM Branch to line 3000
1110 GOSUB 3000
1200 REM Branch to line 4000
1210 GOSUB 4000
1300 REM
2000 PRINT "This is the first program block."
2010 RETURN
2020 REM
3000 PRINT "This is the second program block."
3010 RETURN
3020 REM
4000 PRINT "This is the third program block."
4010 RETURN
4020 REM
```

a. What happens when Program 3.7 is executed?
b. How many times was each program block executed? Why?
c. Did the program cause a syntax error? Why?

4. What happens when you try the following?

```
10 WHILE
20         PRINT "WOW"
30 WEND
```

Why do you suppose this happens?

5. Try to figure out what the following BASIC statements will do. Then enter and try the program. (A control-break gets the computer out of endless loops.)

```
10 TRUE = 1
20 FALSE = 0
30 WHILE TRUE
40        PRINT "WOW!"
50 WEND
```

What did you observe? Why did this happen?

6. Figure out what the following BASIC statements will do, then execute the program.

```
10 TRUE = 1
20 FALSE = 0
30 WHILE FALSE
40        PRINT "WOW!"
50 WEND
```

What actually happened when you executed the program?

7. Enter the following BASIC statements. What happens when they are executed?

```
10 INPUT "Give me a number between 1 and 10"; NUMBER
20 ON NUMBER GOSUB 20, 30, 40, 50, 60, 70, 80, 90, 100
30 PRINT "Ten"
40 PRINT "Twenty"
50 PRINT "Thirty"
60 PRINT "Forty"
70 PRINT "Fifty"
80 PRINT "Sixty"
90 PRINT "Seventy"
100 PRINT "Eighty"
110 PRINT "Ninety"
120 END
```

What happens if you enter 10? Why? What happens if you enter 1? Why?

8. Modify the GOSUB of the last program to

```
20 ON NUMBER GOSUB 30, 40, 50, 60, 70, 80, 90, 100, 110
```

What happens if you enter 10? Why? What happens if you enter 1? Why?

Self-Test

DIRECTIONS

Program 3.4 was developed to show the proper way to write a structured BASIC program. Answer the following questions by referring to it.

Questions

1. What line does the main program block begin at? How many lines does it contain?
2. How many program blocks are there? What do they do?
3. How can the program be modified to show the accumulated value at the end of each year being calculated?

4. What happens if the user enters 6 for the RATE? What is the value of INTEREST?
5. How can the program be modified to allow the program to be repeated?
6. If the END statement is removed from line 550, how is execution of the program changed? Why?

Study Questions

DIRECTIONS

Each problem is presented in a particular area of technology. Use the WHILE-WEND where appropriate to allow an easy repeat of the program.

1. Assume that the cost of labor to produce a certain item is $24 per hour per person. Develop an outline for a block structured program that represents a report that would be printed to the monitor discussing the following:
   a. Cost of labor.
   b. Labor cost per 40-hour workweek if it takes five workers to produce the item.
   c. Labor cost per 40-hour workweek if your company purchases a computer interface to help produce the item for one year.
2. Develop a report in block structured form that outlines a program that would explain to a beginning drafting technology student how to find the areas of the following figures.
   a. Rectangle
   b. Triangle
   c. Circle
   d. Hexagon
3. Develop a block structured outline for a program that would PRINT to the monitor the keyboard symbols that are available on your computer keyboard other than letters of the alphabet and numbers.
4. Develop a block structured outline for a program that would print to the monitor the standard sizes of lumber available for home construction.
5. Write a block structured outline for a program that would PRINT to the monitor the standard resistor color code.
6. Develop an outline for a computer program that would compute the cost of irrigating land in your region. The user inputs are
   a. Number of acres of land to be irrigated.
   b. Irrigation equipment setup cost per acre.
   c. Cost of irrigation per acre per hour.
7. Write an outline for a computer program that would convert a thermometer reading in degrees Fahrenheit to degrees centigrade.
8. A tool requires a specific amount of power to operate in a machine shop. Write the outline of a computer program that will project the energy costs of operating a specified number of these machines. The user inputs are
   a. Number of tools in the shop.
   b. Power requirements of each tool.
   c. Local cost of electrical power in kilowatt-hours.
   d. Number of hours of operation of the machines (assume all are operating at the same time).

9. Using outline blocks, design a block structured BASIC program that would compute the cost of the material of a printed circuit board for a digital computer. The user inputs are
   a. Board size.
   b. Cost per unit size.
   c. Number of boards to be purchased.
10. Create an outline using program stubs that takes a hexadecimal number and converts it into a binary number.
11. Design a structured outline for a program that computes the area of a rectangular piece of property for a potential site. The user inputs are
    a. Length of road frontage.
    b. Angle (in degrees) of property diagonal.
12. Create a structured outline for a program that computes the power dissipation of a resistor. The user inputs are
    a. Value of resistor in ohms.
    b. Voltage drop across the resistor.
13. Write an outline for a program that will compute the amount of power generated by a rural solar power plant in 24 hours. The user inputs are
    a. Area of solar cell bank.
    b. Wattage developed per unit area.
    c. Anticipated number of daylight hours in a 24-hour period.
14. Develop a structured outline for a program that converts ounces to grams.
15. Create a structured outline for a program that converts the sector of a circle to a percentage of the total area of the circle. The user inputs are
    a. Circle radius.
    b. Sector angle in degrees.
16. Construct a flowchart of the appropriate program for Study Questions 10 through 15.
17. Design a structured outline for a program that plays tic-tac-toe. The user is player one and the program is player two. The user always goes first, but may choose to be X or O.
18. Create a flowchart for a simple text editing program. Users may open, create, and save files. While editing a program, the following features are available: cut, paste, delete, find, and replace.

4 Computations and Comparisons

Ken Koder sat at his desk in front of his computer screen. He was staring intently at a few of the statements in the program that implemented the formula to convert between Fahrenheit and Celsius temperatures. He knew the results were incorrect because when he entered 212 degrees Fahrenheit, the converted answer was 349.60 degrees Celsius, instead of 100.

As Ken examined the code, it became obvious what the problem was. He had forgotten to add some parentheses to make sure the order of mathematical operations was processed correctly.

He tested the program again, confident the problem was corrected. This time he received the answer of 85.78 degrees Celsius. Astonished, Ken looked at the code one more time. This time he noticed a typographical error in the formula. He corrected the mistake, and finally the right answer was displayed on the monitor. Ken was very pleased with himself, until he began to wonder whether he had coded the Celsius to Fahrenheit conversion properly in another part of the program.

Objectives

This chapter gives you the opportunity to learn

1. The fundamental properties of numbers in BASIC.
2. Some of the different variables allowed in BASIC and suggestions on how to use them.
3. How to format the screen to display data.
4. The fundamental arithmetic operations in BASIC and their order of precedence.
5. The logical operators and how to use them in BASIC.
6. The elements of logical decision making using IF-THEN and how it looks in structured BASIC.

Introduction

This chapter demonstrates how to use numbers with structured BASIC. You will also see how to do computations and comparisons with numbers. Logical operations are presented here, with some examples of how to apply them in programming.

The last section in this chapter introduces a powerful concept in programming: the IF-THEN statement. It is this statement that makes the computer appear "smart," giving the machine its decision-making capabilities.

4.1 Using the Computer as a Calculator

You can add, subtract, multiply, divide, raise to a power, and take any root with BASIC, essentially using the computer as a calculator.

If you tried addition in BASIC by entering

```
6 + 12
```

BASIC would defer execution because the BASIC interpreter would use the 6 as a **line number.** If you want an immediate answer to a computational problem PRINTed on the screen by BASIC, you must do it without starting with a line number. When you leave the line number off, BASICA and GWBASIC enter **immediate mode.** In QBASIC, press the F6 key to enter immediate mode.

Addition in Immediate Mode

You can perform addition immediately in BASIC by entering

PRINT N_1 + N_2

As soon as you press the ENTER key, the sum of the answers will be displayed. As an example,

```
PRINT 6 + 12
18
```

Subtraction in Immediate Mode

Subtraction in immediate mode is simply

PRINT N_1 - N_2

This yields the difference in N_1 and N_2 after the ENTER key is pressed. The sign of the answer is preserved in this calculation:

```
PRINT 15 - 6
9
```

or

```
PRINT 6 - 15
-9
```

BASIC will also accept combinations of addition and subtraction, yielding the correct sign of the final answer.

```
PRINT 8 + 2 - 5 + 74 - 12
67
```

Multiplication and Division in Immediate Mode

As shown in the examples in Chapter 1, **multiplication** is represented in BASIC with an **asterisk** (*) rather than the traditional × sign. Recall that the reason for this was so X could be used as a variable.

To multiply in immediate mode, use

```
PRINT 3 * 4
12
```

For **division,** the slash (/) is used.

```
PRINT 12/3
4
```

Raising a Number to a Power in Immediate Mode

In BASIC, a number may be raised to a **power** in this way

```
PRINT N ^ X
```

This yields N^X when executed. Note that the ^ symbol is placed on the screen by holding down the SHIFT key at the same time you press the key containing the symbol. On computer keyboards, this symbol usually shares a key with another symbol. To raise 2 to the third power, use

```
PRINT 2 ^ 3
8
```

It is very important to understand the *order of operations* BASIC uses to evaluate complex mathematical expressions. For example, how is this expression evaluated?

```
PRINT 1 + 2 * 3 - 4 ^ 2 + 3
```

If you have difficulty obtaining the correct answer of –6, refer to Figure 4.1 for assistance.

Done First ⟶ ( )

Then ⟶ ^

Then ⟶ * and /

Then ⟶ + and –

Figure 4.1 Order of Operations Followed by BASIC

As indicated in Figure 4.1, anything in parentheses is evaluated first, then powers are evaluated. Multiplication and division are performed next, and finally addition and subtraction. This forces the example expression to be evaluated as if it were written like this:

```
PRINT 1 + (2 * 3) - (4 ^ 2) + 3
```

which simplifies to

```
PRINT 1 + 6 - 16 + 3
```

Since only addition and subtraction operations remain, they are evaluated from left to right. This gives the final result of –6 as previously stated.

Keep the order of operations in mind as you write your own BASIC expressions for evaluation.

Taking Roots in Immediate Mode

You can also take the **root** of a number in BASIC. For example,

```
PRINT 9 ^ 0.5
```

is the same as $\sqrt{9} = 3$. And

```
PRINT 8 ^ (1/3)
```

will take the **cube root** of 8, which is 2.

Square Root Function

In BASIC the function **SQR** returns the square root of the number supplied. This number is called the **argument.** As an example, in

```
PRINT SQR(16)
4
```

the number 16 is the argument for the SQR function. The argument can also be an arithmetic expression, as in

```
PRINT SQR(2 * 8)
4
```

Using E Notation

In BASIC numbers may be represented in **powers of 10.** To do this, the number is written in a standard form that contains two parts. For example, 3E4 means 3 times 10^4. This is 3 times 10,000, or 30,000. BASIC verifies this value in immediate mode with

```
PRINT 3E4
30000
```

It is important to note that BASIC *does not use commas to represent large numbers.*

Negative exponents may also be used, as in

```
PRINT 3E-3
.003
```

Largest and Smallest

BASIC has a largest and smallest number that can be represented. This is

```
1E38
```

(Same as 1×10^{38}.)

The smallest number is

```
1E-38
```

(Same as 1×10^{-38}.)

If a number larger than 1E38 occurs in a program, the BASIC interpreter will cause

```
OVERFLOW ERROR
```

to be displayed.

Integers and Real Numbers

There are two distinct types of numbers. One type is called an **integer,** the other type is called a **real number.** An integer is simply a whole number (a number without any fractional value). As an example, 24 is an integer, 24.3 is not an integer. However, 24 and 24.3 are both real numbers. Any number you can think of is a real number.

The reason for making this distinction in programming is that an integer number will use less computer memory space than a real number. The memory space for a real number must store not only the numerical values of each digit but also the placement of the decimal point. It also takes more computer time to do arithmetic operations with real numbers. Think of multiplying 34.08 by 7.0045; besides doing the indicated multiplication, the computer must also figure out where the decimal point is going to go, and that takes time. So if you need your program to be fast and to conserve memory, use integers where possible.

Some BASICs offer two types of real numbers. These two types are **single precision** and **double precision.** Both single precision and double precision are real numbers. The difference is the number of digits they accommodate. A single-precision number will accommodate seven or fewer digits, whereas a double-precision number will accept up to and including 17 digits. Look at the following examples:

Integers: 12 –8 342 5875
Single Precision: 12.34567 12345.67 –.091
Double Precision: 1234.5678901324 –234.5987

This information may be necessary when working with very large numbers or when many digits of accuracy are required.

Conclusion

In this section, you were introduced to how BASIC does arithmetic operations in the immediate mode, which makes it possible to use the computer as an expensive calculator. You will learn more about this in the interactive exercises. For now, test your new skills in the following Section Review.

4.1 Section Review

1. Is there any advantage to using the computer in immediate mode?
2. Show what commands you would use in immediate mode to add three numbers.
3. Give examples of how the computer handles positive and negative numbers. Do this for addition, subtraction, multiplication, and division.
4. Show how you would correctly calculate 4^2 using BASIC in immediate mode.
5. State how the number 40,000 would be represented in BASIC. What is wrong with writing a number in BASIC as 45,000?
6. What is meant by order of operations?
7. Evaluate this expression: PRINT 10/2 + 3 * 4 ^ 2 – 2.

4.2 Program Constants and Variables

Constants

There are two types of constants used in BASIC. They are **numerical** and **string** constants, both of which will be explained later.

Constants are assigned to a location in memory by the LET statement. As an example,

```
LET A = 8
```

This statement assigns the value of 8 to A. The letter A represents a **unique memory location in RAM** that now contains the number 8. You can see what is in that memory location with a PRINT statement:

```
PRINT A
```

If 8 is stored in A, then this statement, when executed, will display

```
8
```

This process is indicated in Figure 4.2. Note that it is not necessary to use LET to assign a value. The statement

```
10 A = 8
```

is just as acceptable to the BASIC interpreter as

```
10 LET A = 8
```

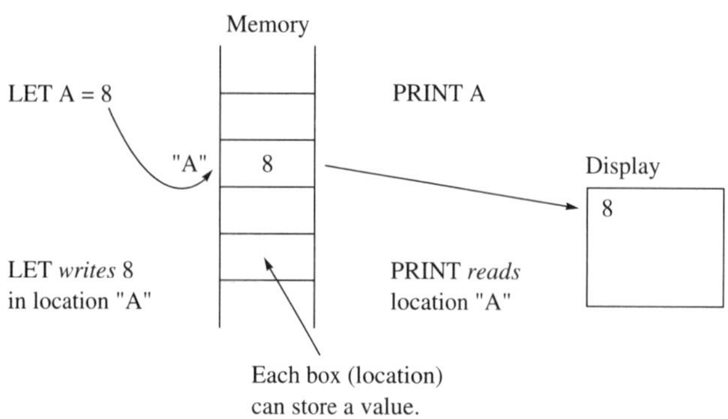

Figure 4.2 Concept of Storing a Value in Memory

The following program stores three different numbers in three different memory locations.

```
10 REM Number storage
20 LET A = 1
30 LET B = 2
40 LET C = 3
50 PRINT A, B, C
```

When this program is executed, three different memory locations in RAM (which you called A, B, and C) will now contain the numbers 1, 2, and 3, respectively. These values will be displayed by the PRINT statement. If you had programmed

```
10 REM Change a number in storage
20 LET A = 1
30 LET B = 2
40 LET C = 3
50 LET A = 4
60 PRINT A, B, C
```

the value stored in the memory location that you called A will wind up with the number 4, not the number 1. This is because the number 4 was the last number assigned to that memory location.

String Constants

A **string,** sometimes called a **character string,** is composed of alphabetic, numeric, or special characters (or a combination of two or all three) enclosed in quotation marks. For example,

```
"abcdefghijklmnopqrstuvwxyz"
```

is a string. So is

```
"0123456789"
```

Note that the digits 0 through 9 are no longer numerical values because they are now enclosed inside quotation marks. This is also a string:

```
"A! +(%$) {d2) |**|:;"
```

To designate that a string is to be stored in memory, you must place a $ after the name you assign the memory location; the $ means a string is to follow. For example,

```
LET A$ = "Secret code."
```

When this statement is executed, the string "Secret code." will be stored in memory beginning at location A$ as shown in Figure 4.3. To see what is in that location, you can again use the PRINT statement, but you must remember to tell BASIC that this is a string you are looking for.

```
PRINT A$
```

This statement will return

```
Secret code.
```

when executed.

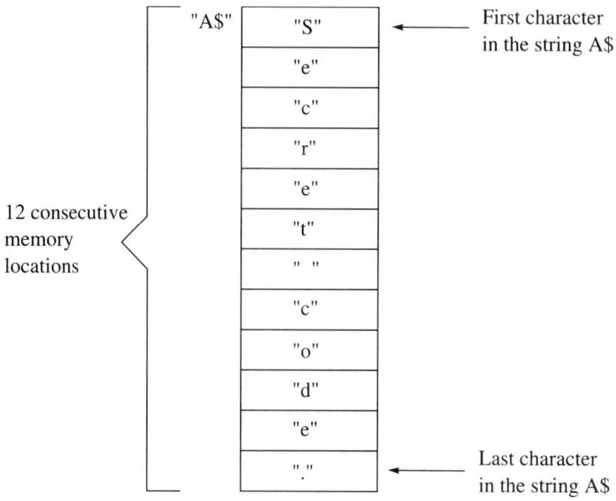

Figure 4.3 Concept of Storing a String in Memory

The following program stores both kinds of variables in memory:

```
100 REM Numerical and string storage.
110 LET A = 25
120 LET A$ = "Your name."
130 PRINT A, A$
```

Line 110 is storing a numeric constant, while line 120 is storing a string constant.

After this program is executed, the following output would be displayed:

```
25 Your name.
```

As you can see, A is a different memory location from A$.

Variables

For the purpose of programming, a **variable** can be thought of as a **unique location in memory.** Recall from Chapter 1 that RAM is used to store information you enter into the computer. (The programmer need not be concerned with where in memory things are stored; the computer will take care of that.)

For a constant, the memory location represented by the name you give it can contain only one value at a time, either numeric or string, and although the value of a *constant* stored in memory never changes during program execution (unless you assign it a new value), a variable does change its value.

An example of a program variable is

```
INPUT A
```

When this statement is executed, whatever value the program user enters will be stored in the memory location named A. Because you don't know what value will be put in A by the user, the value of A can vary; therefore; A is called a **program variable.**

Strings can also be used as variables as shown in the following program:

```
100 REM Numeric and string variables
110 INPUT A
120 INPUT A$
```

This program will wait for the program user to enter a *number* at line 110 and enter *anything* at line 120. No matter what the user enters at line 120 (even just pressing ENTER), it will be treated as a string, but this is not true for line 110, where a number *must* be entered in order for the program to continue. This is a useful feature in programming. Program 4.1 illustrates this function.

Program 4.1

```
100 REM Pausing program execution
110 PRINT "This is the first part of this program."
120 PRINT "If you want to see more, press"
130 PRINT "ENTER"
140 INPUT A$
150 PRINT "Here is the rest of the program."
160 END
```

When Program 4.1 is executed, the user will see

```
This is the first part of this program.
If you want to see more,
press ENTER
?
```

As soon as the ENTER key is pressed, line 150 will be displayed just below the ?.

```
Here is the rest of the program.
```

Variable Names

Any variable name in BASIC must start with a letter of the English alphabet (from A to Z). When you choose a variable name, it makes no difference in BASIC whether the letters are all uppercase, lowercase, or a mixture. BASIC will convert all of them to uppercase. For example,

```
10 LET Apple = 10
20 LET APPLE = 20
```

As far as BASIC is concerned, there is only one variable in the program, and that is APPLE, meaning that Apple and APPLE are the same memory location (and the final value stored there will be 20).

After the first letter, other characters, including all the letters in the English alphabet, may be used. These other characters may include a sequence of numbers and periods. For example, the following are legal BASIC variable names:

```
NUMBER    MY.NUMBER    R12    RESISTOR    V.24.X
```

The advantage of the period is that it helps break up long variable names so that they become more descriptive (the period effectively takes the place of a space, which you cannot use, because if you did, BASIC would think that you had two different variables). BASIC recognizes the first 40 characters of the variable name (some BASICs recognize fewer; check with your system documentation).

You cannot use a BASIC instruction for a variable name. For example, you cannot use PRINT as a variable name, because the computer would confuse this as an instruction for some action. Words that BASIC uses for instructions are generally referred to as **reserved words** or keywords. You cannot use a BASIC reserved word for a variable. However, a BASIC reserved word may be a part of a variable such as PRINTNUMBER.

One last thing about variables. BASIC has a feature that allows you to define your own function. The letters FN are used for this feature. What this means is that none of your variable names may start with the letters FN. If they do, you will get a syntax error.

Hence, to summarize,

- A variable name begins with a letter of the English alphabet.
- After the first letter, numbers, letters, and periods may be used.
- BASIC converts all variable names to uppercase.
- A variable name recognizes the first 40 characters.
- A variable name cannot be a BASIC reserved word.
- A variable name cannot begin with the letters FN.

Types of Variables

Most BASICs have four types of variables. They are

- String variables.
- Integer variables.
- Single-precision variables.
- Double-precision variables.

Recall that a string variable must be followed by the $ symbol. For example, NAME$ is a string variable. A string variable will store any combination of characters in its memory location.

```
10 LET NAME$ = "This is my name!"
```

This statement assigns the string "This is my name!" to the variable NAME$.

If you want a variable to be strictly an integer, then follow the variable name with a %. For example, NUMBER% will ensure that the value represented by NUMBER% will always be an integer. Thus,

```
10 LET NUMBER% = 12.52
```

will recognize only the 12 and ignore the .52.

If you want a variable to be strictly single precision, then follow the variable name with the !. Thus, NUMBER! will always be a single-precision variable. For double precision, use the # and the NUMBER# will always be treated as a double-precision variable. Generally speaking, most of the BASIC variables you will be using will be of two types: standard numerical and string variables. To give you an idea of the difference in these variables, consider the following:

```
10 LET NUMBER% = 3/7
20 LET NUMBER = 3/7
30 LET NUMBER! = 3/7
40 LET NUMBER# = 3/7
50 LET NUMBER$ = "3/7"
60 PRINT "Integer result 3/7 ="; NUMBER%
70 PRINT "Standard number result 3/7 ="; NUMBER
80 PRINT "Single precision result 3/7 ="; NUMBER!
90 PRINT "Double precision result 3/7 ="; NUMBER=#
100 PRINT "String result 3/7 ="; NUMBER$
```

When these statements are executed, the result is

```
Integer result 3/7 = 0
Standard number result 3/7 = .4285714
Single precision result 3/7 = .4285714
Double precision result 3/7 = .4285714285714285
String result 3/7 = 3/7
```

Conclusion

This section showed you what constants and variables are in BASIC. You also saw the difference between a numeric and a string variable, in addition to learning the rules of assigning names to these constants and variables.

In the next section, you will see how to work with these constants and variables and how to display them in a manner that is easy to read and understand. For now, test your knowledge of this section with the following Section Review.

4.2

Section Review

1. Name the two types of constants used in BASIC.
2. Explain what happens when the statement

   ```
   LET R = 5
   ```

   is executed.
3. When the following program is executed

   ```
   10 LET Q = 1
   20 LET W = 5
   30 LET Z = Q + 5
   40 LET Q = Z
   ```

   what will be the values stored in Q, W, and Z?
4. Explain what is meant by a string.
5. Give an example of how you would store the string Hello in a memory location beginning at W$.
6. State the difference between the following two program lines:

   ```
   PRINT K
   PRINT K$
   ```

7. State the rules for naming variables.
8. Which of the following are *not* legal BASIC variable names?

   ```
   Z  THIS.NAME  24SKIDOR  FN.ME  MY/WORD  BIGSCORE!
   ```

4.3 Screen Formatting

Screen formatting is how you design your program to appear on the monitor screen. Putting some time and effort into this can make your program easier to use and understand. This is such an important area in programming that many software companies spend the majority of their development time in the design of screen formatting. Figure 4.4 illustrates a **multiscreen** display using display **windows** to present several different types of information to the program user.

INPUTting with Instructions

The INPUT statement was introduced in Chapter 1 as a means of having the program user enter information into the program.

```
10 REM Input information
20 PRINT "Enter a number."
30 INPUT N
```

Recall that the preceding program would cause the variable N to assume the value entered by the program user (remember, N is a specific memory location that you named). When this program is executed, the following is displayed:

```
Enter a number.
?
```

and the program waits for the user to enter a number.

Another method can be used to explain to the program user what is to be entered. Follow the INPUT statement with a **prompt string:**

```
INPUT "prompt string"; variable
```

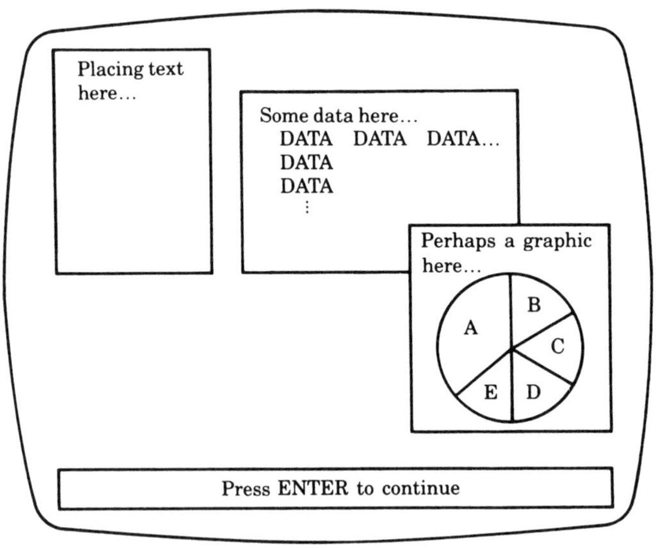

Figure 4.4 Examples of Screen Formatting

Hence, the program could have been written

```
10 REM New input information
20 INPUT "Enter a number"; N
```

When executed, it will display

```
Enter a number?
```

and the program will again wait for the user to input a number and press the ENTER key.

The Comma

The **comma** serves many useful purposes in BASIC screen formatting. For example, you may want the program user to input the value of several resistors. This can be done by using the INPUT statement in its most general form

```
INPUT variable 1, variable 2, . . . variable n
```

where each of the variables can be either numeric or string variables. Program 4.2 is an example of the resistor program.

Program 4.2

```
10 REM Series Resistance Program
20 PRINT "This program solves for the total"
30 PRINT "resistance of three resistors in series."
40 PRINT "Enter the three values separated with"
50 PRINT "commas: #, #, #"
60 INPUT "Value of each resistor ==> "; R1, R2, R3
70 LET RT = R1 + R2 + R3
80 PRINT "The total resistance is "; RT; " ohms."
```

Assume that the value of each resistor entered by the program user will be R1 = 10, R2 = 20, and R3 = 30 ohms. When the program is executed, the following will appear on the screen

```
This program solves for the total
resistance of three resistors in series.
Enter the three values separated with
commas: #, #, #
Value of each resistor ==> ?
```

The user must now enter the value of each resistor with each value separated by a comma. The comma tells BASIC that the user has finished entering the value of one resistor and is ready to enter the value of the next resistor. This is how it would look on the screen after all three resistor values were entered:

```
This program solves for the total
resistance of three resistors in series.
Enter the three values separated with
commas: #, #, #
Value of each resistor ==> ?10,20,30
```

After the last number was entered and the ENTER key pressed, the last line of the program would now be displayed:

```
The total resistance is 60 ohms.
```

You can also input string variables as shown in Program 4.3.

Program 4.3

```
10 REM Inputting strings and numbers
20 PRINT "Input the name and amount of"
30 PRINT "acreage of the crop."
40 INPUT "Crop name, acreage ==> "; C$, A
```

When Program 4.3 is executed, the following will appear:

```
Input the name and amount of string "wheat" and
acreage of the crop.
Crop name, acreage ==> ? wheat, 120
```

This input would cause the string variable C$ to contain the string "wheat" and the numeric variable A to contain the number 120.

Formatting with the PRINT Statement

The **PRINT** statement can also use commas to help in screen formatting. BASIC programs come with **preset tabs** that can be used with the comma. How many preset tabs there are depends on the computer you are using. The interactive exercises for this chapter will show you how to find out. For example, when these two statements are executed:

```
100 REM Preset tab demonstration
110 PRINT "Room 1", "Room 2", "Room 3"
```

the display will look like this:

```
Room 1     Room 2     Room 3
```

Program 4.4 is an example of expanding the use of the preset tabs in BASIC.

Program 4.4

```
100 REM Using preset tabs
110 INPUT "Number of patients in each room"; A, B, C
120 PRINT "Room 1", "Room 2", "Room 3"
130 PRINT A, B, C
```

When Program 4.4 is executed, the following will appear:

```
Number of patients in each room?3,5,2
Room 1     Room 2     Room 3
3          5          2
```

The TAB

BASIC supports the **TAB** function. The TAB function must be used in a PRINT statement, as in

```
PRINT TAB(n)
```

The value of n can be any number in the range of 1 to 255. Consider this statement:

```
100 PRINT "Circles"; TAB(20); "Rectangles"
```

When executed, the following will be displayed:

```
Circles             Rectangles
```

PRINTing Constants and Variables

You have seen several statements that have strings and variables in the same PRINT statements, as in

```
10 PRINT "This contains a variable"; V
```

When executed, the string and the value of the variable are both displayed. The variable *must* be outside the quotation marks, or it will be treated as part of the string. This is shown in Program 4.5.

Program 4.5

```
10 REM String and variable demonstration
20 INPUT "Give me a number ==> "; N
30 PRINT "This is not your number ==>; N"
40 PRINT "This is your number ==>"; N
```

If the user inputs 55 for the number, the program, when executed, will display

```
Give me a number ==> ?55
This is not your number ==>; N
This is your number ==> 55
```

The reason this happens is as follows. Look at program line 30. Note that the N is contained *inside* the quotation marks. Because of this, the letter N will be treated as a part of the string "This is not your number", and not as a separate variable. That is why line 30 prints

```
This is not your number ==>; N
```

It is simply doing as it is told.

Now look at line 40. Here the variable N is placed *outside* the quotation marks. Now the letter N is being treated as a variable. Since N now represents a memory location, the number contained at that location will be displayed.

```
This is your number ==> 55
```

The PRINT USING Statement

When it is necessary to format numerical output, such as the result of a calculation, the **PRINT USING** statement provides a simple solution. Consider these two PRINT statements:

```
100 PRINT "The square root of 2 is "; SQR(2)
110 PRINT USING "The square root of 2 is #.###"; SQR(2)
```

During execution, the following results are displayed:

```
The square root of 2 is  1.414214
The square root of 2 is 1.414
```

The # symbols are used to indicate where numeric digits are allowed in the output of a PRINT USING statement. The least significant digit is rounded accordingly.

Conclusion

This section presented some important aspects of screen formatting. The next section shows how to use the arithmetic operations of BASIC to do some very powerful and interesting calculations. For now, test your understanding of this section with the following Section Review.

4.3 Section Review

1. Explain what is meant by screen formatting.
2. Describe the difference between these two programs:

```
10 REM First program          10 REM Second program
20 PRINT "Your name"          20 INPUT "Your name";N$
30 INPUT N$
```

3. State some of the uses of the comma in BASIC.
4. Explain how the program user would enter the values of the three variables shown in the following program line:

```
50 INPUT "Price of each part (as #,#,#)==>"; P1,P2,P3
```

5. Explain what the following program line would cause to be displayed when executed:

```
50 PRINT "Area of Circle","Volume of Sphere","Totals"
```

6. Describe the purpose of the TAB function in BASIC.
7. What will be displayed on the monitor screen when the following program line is executed?

```
50 PRINT "Acres"; TAB(20); "Crops"
```

8. Describe what will be displayed when the following program is executed:

```
10 LET T = 55
20 PRINT "This is the number T"
30 PRINT "This is the number "; T
```

4.4 Arithmetic Operations

What Arithmetic Operations Do

Arithmetic operations are part of the backbone of any programming language. Arithmetic operations include the operation of addition, subtraction, multiplication, and division. As you will see in this section, they also include some other useful computational tools.

Table 4.1 lists the arithmetic operations used by BASIC and compares them with the standard "everyday" notations.

Strictly speaking, the last three "mathematical operations" in Table 4.1 are really **built-in functions** of BASIC rather than pure mathematical operations. But, for your purposes in this chapter, they will be included here. Presenting the material in this manner will help you see how all of these relate to each other and make your programming easier and more understandable. These last three functions will be explained later in this section.

We briefly looked at order of operations in Figure 4.1. Let us take a closer look now.

Order of Operations

Order of operations is simply the order in which arithmetic operations are performed. As an example, look at the BASIC expression

```
LET X = 5 + 4/2
```

What will the answer be? Will the computer add 5 to 4 first and then divide by 2? Or will the computer divide 4 by 2 first and then add 5? It is important that whatever it does, it does so consistently because if it uses the first order, the answer is 4.5, whereas if it uses the second order, the answer is 7. To tell BASIC which order you want, you can use parentheses.

Table 4.1 BASIC Arithmetic Operations

Mathematical Operation	Symbol Used by BASIC	Programming Example	Standard Notation
Exponentiation	^	3^2 = 9	$3^2 = 9$
Multiplication	*	4*3 = 12	$4 \times 3 = 12$
Division	/	9/4 = 2.25	9/4 = 2.25
Integer Division	\	9\4 = 2	
Modulo	MOD	10 MOD 3 = 1	
Addition	+	4 + 5 = 9	4 + 5 = 9
Subtraction	–	8 – 3 = 5	8 – 3 = 5
Square Root	SQR(N)	SQR(16) = 4	$\sqrt{16} = 4$
Absolute Value	ABS(N)	ABS(3 – 5) = 2	$\|3 - 5\| = 2$
Integer	INT(N)	INT(3.6) = 3	

Parentheses

When **parentheses** are used in a mathematical expression, the operation inside the parentheses is performed first.

```
LET X = (5 + 4)/2
```

This yields 9/2 = 4.5, because the addition of 5 and 4 is done first (it's inside the parentheses).

Parentheses can be **nested**—that is, parentheses can be contained inside parentheses.

```
LET X = 3 *(4 + 2*(6 - 5))
```

This expression will evaluate the innermost expression first: $3 \times (4 + 2 \times 1)$, and then the expression left in the last set of parentheses: $3 \times 6 = 18$.

When using nested parentheses, the number of left parentheses must equal the number of right parentheses. Thus, the following expression is not correct:

```
LET Y = 2*(3 + 7*(2 - 5)))
```

This expression contains two left parentheses and three right parentheses, and a syntax error message will result. It should be noted that different BASIC interpreters are limited in the maximum number of nested parentheses they can handle. The interpreter can keep track of only a certain number of pending operations.

Using Order of Operations

Table 4.2 lists the order of priority for BASIC arithmetic operations.

Consider the following cases:

`LET A = 6 + 12/6` (Division before addition)

When this is computed, it yields

```
A = 6 + 2 = 8
```

`LET N = (6 + 12)/6` (Addition before division due to parentheses)

When the above is computed, it yields

```
N = 18/6 = 3
```

Table 4.2 Priority of BASIC Arithmetic Operations

Priority	**Operation**
First	( ) or BASIC functions (ABS, INT, SQR, etc.)
Second	Exponentiation ^
Third	Negation (assigning a negative number: –N)
Fourth	Multiplication *, Division /
Fifth	MOD \
Sixth	Addition +, Subtraction –

`LET X = 4^2 * 8` (Exponentiation before multiplication)

When that is computed, it yields

```
X = 16 * 8 = 128
```

`Let V = (3 - 5) ^ 2` (Subtraction before exponentiation due to parentheses)

When the above is computed, it yields

```
V = (-2) ^ 2 = 4
```

Some Useful Functions

In BASIC, the absolute function

```
ABS(arithmetic expression)
```

returns the absolute value of the arithmetic expression. For example,

```
LET Y = ABS(-5)
```

assigns a value of 5 to Y, and

```
LET Y = ABS(6 - 9)
```

assigns a value of 3 to Y.

The **integer function** in BASIC

```
INT(arithmetic expression)
```

returns a value that is the largest integer (whole number) *less than* or *equal to* the arithmetic expression. As an example, the expression

```
LET X = INT(22.87)
```

assigns a value of 22 to X.

This function can be a bit tricky when using negative numbers. You shouldn't be surprised that

```
LET Y = INT(-5.78)
```

assigns a value of –6 to Y. It does this because –6 is less than –5.78.

Some Examples

Table 4.3 gives some examples of algebraic expressions on the left and their corresponding BASIC statements on the right.

Table 4.3 Algebraic Expressions in BASIC

Algebraic Expression	BASIC Expression
$\frac{A + B}{C - D}$	(A + B) / (C – D)
$\frac{2(A \times B)^2}{4\sqrt{X - Y}}$	2*(A * B)^2 / (4 * SQR(X – Y))
$\frac{1}{\lvert\sqrt[3]{x}\rvert}$	1 /ABS(X^(1/3)))

Conclusion

This section presented the fundamental arithmetic operations of BASIC. You will use these concepts many times as you develop programs in structured BASIC. Test your understanding of this section by trying the following Section Review.

4.4 Section Review

1. State the four arithmetic operations that are available in BASIC.
2. Name the three built-in functions presented in this section.
3. Explain what is meant by order of operations.
4. Using the order of operations, determine the results of
   a. 3 + 8*2 =
   b. 3*(4 + 2) =
   c. 5 + ABS(–5) =
5. Explain the role that parentheses play in the order of operations.
6. Arrange the following arithmetic operations in the correct order.

   `+, *, (), ^, /, -, INT`

7. Using the results you would obtain with BASIC, state the results of executing Program 4.6.

Program 4.6

```
10 LET X = 5
20 LET Y = 2
30 LET Z = 3
40 LET T = (X + Y)/(Z - 2)^2
50 PRINT T
```

4.5 Introduction to the IF-THEN Statement

Making Decisions

The **IF-THEN** statement gives the computer, through BASIC, its ability to make decisions. One form of this statement is

```
IF (arithmetic expression) THEN (BASIC statements)
```

where `(arithmetic expression)` = any numeric expression
`(BASIC statements)` = one or more BASIC statements

As an example, consider Program 4.7, part of a program that could be used to help the program user identify the colors used by the standard resistor color code.

Program 4.7

```
100 REM IF-THEN demonstration
110 INPUT "Give me a number from 0 to 9"; N
120 IF N = 0 THEN PRINT "0 is represented by black."
```

In this case the color black represents 0. When the program is executed, and the user selects 0, the screen will display

```
0 is represented by black.
```

The program can be expanded to include more colors, as shown in Program 4.8.

Program 4.8

```
100 REM IF-THEN demonstration
110 INPUT "Give me a number from 0 to 2"; N
120 IF N = 0 THEN PRINT "0 is represented by black."
130 IF N = 1 THEN PRINT "1 is represented by brown."
140 IF N = 2 THEN PRINT "2 is represented by red."
```

Using Program 4.8, if the user selects a 0, 1, or 2, the corresponding color will be PRINTed.

The arithmetic expression part of the IF-THEN statement can also use strings. This is because a string is converted into the computer's own number code. Consider Program 4.9. Using this program, if the user types BLACK, BROWN, or RED, the corresponding PRINT statement will be displayed. If the user typed the word *red,* none of the lines would be displayed because the word was typed in lowercase letters.

Program 4.9

```
100 REM IF-THEN new demonstration
110 INPUT "Give me a color and I'll display the number."; C$
120 IF C$ = "BLACK" THEN PRINT "Black is a 0."
130 IF C$ = "BROWN" THEN PRINT "Brown is a 1."
140 IF C$ = "RED" THEN PRINT "Red is a 2."
```

Another example of using a BASIC statement after the THEN of an IF-THEN statement is shown in Program 4.10.

Program 4.10

```
100 REM Another IF-THEN demonstration
110 PRINT "Select by number:"
120 INPUT "1]. Square   2]. Cube "; N
130 INPUT "Give me the value ==> "; V
140 IF N = 1 THEN A = V ^ 2
150 IF N = 2 THEN A = V ^ 3
160 PRINT "Your answer is ==>"; A
```

This is a program that allows the program user to select whether the value (V) is to be squared or cubed. What follows is an execution where the user wants to find the value of 3^3 (3 cubed).

```
Select by number:
1]. Square 2].Cube ?2
Give me the value ==> ?3
Your answer is ==> 27
```

The value of N will determine if the THEN portion of line 140 or line 150 is executed.

Using Relational Operators

Table 4.4 describes the relational operators found in BASIC. A **relational operator** expresses a relationship between two quantities, in the form of a comparison. Relational operators can be used with the IF-THEN statement. Programs 4.11 and 4.12 show some examples.

In Program 4.11, the string "Fever!" will be displayed only if the user has input a value greater than 98.6.

Program 4.11

```
100 REM Example #1 Relational operators
110 REM This program checks to see if your
120 REM body temperature is above normal.
130 INPUT "What is the body temperature ==>"; T
140 IF T > 98.6 THEN PRINT "Fever!"
```

Program 4.12

```
100 REM Example #2 Relational operators
110 REM This program checks a patient's
120 REM temperature reading and gives advice.
130 INPUT "What is the body temperature ==> "; T
140 IF T > 98.6 THEN PRINT "Above normal."
150 IF T = 98.6 THEN PRINT "Normal."
160 IF T < 98.6 THEN PRINT "Below normal."
```

When Program 4.12 is executed, "Above normal", "Normal", or "Below normal" will be displayed depending on the temperature reading.

Program 4.13 could be used in computer-aided manufacturing:

Program 4.13

```
100 REM Example #3 Relational operators
110 REM This program checks to see if
120 REM two parts will fit together and
130 REM informs the operator accordingly.
140 INPUT "Diameter of hole ==>"; DH
150 INPUT "Diameter of part to put through hole ==>"; DP
160 IF DH = DP THEN PRINT "Tight fit!"
170 IF DH < DP THEN PRINT "Part too large!"
180 IF DH > DP THEN PRINT "Easy fit!"
```

Table 4.4 Relational Operations

BASIC Symbol	Example	Meaning
=	A = B	Equality: A equals B.
<> or ><	A<>B	Inequality: A is not equal to B.
<	A < B	Less than: A is less than B.
>	A > B	Greater than: A is greater than B.
<= or =<	A <= B	Less than or equal to: A is less than or equal to B.
=> or >=	A >= B	Greater than or equal to: A is greater than or equal to B.

Using String Variables

The IF-THEN statement works with string variables as well as with numerical variables because every string character is first converted to a number by BASIC. The code used for this is called the **American Standard Code for Information Interchange** and is abbreviated **ASCII.**

The ASCII code uses 128 different numbers and is divided into the following groups:

1. 32 codes for the uppercase letters of the English alphabet, as well as some punctuation symbols.
2. 32 codes used for numbers, spacing, and additional punctuation symbols.
3. 32 codes for the lowercase letters of the English alphabet and some more punctuation symbols.
4. 32 codes used for various control operations.

The complete ASCII code is contained in Appendix A. Table 4.5 lists the ASCII code for the uppercase letters of the English alphabet. Observe from this table that the letters of the English alphabet are in numerical order, to make it easy for a computer to alphabetize. Since all letters are converted to numbers using the ASCII code, it's then an easy matter to compare the numerical value of the letters and sort them accordingly. You'll see exactly how this is done later in the text.

The relational operators use the ASCII number code to make comparisons with string variables. Two strings are actually compared by taking one character at a time from each string and comparing ASCII codes. If the ASCII codes are the same, the strings are equal.

Table 4.5 American Standard Code for Information Interchange for Uppercase Letters

Character	Code	Character	Code
A	65	N	78
B	66	O	79
C	67	P	80
D	68	Q	81
E	69	R	82
F	70	S	83
G	71	T	84
H	72	U	85
I	73	V	86
J	74	W	87
K	75	X	88
L	76	Y	89
M	77	Z	90

Here is an example of two equal strings:

```
"SPECIAL ACCOUNT" = "SPECIAL ACCOUNT"
```

If the ASCII codes are different, the string with the lower ASCII number is less than the string with the higher ASCII number. For example,

```
"A" < "B"
```

and

```
"AB" < "AC"
```

are both true.

During a comparison, when one string is shorter than the other, the alphabetical order, such as in the dictionary, determines which will be considered the smaller of the two. Program 4.14 illustrates this concept.

Program 4.14

```
100 REM Example of a simple character comparison
110 INPUT "Give me a capital letter ==> "; L$
120 IF L$ > "M" THEN PRINT "Last part of the alphabet."
130 IF L$ = "M" THEN PRINT "It's in the middle!"
140 IF L$ < "M" THEN PRINT "First part of the alphabet."
```

Conclusion

This section introduced you to the IF-THEN statement. As you saw, this BASIC statement gives the computer its decision-making capability. You will learn more about this powerful statement later in the text. For now, test your understanding of this section by trying the following Section Review.

4.5 Section Review

1. Explain how the IF-THEN statement operates.
2. State under what conditions the following PRINT statement will be displayed

```
50 IF (X = 3 + 5) THEN PRINT "X equals 8"
```

3. Describe what will be displayed when Program 4.15 is executed.

Program 4.15

```
10 LET A = 3
20 LET B = 5
30 LET C = 10
40 IF (A > B) THEN IF (C < A) THEN PRINT "First statement."
50 IF (B >= A) THEN IF (C >= A) THEN PRINT "Statement two."
60 IF A <= C THEN PRINT "Third statement."
```

4. Explain what is meant by relational operators as used in BASIC.
5. Give the meaning of the following:
   a. =
   b. `<>` or `><`
   c. `=>`
   d. `<=`

6. State what the term ASCII stands for.
7. What does the ASCII code represent?
8. Explain why the ASCII codes for letters of the alphabet are in numerical order.
9. Why is a numeric code, such as the ASCII code, necessary?
10. State what is displayed when Program 4.16 is executed.

Program 4.16

```
10 LET V$ = "C"
20 IF V$ > "A" THEN PRINT "First statement."
30 IF V$ = "A" THEN PRINT "Second statement."
40 IF V$ < "A" THEN PRINT "Third statement."
```

4.6 Logical Operations

Basic Logic

In programming, a **logical** operation can have only two conditions: **true** or **false.** You saw this with the IF-THEN statement, though you may not have realized it. Here is what happens.

With the IF-THEN statement, the THEN part will be executed only when the IF part is true. For example, consider the following program line:

```
10 IF X = 10 THEN PRINT "It's now equal to 10!"
```

The relation X = 10 will be true when the numerical value stored in the computer's memory location called X contains the number 10. When this condition is true, the THEN part will be executed. ("It's now equal to 10!" will be displayed on the screen.)

An IF-THEN statement may be interpreted to mean

```
IF (this expression is true) THEN (cause something to happen)
```

Anytime the expression in the IF-THEN statement is true, the "cause something to happen" portion will execute.

Logical operations can be used in the expression part of the statement, giving you the option of making the computer look very smart. Let us examine the logical operations.

The AND Operation

The first logical operation presented here is the **AND** operation. Its syntax is as follows:

$(expression_1)$ AND $(expression_2)$

You can see that two expressions are used: $expression_1$ and $expression_2$. The whole statement is considered a single expression. The whole expression is true when $expression_1$ and $expression_2$ are both true. If either one or both are false, then the whole expression is false as indicated in Figure 4.5. For example,

```
10 IF (X = 10) AND (Y = 5) THEN PRINT "System is go."
```

Only if both X = 10 and Y = 5 will the string "System is go." be displayed.

Consider Program 4.17. Only if the string "Y" were entered in both places by the user would the string "Go home!" be displayed.

First Input	Second Input	Result of AND Operation
False	False	False
False	True	False
True	False	False
True	True	True

Figure 4.5 Truth Table for the AND Operation

Program 4.17

```
100 REM Demonstration of the logical AND
110 INPUT "Is it after 5 o'clock (type Y or N)"; T$
120 INPUT "Is the system shut down (type Y or N)"; S$
130 IF (T$ = "Y") AND (S$ = "Y") THEN PRINT "Go home!"
```

The OR Operation

The logical **OR** means

(expression$_1$) OR (expression$_2$)

As you can see, the OR operation also consists of two expressions: expression$_1$ and expression$_2$. The whole OR expression will be true if either expression$_1$ is true or expression$_2$ is true or both of them are true as indicated by the truth table in Figure 4.6. Program 4.18 shows an example of this.

Program 4.18

```
100 REM Demonstration of the logical OR
110 INPUT "Has the system been started (type Y or N)"; S$
120 INPUT "Was an error reported by the system (type Y or N)"; E$
130 IF (S$ = "N") OR (E$ = "Y") THEN PRINT "Restart system!"
```

The NOT Operation

The **NOT** operation is just as useful as the AND and OR operations. Figure 4.7 shows how the NOT operation works. Here is one application:

```
10 IF NOT (X = 10) THEN PRINT "Not equal."
```

First Input	Second Input	Output of OR Operation
False	False	False
False	True	True
True	False	True
True	True	True

Figure 4.6 Truth Table for the OR Operation

First Input	Output of NOT Operation
False	True
True	False

Figure 4.7 Truth Table for the NOT Operation

The "Not equal." message will be displayed only if variable X does not contain a 10. The same results could have been obtained with

```
10 IF X <> 10 THEN PRINT "Not equal."
```

But consider the following:

```
10 IF (X = 10) AND (Y = 5) THEN PRINT "They both check!"
20 IF NOT ((X = 10) AND (Y = 5)) THEN PRINT "No pass!"
```

The "No pass!" string will be displayed when the expression

```
NOT ((X = 10) AND (Y = 5))
```

is true. Essentially here is what happens. The NOT changes the logic condition of the AND operation. When the expression following the NOT is false, the NOT will make it true; when the expression following the NOT is true, the NOT will make it false. This is illustrated in Program 4.19.

Program 4.19

```
10 REM Example of the logical NOT
20 INPUT "Is it after 5 o'clock (Enter Y or N)"; T$
30 INPUT "Is the system shut down (Enter Y or N)"; S$
40 IF NOT ((T$ = "Y") AND (S$ = "Y")) THEN PRINT "Stay!"
50 IF (T$ = "Y") AND (S$ = "Y") THEN PRINT "Go home!"
60 IF (T$ = "Y") OR (S$ = "Y") THEN PRINT "At least one is true."
70 IF NOT ((T$ = "Y") OR (S$ = "Y")) THEN PRINT "Neither are done."
```

Table 4.6 shows the different conditions and resulting output.

Table 4.6 Using the NOT Statement (Program 4.19)

Condition of (T$ = "Y")	(S$ = "Y")	**Results Displayed on Monitor**
False	False	Stay! Neither are done.
False	True	Stay! At least one is true.
True	False	Stay! At least one is true.
True	True	Go home! At least one is true.

Conclusion

This section presented the three most common logic statements used in BASIC: AND, OR, and NOT. As you progress through this text, you will find many applications for these powerful BASIC statements. Test your understanding of this section with the following Section Review.

4.6 Section Review

1. State what is meant in BASIC by a logical operation.
2. Explain the meaning of the AND operation.
3. Explain the meaning of the OR operation.
4. Give an example of the use of the AND operation.
5. Give an example of the use of the OR operation.
6. Explain the meaning of the NOT operation.
7. Give an example of the use of the NOT operation.
8. What is displayed when Program 4.20 is executed?

Program 4.20

```
10 LET D = 2
20 LET E = 5
30 LET F = 10
40 IF (D = 2) AND (F > E) THEN PRINT "First statement."
50 IF NOT ((D > 5) AND (F < D)) THEN PRINT "Number two."
60 IF (E = D) OR (F <> E) THEN PRINT "This is three."
```

4.7 The Waveform Viewer Project

The Waveform Viewer program requires many calculations and comparisons. Some of the calculations are as follows:

- Determining the pixel position based on WAV amplitude data.
- Adjusting the beginning and ending waveform points for zooming.
- Scaling the display.

Examine the Waveform Viewer statements shown here to see how the endpoints are adjusted.

```
260 X = 88
270 GOSUB 840:     REM Change starting point
280 SAVEWST = WAVSTART + (X - 88) * WAVSTEP
290 X = 599
300 GOSUB 840:     REM Change ending point
310 WAVEND = WAVEND - (599 - X) * WAVSTEP
320 WAVSTEP = (WAVEND - SAVEWST) / 512
330 WAVSTART = SAVEWST
```

Note the use of parentheses in statements 280, 310, and 320. The calculations performed in each statement would give different (and incorrect) results without them.

Several of the comparisons performed by the Waveform Viewer are:

- Character comparisons for the "L" (left), "R" (right), and "Q" (quit) commands.
- Limit testing during zoom.
- Determining when the last pixel has been drawn.

Examine the following statements to see how limit testing is accomplished.

```
920      IF A$ = "L" OR A$ = "l" THEN GOSUB 970
930      IF A$ = "R" OR A$ = "r" THEN GOSUB 1020
.
.
.
970 REM Move arrow left
980 GOSUB 1070
990 X = X - 1
1000 IF X < 88 THEN X = 88
1010 RETURN
1020 REM Move arrow right
1030 GOSUB 1070
1040 X = X + 1
1050 IF X > 599 THEN X = 599
1060 RETURN
```

The 88 and 599 values represent the horizontal end points of the waveform display. The zoom arrows may not move beyond either end. The value of X represents the current horizontal arrow position. The character code in A$ determines whether an arrow is moved left or right (or not at all).

Conclusion

These and other types of calculations and comparisons are necessary for the proper operation of the Waveform Viewer program. Check your knowledge of this material by trying the following Section Review.

4.7 Section Review

1. What is the value of SAVEWST if WAVSTART equals 100, X equals 90, and WAVSTEP equals 10? Repeat the calculation with the parentheses in statement 280 removed.
2. Explain how the "L" and "R" character keys cause the arrow on the Waveform Viewer display to move.

4.8 Troubleshooting Techniques

Here are several important points to keep in mind:

- BASIC is not case sensitive. The variable names abc and ABC are the same.
- Be aware of a variable's type when performing arithmetic.
- String variables are followed by a "$" character, as in MYSTR$.
- Know how to use the arithmetic order of operations.
- Use AND, OR, and NOT to assist in performing complex comparisons.

Once you have written a number of programs yourself, this type of information will be automatically available, just by thinking about it.

Conclusion

Check your knowledge of this material by trying the following Section Review.

4.8 Section Review

1. What is case sensitivity?
2. Why is the order of operations important?

Interactive Exercises

DIRECTIONS

These exercises require that you have access to a computer that supports BASIC. They are provided here to give you valuable experience and, most importantly, immediate feedback on what the concepts and commands introduced in this chapter will do.

Exercises

1. Enter the following:

   ```
   10 + 5
   ```

   What are the results? Why? What happens when you enter

   ```
   RUN
   ```

   Why does this happen?
2. Try the following:

   ```
   PRINT 3 + 4
   ```

   What results do you get?
3. Enter each of the following. Be sure to record the results of each entry.

   ```
   PRINT 3 ^ 2
   PRINT 9 ^ .5
   PRINT SQR(16)
   PRINT SQR(20+5)
   PRINT -1 ^ 3
   ```

4. Your computer uses an E notation to represent large and small numbers. To discover some facts about this, enter the following:

   ```
   PRINT 3
   PRINT 30
   PRINT 300
   PRINT 3000
   PRINT 30000
   ```

   What is the largest number you can enter without getting back an E notation number? Explain how you did this.
5. Enter the following and record the results.

   ```
   PRINT .3
   PRINT .03
   PRINT .003
   PRINT .0003
   ```

What is the smallest number you can enter without getting back an E notation number? Explain how you did this.

6. Enter the following and record the results.

```
PRINT 5E0
PRINT 5E1
PRINT 5E2
PRINT 5E3
PRINT 5E4
PRINT 5E-1
PRINT 5E-2
PRINT 5E-3
PRINT 5E-4
```

What is the largest number your computer will accept? What is the smallest number your computer will accept? Explain how you did this.

7. What happens when you enter a number that is larger than your computer will accept? What happens when you enter a number that is smaller than your computer will accept?
8. What happens when you enter the following?

```
PRINT 5/0
```

9. Enter Program 4.21 and execute it. The computer will display four results. Explain what each one means. What is the difference between the 5 that is displayed by line 30 and the 5 that is displayed by line 50?

Program 4.21

```
10 LET X = 5
20 LET X$ = "5"
30 PRINT X$
40 PRINT "X$"
50 PRINT X
60 PRINT "X"
```

10. Enter Program 4.22 and execute it. What happens when you try to enter another letter? Why?

Program 4.22

```
10 INPUT "Enter a letter of the alphabet ==> "; L$
20 PRINT "The letter was "; L$
30 INPUT "Enter another letter ==> "; L
```

11. Your computer probably has preset tabs that can be invoked by using the comma. Enter Program 4.23 and execute it. Describe how the output is displayed on your system.

Program 4.23

```
10 LET A = 1
20 LET B = 2
30 LET C = 3
40 LET D = 4
50 PRINT A, B, C, D
```

12. To test the TAB function on your computer, try the following:

```
PRINT TAB(10) "10"
PRINT TAB(20) "20"
PRINT TAB(40) "40"
```

```
PRINT TAB(60) "60"
PRINT TAB(80) "80"
PRINT TAB(100) "100"
PRINT TAB(120) "120"
```

Record the results of each entry. How many columns wide is your system? What happens to the entry when it exceeds the width of your monitor?

13. To test the order of operations on your computer, first predict what you think the answer will be, then enter the computation. Using a sheet of paper, list first your predictions, then your results.

```
PRINT 3* 2 + 2
PRINT 3*(2 + 2)
PRINT 3*2 ^ 2
PRINT (3*2) ^ 2
PRINT 3*2 ^ 2+1
PRINT 3*2 ^ (2+1)
PRINT ABS(-5) + 8
```

14. See how your system responds to logic instructions. Try the following:

```
LET A = 0
LET B = 0
PRINT A OR B
PRINT A AND B
LET B = 1
PRINT A OR B
PRINT A AND B
LET A = 1
PRINT A OR B
PRINT A AND B
PRINT A <> B
PRINT A > B
LET A = 0
PRINT A > B
PRINT B > A
```

15. How many characters does your system allow for representing numeric variable names? What did you do to test this? How many characters does your system allow for representing string variable names? How did you test for this?

Self-Test

DIRECTIONS

Program 4.24 was developed for health technology. It helps compute a hospital bill. Answer the following questions by referring to this program.

Program 4.24

```
100 REM A Program to Compute a Hospital Bill
110 REM
120 REM Developed by: Doctor Programmer
130 REM
140 REM This program computes the total hospital bill
150 REM for three hospital patients.
160 REM The program user must enter the name of the
```

```
170 REM patient, number of days in hospital, patient
180 REM cost per day plus any added expenses.
185 REM
190 REM Variables Used:
200 REM P1$, P2$, P3$ = Names of each patient
210 REM D1, D2, D3    = Cost per day for each patient
220 REM N1, N2, N3    = Number of days for each patient
230 REM E1, E2, E3    = Extra expenses for each
240 REM T1, T2, T3    = Totals for each patient
250 REM T             = Total hospital bills
260 REM
300 REM Explain program to user.
310 PRINT "This program will compute the total hospital bill"
320 PRINT "for three patients."
330 PRINT ""
340 PRINT "The program user must enter the name of each patient,"
350 PRINT "the number of days in the hospital, cost per day, and"
360 PRINT "any additional expenses."
370 REM End of this block.
380 REM
400 REM Get information from user.
410 PRINT "Enter patient name and total days in the hospital."
420 PRINT
430 INPUT "First patient: name, total days ==> "; P1$, N1
440 PRINT
450 INPUT "Second patient: name, total days ==> "; P2$, N2
460 PRINT
470 INPUT "Third patient: name, total days ==> "; P3$, N3
480 PRINT
490 REM
500 REM Get information about additional expenses.
510 PRINT "Cost per day and additional expenses for "; P1$
520 INPUT "==> ", D1, E1
530 PRINT
540 PRINT "Cost per day and additional expenses for "; P2$
550 INPUT "==> ", D2, E2
560 PRINT
570 PRINT "Cost per day and additional expenses for "; P3$
580 INPUT "==> ", D3, E3
590 REM
600 REM Do computations.
610 REM Compute total cost for each patient.
620 LET T1 = (D1 * N1) + E1
630 LET T2 = (D2 * N2) + E2
640 LET T3 = (D3 * N3) + E3
650 REM
660 REM Compute total hospital bill.
670 LET T = T1 + T2 + T3
680 REM
700 REM Display the results.
710 PRINT
720 PRINT "Patient Name", "Total Days", "Expenses each patient"
730 PRINT P1$, N1, T1
740 PRINT P2$, N2, T2
750 PRINT P3$, N3, T3
760 PRINT
```

```
770 PRINT "Total expenses ==> "; TAB(25); T
780 REM
800 REM Display who has the largest bill.
810 IF (T1 > T2) AND (T1 > T3) THEN PRINT P1$; " has the largest bill."
820 IF (T2 > T1) AND (T2 > T3) THEN PRINT P2$; " has the largest bill."
830 IF (T3 > T1) AND (T3 > T2) THEN PRINT P3$; " has the largest bill."
840 REM
900 REM End of program
910 END
```

Questions

1. Explain what Program 4.24 does.
2. What is the purpose of lines 430, 450, and 470? Name the two kinds of variables used here and the reason for the comma that separates them.
3. Explain the reason for the comma before the variable D1 on line 520.
4. How many different variables are used in the program? Name them.
5. Describe the sequence of operations used in the program.
6. What programming lines would you add to Program 4.24 to determine whether any patients have stayed in the hospital for more than a week?
7. Assume there was a hospital tax of 6 percent of the total charges per patient. How would you modify the program to automatically include this charge?
8. State the purpose of the commas between the variables in program lines 730, 740, and 750.
9. Show what changes you would make to the program to show which patient has the smallest bill instead of the largest bill.

Study Questions

1. Describe how you would use the computer as a calculator. What mathematical operations could be performed in this manner? Give an example of an entry that
   a. Gets the sum of three numbers.
   b. Calculates the sales tax of the preceding sum.
   c. Adds the resultant sales tax to the original sum.
2. Explain how you would use the computer as a calculator to
   a. Find the square root of a number.
   b. Get the absolute value of any subtraction.
   c. Take any root of a number.
3. Develop a BASIC program that will find the total resistance of three parallel resistors. The formula is

$$R_T = 1/(1/R_1 + 1/R_2 + 1/R_3)$$

   where R_T = Total resistance in ohms
   R_1, R_2, R_3 = Value of each resistor in ohms

4. Develop a BASIC program that will calculate the surface area of a sphere for a given radius. The formula is

$$A = 4\pi R^2$$

   where A = surface area
   π = constant pi
   R = radius of sphere

5. Create a BASIC program that displays the days of the week for the current month in a standard calendar form.
6. Create a BASIC program that will allow the user to enter the name of a patient and the room number assigned to the patient. Construct the program to take the names of three patients at a time, then have the information displayed as follows:

Patient Name	Room Number
Mary Jones	12
Harold Smith	29
Robert James	16

7. Develop a BASIC program that will inventory five different parts. User input should include the name of the part and the number of parts. Have a minimum number of 10 parts before a reorder is to occur. If the user inputs a number less than 10, then the program should indicate that a reorder is necessary.
8. Create a BASIC program that will compute a 6 percent sales tax on five items. The user should input the following:

   Name of the item
   Price

   The program should then calculate the total cost and state which item was the most expensive and which item was the least expensive.
9. Develop a BASIC program that will alphabetize three letters of the alphabet input by the user.
10. Write a BASIC program that will compute the power dissipation of each of four resistors input by the user. Assume that each resistor is to be connected to the same 24 V voltage source. The formula for the power dissipation is

$$P = V^2/R$$

   where P = power dissipated in resistor
   V = voltage
   R = value of resistor

   Have the program state which of the four resistors dissipates the most power and which of the four resistors dissipates the least.
11. Write a BASIC program that displays the truth tables of the AND, OR, and NOT operations. Be sure to use each operation to generate the truth table outputs.
12. Write a BASIC program that generates the truth table for the following expression:

```
RESULT = (A AND B) OR (B AND NOT C)
```

   The truth table must have eight different TRUE/FALSE input combinations.
13. An automobile manufacturer is designing a system that sounds a buzzer under the following conditions:
    a. The door is open and the key is in the ignition.
    b. The lights are on and the engine is off.

   Write a BASIC program that allows the user to enter the status of the door (open/closed), the ignition key (in/out), the engine (running/off), and the lights (on/off). Display the message "BUZZ" if either condition is true.
14. Write a BASIC program that converts an input number into hexadecimal. For example, if the user enters 100, the program displays 64H.
15. Write a BASIC program that determines whether an input number is even or odd.

5 Making Decisions—Branch Blocks

Ken Koder was using the flowchart symbols in Microsoft Word to create a flowchart for the program he was designing. He usually did not bother with this step, but the customer had specifically requested that a flowchart be produced. As he connected all the parts together, he noticed that it helped him understand the process better.

Don, the senior technician, looked over Ken's shoulder and commented, "I didn't know that Word had flowchart symbols in it."

Ken, turning around to talk to Don, stated, "I've never used them before, but I had seen them on the drawing toolbar. They are every easy to use and I am happy about the way the flowchart is turning out."

When Ken began writing the code using the flowchart as a guide, the process went very smoothly. So smoothly in fact, that Ken began to reconsider the importance of creating a flowchart for any type of program development.

Objectives

This chapter will show you how to

1. Use open and closed branches.
2. Structure the branch statement.
3. Use the IF-THEN-ELSE statement.
4. Make use of GOSUB in program branching.
5. Construct a case statement block.
6. Design programs using multiple branches.
7. Analyze a complex program in computer-aided troubleshooting that uses different branching techniques.

Introduction

This chapter shows you the secrets of what makes a computer appear "smart"—the ability to *simulate decision making.* Without this ability, the computer would be little more than a very fast preprogrammable calculator. However, as you will discover in this chapter, a BASIC computer program can be constructed so that what it will execute depends on a prior condition. You have worked a little bit with the IF-THEN statement. This statement can be used to give your BASIC program decision-making capabilities.

The concepts presented in this chapter are important because they are concepts that are used in all major programming languages. Be sure to take your time and carefully practice the processes presented in this chapter.

5.1 Making Choices

Basic Idea

Figure 5.1 shows a flowchart concept of a program branch.

As you can see from Figure 5.1, the program may take one of two routes, depending on the results of a **test condition.** The test condition is a BASIC statement that can have either a TRUE condition or a FALSE condition. If the test condition is FALSE, then, in the figure, program execution continues to the left; if the test condition is TRUE, then program execution continues to the right. Also notice from the figure that no matter which *branch* is taken (the one to the left or the one to the right), the program will continue forward.

An Example—Open Branch

There are two types of program branches. One is called an **open branch** and the other is called a **closed branch.** Consider first an open branch. Look at Program 5.1.

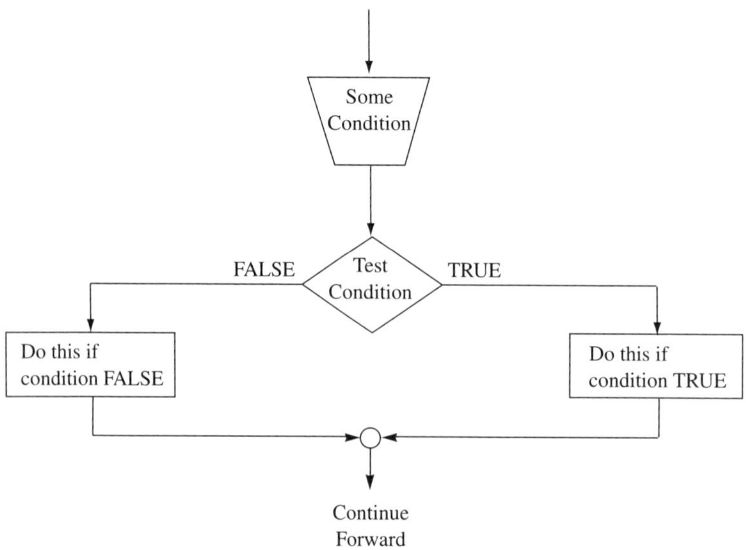

Figure 5.1 Flowchart of a Branch Block

Program 5.1

```
100 INPUT "Give me a number from 1 to 100 => "; NUMBER
110 IF (NUMBER > 50) THEN PRINT "Greater than 50!"
120 PRINT "Thank you for your number."
```

In Program 5.1, the user is asked to input a number from 1 to 100. If the number is greater than 50, then the screen will display

```
Greater than 50!
Thank you for your number.
```

However, if the user inputs a number equal to or less than 50, the screen will then display

```
Thank you for your number.
```

The reason Program 5.1 is an example of an *open branch* is because there is only one option contained in the branch.

The decision-making statement for Program 5.1 is line 110:

```
110 IF (NUMBER > 50) THEN PRINT "Greater than 50!"
```

If the condition (NUMBER > 50) is TRUE, then PRINT "Greater than 50!" will be executed. If, however, the condition (NUMBER > 50) is FALSE, the PRINT statement will not be executed. In either case, line number 120

```
120 PRINT "Thank you for your number."
```

is always executed. Figure 5.2 presents the flowchart representation of Program 5.1.

As you can see from the flowchart in Figure 5.2, there is just one branching option.

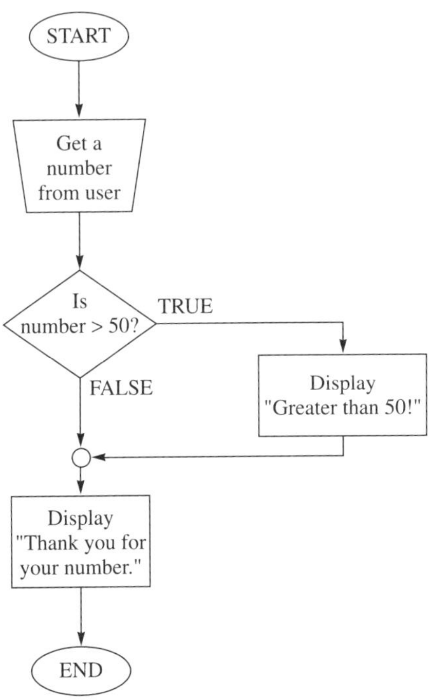

Figure 5.2 Flowchart of Program 5.1

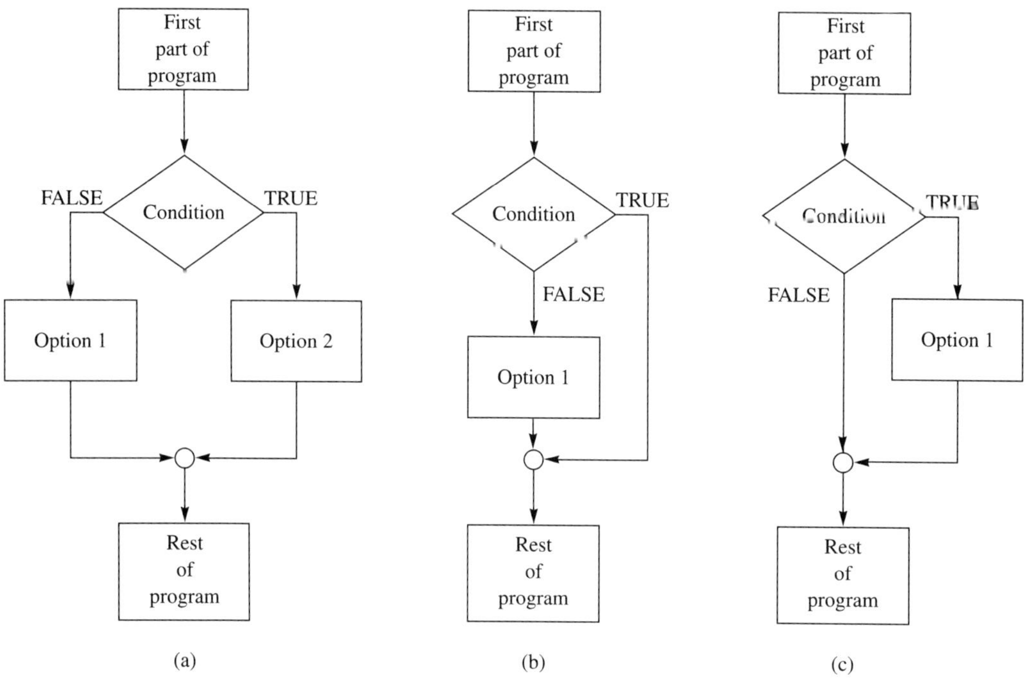

Figure 5.3 Three Types of Branches

Other Types of Branches

Consider Figure 5.3. In this figure, three types of branches are illustrated.

As shown in Figure 5.3a, the first type of branch is a *closed branch.* The reason it is called a closed branch is that one of *two* options will take place, and then the program will continue on. The next two types of branches are *open branches.* The reason the last two are open branches is that only one option is available: either the option will be selected or it will not, and the program will continue on. Note from Figure 5.3 that the single option of the open branch can take place from either a FALSE condition (Figure 5.3b) or a TRUE condition (Figure 5.3c).

Conclusion

In this section you were introduced to using a decision-making process in BASIC. Some of this material was a review of the IF-THEN statement, set in the context of an open or a closed branch. Check your understanding of this section by trying the following Section Review.

5.1 Section Review

1. Describe what is meant by a program branch.
2. What is an *open branch?*
3. Name the different types of program branches.
4. Can an open branch have an option activated on a FALSE condition?
5. What is the difference between an open branch and a closed branch? Explain.

5.2 More Choices

The Closed Branch

Program 5.2 is an example of a closed branch.

Program 5.2

```
100 INPUT "Give me a number from 1 to 100 => "; NUMBER
110 IF NUMBER > 50 THEN PRINT "Greater than 50!" ELSE PRINT "50 or less!"
120 PRINT "Thank you for your number."
```

Program 5.2 represents a closed branch because two separate choices are available. A flowchart of Program 5.2 is illustrated in Figure 5.4.

As you can see from Figure 5.4, two options are available in the program. One option is PRINT "Greater than 50!" while the other option is PRINT "50 or less!".

If the user inputs a number greater than 50, the resulting output will be

```
Greater than 50!
Thank you for your number.
```

And if the user inputs a number that is 50 or less, the resulting output will be

```
50 or less!
Thank you for your number.
```

The condition is tested by the IF-THEN-ELSE statement.

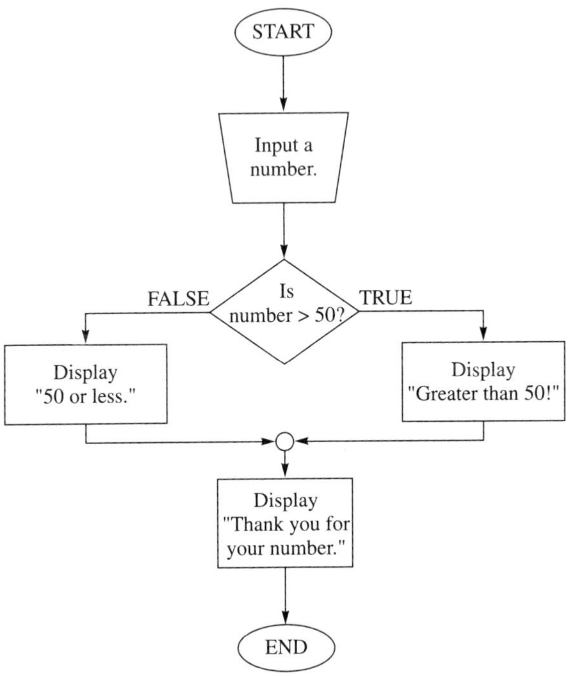

Figure 5.4 Flowchart of Program 5.2

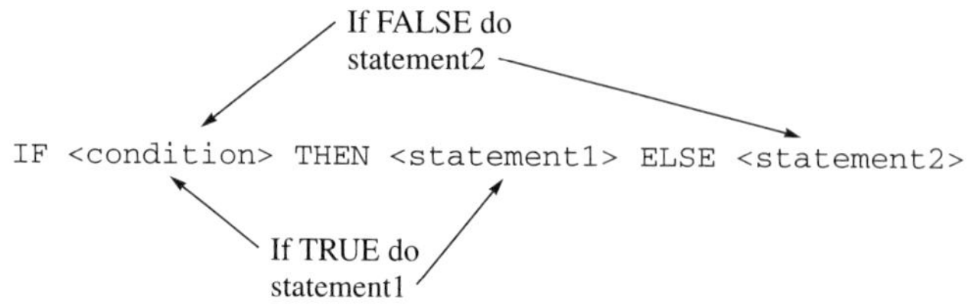

Figure 5.5 Operation of the IF-THEN-ELSE Statement

The IF-THEN-ELSE Statement

The BASIC IF-THEN-ELSE statement has the following characteristics:

```
IF <condition> THEN <statement1> ELSE <statement2>
```

where `condition` = Any legal BASIC expression that has a TRUE or a FALSE condition

`statement1, statement2` = Any legal BASIC statements

Figure 5.5 shows the operation of the IF-THEN-ELSE statement.

As shown in Figure 5.5, the IF-THEN-ELSE statement always contains two branches.

Making Things Easier to Read

Program 5.2 is somewhat awkward to read because of the long line required by the IF-THEN-ELSE statement. Most BASICs have a feature that allows you to continue your program line onto another new line, without BASIC thinking that you actually have a new line. You can continue BASIC statements in BASICA and GWBASIC onto another line as a *continuation* of the existing line by using CTRL-J. CTRL-J means that while holding down the CTRL key you press the J key. Using CTRL-J while in the BASIC editor will cause the cursor to be brought down one line and to the left of the screen. However, BASICA and GWBASIC will treat this "new line" as an extension of the last line number (up to a maximum of 255 characters and spaces).

As an example, line 110 of Program 5.2 could have been entered as

```
110 IF NUMBER > 50                    <CTRL-J>
    THEN PRINT "Greater than 50!"     <CTRL-J>
    ELSE PRINT "50 or less!"          <ENTER>
```

This may not work in all versions of BASICA or GWBASIC. Therefore, it is not recommended.

In QBASIC it is not necessary to use any special characters to create continuation lines. Simply enter the BASIC statements as you want them to appear. However, the last continuation line must always be END IF.

Using continuation lines creates a programming structure that is easier to read and easier to debug. Program 5.3 illustrates the new structure.

Program 5.3

```
100 INPUT "Give me a number from 1 to 100 => "; NUMBER
110 IF NUMBER > 50
      THEN PRINT "Greater than 50!"
      ELSE PRINT "50 or less!"
120 PRINT "Thank you for your number."
```

Using GOSUB with Branching

You can use the GOSUB statement when doing program branching. As a matter of fact, the use of GOSUB is often advisable because it usually results in a better program structure. Consider a program that will compute the total current for one of two electrical circuits. These circuits are shown in Figure 5.6.

As shown in Figure 5.6, each circuit consists of a single voltage source (designated as V) and two resistors (designated as R_1 and R_2). Both of the circuits shown are series circuits, meaning that there is only one path for current flow from the voltage source. To calculate the total current in a series circuit consisting of two resistors, you use

```
I = V /(R1 + R2)
```

where `I` = The total circuit current in amps
`V` = The source voltage in volts
`R1, R2` = The value of each resistor in ohms

Program 5.4 illustrates a method of solving for the total current in either circuit.

Program 5.4

```
100 INPUT "Give me the circuit number (1 or 2) => "; CIRCUIT.NUMBER
110 REM
120 IF CIRCUIT.NUMBER = 1
      THEN V = 5: R1 = 100: R2 = 200
      ELSE V = 9: R1 = 500: R2 = 800
130 REM
140 REM Calculate current
150 I = V / (R1 + R2)
160 REM
170 PRINT "The total current is "; I; " amps."
```

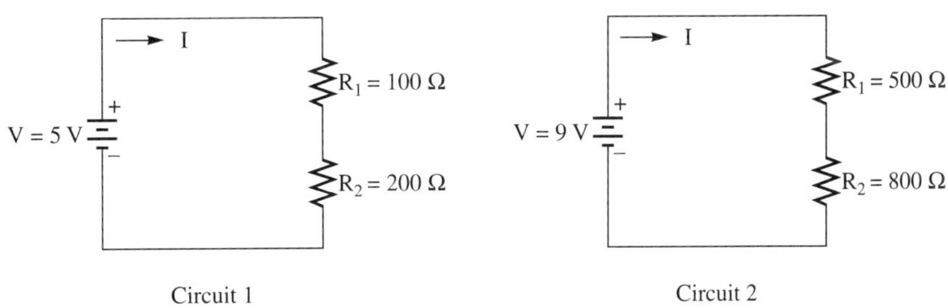

Figure 5.6 Electrical Circuits for Total Current (I)

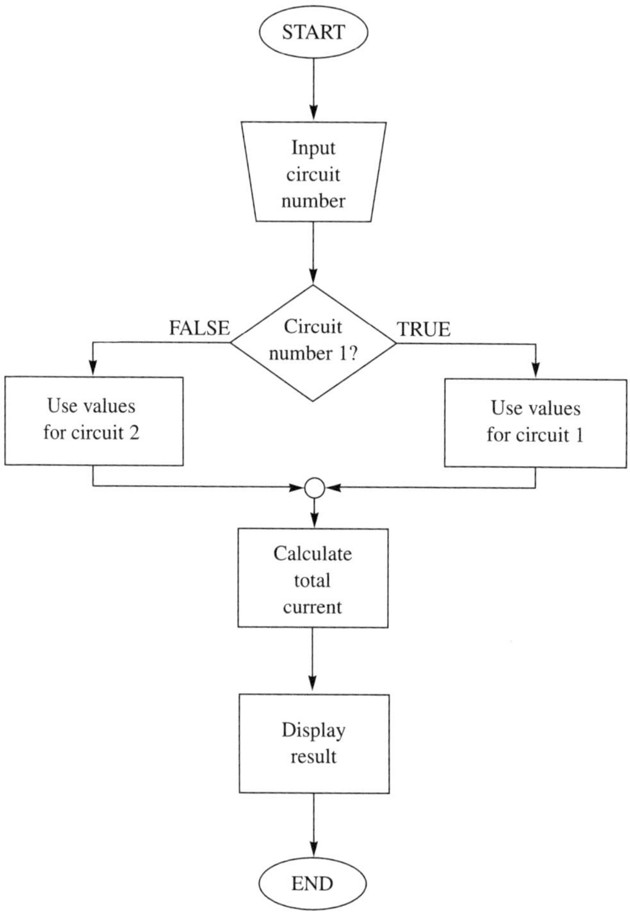

Figure 5.7 Flowchart of Program 5.4

Note the structure of Program 5.4. The IF-THEN-ELSE statement is written as follows:

```
IF CIRCUIT.NUMBER = 1
   THEN V = 5: R1 = 100: R2 = 200
   ELSE V = 9: R1 = 500: R2 = 800
```

The colon (:) allows you to place more than one BASIC statement in the same program line. CTRL-J is also used to create a new line for ease of reading. The circuit values are set according to the circuit chosen (either circuit 1 or *any other number*).

A flowchart of Program 5.4 is shown in Figure 5.7.

As shown in the flowchart, Program 5.4 will give the correct circuit values for either circuit. In both cases, the same formula is used because it applies to either circuit.

The same program could have been written using GOSUBs as shown in Program 5.5.

Program 5.5

```
100 INPUT "Give me the circuit number (1 or 2)=> "; CIRCUIT.NUMBER
110 IF CIRCUIT.NUMBER = 1 THEN GOSUB 200 ELSE GOSUB 300
120 REM Calculate current
```

```
130 I = V / (R1 + R2)
140 PRINT "The total current is "; I; " amps."
150 END
200 REM Circuit 1
210 V = 5
220 R1 = 100
230 R2 = 200
240 RETURN
300 REM Circuit 2
310 V = 9
320 R1 = 500
330 R2 = 800
340 RETURN
```

The main feature of Program 5.5 is the use of GOSUB for options in the program branch. The key statement is line 110:

```
110 IF CIRCUIT.NUMBER = 1 THEN GOSUB 200 ELSE GOSUB 300
```

Notice the IF-THEN-ELSE statements make use of GOSUB. By using GOSUB to branch to another section of the program, you can create very large program sections and still preserve the block structure of your program.

Conclusion

In this section you learned more about program branching. You saw the use of the IF-THEN-ELSE statement. You also saw methods of structuring your program to keep it easy to read, modify, and debug. Use of GOSUB in program branching was also introduced.

Check your understanding of this material by trying the following Section Review.

5.2 Section Review

1. Describe what is meant by a *closed branch.*
2. What method may be used to create a new line in the BASIC editor without having to add a new line number?
3. What are the limitations, if any, for creating a new line as in Question 2 above?
4. Can you have more than one BASIC statement for a given program line? Explain how this is done.
5. What is the advantage of using GOSUB in a program branch?

5.3 Making Multiple Choices

Multiple Choices—The Case Structure

The **case structure** gives the program the power to choose between alternatives. This differs from the open branch in that in the **case,** one of the alternatives must be selected or an error will occur (the intended results will not be achieved). An example of the kind of programming that lends itself to the case structure is shown in Program 5.6.

Program 5.6

```
10 INPUT "What is the number (0 to 2)"; N
20 IF N = 0 THEN C$ = "Black"
30 IF N = 1 THEN C$ = "Brown"
40 IF N = 2 THEN C$ = "Red"
50 PRINT "Color is "; C$
```

Resistor Color Code Program

Program 5.7 illustrates the use of the case structure. There are several important features in this program. First, there is a *subroutine* using the case structure in the programming block beginning at line 5000.

Program 5.7

```
100 REM Resistor Color Code
110 REM
120 REM Developed by:
130 REM A. Technology Student
140 REM
150 REM This program will compute the standard color code
160 REM of a resistor.
170 REM The program user must enter the value of the first
180 REM two numbers and then the place value of the total
190 REM number. As an example:
200 REM    1200 = Value of the first two numbers is 1 and 2.
210 REM           Place value is 3 (10 to the 3rd power).
220 REM    120  = Value of first two numbers is 1 and 2.
230 REM           Place value is 2 (10 to 2nd power).
240 REM
250 REM Variables used:
260 REM N = Variable for all numbers.
270 REM C1 = Value of first number.
280 REM C2 = Value of second number.
290 REM C3 = Value of place value.
300 REM C1$ = Color of first number.
310 REM C2$ = Color of second number.
320 REM C3$ = Color of third number.
330 REM C$ = Computed color.
340 REM V1 = Value of first digit.
350 REM V2 = Value of second digit.
360 REM V3 = Place value of the number.
370 REM CT$ = Complete color code.
380 REM AGAIN$ = Variable for program repeat.
390 REM
400 REM Main Program Block
410 REM Explain program to user.
420 GOSUB 1000
430 AGAIN$ = "Y":       REM Set initial value of AGAIN$
440 WHILE AGAIN$ = "Y"
450    REM Get values from user and compute colors
460    GOSUB 2000
```

```
470    REM Display answers
480    GOSUB 3000
490    REM Program repeat
500    GOSUB 6000
510 WEND
520 END
1000 REM Explain program to user.
1010 PRINT "This program will convert numbers into the standard"
1020 PRINT "colors of the resistor color code."
1030 PRINT
1040 PRINT "You must enter the first two digits of the number and"
1050 PRINT "then the power of ten for that number if it were"
1060 PRINT "expressed in scientific notation."
1070 PRINT
1080 PRINT "As an example: 1200 would be entered as -"
1090 PRINT "1 for the first number; 2 for the second"
1100 PRINT "and three for the power of ten (as if it were"
1110 PRINT "expressed as 1.2 * 10 ^ 3)."
1120 PRINT
1130 INPUT "Press ENTER to continue."; A$
1140 RETURN
1150 REM
2000 REM Get values from user and compute colors
2010 PRINT
2020 INPUT "What is the first number "; N
2030 LET C1 = N
2040 REM Compute the color
2050 GOSUB 5000
2060 LET C1$ = C$
2070 INPUT "What is the second number "; N
2080 LET C2 = N
2090 REM Compute the color
2100 GOSUB 5000
2110 LET C2$ = C$
2120 INPUT "What is the place value "; N
2130 LET C3 = N - 1
2140 LET N = N - 1
2150 REM Compute the color
2160 GOSUB 5000
2170 LET C3$ = C$
2180 RETURN
2190 REM
3000 REM Display answers
3010 PRINT
3020 REM Compute numerical value
3030 REM Put first digit in tens place
3040 LET V1 = 10 * C1
3050 REM Combine into a number
3060 LET V2 = V1 + C2
3070 REM Compute place value for number
3080 LET V3 = V2 * 10 ^ C3
3090 REM Complete computations
3100 REM Prepare the color code for display
```

```
3110 LET CT$ = C1$ + " " + C2$ + " " + C3$
3120 REM Complete preparations
3130 REM Show problem and answer
3140 PRINT "The color code for the number ==>"; V3
3150 PRINT "is ==> "; CT$
3160 REM Display complete
3170 RETURN
3180 REM
5000 REM Compute color subroutine
5010 REM Case of N
5020 IF N = 0 THEN C$ = "Black"
5030 IF N = 1 THEN C$ = "Brown"
5040 IF N = 2 THEN C$ = "Red"
5050 IF N = 3 THEN C$ = "Orange"
5060 IF N = 4 THEN C$ = "Yellow"
5070 IF N = 5 THEN C$ = "Green"
5080 IF N = 6 THEN C$ = "Blue"
5090 IF N = 7 THEN C$ = "Violet"
5100 IF N = 8 THEN C$ = "Gray"
5110 IF N = 9 THEN C$ = "White"
5120 REM End case
5130 RETURN
5140 REM
6000 REM Program repeat
6010 PRINT
6020 PRINT
6030 PRINT "Do you want to repeat the program?"
6040 PRINT
6050 INPUT "Your response (Y/N) =>"; AGAIN$
6060 RETURN
```

Program block 5000, using a **case structure,** offers a choice between alternatives, and one of the alternatives must be selected. The variable N will have only one value; if that value is an integer from 0 to 9, the string variable C$ will be assigned a unique string that, in this case, represents the "color" of the number. If the variable N is any value other than an integer from 0 to 9, the intended results of the program block will not be achieved.

IF-THEN Case Structure

The program block in Program 5.7 starting at line number 5000 is an example of a case structure, in which a single choice between more than two alternatives must be made. Notice that there are 10 values of the variable N that must be tested (from 0 to 9). The string variable C$ is set to the correct color string according to the value of N selected by the program user.

ON-GOSUB

There is a statement in BASIC that allows the computer to select a particular subroutine. The case statement of the program block that computed the resistor color code was used several times by another program block. In this new application, the program will have several different program blocks used as subroutines, but only one of these blocks will be selected for a particular program application. The statement that performs this function is

ON <exp> GOSUB N_1, N_2, . . . N_x

where <exp> = An arithmetic expression
N_1, N_2 . . . N_x = Line numbers that represent the first line number of a subroutine for x subroutines

Program 5.8

```
10 REM ON-GOSUB application
20 INPUT "Select a number from 1 to 3 "; N
30 ON N GOSUB 100, 200, 300
40 PRINT "This completes the demonstration."
50 END
60 REM
100 REM First subroutine
110 PRINT "You have selected the first"
120 PRINT "subroutine of this program."
130 RETURN
140 REM
200 REM Second subroutine
210 PRINT "This is the second subroutine"
220 PRINT "of this program. You selected it."
230 RETURN
240 REM
300 REM Third subroutine
310 PRINT "Here is subroutine number three."
320 PRINT "You just selected it."
330 RETURN
```

Program 5.8 illustrates the action of the ON-GOSUB. When executed, it displays

```
Select a number from 1 to 3 ? 2
This is the second subroutine
of this program. You selected it.
This completes the demonstration.
```

or, if a different number were selected,

```
Select a number from 1 to 3 ? 3
Here is subroutine number three.
You just selected it.
This completes the demonstration.
```

Note that in all cases, the program always RETURNs to the program block containing the ON-GOSUB command; this is necessary to maintain structure.

Conclusion

This section presented more decision-making methods and their use in structured BASIC. The next section presents an application program showing many of the decision-making techniques presented in this chapter. Check your understanding by trying the following Section Review.

5.3 **Section Review**

1. What will the results be for the following program lines when the program is executed

```
10 IF A > 8 THEN PRINT "Value is larger than 8."
20 PRINT "This program will continue."
```

   when
   a. A = 8?
   b. A > 8?
2. Explain a case structure and give an example.
3. Explain the operation of

```
ON K GOSUB 100, 200, 300, 400
```

4. In structured programming, can the program ever leave the block other than at the end of the block? Explain.
5. Explain why the intended results of a case statement may not be achieved. How can this problem be avoided?

5.4 Using Branch Blocks

This section presents an example program that requires many decisions in order to complete its intended task; many different forms of branch blocks are used in this program. An analysis of the various blocks of the program is presented at the end of this section.

Example Branch Program

Program 5.9 represents a **computer-aided troubleshooting (CAT)** program. It simulates a troubleshooting procedure used on a hypothetical robot. This kind of program is gaining wide popularity in industry. The computer hardware is usually connected directly to the system being tested so that the technician does not have to make the measurements. In this program, it is assumed that the technician is making the required measurements and entering the measured values into the computer.

Program 5.9

```
100 REM Robot Troubleshooter
110 REM
120 REM Developed by:
130 REM A. Test Technician
140 REM
150 REM This program was developed to demonstrate the proper
```

```
160 REM structure of different types of branch blocks
170 REM encountered in structured BASIC.
180 REM It simulates computer-aided troubleshooting (CAT) by
190 REM leading the program user through a simulated
200 REM troubleshooting exercise of a hypothetical robot.
210 REM The program user plays the game by entering choices
220 REM and measurements as if the robot were actually being
230 REM tested.
240 REM
250 REM Variables used:
260 REM S = User selection
270 REM V1, V2, . . ., Vn = Voltage values
280 REM A$ = Dummy variable
290 REM
300 REM Main program block
310 REM Explain program to user
320 GOSUB 1000
330 REM Start testing sequence
340 GOSUB 2000
350 END
1000 REM Explain program to user
1010 PRINT
1020 PRINT "This program will assist you in troubleshooting the"
1030 PRINT "HPT-100 Robot (Hypothetical Robot)."
1040 PRINT
1050 PRINT "Just follow the directions on the screen and make"
1060 PRINT "the requested measurements. Then enter the measurement"
1070 PRINT "values. The program will direct you as to what to"
1080 PRINT "do next."
1090 PRINT
1100 INPUT "Press ENTER to continue"; A$
1110 RETURN
1120 REM
2000 REM Start testing sequence
2010 REM Clear the screen
2020 CLS
2030 REM Select area of difficulty
2040 PRINT "Where is the area of difficulty?"
2050 PRINT "1]. Robot arm     2]. Robot torso"
2060 INPUT "Select (1 or 2) by number ==>"; S
2070 REM Arm or torso routine
2080 ON S GOSUB 3000, 4000
2090 RETURN
2100 REM
3000 REM Robot Arm routine
3010 PRINT
3020 PRINT "Measure the voltage at Test Point #1"
3030 INPUT "Enter the value ==>"; V1
3040 REM Case of V1
3050 REM Arm drive disconnect
```

```
3060 IF V1 < 30 THEN GOSUB 10000
3070 REM Light check
3080 IF V1 >= 30 AND V1 <= 35 THEN GOSUB 11000
3090 REM Power unit test
3100 IF V1 > 35 THEN GOSUB 12000
3110 RETURN
3120 REM
4000 REM Torso routine
4010 PRINT
4020 PRINT "Refer to #'Torso Service Routine'# . . ."
4030 RETURN
4040 REM
10000 REM Arm drive disconnect
10010 PRINT "Disconnect arm drive and remeasure voltage at"
10020 PRINT "test point #1."
10030 INPUT "Enter the value ==> "; V2
10040 IF V2 < 30 THEN PRINT "Replace arm drive circuit board."
10050 IF V2 >= 30 THEN PRINT "Replace arm power unit."
10060 RETURN
10070 REM
11000 REM Light check
11010 PRINT
11020 PRINT "Select status of light indicator"
11030 PRINT "1]. Red 2]. Green 3]. Light is off"
11040 INPUT "Input by number ==> "; S
11050 ON S GOSUB 11100, 11200, 11300
11060 REM Exit block
11070 RETURN
11100 REM Light is Red
11110 PRINT "Disconnect power and replace fuse F1."
11120 PRINT "Repeat service routine."
11130 REM End light check
11140 RETURN
11150 REM
11200 REM Light is Green
11210 PRINT "Disconnect power and replace drive board B-12."
11220 PRINT "Repeat service routine."
11230 REM End light check
11240 RETURN
11250 REM
11300 REM Light is off
11310 PRINT "Replace bulb and continue service routine."
11320 REM End light check
11330 RETURN
11340 REM
12000 REM Power unit test
12010 PRINT
12020 PRINT "Disconnect power, replace power unit."
12030 PRINT "Repeat service routine after replacement."
12040 RETURN
```

Troubleshooting Chart

As shown in the chart in Figure 5.8, the technician starts at the top of the flowchart, makes the required measurement and, based on the value of that measurement, proceeds to the block based on the measurement. As an example, in the **robot arm routine block,** the technician must measure the voltage; if the value is less than 30 volts, the next step is to follow the instructions in the **arm drive disconnect block.** You should observe that this kind of troubleshooting lends itself to **branching;** the troubleshooting chart shows just where to branch depending on a prior condition.

Troubleshooting Program

Program 5.9 was constructed from the troubleshooting chart in Figure 5.8. The program uses several different kinds of branch blocks.

Program Block 2000	Uses an ON-GOSUB in line 2080.
Program Block 3000	Uses an IF-THEN GOSUB in lines 3060, 3080, and 3100.
Program Block 10000	Uses a closed branch.

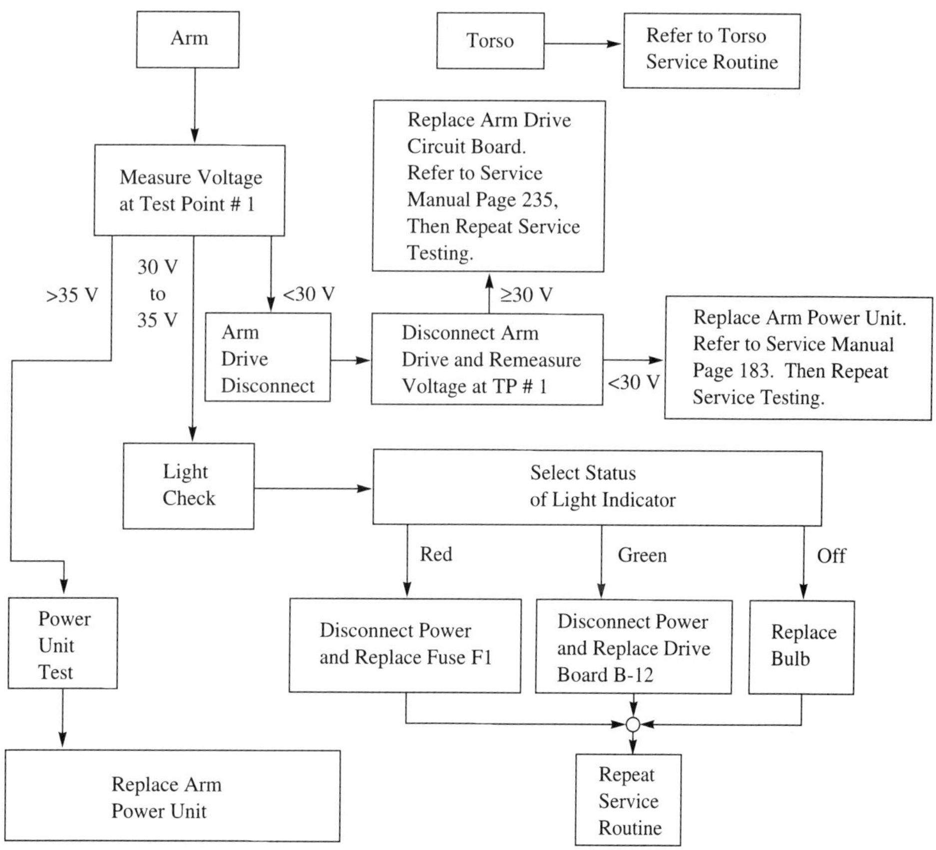

Figure 5.8 Troubleshooting Chart for Robot

Conclusion

The program presented in this section used different types of branch blocks. The rules of structured BASIC were preserved in a complex program using extensive decision making. In the next chapter, you will see how to structure loop blocks. These blocks add even more power to your programming ability. Now, try the following Section Review.

5.4 **Section Review**

The following questions refer to the Robot Troubleshooter program, Program 5.9.

1. When will the GOSUB statement in line 3060 be executed?
2. State the purpose of the logical AND in line 3080.
3. Explain how the ON S GOSUB . . . statement works in line 11050.
4. Can the three IF statements in lines 3060, 3080, and 3100 be replaced by two equivalent IF statements, or even a single IF statement?

5.5 The Waveform Viewer Project

The Waveform Viewer program requires input from the user in the following order:

1. The name of the WAV file to display.
2. "Q" or "q" to quit, or any other key to continue.
3. "L" or "R" as many times as necessary to set the new beginning point of the waveform.
4. The SPACE key must be pressed to allow the ending point to be moved.
5. "L" or "R" as necessary to set the new ending point of the waveform.
6. The Space key must be pressed to redisplay the waveform and go back to step 2.

Enforcing this order is a simple matter of calling the appropriate GOSUBs and using IF-THEN statements to process user commands.

The main loop in the Waveform Viewer looks like this:

```
130 A$ = "Y"
140 WHILE A$ = "Y"
150      GOSUB 360:      REM Draw axis
160      GOSUB 720:      REM Draw waveform
170      GOSUB 200:      REM Move pointers
180 WEND
```

The subroutine at line 200 is responsible for updating the value of A$ so that an exit is possible from the WHILE-WEND loop. This is where user input is required. A function called INKEY$ is used to check for a keypress. INKEY$ returns " " (the empty string) if no key has been pressed, or the ASCII code of the key that has been pressed. Examine the following statements to see how INKEY$ is used.

```
200 REM Move pointers or quit
210 A$ = INKEY$
220 WHILE A$ = ""
230      A$ = INKEY$
240 WEND
250 IF A$ = "Q" or A$ = "q" THEN RETURN
```

The WHILE-WEND loop beginning at statement 220 forces the program to wait until a key is pressed. The IF statement processes the quit command.

If the user does not quit, the starting and ending points must be adjusted. This is done with the following code:

```
850 MOVING$ = "Y"
860 WHILE MOVING$ = "Y"
870     GOSUB 1140
880     A$ = INKEY$
890     WHILE A$ = ""
900        A$ = INKEY$
910     WEND
920     IF A$ = "L" or A$ = "l" THEN GOSUB 970
930     IF A$ = "R" or A$ = "r" THEN GOSUB 1020
940     IF A$ = " " THEN MOVING$ = "N"
950 WEND
```

The first two IF statements branch to the appropriate subroutine (move left or move right), or to neither (in the case that a SPACE is entered). The last IF statement causes the loop to exit when a SPACE is entered.

Conclusion

Processing user commands requires combinations of logical statements that process acceptable inputs. Check your knowledge of this material by trying the following Section Review.

5.5 **Section Review**

1. What happens if keys other than "Q", "L", "R", or SPACE are entered?
2. Consider replacing these two statements:

```
920     IF A$ = "L" or A$ = "l" THEN GOSUB 970
930     IF A$ = "R" or A$ = "r" THEN GOSUB 1020
```

with this statement:

```
920     IF A$ = "L" or A$ = "l" THEN GOSUB 970 ELSE GOSUB 1020
```

Is it possible?

5.6 Troubleshooting Techniques

Now that your BASIC programs include decision-making abilities, it is more important than ever to remember to use comments and good structured programming techniques. For example, when coding a branch block, remember to indent all of the lines inside of it so that any programmer can identify all the conditional statements very easily. Similarly, in an IF-THEN-ELSE statement, all the statements in the THEN and ELSE portions are also indented. When it is necessary to execute many statements in a branch block, the GOSUB is used to call the routine, execute all necessary statements, and then return. This keeps the program structured and aids in readability.

Conclusion

Test your knowledge of this material by trying the following Section Review.

5.6 Section Review

1. Is any special coding required when writing branch blocks? Explain.
2. When is it necessary to use a GOSUB statement inside an IF-THEN-ELSE statement?
3. Why is it important for conditional statements to be structured properly?

Interactive Exercise

DIRECTIONS

To complete this exercise, you must have access to a computer that supports BASIC. This exercise is provided here to give you valuable experience and immediate feedback on what the concepts and commands introduced in this chapter will do.

Exercise

1. The IF-THEN statement depends on a true condition. In BASIC, the number 0 is considered to be the false condition. Any number other than 0 is considered to be the true condition. To see how your computer system responds, enter the following in immediate mode:

```
IF 1 THEN PRINT "True"
IF 0 THEN PRINT "False"
IF NOT 0 THEN PRINT "True"
IF -1 THEN PRINT "True"
IF 0.2 THEN PRINT "True"
IF 1 AND 0 THEN PRINT "True"
IF 1 AND 1 THEN PRINT "True"
IF 1 OR 0 THEN PRINT "True"
IF 0 OR 0 THEN PRINT "True"
IF NOT(1 AND 0) THEN PRINT "True"
IF NOT(NOT 0) THEN PRINT "True"
```

Self-Test

DIRECTIONS

Program 5.10 was developed to illustrate many of the concepts presented in this chapter. Answer all the following questions by referring to this program.

Program 5.10

```
100 REM Geometry Examples
110 ANSWER$ = "Y":      REM Set initial value of ANSWER$
120 WHILE ANSWER$ = "Y"
```

```
130     PRINT "Select the structure you wish to work with:"
140     PRINT "1] Square"
150     PRINT "2] Rectangle"
160     PRINT "3] Triangle"
170     PRINT "4] Circle"
180     INPUT "Choice? ==> "; ITEM
190     ON ITEM GOSUB 300, 400, 500, 600
200     PRINT "The area of the "; ITEM$; " is "; AREA; " square units."
210     PRINT
220     INPUT "Find another area (Y/N)? ==> "; ANSWER$
230 WEND
240 PRINT "End of geometry examples"
250 END
260 REM
300 REM Area of a square
310 PRINT
320 INPUT "What is the length of one side of the square? ==> "; SLENGTH
330 AREA = SLENGTH ^ 2
340 ITEM$ = "square"
350 RETURN
360 REM
400 REM Area of a rectangle
410 PRINT
420 INPUT "What is the length of the rectangle? ==> "; RLENGTH
430 INPUT "What is the width of the rectangle? ==> "; RWIDTH
440 AREA = RLENGTH * RWIDTH
450 ITEM$ = "rectangle"
460 RETURN
470 REM
500 REM Area of a triangle
510 PRINT
520 INPUT "What is the base of the triangle? ==> "; TBASE
530 INPUT "What is the height of the triangle? ==> "; THEIGHT
540 AREA = .5 * TBASE * THEIGHT
550 ITEM$ = "triangle"
560 RETURN
570 REM
600 REM Area of a circle
610 PRINT
620 INPUT "What is the radius of the circle? ==> "; CRADIUS
630 AREA = 3.14159 * CRADIUS ^ 2
640 ITEM$ = "circle"
650 RETURN
660 REM
```

Questions

1. Explain what Program 5.10 does.
2. How many variables does the program use?
3. Describe the sequence of operations used in the program.
4. What happens if the user enters an invalid choice in line 180 such as 1.4 or 5 or –10?
5. How many program blocks are used in this program? Name each one.
6. Describe the use of the ON-GOSUB statement.

Study Questions

1. Create a structured BASIC program where the price of the following items is already entered:
   a. Soap 12.50
   b. Powder 11.75
   c. Asphalt 27.56
   d. Glue 2.33
   e. Gum 18.49

   The user need only select the item by letter and the quantity of the selected item. The program computes the total cost.
2. Develop a structured BASIC program that demonstrates to the user all the forms of the branch presented in this chapter.
3. Create a structured BASIC program that will allow the user to compute the voltage across each of three resistors in series. The relationships are

$$R_T = R_1 + R_2 + R_3$$
$$I_T = V_T/R_T$$
$$V_x = I_T R_x \ (x = 1, 2, \text{ or } 3)$$

where R_T = total circuit resistance
R_1,R_2,R_3 = values of each resistor
I_T = total circuit current
V_T = total applied voltage

4. Develop a flowchart of the structured BASIC program used in the self-test section of this chapter.
5. Develop a structured BASIC program that will simulate computer-aided troubleshooting of a hypothetical diesel engine. The troubleshooting chart is shown in Figure 5.9.

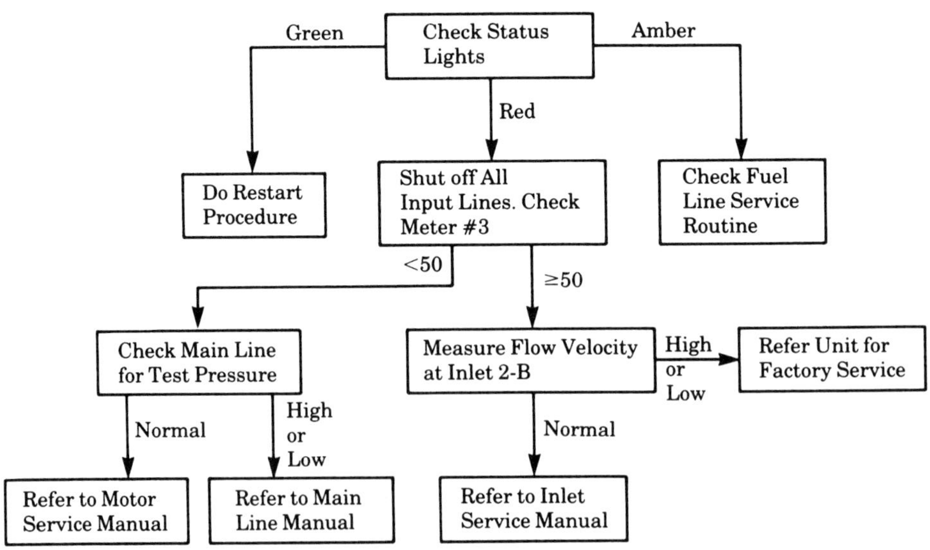

Figure 5.9 Troubleshooting Chart for Diesel Engine

6. Create a structured BASIC program that will allow the user to convert from or to metric. The user can then choose length, volume, or weight for the conversion.
7. Develop a structured BASIC program that will compute the weight of a machined part. The program user can select from three forms—cylinder, rectangle, or cone—and three materials—copper, aluminum, or steel. The program must automatically compute the volume and, using the density of the selected material, compute the total weight.
8. Modify Study Question 1 so that a sales tax of 6 percent is automatically added to the cost of the asphalt and glue only.
9. Create a flowchart of the program developed in Study Question 2.
10. Modify the program developed in Question 3 so that the power dissipated by any of the three resistors in the circuit can also be calculated. The user can select the unknown variable. The formula for power dissipation is

$$P = I^2R$$

where P = power dissipated in the resistor
I = resistor current
R = value of resistor

11. Develop a structured BASIC program that will compute the volume of three different solids. Use an example of the case format in your program.
12. Modify the program you developed in Study Question 5 so that the program contains an example of an ON-GOSUB.
13. Expand the program in Study Question 6 so that the user may also convert to and from degrees Fahrenheit and degrees centigrade.
14. Modify the program developed in Study Question 7 so that it contains an IF-THEN GOSUB and a closed branch containing an IF-THEN ELSE.
15. Develop a structured BASIC program that will allow the user to select information concerning three different investment accounts and two different payment methods for each of the three investment accounts. The information about the accounts and their payments need not be any more detailed than the PRINTing of "This is investment account #1" and "This is payment method #2."
16. Create a structured BASIC program that gives an example of each type of program decision making presented in this chapter. Develop a flowchart for the program.
17. Use a WHILE-WEND loop and an IF-THEN statement to perform division by repeatedly subtracting the value stored in B from the input value A. As long as A is greater than or equal to B, keep subtracting.
18. Show how a WHILE-WEND loop, together with an IF-THEN statement, can be used to guarantee that the user enters a number between 10 and 50.

6 Loop Blocks

Ken Koder spent some of his free time looking at the library of programs developed for RWA Software customers. One of the programs he examined contained code that executed the same routine 15 times in a row. He wondered why the programmer would write code like that and not use a loop.

Later that day, Ken ran into Don, the senior technician. Ken explained to Don how he had noticed some other BASIC code in the library that did not appear to be properly written.

Don replied, "The former programmer whose work you have already been fixing unfortunately wrote plenty of other code, too. It's not pretty, but it works. Someday we might have to rewrite some of that older code but, for now, concentrate on getting the new stuff out the door."

Objectives

This chapter will introduce you to

1. The concept of repeating a process many times.
2. The common features contained in all programming loops.
3. Several different methods used to create programming loops.
4. The kinds of loops available and how each type is used.
5. How to use the FOR-NEXT statement to create a loop block.
6. Various ways of incrementing loop variables.
7. How to use the WHILE-WEND statement.
8. How to create nested loops.
9. How to structure nested loop blocks.

Introduction

This chapter shows how you can use one of the major strengths of the computer, the ability to repeat the same statements over and over again. This is called **looping,** and in structured BASIC, looping is done with **loop blocks.**

By using loop blocks you will discover one of the strengths of using a computer for analysis and solution of many types of problems. The loop block allows you to quickly test conditions for a range of values, perform calculations on a range of numbers, or run a program multiple times.

In this chapter, you will learn the correct method of structuring loop blocks. When you complete this chapter, you will be able to develop very powerful structured BASIC programs, which will be easy to understand, modify, and debug.

As with all the other chapters in this text, the skills you learn in this chapter will be easily transferred to other high-level programming languages and computer systems.

6.1 Introductory Concepts

Remember there are only three kinds of blocks needed for any computer program, no matter how complex: **action blocks, branch blocks,** and **loop blocks.** This section will introduce you to the reasons loop blocks are used in programming, what they look like, and how they differ from branch blocks.

General Idea

Suppose you wanted to know the distance an object would fall toward Earth after a certain number of seconds (disregarding air resistance). The equation for the distance traveled by an object starting at rest toward Earth, disregarding air resistance, is

$$S = 0.5\ at^2$$

where S = distance traveled by the object (in feet)
a = acceleration of the object due to gravity (32 ft/sec^2)
t = time (in seconds) the object is falling

For example, you want to know the distance a falling object would cover for the first three seconds of the fall and you specifically want to know the distances at one seconds, two seconds, and three seconds. Program 6.1 shows one way you could write the program.

Program 6.1

```
100 REM Falling Body Analysis
110 REM
120 REM Developed by: G. Galileo
130 REM
140 REM This program computes the distance traveled by an object
150 REM falling toward Earth.
160 REM
170 REM Variables used:
180 REM S = Distance in feet
```

```
190 REM T = Time in seconds
200 REM
210 REM Constants used:
220 REM Acceleration due to gravity
230 LET A = 32
240 REM
250 GOSUB 2000: REM Compute and display answer
260 END
2000 REM Compute and display answer
2010 LET T = 1
2020 GOSUB 3000: REM Compute S
2030 LET T = 2
2040 GOSUB 3000: REM Compute S
2050 LET T = 3
2060 GOSUB 3000: REM Compute S
2070 RETURN
2080 REM
3000 REM Compute and display S
3010 LET S = .5 * A * T ^ 2
3020 PRINT "The distance at "; T; " seconds is "; S; " feet."
3030 RETURN
```

When Program 6.1 is executed, it will display

```
The distance at 1 seconds is 16 feet.
The distance at 2 seconds is 64 feet.
The distance at 3 seconds is 144 feet.
```

You will get these answers for the three different values of time.

Program 6.1 performs what you would do to solve this problem if you were using a pocket calculator, pencil, and paper. You would do what is being done in the subroutine starting at line 3000, and you would do it three times, once for each of the three values of T.

You would solve the same formula for each value of T required and each time record the corresponding answer. It could be said, if you were solving a problem like this without a computer, that you were looping. That is, once you solved the problem for T = 1, you would then loop back and solve the same problem over again for T = 2. You would repeat this process until you calculated the last value of T required, which in this case is T = 3. You would repeat the same process three times, as shown in Figure 6.1.

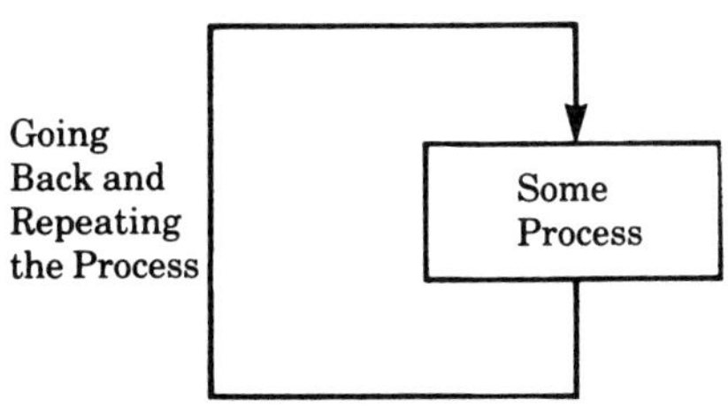

Figure 6.1 Idea of Looping

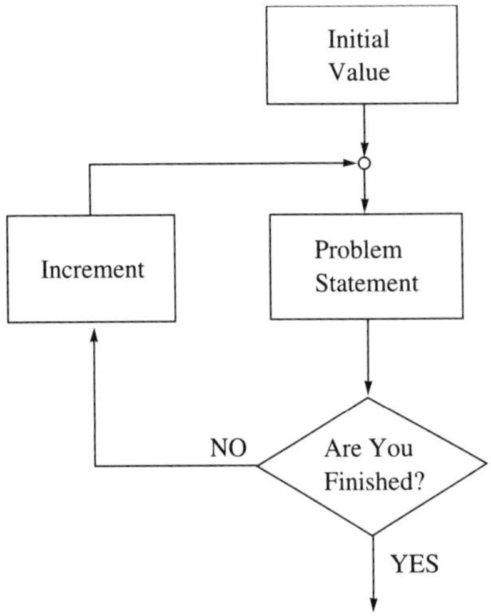

Figure 6.2 Steps in a Program Loop

What You Need to Know

To use a loop, you need to define four things:

1. The initial value at which the loop starts.
2. Action to be taken within the loop (the problem statement).
3. The value to end the loop.
4. Increments used for each pass through the loop.

Figure 6.2 illustrates the process of steps in a program loop.

Returning to the example of the velocity program, here is how each of the four items required in a loop were used.

1. The initial value for the loop:

   The initial value of T = 1

2. Action to be taken within the loop.

```
LET S = .5 * 32 * T ^ 2
PRINT "The distance at ";T; " seconds is ";S; "feet."
```

3. The final value for ending the loop.

   The final value of T = 3

4. Increments used for each pass through the loop.

   T was increased by 1 each time.
   (T = 1, T = 2, and T = 3)

In this example, T could have been increased by increments of 2 and solved for T = 1, T = 3, and T = 5. From this, you can correctly conclude that a loop block requires the following four kinds of information: where to start, what to do, when to end, and how much to change each time.

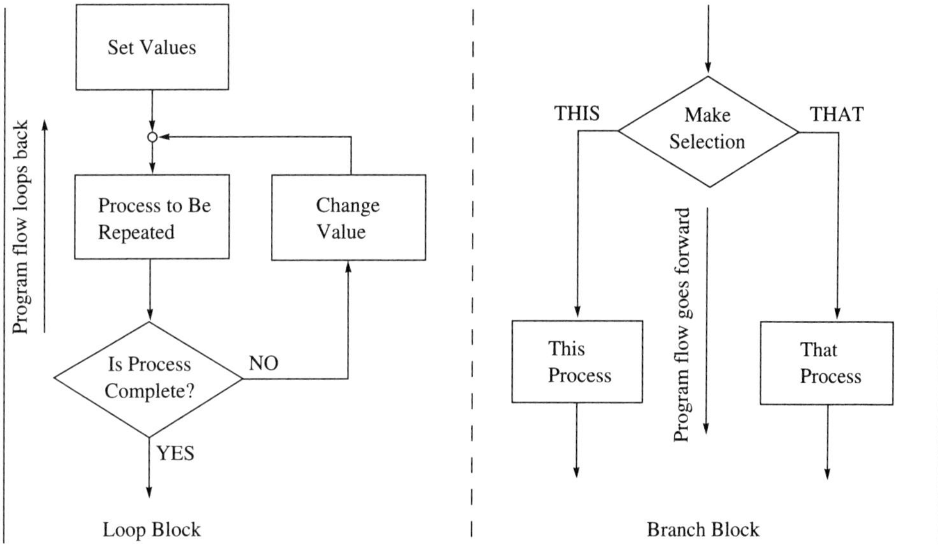

Figure 6.3 Comparing the Loop and Branch Blocks

Loop and Branch Compared

In a loop block the program has the potential to go back and repeat the same process. In a branch block the program always advances forward and makes a decision between alternatives. Flowcharts of the two are compared in Figure 6.3.

Why Loops Are Needed

Program 6.1 is not very efficient. Suppose you wanted the program to print out the distance of a falling object every millisecond (one thousandth of a second) for the first three seconds. This would result in more than 6000 program lines consisting of the text shown in Program 6.2.

Program 6.2

```
10 T = .001
15 GOSUB 11000: REM Compute S
20 T = .002
25 GOSUB 11000: REM Compute S
30 T = .003
35 GOSUB 11000: REM Compute S
40 REM Six
50 REM Thousand
60 REM Program
70 REM Lines
10000 T = 3
10005 GOSUB 11000
10010 REM
10020 END
11000 REM Compute S
```

```
11010 S = .5 * 32 * T ^ 2
11020 PRINT "The distance at "; T; " seconds is "; S; " feet."
11030 RETURN
```

Obviously, this method of programming is not very efficient. Repeating a process by duplicating program statements over and over (doing what you and I would do if we were solving the same problem with pencil and paper) has practical limitations on the computer memory and taxes the patience of the programmer.

Conclusion

In this section you saw some examples of why we need loop blocks and what we need to know about them. Test your understanding of this section by trying the following Section Review.

6.1 Section Review

1. Name the three different kinds of programming blocks.
2. State why Program 6.2 is not practical.
3. Define a loop block.
4. Explain the difference between a loop block and a branch block.

6.2 The Loop Block

In the last section, you were shown why loop blocks were necessary and what they had to contain. You also saw the difference between a loop block and a branch block. In this section, you will see the construction of a loop block and be introduced to two important and powerful kinds of loop blocks.

Armed with the knowledge presented in this section, you will be able to use the full power of the computer. You will have the ability to structure a program that contains action blocks, branch blocks, and loop blocks.

An Important Concept

An easy way to change the value of a variable is to simply use the following statement:

```
LET T = T + 1
```

This statement is not an algebraic equation! It is an instruction to the computer to increment T, as shown in Figure 6.4. The instruction means:

> Take the number that is stored in the memory location designated by T, add 1 to it, and store the result back in the same memory location.

If you want to increase T by 2 you only need

```
LET T = T + 2
```

or to increase it by 0.5

```
LET T = T + .5
```

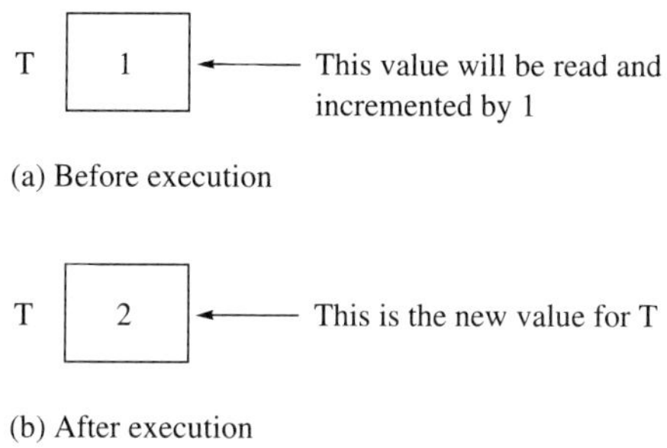

Figure 6.4 Meaning of LET T = T + 1

or even to decrease it by 3

```
LET T = T - 3
```

Program 6.3 shows the result of incrementing T by 1 over and over.

Program 6.3

```
1000 LET TRUE = 1
1010 A = 32
2000 REM Loop block
2010 REM Set initial condition
2020 LET T = 1
2030 WHILE TRUE
2040    REM Compute S
2050    GOSUB 3000
2060    REM Increase T by one
2070    LET T = T + 1
2080 WEND
2090 END
3000 REM Compute and display S
3010 LET S = .5 * A * T ^ 2
3020 PRINT "The distance at "; T; " seconds is "; S; " feet."
3030 RETURN
```

When executed, the program displays:

```
The distance at 1 seconds is 16 feet.
The distance at 2 seconds is 64 feet.
The distance at 3 seconds is 144 feet.
The distance at 4 seconds is 256 feet.
The distance at 5 seconds is 400 feet.
The distance at 6 seconds is 576 feet.
The distance at 7 seconds is 784 feet.
The distance at 8 seconds is 1024 feet.
The distance at 9 seconds is 1296 feet.
                .
                .
                .
```

As you can see in Program 6.3, the WHILE-WEND loop condition is always TRUE and thus will continue forever. The value of T changes for each calculation. Something is needed to make the computer know how many times it is to repeat the loop and under what conditions to stop. Let us look at a predefined looping structure called the FOR-NEXT loop.

FOR-NEXT Loops

A statement available in BASIC for beginning a loop block is

```
FOR (starting value) TO (ending value) STEP (step value)
```

where `(starting value)` = initial value of the loop variable
`(ending value)` = final value of loop variable
`(step value)` = the amount to change the loop variable each time through the loop (optional)

The next thing that is needed are the statements to be performed each time. The loop is completed with a NEXT statement. To use the FOR-NEXT loop, simply place the FOR statement at the beginning, the statements to be executed during each loop in the middle, and the statement NEXT(variable name) at the end. For example,

```
FOR N = (starting value) TO (ending value) STEP (value)
```

[Statements to be repeated]

```
NEXT N
```

Program 6.4 is an example of a FOR-NEXT loop.

Program 6.4

```
10 REM FOR-NEXT demonstration
20 REM Begin loop
30 FOR X = 1 TO 5 STEP 1
40   PRINT X
50 NEXT X
60 REM End loop
```

When executed, the program displays:

```
1
2
3
4
5
```

Recall that for any program loop block, the computer must know four things:

1. The value at which the loop starts.
2. The value to end the loop.
3. The statements to be repeated.
4. How much to increment the loop counter.

Consider this FOR statement:

```
FOR X = 1 TO 5 STEP 1
```

This statement tells the loop where to start and where to end. (Start with X = 1, end with X = 5.)

```
STEP 1
```

tells the loop how much to increment (X + 1). Finally,

```
NEXT X
```

does two things:

1. It defines the end of the loop statement.
2. It actually increments X by 1. (Just like X = X + 1.)

Applying the FOR-NEXT Loop

Returning to the original problem of solving for the distance of a falling object every second for nine seconds, using the FOR-NEXT statement to develop the loop produces Program 6.5.

Program 6.5

```
2000 LET A = 32
2010 REM Begin loop
2020 FOR T = 1 TO 9 STEP 1
2030    GOSUB 3000
2040 NEXT T
2050 REM End loop
2060 END
2070 REM
3000 REM Compute S
3010 LET S = .5 * A * T ^ 2
3020 PRINT "The distance at "; T; " seconds is "; S; " feet."
3030 RETURN
```

To simplify this program, you can place the subroutine part of the program within the actual loop and omit an extra program block, as shown in Program 6.6.

Program 6.6

```
2000 LET A = 32
2010 REM Begin loop
2020 REM
2030 FOR T = 1 TO 9 STEP 1
2040   S = .5 * A * T ^ 2
2050   PRINT "The distance at "; T; " seconds is "; S; "feet."
2060 NEXT T
2070 REM End loop
2080 REM
```

This program, when executed, will produce the following:

```
The distance at 1 seconds is 16 feet.
The distance at 2 seconds is 64 feet.
The distance at 3 seconds is 144 feet.
The distance at 4 seconds is 256 feet.
The distance at 5 seconds is 400 feet.
The distance at 6 seconds is 576 feet.
The distance at 7 seconds is 784 feet.
The distance at 8 seconds is 1024 feet.
The distance at 9 seconds is 1296 feet.
```

Conclusion

Now you have learned the secrets of constructing loop blocks. In the next section you will learn some of the most common uses of loop blocks and how to structure them. Test your understanding of this section by trying the following Section Review.

6.2 Section Review

1. Explain what the following program line means:

   ```
   LET V = V + 2
   ```

2. State the four things that must be present in a loop block.
3. Construct a simple loop block using a WHILE-WEND statement that will PRINT the value of a number starting at 8 and ending at 0 in steps of –2.
4. Construct a simple loop block using the FOR-NEXT statement that will PRINT the value of a number starting at 10 and ending at 18 in steps of 0.5.

6.3 Using Loop Blocks

In this section, you will discover some of the practical uses of loop blocks. You will learn how to have the program user easily repeat a structured BASIC program and how to prevent the program user from entering the wrong kind of data. You will also see a sample program that lets the program user decide the beginning, ending, and stepping of the loop block variables and a modification that lets the computer decide the same limits.

Omitting the STEP

When you use the FOR-NEXT portion statement in a loop block, if the STEP is not specified, the variable will automatically be incremented by 1. Program 6.7 illustrates a loop block where the STEP has been omitted.

Program 6.7

```
10 REM Omitting the STEP
20 REM Begin loop
30 FOR X = 1 TO 5
40    PRINT X
50 NEXT X
60 REM End loop
```

When executed, Program 6.7 displays

```
1
2
3
4
5
```

Note that when the STEP isn't specified, the variable (in this case X) is automatically incremented by 1.

STEPping with Values

When you include the STEP in the FOR-NEXT statement, you can perform many different increments. You could increase the count by a fractional amount, as shown in Program 6.8.

Program 6.8

```
10 REM FOR-NEXT STEP demonstration
20 REM Begin loop
30 FOR N = 0 TO 6 STEP 1.5
40    PRINT N
50 NEXT N
60 REM End loop
```

This results in the following execution:

```
0
1.5
3
4.5
6
```

You can also create a loop that decrements. Simply make the changes shown in Program 6.9. Note that now the counting variable N starts at a larger number (6) and ends at a smaller number (0). Also note that the STEP number is a –2.

Program 6.9

```
10 REM FOR-NEXT demonstration
20 REM Begin loop
30 REM
40 FOR N = 6 TO 0 STEP -2
50   PRINT N
60 NEXT N
70 REM End loop
```

When this program is executed, the results are

```
6
4
2
0
```

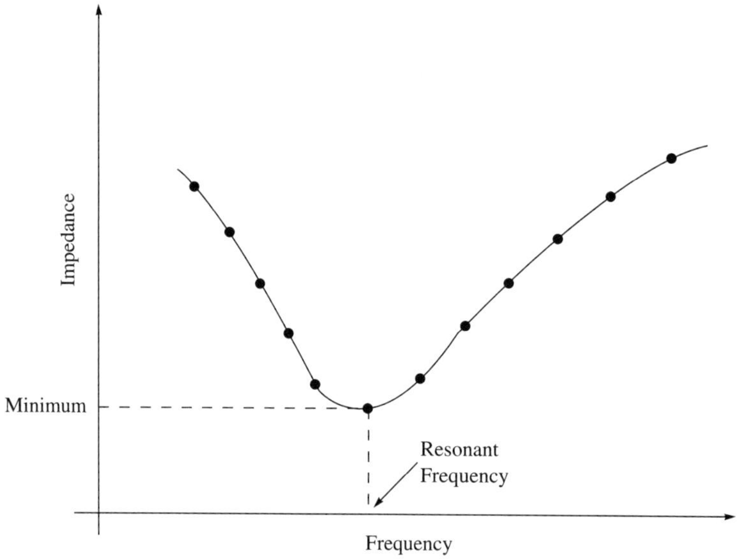

Figure 6.5 Impedance Versus Frequency Relationship of Series RLC Circuit

User Control of Loop Parameters

Loop blocks are even more useful when the user decides the beginning, ending, and increment values. Program 6.10 illustrates this. The program computes the impedance of a series resonant circuit consisting of a resistor, an inductor, and a capacitor. The opposition to current flow of this electrical circuit will change with the applied frequency. As the applied frequency is increased, its opposition to current flow, called impedance, will begin to decrease. At a certain frequency the circuit impedance will arrive at a minimum value. This frequency is called the resonant frequency. Further increasing the applied frequency will cause the circuit impedance to begin to increase. A graph of this action is presented in Figure 6.5.

Program 6.10

```
100 REM A Series Resonant Circuit
110 REM
120 REM Developed by: A. Series Student
130 REM
140 REM      This program will calculate the impedance
150 REM of a series resonant circuit consisting of
160 REM a resistor, capacitor, and inductor.
170 REM
180 REM      The program user must enter the value of
190 REM the resistor, capacitor, and inductor.
200 REM
210 REM      The program will then ask for the lowest
```

```
220 REM frequency and the highest frequency as well
230 REM as the change in frequency for each calculation.
240 REM
250 REM      The value of the circuit impedance is then
260 REM calculated for each frequency.
270 REM
280 REM Variables used:
290 REM  R = Value of resistor in ohms
300 REM  L = Value of inductor in henrys
310 REM  C = Value of capacitor in farads
320 REM  F = Frequency for calculation
330 REM FL = Low frequency
340 REM FH = High frequency
350 REM FI = Incremental frequency change
360 REM A$ = Temporary variable
370 REM  Z = Circuit impedance
380 REM
400 REM Constants used:
410 PI = 3.14159:       REM Value of PI
420 REM
1000 REM Main program block
1010 GOSUB 2000: REM Explain program to user
1020 REPEAT$ = "Y"
1030 WHILE REPEAT$ = "Y"
1040    GOSUB 3000:     REM Get values from user
1050    GOSUB 4000:     REM Calculate and display impedance
1060    GOSUB 5000:     REM Ask for program repeat
1070 WEND
1080 END
1090 REM
2000 REM Explain program to user
2010 CLS :      REM Clear the screen
2020 PRINT
2030 PRINT "This program will compute the impedance of a series"
2040 PRINT "RLC circuit for a range of frequencies."
2050 PRINT
2060 PRINT "You must enter the value of the resistor in ohms,"
2070 PRINT "the value of the inductor in henrys, and the"
2080 PRINT "capacitor in farads."
2090 PRINT
2100 PRINT "The program will then ask for the minimum frequency"
2110 PRINT "to begin calculation, the maximum frequency to end"
2120 PRINT "the calculation, and the incremental frequency change"
2130 PRINT "for each calculation."
2140 PRINT
2150 PRINT "Press ENTER to continue."; A$
2160 RETURN
2170 REM
3000 REM Get values from user
3010 CLS :      REM Clear screen again
```

```
3020 PRINT
3030 INPUT "Value of resistor in ohms    => "; R
3040 INPUT "Value of inductor in henrys  => "; L
3050 INPUT "Value of capacitor in farads => "; C
3060 INPUT "Lowest frequency to start calculation      => "; FL
3070 INPUT "Highest frequency to end calculation       => "; FH
3080 INPUT "Increase in frequency for each calculation => "; FI
3090 RETURN
3100 REM
4000 REM Calculate and display impedance
4010 REM Begin loop
4020 REM
4030 FOR F = FL TO FH STEP FI
4040     XL = 2 * PI * F * L :                REM Compute inductive reactance
4050     XC = 1 / (2 * PI * F * C) :          REM Compute capacitive reactance
4060     Z = SQR((XL - XC) ^ 2 + R ^ 2):    REM Compute circuit impedance
4070     PRINT "Frequency = "; F; " Hz Impedance = "; Z; " ohms"
4080 NEXT F
4090 REM End loop
4100 RETURN
4110 REM
5000 REM Ask for program repeat
5010 INPUT "Do you wish to repeat the program? (Y/N) ==> "; REPEAT$
5020 RETURN
5030 REM
5040 REM End of program
```

Note that the Explain program to user block is not repeated if the program user wants to repeat the program; it is assumed that the user now understands the purpose of the program and does not need to see the directions again.

A sample execution of Program 6.10 is as follows:

```
Value of resistor in ohms   ====> ? 10
Value of inductor in henrys ===> ? .001
Value of capacitor in farads ==> ? .000001
Lowest frequency to start calculation      ==> ? 1000
Highest frequency to end calculation      ===> ? 10000
Increase in frequency for each calculation ==> ? 1000
Frequency = 1000 Hz Impedance = 153.1986 ohms
Frequency = 2000 Hz Impedance = 67.75321 ohms
Frequency = 3000 Hz Impedance = 35.63407 ohms
Frequency = 4000 Hz Impedance = 17.7426 ohms
Frequency = 5000 Hz Impedance = 10.0861 ohms
Frequency = 6000 Hz Impedance = 14.99471 ohms
Frequency = 7000 Hz Impedance = 23.48159 ohms
Frequency = 8000 Hz Impedance = 31.97501 ohms
Frequency = 9000 Hz Impedance = 40.13062 ohms
Frequency = 10000 Hz Impedance = 47.97019 ohms
Do you wish to repeat the program? (Y/N) ==>
```

From the program output, observe that the impedance of the circuit is at a minimum at 5000 Hz. Below this frequency and above this frequency the impedance of the circuit increases, as was predicted by the graph in Figure 6.5.

Setting Loop Parameters Automatically

Often the user is not sure of the range of values to be used for the best type of analysis. For example, in Program 6.10, depending on the input values of the inductor and capacitor, the program user may not have had the program reach the point of minimum circuit impedance. If the range of frequencies selected had been from 10,000 Hz to 20,000 Hz, the minimum circuit impedance would have been missed completely. For this type of circuit, the frequencies around and at the minimum circuit impedance (called circuit resonance) are usually the area of interest for circuit analysis.

If the user could enter the circuit values as before, yet have an option that would let the computer decide what the minimum and maximum frequencies should be, it would ensure that the circuit resonant frequency would be displayed within the range, as shown in Figure 6.6.

To ensure display of the resonant frequency, additional calculations are required. First, the resonant frequency of the circuit is calculated using the formula:

$$f_r = 1/(2\pi\sqrt{LC})$$

This determines the point where the impedance of the circuit will be at a minimum. Thus, the area of most interest has been determined by the computer. What is left now is to determine the range of frequencies (minimum and maximum values for the loop). There are many ways of doing this. For the purpose of this demonstration, the selected range will be 10 percent above and 10 percent below the calculated resonant frequency.

Once the beginning and ending values of the loop have been determined, all that is necessary is to determine the value of the increment for the loop.

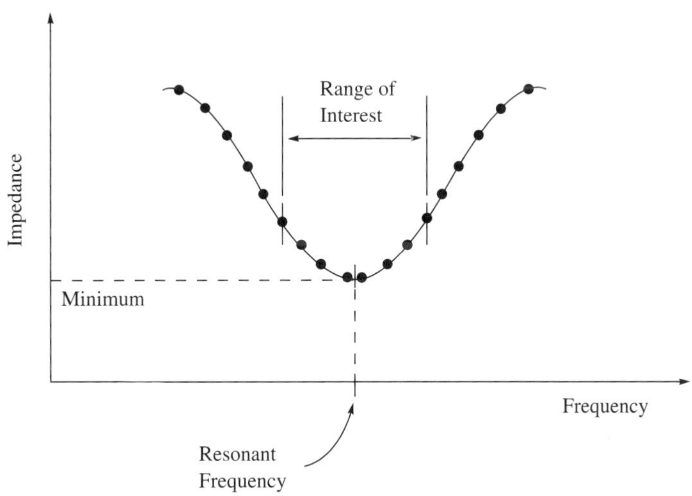

Figure 6.6 Area of Resonant Frequencies

The range between the lowest frequency and the highest frequency is divided into 10 parts. The result is the incremental value to be used by the STEP part of the FOR-NEXT loop. The completed changes are shown in Program 6.11. When Program 6.11 is executed, the computer will determine the beginning and ending values of the loop, as well as the STEP value.

Program 6.11

```
100 REM A Series Resonant Circuit
110 REM
120 REM Developed by: A. Series Student
130 REM
140 REM      This program will calculate the impedance
150 REM of a series resonant circuit consisting of
160 REM a resistor, capacitor, and inductor.
170 REM
180 REM      The program user must enter the value of
190 REM the resistor, capacitor, and inductor.
200 REM
210 REM      The program will then compute the lowest
220 REM frequency and the highest frequency as well
230 REM as the change in frequency for each calculation.
240 REM
250 REM The value of the circuit impedance is then
260 REM calculated for each frequency.
270 REM
280 REM Variables used:
290 REM  R = Value of resistor in ohms
300 REM  L = Value of inductor in henrys
310 REM  C = Value of capacitor in farads
320 REM  F = Frequency for calculation
330 REM FL = Low frequency
340 REM FH = High frequency
350 REM FI = Incremental frequency change
360 REM A$ = Temporary variable
370 REM  Z = Circuit impedance
380 REM
400 REM Constants used:
410 PI = 3.14159:      REM Value of PI
420 REM
1000 REM Main program block
1010 GOSUB 2000: REM Explain program to user
1020 REPEAT$ = "Y"
1030 WHILE REPEAT$ = "Y"
1040     GOSUB 3000:     REM Get values from user
1050     GOSUB 4000:     REM Calculate and display impedance
1060     GOSUB 5000:     REM Ask for program repeat
1070 WEND
1080 END
1090 REM
2000 REM Explain program to user
2010 CLS :    REM Clear the screen
```

```
2020 PRINT
2030 PRINT "This program will compute the impedance of a series"
2040 PRINT "RLC circuit for a range of frequencies."
2050 PRINT
2060 PRINT "You must enter the value of the resistor in ohms,"
2070 PRINT "the value of the inductor in henrys, and the"
2080 PRINT "capacitor in farads."
2090 PRINT
2100 PRINT "The program will then compute the minimum frequency"
2110 PRINT "to begin calculation, the maximum frequency to end"
2120 PRINT "the calculation, and the incremental frequency change"
2130 PRINT "for each calculation."
2140 PRINT
2150 PRINT "Press ENTER to continue."; A$
2160 RETURN
2170 REM
3000 REM Get values from user
3010 CLS :     REM Clear screen again
3020 PRINT
3030 INPUT "Value of resistor in ohms    => "; R
3040 INPUT "Value of inductor in henrys  => "; L
3050 INPUT "Value of capacitor in farads => "; C
3090 RETURN
3100 REM
4000 REM Calculate and display impedance
4010 REM
4020 REM Compute resonant frequency
4030 LET FR = 1 / (2*PI * SQR(L * C))
4040 REM
4050 REM Calculate minimum and maximum frequencies
4060 REM 10% below FR
4070 LET FL = FR - .1 * FR
4080 REM 10% above FR
4090 LET FH = FR + .1 * FR
4100 REM
4110 REM Compute frequency changes per step
4120 REM Do 10 steps
4130 LET FI = (FH - FL) / 10
4140 REM
4150 REM Begin loop
4160 FOR F = FL TO FH STEP FI
4170     REM Compute inductive reactance
4180     LET XL = 2 * PI * F * L
4190     REM Compute capacitive reactance
4200     LET XC = 1 / (2 * PI * F * C)
4210     REM Compute circuit impedance
4220     LET Z = SQR((XL - XC) ^ 2 + R ^ 2)
4230     PRINT "Frequency = "; F; " Hz, Impedance = "; Z; " ohms."
4240 NEXT F
4250 REM End loop
4260 RETURN
```

```
5000 REM Ask for program repeat
5010 INPUT "Do you wish to repeat the program? (Y/N) ==> "; REPEAT$
5020 RETURN
5030 REM
5040 REM End of program
```

Conclusion

In this section you saw how to create a loop block that allowed the program user to decide the loop parameters. You also saw an example of the program itself calculating the loop parameters. In the next section you will see examples of nested loops. Test your understanding of this section by trying the following Section Review.

6.3 Section Review

1. Explain the purpose of the STEP part of the FOR-NEXT statement.
2. State the output of the following statements:

```
10 FOR N = 1 TO 2 STEP .5
20       PRINT N
30 NEXT N
```

3. State the output of the following statements:

```
10 FOR N = 2 TO 1 STEP -.5
20       PRINT N
30 NEXT N
```

4. What happens when the STEP parameter is eliminated?
5. What program line is necessary to complete the following?

```
10 FOR N = 1 TO 10 STEP X
20       PRINT N
30 NEXT N
```

6.4 Nested Loops

This section presents the concept of having one loop inside another. Here you will see methods to help you structure nested loops to make them easy to read and less prone to error.

General Idea

A **nested loop** is simply one loop inside another. Program 6.12 shows a simple nested loop.

Program 6.12

```
10 REM Nested loop example
20 REM
30 REM This is the outer loop
40 FOR B = 1 TO 5
50      REM
```

```
60      REM This is the nested loop
70      FOR P = 1 TO 4
80              V = B ^ P
90              PRINT V,
100     NEXT P
110     REM End nested loop
120     REM
130     PRINT
140 NEXT B
150 REM End of outer loop
```

This program calculates the value of a number B raised to different powers of P. The first time through the **outer loop** B = 1; the **inner loop** will then calculate: 1^1, 1^2, 1^3, 1^4 and PRINT each answer. This will then complete the inner loop and the NEXT B (line 140) of the outer loop will increase the value of B by 1 and the inner loop will again go through its four steps and calculate: 2^1, 2^2, 2^3, and 2^4. The outer loop will then increase B by 1 more again and cause the inner loop to do four more calculations of 3^1, 3^2, 3^3, and 3^4. This process continues until B = 5. The output values for Program 6.12 are

```
1          1          1          1
2          4          8          16
3          9          27         81
4          16         64         256
5          25         125        625
```

As you can see, 20 calculations are performed by the nested loop structure.

Nested Loop Structure

The **structure** of a nested loop is important. You need to know which loop is the nested loop and which loop is the outer loop. That is why indentations are used to offset each loop block.

When structuring nested loops, the FOR and the NEXT part of the same loop should be lined up vertically. Note from this structure that the FOR part of the outer loop is lined up with the NEXT B, and the FOR part of the nested loop is lined up with the NEXT P of the nested loop. Structuring nested loops (or any loop) in this way is a great aid in allowing the loop statements to be easily identified.

Nested Loop Rule

The most important rule concerning nested loops is that the FOR and NEXT parts of the loops must not cross. In other words, the variable found in any NEXT statement must be the same as the variable used in the most recent FOR statement.

Nesting WHILE-WEND

The WHILE-WEND loop may also be nested. It is important that each WHILE part have a matching WEND part. Interpreters automatically look for this. Program 6.13 is an illustration of a nested WHILE-WEND application.

Program 6.13

```
10 REM Nested WHILE-WEND loop example
20 REM
30 REM This is the outer loop
40 X = 0
50 WHILE X < 3
60        PRINT "X = "; X,
70        X = X + 1
80        REM This is the nested loop
90        Y = 0
100       WHILE Y < 4
110             PRINT "Y = "; Y,
120             Y = Y + 1
130       WEND
140       REM End of the nested loop
150       PRINT
160 WEND
170 REM End of the outer loop
```

When this program is executed, the output is

```
X = 0          Y = 0          Y = 1          Y = 2          Y = 3
X = 1          Y = 0          Y = 1          Y = 2          Y = 3
X = 2          Y = 0          Y = 1          Y = 2          Y = 3
```

Note the importance of the program structure in the WHILE-WEND loop. Also notice that the comma at the end of the variables of the PRINT statements causes the output data to be tabulated.

Conclusion

This section presented the concept of nested loops. You saw that if proper program structure was observed, it made the visualization of what these loops were doing very easy. Test your understanding of this section with the following Section Review.

6.4 Section Review

1. Describe what is meant by a nested loop.
2. State what Program 6.14 will output when it is executed.

Program 6.14

```
10 FOR A = 1 TO 3
20     FOR B = 1 TO 3
30         LET C = A + B
40         PRINT C,
50     NEXT B
60 NEXT A
```

3. Show how the structure of Program 6.14 could be improved.
4. How many times does line 110 of Program 6.15 execute?

Program 6.15

```
10 REM Multiple nested loop example
20 REM
30 REM Outer loop
40 FOR A = 1 TO 10
50    REM First inner loop
60    FOR B = 1 TO 10
70       REM Second inner loop
80       FOR C = 1 TO 10
90          REM Third inner loop
100         FOR D = 1 TO 10
110            LET V = A * B + C * D
120            PRINT V,
130         NEXT D
140         REM End third inner loop
150      NEXT C
160      REM End second inner loop
170   NEXT B
180   REM End first inner loop
190 NEXT A
200 REM End outer loop
```

5. If there is an error in the nested loop shown in Program 6.16, state what it is.

Program 6.16

```
10 FOR X = 1 TO 50 STEP 3
20    FOR Y = 3 TO 12 STEP 2
30        T = X * Y
40    NEXT X
50 NEXT Y
```

6. Is it possible to nest more than one loop? If so, what are the rules for doing so?
7. What will be the output when Program 6.17 is executed?

Program 6.17

```
10 WHILE X < 3
20     PRINT "X = "; X
30     LET X = X + 1
40     WHILE Y < 4
50        Y = Y + 1
60        PRINT "Y = "; Y,
70     WEND
80 WEND
```

6.5 The Waveform Viewer Project

The specification for the Waveform Viewer limits the maximum size of a waveform to the first 8192 samples read from the WAV file. Since a loop will be used to read data from the WAV file, there are two conditions that may cause the loop to terminate. They are:

1. 8192 samples have been read.
2. The end of the WAV file has been reached.

Although file I/O is not covered until Chapter 10, you should be able to make sense of the following WHILE-WEND loop (which loads the WAV samples).

```
1260 OPEN F$ FOR RANDOM AS #1 LEN = 1
1270 FIELD #1, 1 AS W$
1280 WAVLEN = 0
1290 WHILE (WAVLEN < MAXLEN) AND NOT EOF(1)
1300      GET #1
1310      WAVBUFF(WAVLEN) = ASC(W$)
1320      WAVLEN = WAVLEN + 1
1330 WEND
1340 CLOSE #1
```

The EOF function returns TRUE when the end of the WAV file has been reached. This provides an alternate exit if the WAV file has fewer than 8192 samples.

Conclusion

Check your knowledge of this material by trying the following Section Review.

6.5 Section Review

1. How is the length of the waveform maintained?
2. Why are two exits from the WHILE-WEND loop necessary?

6.6 Troubleshooting Techniques

Whenever you use a loop to solve a programming problem, it pays to know exactly how many times the statements in the loop will execute. For a simple FOR-NEXT loop, this is relatively easy to determine. For example, the following loop executes statement 110 five times:

```
100 FOR K = 1 TO 5
110      P = P + 3
120 NEXT K
```

A nested loop, however, provides a bigger challenge. How many times does statement 120 execute in the nested loop shown here?

```
100 FOR K = 1 TO 5
110      FOR L = 1 TO 4
120           P = P + 3
130      NEXT L
140 NEXT K
```

If your answer is 20 you are correct. The outer loop causes the inner loop to execute five times. The inner loop executes statement 120 four times. So, five groups of four give a total of 20 executions of statement 120.

Try this next example, which has a slight twist thrown in.

```
100 FOR K = 1 TO 5
110      FOR L = 1 TO K
120           P = P + 3
130      NEXT L
140 NEXT K
```

Now you are correct if your answer is 15. This is because the value of K from the outer loop determines how many times the inner loop executes. Do you see that statement 120 executes once, then twice, then three times, four times, and finally five times?

In general, pay attention to the types of loops you use in your programs so that you do not get caught executing the innermost loop statements more often than necessary.

Conclusion

Check your understanding of this material by trying the following Section Review.

6.6 **Section Review**

1. How many times does statement 220 execute?

```
210 FOR K = 5 TO 11
220     P = P + 3
230 NEXT K
```

2. Why does the innermost statement of a nested loop execute so many times?

Interactive Exercises

DIRECTIONS

To complete these exercises, you need access to a computer that supports BASIC. They are provided here to give you valuable experience and immediate feedback on what the concepts and commands introduced in this chapter will do.

In the latter part of these exercises some **screen formatting** commands are introduced. This is the best place to introduce them since each computer system handles them a little differently. You should have fun with these and learn some useful tricks too.

Exercises

1. Here is an interesting display:

```
10 FOR N = 1 TO 70 : PRINT TAB(N) "-" : NEXT
```

   Note that the NEXT N omits the N. Does this make any difference?

2. What happens to the output when you place a comma after the string in the program from Exercise 1?

```
10 FOR N = 1 TO 70 : PRINT TAB(N) "-", : NEXT
```

3. Program 6.18 gives some interesting results. What use does this program have? Try transferring the output of this program to your printer.

Program 6.18

```
10 FOR Y = 1 TO 10
20     FOR X = 1 TO 70 STEP 5
30             PRINT TAB(X); "|";
40     NEXT X
50 NEXT Y
```

4. Program 6.19 is another useful example. What applications would this program have? Try to transfer the output of Program 6.19 to your printer.

Program 6.19

```
10 FOR Y = 1 TO 10
20     FOR Z = 1 TO 70
30       PRINT TAB(Z); "-";
40     NEXT Z
50     FOR X = 1 TO 70 STEP 5
60       PRINT TAB(X); "|";
70     NEXT X
80 NEXT Y
```

5. Program 6.20 has its loops crossed. How does your system respond to this kind of program?

Program 6.20

```
10 FOR X = 1 TO 5
20     FOR Y = 1 TO 5
30     NEXT X
40 NEXT Y
```

Self-Test

DIRECTIONS

Answer the following questions in reference to Program 6.11.

Questions

1. What is the resonant frequency if the user enters R = 100, L = .035, and C = 1e-6?
2. How can Program 6.11 be modified to display the message

   ```
   RESONANCE!
   ```

   when the resonant frequency is printed?
3. How might the user select a different range of frequencies other than +/– 10 percent?
4. Is there a nested loop in Program 6.11?
5. Can the STEP parameter be eliminated from the FOR-NEXT loop without changing execution?

Study Questions

1. Develop a structured BASIC program that will display the interest compounded annually from one to 30 years. The user must input the principal and the rate of interest. The mathematical relationship is

   $$Y = A(1 + N)^{T}$$

   where Y = the amount
   A = the principal invested
   N = interest rate
   T = number of years

2. Create a structured BASIC program that will find different roots of a number entered by the user. The range of roots is from the square root to the tenth root.

3. Construct a structured BASIC program that will compute the power dissipation of a resistor for a range and increments of currents selected by the user. The user enters the value of the resistor. The mathematical relationship is

$$P = I^2 R$$

where P = power
I = current
R = value of resistor

4. You are required to develop a structured BASIC program that will show the relationship of the change in volume of a sphere for a given change in radius. The user selects the initial, incremental, and ending values of the radius. The mathematical relationship is

$$V = (4/3)\pi R^3$$

where V = volume
π = constant pi
R = radius of the sphere

5. You have been assigned to construct a program using structured BASIC that will demonstrate the change in volume of a cylindrical water tank as the amount of water in the tank changes (increases or decreases). The user is to input the radius and height of the water tank as well as the incremental increase or decrease of the amount of water in the tank.
6. It is necessary for a health science class to develop a structured BASIC program that will display the value of a range of temperatures in degrees Fahrenheit and degrees centigrade. The user is to select the lowest, highest, and incremental temperature change. The mathematical relationship is

$$F = (9/5)C + 32$$

where F = temperature in degrees Fahrenheit
C = temperature in degrees centigrade

7. Develop a structured BASIC program that will show the change in the volume of a metal cone as it is machined. Assume that the machining reduces the height of the metal cone. The user enters the dimensions of the cone as well as the incremental changes in the cone height. The mathematical relationship is

$$V = h/3(A_1 + A_2 + \sqrt{A_1 A_2})$$

where V = volume of the cone
h = height of cone
A_1 = area of lower base
A_2 = area of upper base

8. Modify Study Question 1 so that the program contains an inner loop that will display the interest for different amounts of money. The user would now select the range for the principal and the incremental difference as well as entering the rate of interest.
9. Modify Study Question 5 so that the computer will warn the user when the water tank is overflowing or is empty.
10. Modify Study Question 3 by adding an inner loop so that the program user may observe the power dissipation for a range of resistors as well as a range of current. The user would now select the current range and resistance range as well as the incremental values for each.
11. Create a structured BASIC program that will display a range of the same lengths in feet, meters, and inches. The user can select the beginning, ending, and incremental measurements in feet.
12. The relationship between the number of units of fertilizer and the expected crop yield is

$$Y = F/(2 \wedge F) + 1$$

where Y = the yield improvement factor
F = arbitrary units of fertilizer per acre

Develop a structured BASIC program to find what value of F produces a maximum value of Y.

13. Create a structured BASIC program that will display the heartbeat of a patient over a range of beats per minute, beats per hour, and beats per day. The user can enter the minimum and maximum number of beats per minute and the value of the increment.
14. Develop a structured BASIC program that will show a range of weights in pounds and kilograms. The user can enter the minimum and maximum numbers of the weight along with the increment value either in pounds or in kilograms.
15. Write a structured BASIC program that will compute the sales tax for a range of values and round the result off to the nearest cent. The user can input the minimum and maximum dollar amounts, and the percentage of sales tax. The increment is to be determined by the program so that a printout is given for every one-cent change in the total amount.
16. Modify the example problem of the series resonant circuit used in this chapter so that the user can select between a series resonant or a parallel resonant circuit.
17. Write a BASIC program that simulates the operation of a simple vending machine. The user is allowed to enter nickels (N), dimes (D), and quarters (Q). When done, the user enters P to purchase a product. Products all cost 50 cents. If any change is due, display the minimum number of coins required to make change. An example is as follows:

```
Enter N, D, Q, or P ==> ? Q
Enter N, D, Q, or P ==> ? N
Enter N, D, Q, or P ==> ? D
Enter N, D, Q, or P ==> ? Q
Enter N, D, Q, or P ==> ? D
Enter N, D, Q, or P ==> ? P

Your change is 1 Quarter.
```

18. Modify the vending machine program of Question 17 so that a choice of three products is available, whose prices are as indicated:

    Product 1: \$0.50
    Product 2: \$0.65
    Product 3: \$1.25

19. The following sequence shows the first 10 Fibonacci numbers:

```
1   1   2   3   5   8   13   21   34   55
```

    Show a BASIC program containing a loop that generates these numbers.
20. Modify the Fibonacci program from Study Question 19 so that the user is allowed to enter the specific Fibonacci number to display. For example, the user enters 7 and gets 13 as the result.
21. Use nested loops to generate the following sequence of numbers:

```
0   0   0
0   0   1
0   1   0
0   1   1
1   0   0
1   0   1
1   1   0
1   1   1
```

22. The equation for a straight line is

$$Y = 5X - 6$$

    Write a BASIC program that shows the resulting X-Y coordinates when X is stepped from 0 to 10 by 1.

7 Arrays

Ken Koder was sitting at his desk when Don, the senior technician, walked up and handed him a 40-page document filled with numbers.

"Ken, this data represents a digitized sample of an insect's chirping sound. I need a program that will display the data as an analog waveform, with simple zoom capability. Think you can do it?"

Ken leafed through the pages of data. "How much time do I have?"

"Two weeks. Do you think you can do it?" Don asked again.

"Yes, Don, I think so."

By the following afternoon, Ken was finished and was demonstrating the program to Don, who was flummoxed.

"How did you enter all the data so fast?" he asked. "You must have been up all night typing."

"Actually," Ken replied, "it took me only three hours to enter all the data. I scanned each page and used optical character recognition to extract the numbers."

Don didn't bother asking any more questions.

Objectives

This chapter will teach you

1. The definition and use of an array.
2. How to use READ and DATA statements.
3. When and how to DIMension array variables.
4. How the pointer works in READ and DATA statements and how to RESTORE it.
5. Methods of entering and displaying array data.

Introduction

A very important concept, the **array,** is presented in this chapter. An array is an easy way of keeping track of many different data items.

The word array comes from the word *arrangement.* You will see that an array is an easy way of arranging things. Once you have data arranged, you can use it in many useful ways. You will see that some programs cannot be written without the use of arrays. So, read on to see what is necessary to work with arrays.

7.1 What Is an Array?

An array is a collection of data items that are all associated with a single variable name. Consider the following BASIC statements:

```
10 N0 = 16
20 N1 = 18
30 N2 = 30
40 N3 = -12
50 N4 = 9
```

The programmer is using five different variables (N0 through N4) to keep track of a series of numbers. By using an array, all five numbers may be associated with a single variable (called an *arrayed* variable). Figure 7.1 illustrates this principle.

The name of the array in Figure 7.1 is simply N. Individual values (called *elements*) stored within array N are referenced by the use of an integer *subscript* (or *index*) that points to its position in the array. For example, N(0) is the first element of the array and has the value 16. The element subscript is placed within parentheses to indicate that N is an array variable. Note that BASIC begins numbering elements with 0, not 1 as we might be accustomed to.

N(4) is the fifth element of the array and has the value 9. How did the element values get loaded into the array in the first place? One way is as follows:

```
10 N(0) = 16
20 N(1) = 18
30 N(2) = 30
40 N(3) = -12
50 N(4) = 9
```

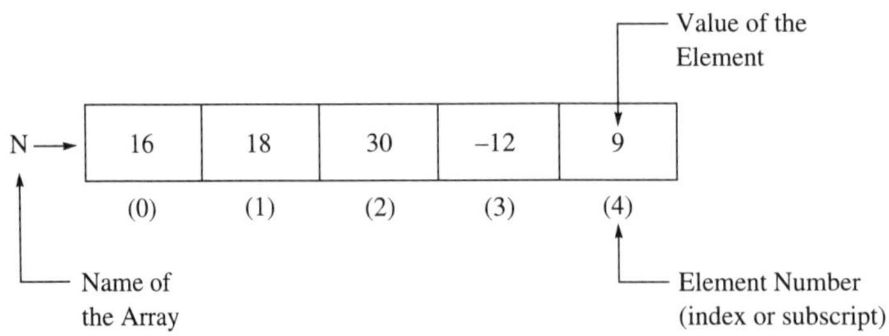

Figure 7.1 A Five-Element Array

Array elements may be assigned values just like any other variable. A second, preferred, method to initialize the array is to use a loop, as in

```
10 FOR K = 0 TO 4
20     INPUT N(K)
30 NEXT K
```

Here we see that the INPUT statement allows us to directly enter a number into a specific element (the element whose subscript equals the current value of K).

What advantage is there in using an array? To answer this question, let us return to our five variables N0 through N4. We might write a statement to find the average of the five numbers stored in N0 through N4 like this:

```
60 AVE = (N0 + N1 + N2 + N3 + N4) / 5
```

When using an array, the statement is very similar:

```
60 AVE = (N(0) + N(1) + N(2) + N(3) + N(4)) / 5
```

This does not seem to be an advantage, and actually requires more typing by the programmer. But suppose that we need to find the average of 500 numbers. Using individual variables, we would end up writing a program with hundreds or even thousands of lines. This is where using an array has an advantage. BASIC will allow us to create an array of 500 elements *with a single statement!* Then, through the use of a loop, the sum of *all* numbers in the array will be easily accomplished with only a few additional statements. Thus, we see there are times when it may be difficult, or even impossible, to write a BASIC program without the use of an array.

The array N in Figure 7.1 is called a **one-dimensional** array. BASIC allows the use of **multidimensional** arrays as well. Figure 7.2 shows an example of a two-dimensional array containing three rows and five columns of elements.

Once again we see that BASIC begins numbering elements at 0. Since there are two dimensions to the array NUMS, the programmer must supply two subscripts (one for the row and the other for the column), as in NUMS(1, 3). BASIC will allow as many subscripts as you require, as long as there is enough memory for the array.

Working with multidimensional arrays usually requires some sort of nested loop structure. For example, to display the contents of the NUMS array shown in Figure 7.2, the following statements are necesssary:

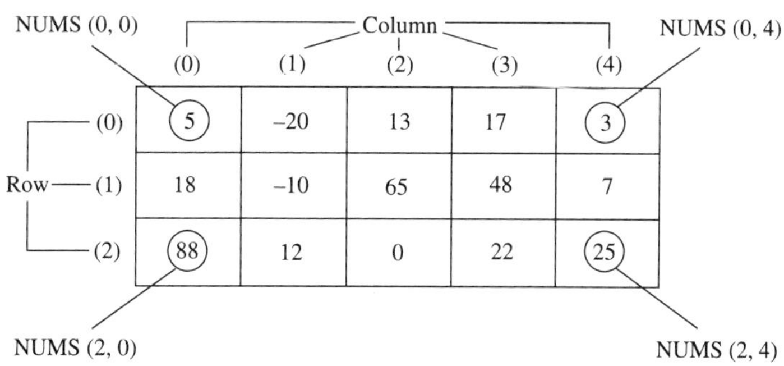

Figure 7.2 A Two-Dimensional Array Called NUMS

```
100 FOR ROW = 0 TO 2
110     FOR COL = 0 TO 4
120        PRINT NUMS(ROW,COL),
130     NEXT COL
140     PRINT
150 NEXT ROW
```

The PRINT statement on line 140 is needed to force a carriage return after the end of each row of data.

Most of the examples in this chapter will use one-dimensional arrays. Before you see what they are, try the following Section Review.

7.1 Section Review

1. Explain the origin of the word *array*.
2. Give an example of using a subscript.
3. State the advantage of using subscripts.
4. How does BASIC use subscript notation?
5. What are the subscript values for the first element of a two-dimensional array?

7.2 The READ and DATA Statements

Up to now we have only used one method to input data into a program: the use of an INPUT statement to read in a value. In this section we examine a second method that uses READ and DATA statements. We will also see that the READ and DATA statements provide an easy way to initialize an array with preset values.

Assigning Values with READ and DATA

The use of the **READ** and **DATA** statements is as follows:

```
10 READ A
20 DATA 3
```

These two statements are equivalent to

```
10 LET A = 3
```

It's important to understand how the READ and DATA statements work. Both of the following groups of statements will assign a value of 5 to the variable A:

```
10 READ A
20 DATA 5
```

or

```
10 DATA 5
20 READ A
```

Note that it makes no difference where in the program the DATA statement is found. What happens if there is more than one DATA statement?

```
10 DATA 5
20 READ A
30 DATA 6
```

This program will assign the value of 5 to the variable A because the first DATA statement in the program will be read first.

The DATA Statement

The DATA statement contains data separated by commas.

```
10 READ A
20 DATA 10, 20, 30, 40
```

When these statements are executed, the first piece of data (10) will be assigned to the variable A, but when the variable in the READ statement is put into a programming loop, something different happens.

Program 7.1

```
10 FOR V = 1 TO 4
20      READ A
30 NEXT V
40 REM
50 PRINT "DATA equals "; A
60 REM
70 DATA 10, 20, 30, 40
```

When Program 7.1 is executed, the result is

```
DATA equals 40
```

The final value of the variable A in the READ statement will now contain the fourth piece of data in the DATA statement on line 70. Because the FOR-NEXT loop contained the READ A statement, the first time through the loop the variable A was assigned the first piece of data in the DATA statement (the value 10). The second time through the loop, the READ A statement assigned the second piece of data in the DATA statement (the value 20). This process continued until the fourth and last time through the loop, where the variable A was assigned the fourth piece of data in the DATA statement (the value 40).

It's convenient to think of the READ and DATA statements as containing an imaginary **pointer** that starts out by pointing to the first piece of data following the DATA statement. Each time the READ A statement in the FOR-NEXT loop is executed, this imaginary pointer is incremented by 1 and the next piece of data following the DATA statement is read into the variable following the READ statement. This process is illustrated in Figure 7.3.

Loading Arrays with READ and DATA

A practical application of the READ and DATA statements results when an array is used in the READ statement inside a FOR-NEXT loop.

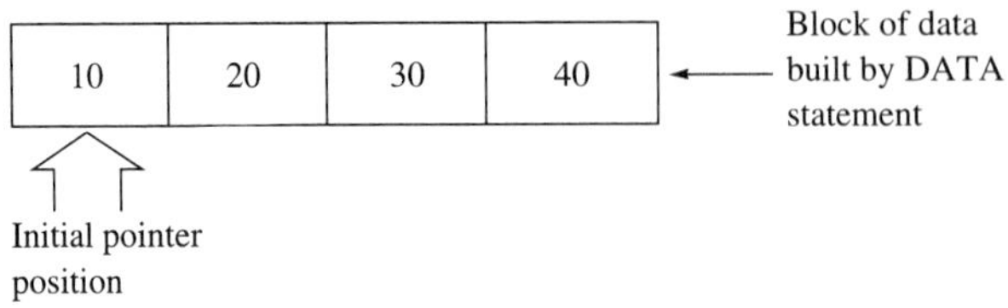

(a) Pointer and data at beginning of execution

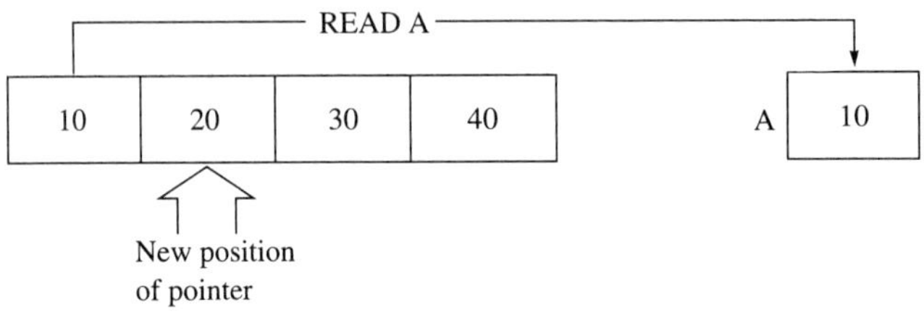

(b) Pointer and contents of variable A
after first READ statement

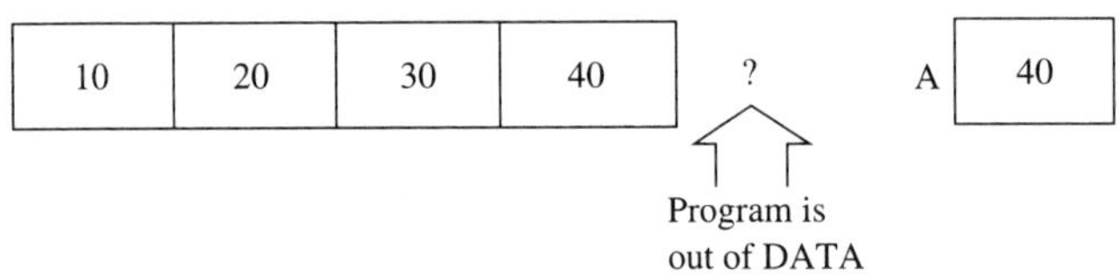

(c) Pointer and contents of variable A
after the fourth READ statement

Figure 7.3 Using a Pointer to Locate Data for READ

Program 7.2

```
10 FOR V = 1 TO 4
20     READ A(V)
30 NEXT V
40 REM
50 PRINT A(1), A(2), A(3), A(4)
60 REM
70 DATA 6, 7, 5, 2
```

When executed, Program 7.2 gives

```
6    7    5    2
```

Note that the first time through the loop, the variable A(1) was assigned the value of 6. The second time through the loop, the variable A(2) was assigned the value of 7 because the imaginary pointer was now pointing at the second piece of data in the DATA statement. This process continued and the PRINT statement printed the values of each of the array elements.

Printing an Array

It is useful to place the PRINT statement in a loop as well as the READ statement, as shown in Program 7.3.

Program 7.3

```
10 FOR V = 1 TO 4
20    READ A(V)
30 NEXT V
40 REM
50 FOR V = 1 TO 4
60    PRINT A(V),
70 NEXT V
80 DATA 6, 7, 5, 2
```

When executed, Program 7.3 will give the same display as Program 7.2:

```
6    7    5    2
```

If the comma is omitted from the end of line 60, the output of Program 7.3 will look like this:

```
6
7
5
2
```

Care must be used when displaying array data from a loop.

Using Strings in READ and DATA Statements

The READ and DATA statements used up to this point have been involved with numbers. You can also use strings.

Program 7.4 illustrates using READ and DATA statements with strings.

Program 7.4

```
10 FOR V = 1 TO 4
20   READ N$(V)
30 NEXT V
40 REM
50 FOR V = 1 TO 4
60   PRINT N$(V),
70 NEXT V
80 REM
90 DATA "Jones", "Smith", "Proctor", "McDaniels"
```

When executed, the output will be

```
Jones     Smith     Proctor     McDaniels
```

and if the comma is left out of line 60, the output will be

```
Jones
Smith
Proctor
McDaniels
```

Note the important changes necessary to read string variables. First, the array must be a string (N$). Second, the data in the DATA statement must be enclosed in quotation marks as with any string variable. The PRINT statement must also reference the string variable.

If the string data does not contain any spaces, quotation marks are not necessary. As an example, the data statement of line 90 in Program 7.4 could have been entered as

```
90 DATA Jones, Smith, Proctor, McDaniels
```

However, if there are any commas, semicolons, or significant leading or trailing blanks, quotation marks must be used. Quotation marks will be used for the examples in this text.

Type Mismatch

If you use a numerical variable to try and read a string, an error will occur. Examine the following statements:

```
10 FOR X = 1 TO 3
20     READ A(X)
30 NEXT X
40 REM
50 DATA 12, 15, "TOM"
```

The last piece of data is a string, and the array A is not a string array. Note that the following statements do not produce an error because numbers can be read as string characters.

```
10 FOR X = 1 TO 3
20     READ A$(X)
30 NEXT X
40 REM
50 DATA 12, 15, "TOM"
```

READing More than One Type of DATA

A powerful feature of the READ and DATA statements allows you to read more than one type of data. The data can even be a mixture of numerical and string data without giving you an error for a **type mismatch.** Consider Program 7.5.

Program 7.5

```
10 FOR V = 1 TO 4
20      READ N$(V), D(V)
30 NEXT V
40 REM
50 FOR V = 1 TO 4
60      PRINT N$(V), D(V)
70 NEXT V
80 REM
90 DATA "Jones", 3, "Smith", 6, "Proctor", 1, "McDaniels", 5
```

When Program 7.5 is executed, the output is

```
Jones          3
Smith          6
Proctor        1
McDaniels      5
```

In Program 7.5, the READ statement of line 20 is followed by two array variables separated by a comma. The first, N$(V), is a string variable and the second, D(V), is a numeric variable, requiring that the DATA statement on line 90 has its data pieces arranged the same way.

Conclusion

In this section we saw how a second method may be used to get data into a program, through the use of the READ and DATA statements. Test your understanding of this material by trying the following Section Review.

7.2 Section Review

1. Give an example of how the READ and DATA statements are the same as the LET statement.
2. If there is more than one DATA statement in a BASIC program, which DATA statement will the READ statement use first?
3. Can you have a DATA statement in a BASIC program without any READ statement? Explain.
4. Can you have a READ statement in a BASIC program without a DATA statement? Explain.
5. Show how an array of eight elements can be initialized with READ and DATA statements.

7.3 Restoring and Resuming

The Pointer

Section 7.2 showed how the READ and DATA statements caused an imaginary pointer to move to the next piece of data each time the READ statement was executed. This pointer is reset to the beginning of the data every time the program is executed. There may be times when you want the pointer reset while you are still in the program so that you can use the data over. The command to do this is

```
RESTORE
```

RESTORing the Pointer

The **RESTORE** command will cause the next READ statement to begin reading the data from the first DATA statement in the program. Consider Program 7.6.

Program 7.6

```
10 FOR V = 1 TO 2
20    READ N$(V), D(V)
30 NEXT V
40 REM
50 RESTORE
60 REM
```

```
70 FOR V = 3 TO 4
80     READ N$(V), D(V)
90 NEXT V
100 REM
110 FOR V = 1 TO 4
120     PRINT N$(V), D(V)
130 NEXT V
140 REM
150 DATA "Jones", 3, "Smith", 6, "Proctor", 1, "McDaniels", 5
```

When Program 7.6 is executed, the output is

```
Jones   3
Smith   6
Jones   3
Smith   6
```

Notice what has happened here. The RESTORE statement on line 50 has caused the pointer to be reset, or RESTOREd, to again start reading the first piece of data defined by the DATA statements. Therefore, when the READ statement is again used with the loop beginning at line 70, the first set of data is read again. Figure 7.4 illustrates this concept.

Running Out of Data

Look at the loop in Program 7.7 that starts at line 20. Note that it will loop five times. However, there are only four pieces of data in the DATA statement.

Program 7.7

```
10 REM Too many reads
20 FOR N = 1 TO 5
30      READ D
40 NEXT N
50 REM
60 PRINT D
70 DATA 2, 4, 6, 8
```

When this program is executed, the computer will display

```
Out of DATA in 30
```

and the program will stop execution. The PRINT statement on line 60 is never executed. As you can see from the above example, when the pointer is incremented beyond the available data, an error will occur and program execution will stop. There are some easy ways of dealing with this problem when it occurs.

Data Terminators

One way to prevent an "Out of DATA" error is to place the READ statement inside a loop containing an IF-THEN statement that examines the data as it is read in.

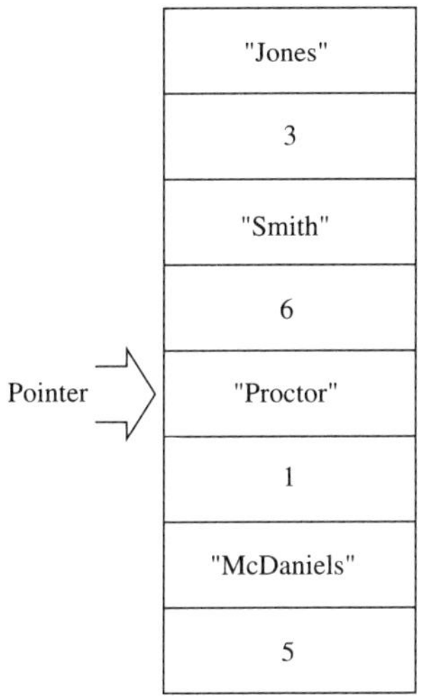

(a) Position of pointer at end of first loop

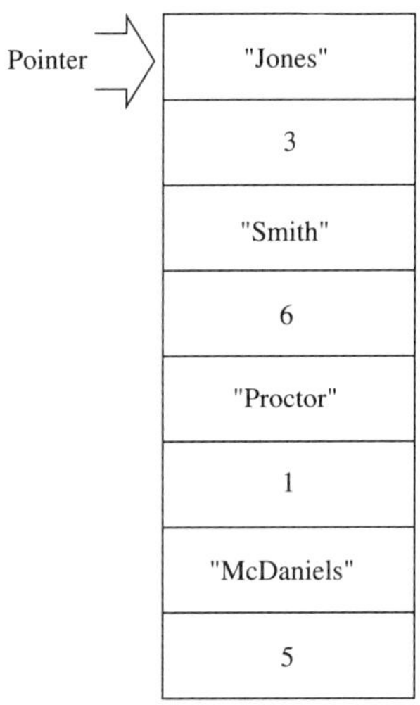

(b) Position of pointer after RESTORE

Figure 7.4 Using the RESTORE Statement

Program 7.8

```
10 REM Avoiding the out of data error
20 STOPPED = 0: REM Initialize STOPPED flag
30 WHILE STOPPED <> 1
40       READ D
50       PRINT D
60       IF D = 0 THEN STOPPED = 1
70 WEND
80 DATA 2, 4, 0
```

When Program 7.8 is executed, the result is

```
2
4
0
```

Note now that there is no error in the program. The IF-THEN statement on line 60 tested for a **data terminator,** a number whose value indicated that there was no more data to follow. A data terminator can be any number that would not normally appear as a value following the DATA statement. For example, if all data following the data statement were positive numbers, the value of the terminator could be a negative number, such as –1. Using a data terminator means the user (or programmer) does not have to count the data, or tell the program how many data items to read.

You can also do the same thing when using string variables. The data terminator for Program 7.9 is the string "XXX." The terminator could be any string variable, but the string "XXX" is a good choice because it is unlikely that anyone's last name would be "XXX."

Program 7.9

```
10 REM Avoiding the out of data error
20 STOPPED = 0: REM Initialize STOPPED flag
30 WHILE STOPPED <> 1
40       READ D$
50       PRINT D$
60       IF D$ = "XXX" THEN STOPPED = 1
70 WEND
80 DATA "Jones", "Smith", "Proctor", "McDaniels", "XXX"
```

Conclusion

Using the RESTORE command and data terminators in a BASIC program helps avoid troublesome out-of-data errors that often show up when dealing with arrays. Test your knowledge of these data management techniques with the following Section Review.

7.3 Section Review

1. State the action of the RESTORE statement.
2. Explain what happens when a BASIC program runs out of data in READ and DATA statements.
3. Discuss the use of a data terminator in READ and DATA statements.
4. Can a FOR-NEXT loop be used with a data terminator?
5. What is necessary to prevent the data terminators from being displayed in Programs 7.8 and 7.9?

7.4 The DIMension Statement

When you enter a BASIC program that uses arrays, the computer automatically reserves eleven memory locations (labeled 0 through 10) for the data you will put into the array. This is done for each array and each dimension of the array. However, if you want to enter more than eleven items, you must tell the computer ahead of time, or an out-of-range error will occur.

Program 7.10

```
100 REM Out of range error
110 FOR X = 0 TO 11
120     READ D(X)
130 NEXT X
140 REM
500 DATA 1, 2, 3, 4, 5, 6, 7, 8, 9, 10, 11, 12
```

For example, when Program 7.10 is executed, the computer will display

```
Subscript out-of-range error in 120
```

This means that the computer did not reserve enough memory to read more than eleven separate units of arrayed data. When the subscript in line 120 became 11 (D(11)), meaning that there were now twelve pieces of data (D(0) through D(11)), the "Subscript out-of-range error" occurred. To prevent this error, there must be a DIMension statement at the beginning of the program.

The DIMension statement has the following syntax:

```
DIM V(N)
```

where V = variable to be DIMensioned
N = maximum value of the subscript for the array

A DIM statement is needed only once in a program for each **dimensioned variable.** DIMensioned variables are placed in the programmer's block in much the same way that constants are placed.

A DIMension statement could have been added to Program 7.10, causing the computer to set aside twelve (0 through 11) memory locations for the arrayed variable D.

```
90 DIM D(11)
```

DIMension Sizes

The maximum size of the DIMension statement is limited by the size of the computer memory. As a general rule, use the smallest number in the DIMension statement that will accommodate all the arrayed variable requirements.

You can also use the DIMension statement for **multidimensional** arrays. For instance,

```
50 DIM F(20,30,50)
```

will reserve $21 \times 31 \times 51 = 33{,}201$ memory locations (remember that F(0,0,0) is the first element).

You can also DIMension more than one variable at a time with the same DIMension statement (strings as well as numeric), as in

```
50 DIM S$(35), P(40), X(27)
```

Note that the variables are separated by commas.

One last point concerning the DIM statement: the elements of the DIMensioned array are all set to 0 automatically. Program 7.11 DIMensions the V array to 25 elements (0 through 24).

Program 7.11

```
10 REM Automatic array initialization
20 DIM V(24)
30 FOR K = 0 TO 24
40     PRINT V(K),
50 NEXT K
```

When executed, Program 7.11 displays the following:

```
0             0             0             0             0
0             0             0             0             0
0             0             0             0             0
0             0             0             0             0
0             0             0             0             0
```

This clearly demonstrates that each array element has been set to 0, since there are no assignment statements in Program 7.11.

Test your understanding of the DIM statement in the following Section Review.

7.4 Section Review

1. How many memory locations does BASIC automatically save for arrays?
2. What is the purpose of a DIMension statement?
3. Explain what an out-of-range error means.
4. What are the contents of each element in an array when it is first DIMensioned?

7.5 Array Applications

We complete our study of arrays by examining a few additional applications that perform useful and common operations on arrays. These operations involve searching an array, sorting, and analysis of array data.

Searching an Array

There are many times when it is necessary to search an array. For example, an array of names and telephone numbers might be searched for a particular person or number. Or we might want to search an array of numbers to determine the smallest or largest number. Finding the largest value in an array is useful when performing a technique called *normalization*. To normalize a set of numbers is to divide each number in the set by the largest number. This always results in a set of normalized values between 0 and 1.

Program 7.12 shows how an array of ten elements is searched for the highest element value.

Program 7.12

```
10 REM Searching an array
20 FOR K = 1 TO 10
30      READ N(K)
40 NEXT K
50 HIGHEST = N(1):      REM Set initial value
60 REM Search the rest of the array
```

```
70 FOR K = 2 TO 10
80       IF N(K) > HIGHEST THEN HIGHEST = N(K)
90 NEXT K
100 PRINT "The highest value in the array is "; HIGHEST
110 REM
120 DATA 10, 4, 25, 16, 30, 5, 20, 12, 0, 27
```

To determine the highest value, the variable HIGHEST is initialized to the value of the first element N(1). It is not correct to initialize HIGHEST to 0, since the array may contain negative numbers. The remaining array elements are then checked to see if any are larger than HIGHEST. If so, the value of the current array element N(K) replaces the value stored in HIGHEST. A similar method may be used to find the lowest value.

When executed, Program 7.12 displays the following:

```
The highest value in the array is 30
```

Note that we may want to search the array for a certain number as well. Does the array contain the value 55? The search would then return a true or false response, or possibly the position of the data element within the array if found.

Sorting an Array

One of the simplest sorting techniques found in programming is the **bubble sort.** This sort technique makes many passes over the sets of numbers, partially sorting them with each pass. Eventually, the numbers all *bubble* into their correct positions. The bubble sort uses a simple comparison to determine when to swap two numbers in the array. Let us see how this works. Suppose we have the following array elements to begin with:

```
7    5    1    3
```

First, the 7 and 5 are compared. Since 7 is larger than 5, both numbers are swapped within the array, giving

```
5    7    1    3
```

Next, the 7 and 1 are compared and swapped. Now we have

```
5    1    7    3
```

Finally, the 7 and the 3 are compared and swapped, resulting in

```
5    1    3    7
```

This completes the first pass over the set of numbers. Notice that the largest number, 7, has been pushed into its correct position. The other numbers in the array are not yet in their proper places, which is why multiple passes are needed.

At the end of the second complete pass, the array looks like this:

```
1    3    5    7
```

Every number is now in its correct position! The array has been sorted into ascending order. Some arrays will require additional passes to get all of the numbers sorted, so, in general, the bubble sort makes N – 1 passes over a set of N numbers. This means that ten input numbers will require nine passes to guarantee that they are completely sorted. Program 7.13 implements a bubble sort on an array of ten numbers.

Program 7.13

```
10 REM Sorting an array
20 FOR K = 1 TO 10
30      READ N(K)
40 NEXT K
50 FOR K = 1 TO 9
60      FOR J = 1 TO 10 - K
70              IF N(J) > N(J + 1) THEN GOSUB 200
80      NEXT J
90 NEXT K
100 PRINT "The sorted array is:"
110 FOR K = 1 TO 10
120      PRINT N(K);
130 NEXT K
140 END
150 REM
200 TEMP = N(J)
210 N(J) = N(J + 1)
220 N(J + 1) = TEMP
230 RETURN
250 REM
300 DATA 10, 4, 25, 16, 30, 5, 20, 12, 0, 27
```

Nested FOR loops are used to perform the required number of passes over the array. The IF-THEN statement uses a subroutine to swap two elements of the array (elements N(K) and N(K + 1)) whenever the conditional test is true. An execution of Program 7.13 is as follows:

```
The sorted array is:
0 4 5 10 12 16 20 25 27 30
```

The bubble sort is not very efficient when large groups of numbers must be sorted, but it still performs a needed and useful array function.

Finding the Standard Deviation

The standard deviation of a set of numbers tells us important characteristics about the entire set of numbers. For instance, a teacher may want to find the standard deviation of a set of test grades. Based on the results, the cutoffs for As, Bs, and Cs can be determined fairly. To find the standard deviation of a set of numbers, it is first necessary to find the average. Once found, the average is then subtracted from each number in the set. The differences are squared and added together. The final sum is divided by the size of the set. Taking the square root of the result gives the standard deviation. The formula representing this process is illustrated mathematically in Figure 7.5.

Program 7.14 finds the standard deviation of a set of ten numbers that represent some sample test scores.

$$\text{S.D.} = \sqrt{\frac{1}{N-1}\left(\sum_{i=1}^{N}(X_i - A)^2\right)}$$

Figure 7.5 Standard Deviation Formula

Program 7.14

```
10 REM Finding standard deviation
20 SUM = 0
30 FOR K = 1 TO 10
40      READ N(K)
50      SUM = SUM + N(K)
60 NEXT K
70 AVE = SUM / 10
80 SUM = 0
90 FOR K = 1 TO 10
100     SUM = SUM + (N(K) - AVE) ^ 2
110 NEXT K
120 SDEV = SQR(SUM / 9)
130 PRINT "The average is "; AVE
140 PRINT "The standard deviation is "; SDEV
150 REM
160 DATA 72, 84, 96, 88, 91, 75, 79, 100, 76, 99
```

The execution gives these results:

```
The average is 86
The standard deviation is 10.34945
```

It is easy to verify the average. Just add each number together and divide by 10. A little more work is involved in finding the standard deviation, so it would be worthwhile to add a few PRINT statements to Program 7.14 to display intermediate results as the program does its work.

Generating a Histogram

Scientists who work with image data from distant space probes require sophisticated algorithms to clean up received images. The images are usually degraded by noise and reduced signal strength. Before the image can be cleaned up mathematically, it is necessary to examine every piece of the image and tabulate the number of identical pieces. On a simpler scale, count for yourself the number of 7s in the following set of data:

```
2    7    6    7    9    8    9    4    3    2    7    7    6
```

There are four, right? There are also two 2s, one 3, one 4, two 6s, one 8, and two 9s. In summary, we have:

2: 2
3: 1
4: 1
6: 2
7: 4
8: 1
9: 2

This represents a **histogram** of the input set. Program 7.15 performs this process over a set of fifty numbers that range in value from 0 to 9.

Program 7.15

```
10 REM Making a histogram
20 FOR K = 1 TO 50
30      READ N
40      VALS(N) = VALS(N) + 1
50 NEXT K
60 PRINT "The histogram for the data block is:"
70 FOR K = 0 TO 9
80 PRINT "Data value "; K; " : "; VALS(K); " items"
90 NEXT K
100 END
110 REM
200 DATA 1, 7, 6, 7, 5, 4, 3, 5, 4, 6
210 DATA 0, 8, 9, 0, 4, 3, 9, 7, 6, 8
220 DATA 5, 6, 6, 3, 4, 8, 7, 9, 2, 4
230 DATA 3, 8, 6, 0, 1, 9, 4, 7, 5, 6
240 DATA 1, 7, 7, 8, 5, 9, 0, 2, 0, 3
```

The array VALS is used to keep track of the individual counts for each number in the input set. Each input value is used as a subscript into VALS for the purpose of incrementing a particular element. The execution of Program 7.15 is as follows:

```
The histogram for the data block is:
Data value 0 : 5 items
Data value 1 : 3 items
Data value 2 : 2 items
Data value 3 : 5 items
Data value 4 : 6 items
Data value 5 : 5 items
Data value 6 : 7 items
Data value 7 : 7 items
Data value 8 : 5 items
Data value 9 : 5 items
```

Verify for yourself that Program 7.15 accurately counts the frequency of occurrence for each data item.

Conclusion

The array applications presented in this section illustrate just a few of the many things you can do with arrays. Test your understanding of the principles just presented with the following Section Review.

7.5 Section Review

1. Why is it necessary to set HIGHEST equal to N(1) in Program 7.12?
2. How many passes should be made over a set of 25 data values when performing a bubble sort?
3. Why must the TEMP variable be used in the swap subroutine of Program 7.13?
4. Find, by hand, the standard deviation of the following set of numbers:

   ```
   10    12    8    10    12
   ```

   Use Program 7.14 to verify your calculations.
5. What is a histogram?

7.6 The Waveform Viewer Project

The WAV samples displayed by the Waveform Viewer are stored in an array called WAVBUFF, which originally is allocated 8300 locations. Even though only 8192 locations are required for WAV samples, additional information from the WAV file is saved in WAVBUFF as well. The first 44 locations of WAVBUFF contain the WAV file *header* information, a group of data values that specify WAV parameters such as bits per sample, the sampling rate, the number of channels, and encoding format.

Two index pointers, WAVSTART and WAVEND, are used to indicate where the display routine should access the array. The initial value of WAVSTART is 44, which allows the header data to be skipped over. The initial value of WAVEND is the index of the last (or 8192nd) sample. During a zoom operation WAVSTART may be increased and WAVEND decreased.

The reason for limiting the maximum size to 8192 bytes is that some WAV files are very large and it is not possible to dynamically allocate memory to accommodate every possible file size. To view the contents of large WAV files, two methods can be used:

1. Read and display 8192 samples at a time.
2. Maintain a *sliding window* of 8192 samples.

The sliding window method requires a different WAV file access method and more complex index pointer manipulation. The reward is a greater flexibility while zooming.

The code for loading the WAV file and setting the initial waveform parameters is:

```
1210 REM Load WAV data
1220 WAVSTART = 44
1230 MAXLEN = 8192 + WAVSTART
1240 INPUT "Enter WAV file to display --> "; F$
1250 F$ = F$ + ".WAV"
1260 OPEN F$ FOR RANDOM AS #1 LEN = 1
1270 FIELD #1, 1 AS W$
1280 WAVLEN = 0
1290 WHILE (WAVLEN < MAXLEN) AND NOT EOF(1)
1300     GET #1
1310     WAVBUFF(WAVLEN) = ASC(W$)
1320     WAVLEN = WAVLEN + 1
1330 WEND
1340 CLOSE #1
1350 WAVEND = WAVLEN
1360 WAVLEN = WAVLEN - WAVSTART
1370 WAVSTEP = WAVLEN / 512
1380 RETURN
```

In statement 1310 data is being written into WAVBUFF. When the waveform is displayed, data is read out of WAVBUFF and converted into a screen coordinate. This is done as follows:

```
720 REM Draw waveform
730 K = 88
740 SAVEWST = WAVSTART
750 WHILE K <= 600
760     D = 255 - WAVBUFF(WAVSTART)
770     D = INT(.5 + D / 2)
780     PSET (K, 20 + D)
790     K = K + 1
```

```
800      WAVSTART = WAVSTART + WAVSTEP
810 WEND
820 WAVESTART = SAVEWST
830 RETURN
```

The calculations in statements 760 through 780 are used to scale and translate the waveform point to the correct screen coordinate.

Conclusion

Check your knowledge of this material by trying the following Section Review.

7.6 Section Review

1. Why is an array required in the Waveform Viewer? The data is already stored in a file, so why not translate file data directly to the screen?
2. What is the second screen coordinate in the PSET function if the value read out of WAVBUFF is 0? What if it is 255?

7.7 Troubleshooting Techniques

One of the most common problems encountered when working with arrays is the use of improper index values. BASIC is not able to guarantee that an index is valid, since the index value may not be known until runtime. For example, the statement:

```
250 SUM = SUM + VALUES(K)
```

contains the index variable K that may take on any value at runtime. If the value of K is larger than the associated array dimension, the data pointed to by the index variable will not be valid. It is therefore necessary for the programmer to enforce the proper index values at runtime. This is referred to as **bounds checking.**

For sequential access to an array, the index values can be bounded by the parameters of a loop, as in:

```
10 FOR K = 1 TO 3
20     SUM = SUM + ARRAY(K)
30 NEXT K
```

In this case the value of the index variable K is limited to 1, 2, and 3.

When the index variable is based on data provided by the user, a different method must be used to perform the bounds checking. For example, the program might ask the user to enter an item number in a database. The item number entered by the user might be greater than the number of items stored in the database.

Consider an array defined as follows:

```
10 DIM SPEEDS(10)
```

Legal index values for SPEEDS are 0 through 10. Bounds checking can be applied to any access to SPEEDS using this technique.

```
IF ((K = 0) AND (K < 11))
     ACCESS TO SPEEDS(K)
```

Conclusion

Test your understanding of this material by trying the following Section Review.

7.7 **Section Review**

1. What is bounds checking?
2. What happens if an illegal value is used during runtime?
3. Tell how bounds checking can be performed on a two-dimensional array defined like this:

```
10 DIM POINTS(4,7)
```

Interactive Exercises

DIRECTIONS

These exercises require that you have access to a computer that supports BASIC. They are provided here to give you valuable experience and, most importantly, immediate feedback on the concepts and statements introduced in this chapter.

Exercises

1. Enter the following:

```
10 FOR X = 1 TO 100
20     PRINT N(X)
30 NEXT X
```

   What are the results? Why?

2. Try the following:

```
10 FOR X = 1 TO 100
20     DIM N(X)
30 NEXT X
```

   What results do you get? Why do you get these results? (Try the next exercise; it may help you answer this one.)

3. Enter the following multiple DIMension statements.

```
10 DIM N(5)
20 DIM N(6)
```

   Do you get the same results as in Exercise 2 above? Explain what is happening.

4. What happens when you execute the following statement?

```
10 DIM N(0,0)
```

5. How large can you make the variable X for your system?

```
10 DIM N(X)
```

6. How far can your computer system carry out the series in Program 7.16? How much memory does the largest dimension used by your computer require?

Program 7.16

```
10 DIM A(1, 1)
20 DIM B(1, 1, 1)
30 DIM C(1, 1, 1, 1)
40 DIM D(1, 1, 1, 1, 1)
50 REM Keep adding subscripts until you get an error
```

7. What will be displayed when Program 7.17 is executed? Why does this happen?

Program 7.17

```
10 DATA 5
20 DATA 8
30 DATA 10
40 READ X
50 PRINT X
```

8. Is there any difference in the results of Programs 7.18 through 7.20 when they are executed? Why or why not?

Program 7.18

```
10 DATA 2,4,6
20 READ X
30 PRINT X
```

Program 7.19

```
10 DATA 2
20 DATA 4
30 DATA 6
40 READ X
```

Program 7.20

```
10 READ X
20 PRINT X
30 DATA 2, 4, 6
40 PRINT X
```

9. What happens when Program 7.21 is executed? How does the output of Program 7.21 differ from that of Program 7.22? If the two outputs are different, explain why they are different, using the concept of the pointer in your explanation.

Program 7.21

```
10 DATA 4, 6, 8, 9, 12, 18
20 READ X, Y
30 PRINT X, Y
```

Program 7.22

```
10 DATA 4, 6, 8, 9, 12, 18
20 FOR N = 1 TO 3
30      READ X, Y
40 NEXT N
50 PRINT X, Y
```

10. What is the output of Program 7.23? Why is the output of this program different from that of Program 7.21 or 7.22?

Program 7.23

```
10 DATA 4, 6, 8, 9, 12, 18
20 FOR N = 1 TO 3
30    READ X, Y
40    RESTORE
50 NEXT N
60 PRINT X, Y
```

11. Enter Program 7.24. What value is PRINTed when the program is executed? Why does this happen? What is the final value of N?

Program 7.24

```
10 DATA 4, 6, 8, 9, 12, 18
20 FOR N = 1 TO 3
30      READ X(N)
40 NEXT N
50 PRINT X(N)
```

12. Modify Program 7.24 by changing line 50:

    ```
    50 PRINT X(2),X(3),X(1)
    ```

    Now what is the output of the program when it is executed?
13. What output do you get when Program 7.25 is executed? Why do you get this output?

Program 7.25

```
10 DATA 4, 6, 8, 9, 12, 18
20 FOR N = 1 TO 3
30    READ X(N), Y(N)
40 NEXT N
50 PRINT Y(3), X(1)
```

14. Show how you would change Program 7.25 to get the following output:

    ```
    12 8 18 4
    ```

15. Explain what happens to Program 7.25 if you change line 20 to

    ```
    20 FOR N = 1 TO 4
    ```

    Why does this happen?
16. Enter Program 7.26. What happens when it is executed? Why does this happen?

Program 7.26

```
10 FOR N = 1 TO 3
20 READ N$(N)
30 NEXT N
40 DATA "TOM", "DICK", 4
```

17. Change line 40 of Program 7.26 to

    ```
    40 DATA "TOM", "DICK", "HARRY"
    ```

    What happens when the program is executed? Why does this happen?

Self-Test

DIRECTIONS

Program 7.27 was developed to test your skill at analyzing what goes on in a two-dimensional array. The program requires that you enter an odd number for N. Run the program for values of N equal to 3, 5, and 7, and then answer the following questions.

Program 7.27

```
100 INPUT "Enter size of magic square ===> "; N
110 K = 2
120 ROW = 0
130 COL = (N - 1) / 2
140 MAGIC(ROW, COL) = 1
```

```
150 WHILE K < 1 + N ^ 2
160     IF ROW - 1 < 0 THEN X = N - 1 ELSE X = ROW - 1
170     IF COL - 1 < 0 THEN Y = N - 1 ELSE Y = COL - 1
180     IF MAGIC(X, Y) <> 0 THEN GOSUB 500
190     MAGIC(X, Y) = K
200     ROW = X
210     COL = Y
220     K = K + 1
230 WEND
240 FOR ROW = 0 TO N - 1
250     FOR COL = 0 TO N - 1
260             PRINT MAGIC(ROW, COL),
270     NEXT COL
280     PRINT
290 NEXT ROW
300 END
500 IF ROW + 1 < N THEN X = ROW + 1 ELSE X = 0
510 Y = COL
520 RETURN
```

Questions

1. When an input value of 3 is used, what is the sum of elements in each row, column, and diagonal?
2. What is the sequence of ROW and COL numbers generated with an input value of 3?
3. What statement is responsible for ensuring that an illegal ROW subscript is not generated?
4. What is the purpose of line 180? What happens when MAGIC(X,Y) does not equal 0?
5. When an input value of 5 is used, what is the sum of elements in each row, column, and diagonal?
6. When an input value of 7 is used, what is the sum of elements in each row, column, and diagonal? Does the PRINT statement in line 260 need to be rewritten now?
7. How can Program 7.27 be modified so that the input number N is tested to ensure that it is an odd number?
8. What happens when you enter a value of 4 for N?

Study Questions

1. Develop a structured BASIC program that will display the amount of money in any safe deposit box that is contained in a wall that has ten rows by eight columns of these boxes.
2. Create a structured BASIC program that will take a 4 × 5 array and multiply the first column by any other column and display the sum of the products.
3. The circuit shown in Figure 7.6 is a parallel-series circuit. Develop a structured BASIC program that will compute the total resistance of any branch selected by the user. The total resistance of any one of the branches is

$$R_T = R_1 + R_2 + R_3$$

where R_T = total branch resistance in ohms
R_1, R_2, R_3 = value of each resistor in the branch in ohms

4. Create a structured BASIC program that will give the user the color of an area of the grid system shown in Figure 7.7. The user must enter the row and column number of the grid.

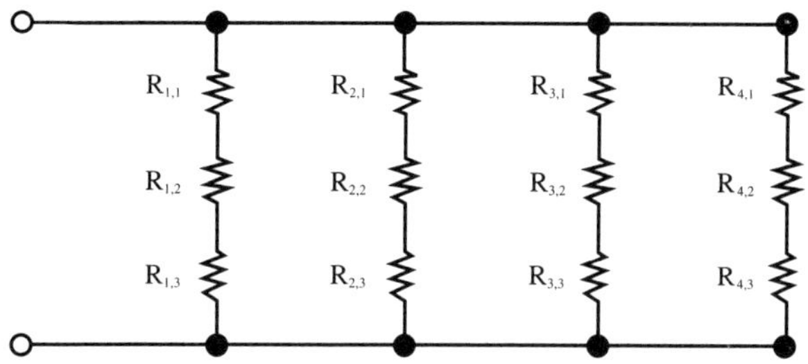

Figure 7.6 Circuit for Study Question 3

5. Develop a structured BASIC program that will rate dairy cows according to their age, milk-producing ability (quarts per day), and cost of feed per day. The user must be able to access the name of any dairy cow by milk-producing ability, age, or cost of feed per day.
6. A pharmacist needs a structured BASIC program that will allow her to find any prescription by (1) name of medication, (2) name of patient, or (3) cost of medication. The user must be able to locate all of this information by entering any one of the above three items.
7. A robotics company requires a structured BASIC program that will produce the following information about factory workers on an assembly line: (1) name of worker, (2) hourly wages, (3) hours worked per week, and (4) total weekly pay. The user must be able to locate all of the above information by entering any one of the above items.
8. Change the program in Study Question 1 so that the user may enter the amount of money in each safe deposit box.

Row \ Column	1	2	3	4
1	Red	Green	Blue	White
2	Violet	Amber	Brown	Black
3	Orange	Pink	Magenta	Yellow
4	Silver	Gold	Slate	Pink

Figure 7.7 Grid System for Study Question 4

9. Change the program in Study Question 2 so that the user may select any column to be multiplied by any other column and the sum of the products to be displayed as the answer.
10. Expand the program in Study Question 3 so that the user may enter the values of each resistor in the parallel-series circuit.
11. Modify the program in Study Question 4 so that the coordinates of all the areas of the same color will be displayed for the user. The user need only enter the color and all the coordinates for that color will be displayed.
12. Modify the program in Study Question 5 so that all cows that produce above or below a user-specified number of quarts of milk per day can be listed.
13. Modify the program in Study Question 6 so that the user may find the total cost of all medications for any selected patient.
14. Modify the program in Study Question 7 so that the user may find the total wages paid for the week to any factory worker. The program must allow the user to locate any factory worker by his/her weekly income earnings, or by those who have made less than a specified amount or those who have made more than a specified amount.
15. A bookkeeping firm needs a structured BASIC program that will display the amount entered for any entry of a 20 × 20 spreadsheet. The user must be able to select the row and column and then make the entry. The program must allow the user to get the total of any column or row.
16. Write a BASIC program that will normalize the 20 numbers saved in the array STATS. To normalize an array of numbers, first find the largest number in the array, then divide each number in the array by the largest number. Each resulting value will then be between 0 and 1.
17. Figure 7.8 shows the schematic of a low-pass filter. The corner frequency of the filter is found by the formula $F_C = 1/(2\pi RC)$. The operation of the low-pass filter is as follows: Input signals whose frequencies are lower than F_C pass through the filter with a small loss in amplitude. Signals whose frequencies are larger than F_C pass through with a large loss in amplitude. The output voltage of the low-pass filter is found by the formula:

    $$V_o = V_i/(\text{sqrt}(1 + (F/F_c) \wedge 2))$$

    where F is the applied frequency. Write a BASIC program that will display the frequency and output voltage for a low-pass filter at the following frequencies:

    $$0.1{*}F_c \quad 0.25{*}F_c \quad 0.5{*}F_c \quad 0.75{*}F_c \quad 0.9{*}F_c$$
    $$F_c \quad 2{*}F_c \quad 5{*}F_c \quad 7.5{*}F_c \quad 10{*}F_c$$

    Let V_i = 100 volts, R = 1000 ohms, and C = 0.1 microfarads. Save each frequency/voltage pair in an array and scan the array for the frequency at which V_o is closest to 70.7 V. Display the resulting frequency value.
18. Write a BASIC program that will match each resistor from list A with each resistor from list B (totaling 20 pairs), and compute the total resistance, the current supplied by a 50-V battery to

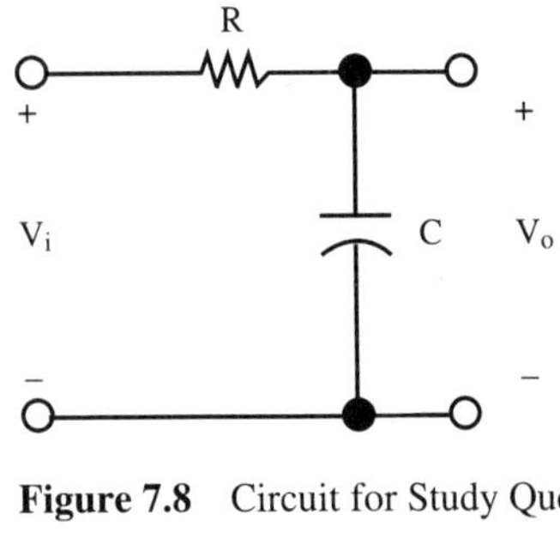

Figure 7.8 Circuit for Study Question 17

the total resistance, and the voltage across each resistor. For example, the first pair of resistors is 100 ohms, 270 ohms. The resulting display should be

```
R1      R2      Rt      I         V1        V2
100     270     370     0.135     13.5      36.5
```

The lists of resistor values are as follows:

List A	*List B*
100	270
150	330
220	470
270	560
330	

19. A five-card poker hand is represented by the two-dimensional integer array CARDS(2,5). The first row in CARDS contains the card numbers:

2 through 10	:2 through 10
Jack	:11
Queen	:12
King	:13
Ace	:14

The second row contains the suit number for each card. The suit numbers are defined as

Clubs	:1
Diamonds	:2
Hearts	:3
Spades	:4

Write a BASIC function that will analyze the poker hand and determine if any of the following are present:

Royal flush (10, J, Q, K, A of same suit)
Straight flush (any consecutive group of five cards in same suit)
Four of a kind
Full house (three of a kind and two of a kind)
Flush (all five cards in same suit)
Straight (any consecutive group of five cards from any suit)
Three of a kind
Two pair
One pair

Assign any values you want to the poker hands shown.

20. The knight on a chess board may move from its current position to any of the positions shown in Figure 7.9. Assuming row and column numbers are from 1 to 8, write a function that determines if a knight is being legally moved from OldRow, OldColumn to NewRow, NewColumn.
21. Write a BASIC program that computes all factors of a user-supplied integer. Store the factors in an array called FACTORS.
22. Modify the program in Study Question 21 to determine if the input number is a *perfect* number. A perfect number is a number whose factors add up to itself. For example, 6 is a perfect number, because its factors (1, 2, and 3) add up to 6. The number itself is not considered a factor in this case.
23. Another technique used to sort numbers is called *insertion* sort. In this technique, each new number is inserted into the correct position of an in-order array. For example, given the array

5 6 9 12 24 39 52

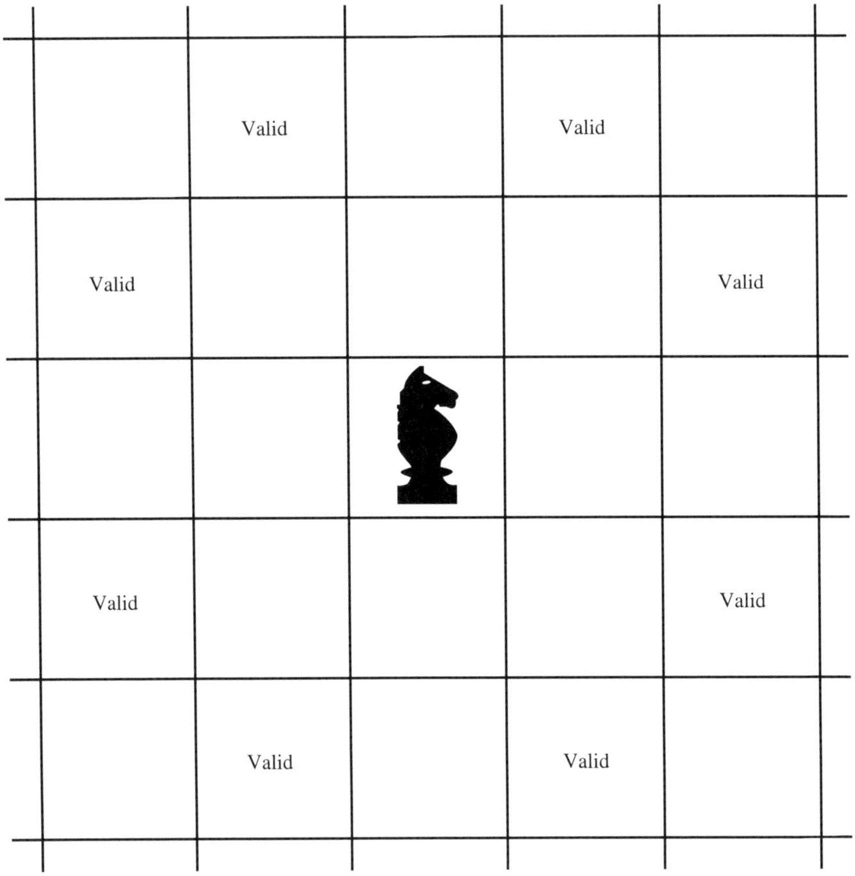

Figure 7.9 Diagram for Study Question 20

the new value 18 will be inserted between the 12 and the 24 by moving elements 24, 39, and 52 up one position in the array. Write a BASIC program that performs an insertion sort. Use the example array as the initial array. Allow the user to enter three numbers, one at a time. Show the resulting array after each insertion.

24. A two-dimensional array LINES(3,4) contains a set of three end-point coordinates. For example, if the first row of LINES contains the numbers 10, 20, 100, and 20, the end points of the first line are (10,20) and (100,20). Write a BASIC program that determines if the three lines form a triangle.
25. Write a BASIC program that transposes a square matrix. For example, given the matrix:

```
1 2 3
4 5 6
7 8 9
```

your program should create the following transposed matrix:

```
1 4 7
2 5 8
3 6 9
```

8 String Manipulation and Sorting

Ken Koder was experimenting with sort subroutines. He found a simple algorithm in a reference book and wrote the necessary code to test it. He entered several short lists of numbers to sort, and the results were correct each time.

Just for fun he decided to sort the 4096-sample array created for the Waveform Viewer program. When he pressed ENTER to begin the sort, he was surprised to see that the program did not finish quickly, as it had for the other test numbers. Ken waited for a few minutes but nothing seemed to be happening. To see what was going on, Ken added statements to display the progress of the sort algorithm and ran the program again. Five minutes later the program had performed only twenty six passes over the 4096-element data array.

Ken did a quick calculation and was horrified to discover that it would take several hours to sort the data.

He began looking for another sort algorithm.

Objectives

This chapter gives you a chance to learn

1. The meaning of *string manipulation.*
2. The most common string functions used in BASIC.
3. The most common string-related functions used in BASIC.
4. Specialized string functions found in some versions of BASIC.
5. The fundamental concepts of sorting.
6. How to develop a simple sort program in structured BASIC.
7. A method of sorting strings and how to apply this to technology applications.

Introduction

This chapter shows you how to work with words, or strings of characters. In the previous chapters, the focus was on calculations and using numbers; in this chapter, you will see how to work with everyday words as well as the technical words of your specialty.

Here you will also see the "mysteries" of sorting unlocked. You will learn how to develop structured BASIC programs that sort numerical data as well as strings, all very useful in keeping track of people, places, and things.

8.1 String Functions

BASIC contains many built-in functions to manipulate string variables. As you have learned, a string is a sequence of characters, words, or other elements. An example of a string is

```
"Hello."
```

Introduction to String Functions

Your computer stores string information just like any other information, as numbers. The ASCII code for the capital letters of the English alphabet is shown in Table 8.1.

BASIC contains a function that converts the ASCII code to its character equivalent. The function is

```
CHR$(N)
```

where `N` = any integer from 0 to 255

As an example,

```
PRINT CHR$(65)
```

will return the letter

```
A
```

Program 8.1 demonstrates the CHR$ function.

Table 8.1 American Standard Code for Information Interchange (Uppercase Letters Only)

Character	Code	Character	Code	Character	Code
A	65	J	74	S	83
B	66	K	75	T	84
C	67	L	76	U	85
D	68	M	77	V	86
E	69	N	78	W	87
F	70	O	79	X	88
G	71	P	80	Y	89
H	72	Q	81	Z	90
I	73	R	82		

Program 8.1

```
100 REM ASCII code conversion
110 FOR N = 65 TO 70
120     W$ = CHR$(N)
130     PRINT W$; " [W$ = CHR$("; N; ")]"
140 NEXT N
```

Execution of Program 8.1 displays

```
A [W$ = CHR$(65)]
B [W$ = CHR$(66)]
C [W$ = CHR$(67)]
D [W$ = CHR$(68)]
E [W$ = CHR$(69)]
F [W$ = CHR$(70)]
```

Program 8.1 is more interesting when the variable N is given the values of 0 to 255, causing the program loop to convert all of the ASCII codes (including special codes that control other functions of your computer and external equipment, such as the printer), and display each ASCII character.

Selecting Portions of a String

BASIC contains three string functions to select specific parts of a string. These are

```
LEFT$(W$, N)
RIGHT$(W$, N)
MID$(W$, N, M)
```

As you might expect, **LEFT$** works with the left part of a string, **RIGHT$** works with the right part of a string, and **MID$** works in the middle of a string. The string function

```
LEFT$(W$, N)
```

where N = any integer from 0 to 255

returns the leftmost N characters of the string W$. Program 8.2 demonstrates this principle.

Program 8.2

```
100 REM LEFT$ demonstration
110 W$ = "Mega ohms"
120 G$ = LEFT$(W$, 4)
130 PRINT G$
```

Program 8.2, when executed, will display

```
Mega
```

Program 8.3 displays the same result.

Program 8.3

```
100 REM LEFT$ demonstration
110 W$ = LEFT$("Mega ohms", 4)
120 PRINT W$
```

The complement of the LEFT$ function is the function

```
RIGHT$(W$, N)
```

where `N` = any integer from 0 to 255

This function returns the rightmost N characters of the string W$. This is shown in Program 8.4.

Program 8.4

```
100 REM RIGHT$ demonstration
110 W$ = "Mega ohms"
120 G$ = RIGHT$(W$, 4)
130 PRINT G$
```

Program 8.4, when executed, displays

```
ohms
```

Again, the same result could have been achieved with Program 8.5.

Program 8.5

```
100 REM RIGHT$ demonstration
110 W$ = RIGHT$("Mega ohms", 4)
120 PRINT W$
```

To work in the middle of a string, use

```
MID(W$, N, M)
```

where `N` = any integer from 1 to 255
`M` = any integer from 0 to 255

The MID$ command selects a section of a given string, by starting at position N of the string and selecting M characters from that position.

Program 8.6 shows how the MID$ function is used.

Program 8.6

```
100 REM MID$ demonstration
110 W$ = "micro milli Kilo Mega"
120 G$ = MID$(W$, 7, 5)
130 PRINT G$
```

Program 8.6, when executed, displays

```
milli
```

Position 7 of the string "micro **milli** Kilo Mega" holds the m of milli. Five characters starting from the "m" produce the string "milli". Figure 8.1 illustrates the operation of LEFT$, RIGHT$, and MID$.

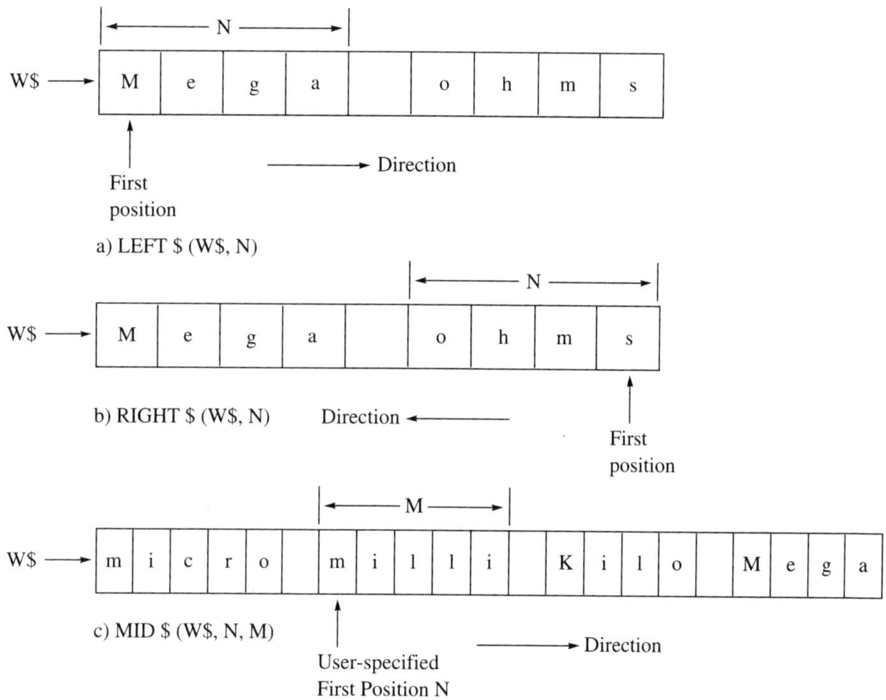

Figure 8.1 Concepts of Built-in String Functions

The STRING$ Function

Another useful string function is

`STRING$(N, W$)` or `STRING$(N, M)`

where `N, M` = an integer from 0 to 255
`W$` = any string expression

This string function returns a string of length N whose characters all have the same ASCII code given by M or the first character of the string W$. An example of STRING$ is given in Program 8.7.

Program 8.7

```
100 REM STRING$ example repeating first character
110 S$ = "*"
120 L$ = STRING$(10, S$)
130 PRINT L$; "RESISTOR VALUES"; L$
```

When Program 8.7 is executed, it displays

```
**********RESISTOR VALUES**********
```

The second form of the STRING$ function is used in Program 8.8.

Program 8.8

```
100 REM STRING$ example using the ASCII code
110 L$ = STRING$(10, 45)
120 PRINT L$; "RESISTOR VALUES"; L$
```

The ASCII character for 45 is the dash (-); execution of Program 8.8 will cause the display to be

```
----------RESISTOR VALUES----------
```

Specialized String Functions

The **INKEY$** function is used to enter data from the keyboard. This function is not available on all versions of BASIC. The interactive exercises will help you determine if INKEY$ is available on your system. The function is used like this:

```
S$ = INKEY$
```

INKEY$ reads a single character and must be assigned to a string variable. Program 8.9 is an example of the use of the INKEY$ function.

Program 8.9

```
100 PRINT "Enter a C to continue:"
110 KY$ = ""
120 WHILE KY$ <> "C"
130    KY$ = INKEY$
140 WEND
150 PRINT "Continuing now..."
```

If you want the user's INKEY$ entry to be displayed on the screen, you must use a PRINT statement. The INKEY$ function, by itself, does not echo to the screen.

In Program 8.9, the WHILE-WEND loop will continue until the string variable KY$ is equal to the letter "C". This means the program will repeat line 130 until the user enters a capital "C" on the keyboard; then the program will continue. Otherwise, pressing any other key will keep the program inside the WHILE loop.

Conclusion

This section introduced some common string functions found in BASIC. The next section will introduce you to string-related functions. For now, test your skills in the following Section Review.

8.1 Section Review

1. What is a string?
2. What are the ASCII codes for your first name?
3. State the relationship between the letters of the English alphabet and their corresponding ASCII codes.
4. Predict what Program 8.10 will display when executed.

Program 8.10

```
10 FOR V = 90 TO 87 STEP -1
20    PRINT CHR$(V)
30 NEXT V
```

5. Explain the difference between the following two string functions.

   `LEFT$(W$, N)`   `RIGHT$(W$, N)`

6. State what will be displayed when Program 8.11 is executed.

Program 8.11

```
10 Q$ = "Technical Applications"
20 D$ = MID$(Q$, 5, 5)
30 E$ = MID$(Q$, 16, 8)
40 PRINT D$ + E$
```

7. Write a program line that uses a string function to cause the following to be displayed: ++++++++++

8.2 String-Related Functions

In this section, you will see the use of some common string-related functions found in BASIC.

Getting the ASCII Code

The function CHR$(N) will return the ASCII character represented by the number N. The complement to the function CHR$(N) is the string-related function

`ASC(W$)`

where `W$` = any string expression

The function ASC(W$) will return the ASCII code for the first character of the string W$. Program 8.12 shows the use of this string-related function.

Program 8.12

```
100 REM ASC(W$) example
110 W$ = "ABCDEFG"
120 PRINT ASC(W$)
```

When executed, Program 8.12 displays

`65` [The ASCII code for "A"]

Figure 8.2 shows the operation of CHR$ and ASC.

Inside Strings

An interesting string-related function in BASIC is

`INSTR(N, A$, B$)`

where `N` = an integer from 1 to 255
`A$, B$` = string variables, expressions, or constants

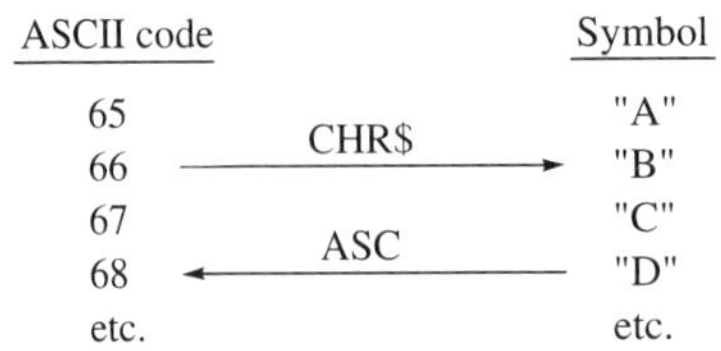

Figure 8.2 Operation of CHR$ and ASC

This function searches for the first occurrence of string B$ in the string A$, and returns a number that is equal to the position where the match is found. The number N is optional, and when used, starts the search at the position given by the value of N.

Program 8.13 searches to see if the user's name is on a selected list. When this program is executed, line 130 searches to see if the string entered by the user is contained in the list on line 120. If it is, the value of variable V will indicate its numerical position in the string defined by line 120; V will then have a value greater than 0 and the message "You're on the list." will be displayed. If the user's name is not on the list, line 130 will return a value of 0 for V and there will be no display.

Program 8.13

```
100 REM Search example
110 INPUT "Enter your last name ==>"; N$
120 C$ = "Jones Smith Frank Warren"
130 V = INSTR(C$, N$)
140 IF V > 0 THEN PRINT "You're on the list."
```

Finding the Length of Strings

There is a function in BASIC that will return the length of a string. It is

```
LEN(W$)
```

where `W$` = any string expression

This function returns the number of characters in the string W$. All characters and blanks, including unprintable characters, are included in the count. Program 8.14 shows how LEN is used.

Program 8.14

```
100 REM String length demonstration
110 INPUT "Enter customer's name ==> "; N$
120 L = LEN(N$)
130 PRINT N$; " contains "; L; " characters."
```

When executed, Program 8.14 displays

```
Enter customer's name ==> ? Bill Williams
Bill Williams contains 13 characters.
```

Converting Between Numbers and Strings

There are two functions in BASIC that allow you to convert between numbers and strings.

`STR$(N)` and `VAL(W$)`

where `N` = any numeric expression
`W$` = a string expression

These two functions are **complementary;** each does the opposite of the other. The STR$(N) function returns a string representation of the value of N; the VAL(W$) function returns the numerical value of the string W$. Program 8.15 demonstrates the STR$ function.

Program 8.15

```
100 REM STR$ demonstration
110 INPUT "Enter the value ==>"; V
120 W$ = STR$(V)
130 L = LEN(W$)
140 PRINT "The number "; V; " used "; L; " spaces"
```

Program 8.15 returns the length of the number entered, and when executed displays

```
Enter the value ==> ? 345678
The number  345678 used 7 spaces
```

Wouldn't you think that the number 345678 would return six spaces instead of seven? The reason for the extra space is to allow for a sign (+ or –). If the user had entered

```
+345678
```

or

```
-345678
```

the program would also have returned seven spaces.

The VAL function converts a string containing numerical digits into an actual number. Program 8.16 shows how this is done.

Program 8.16

```
100 REM VAL demonstration
110 INPUT "Enter value of the resistor ==> "; R$
120 V = VAL(R$)
130 I = 40 / V
140 PRINT "The circuit current is "; I; " amps."
```

When executed, Program 8.16 displays

```
Enter value of the resistor ==> ? 20 ohms
The circuit current is 2 amps.
```

The user entered 20 ohms as the value of the resistor. The variable for the INPUT statement of line 110 must be a string (R$), so the program can accept a user input that includes nonnumeric characters (20 ohms). If the INPUT statement of line 110 had a numerical variable (such as R), it would not accept the user input of 20 ohms. Remember that a numerical variable must contain only a number and no strings. However, a string variable can contain any sequence of characters.

Program line 120 performs the job of stripping the number from the string and assigning it to the numerical variable V. This must be done before any numerical operation is performed, such as in line 130.

An important aspect of the VAL function is that it strips blanks, tabs, and line feeds from the argument string to determine the result, and it will give a result of 0 if there are any string characters before the numerical value.

Conclusion

This section presented some commonly used string-related functions. Test your understanding of this section by trying the following Section Review.

8.2 Section Review

1. Give the complement of the string function CHR$(N). State what it does.
2. Explain what execution of the following will display on the screen:

```
10 W$ = "0123456789"
20 N = INSTR(W$, "5")
30 PRINT N
```

3. State what will be displayed upon execution of these statements:

```
10 W$ = "0123456789"
20 N = INSTR(3, W$, "5")
30 PRINT N
```

4. State what will be displayed when the following statement is executed.

```
100 PRINT LEN("012345-ABC, BASIC!")
```

5. Explain what will be displayed when Program 8.17 is executed:

Program 8.17

```
100 LET N1 = 4 * 5
110 J$ = STR$(N1)
120 PRINT J$ + J$
```

6. State what each of the following groups of statements will display:

```
5 REM Program One            5 REM Program Two
10 P$ = "23 skidoo."         10 P$ = "skidoo 23."
20 PRINT VAL(P$)             20 PRINT VAL(P$)
```

8.3 Sorting Strings

Basic Idea

Chapter 2 introduced the concept of using relational operations with string variables. Since the ASCII code for letters of the alphabet is in numerical order, it is easy for the computer to recognize that

`"A" < "B"` and `"AB" < "AC"`

Because of this, the program used for sorting numbers requires only a simple modification to sort strings: All array variables must be converted into string variables.

The modifications shown in Program 8.18 are required to process string data. These changes allow all the input data to be handled as strings. Note that the user could still enter numerical data in the DATA statement; it would also be treated as a string.

Program 8.18

```
10 REM Sorting an array of strings
20 FOR K = 1 TO 9
30      READ N$(K)
40 NEXT K
50 FOR K = 1 TO 8
60      FOR J = 1 TO 9 - K
70         IF N$(J) > N$(J + 1) THEN GOSUB 200
80      NEXT J
90 NEXT K
100 PRINT "The sorted string array is:"
110 FOR K = 1 TO 9
120     PRINT N$(K)
130 NEXT K
140 END
150 REM
200 TEMP$ = N$(J)
210 N$(J) = N$(J + 1)
220 N$(J + 1) = TEMP$
230 RETURN
240 REM
300 DATA "Michele", "Kristen", "James", "Sue", "Ken", "Turner"
310 DATA "Kimberly", "Mike", "Kenny"
```

When executed, Program 8.18 displays the following sorted list of names:

```
The sorted string array is:
James
Ken
Kenny
Kimberly
Kristen
Michele
Mike
Sue
Turner
```

Sorting names is a useful operation and is a required function when working with databases. As long as a sort routine is available, the user may enter names in any order.

Suppose that along with the array of names we are sorting is a second array containing phone numbers for the people in the first array. It is necessary to sort the second array in an identical fashion. This is easily accomplished by adding a few statements to the subroutine that swaps array elements. Program 8.19 shows this new addition.

Program 8.19

```
10 REM Sorting a phone directory
20 FOR K = 1 TO 9
30      READ N$(K), P(K)
40 NEXT K
50 FOR K = 1 TO 8
60      FOR J = 1 TO 9 - K
70              IF N$(J) > N$(J + 1) THEN GOSUB 200
80      NEXT J
90 NEXT K
100 PRINT "The sorted phone directory is:"
110 FOR K = 1 TO 9
120     PRINT N$(K), P(K)
130 NEXT K
140 END
150 REM
200 TEMP$ = N$(J)
210 N$(J) = N$(J + 1)
220 N$(J + 1) = TEMP$
230 T = P(J)
240 P(J) = P(J + 1)
250 P(J + 1) = T
260 RETURN
270 REM
300 DATA "Michele", 5702, "Kristen", 3586, "James", 5122, "Sue", 5000
310 DATA "Ken", 5257, "Turner", 4088, "Kimberly", 4858, "Mike", 7015
320 DATA "Kenny", 9771
```

When executed, Program 8.19 displays a sorted list of names and phone numbers:

```
James           5122
Ken             5257
Kenny           9771
Kimberly        4858
Kristen         3586
Michele         5702
Mike            7015
Sue             5000
Turner          4088
```

Remember, only the names are sorted. The phone numbers are carried along as swaps are made between array elements.

SWAPping Data

In many forms of BASIC a **SWAP** function can be used to switch the values of two variables. The statement is

```
SWAP V1, V2
```

where `V1, V2` = any two variables

and the statement exchanges the values of the two variables, as shown in Figure 8.3.

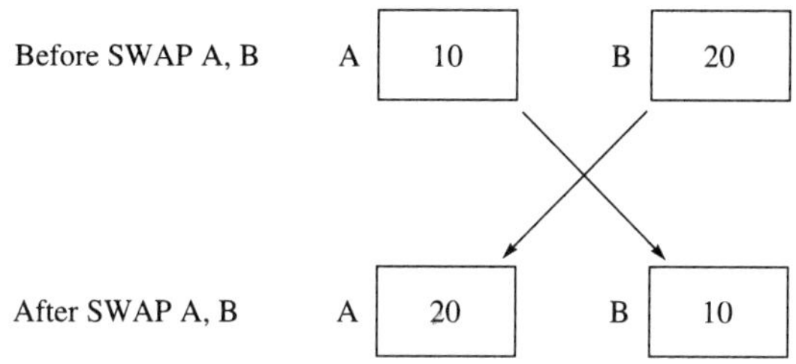

Figure 8.3 Using the SWAP Statement

This statement may be used in the swapping subroutine with a resulting saving of program lines.

The use of the SWAP statement reduces the six programming lines in Program 8.19 to two lines:

```
200 SWAP N$(J), N$(J + 1)
210 SWAP P(J), P(J + 1)
```

This simplifies the structure of the program and eliminates the need for temporary variables. Program 8.20 executes identically to Program 8.19.

Program 8.20

```
10 REM Sorting a phone directory
20 FOR K = 1 TO 9
30      READ N$(K), P(K)
40 NEXT K
50 FOR K = 1 TO 8
60      FOR J = 1 TO 9 - K
70              IF N$(J) > N$(J + 1) THEN GOSUB 200
80      NEXT J
90 NEXT K
100 PRINT "The sorted phone directory is:"
110 FOR K = 1 TO 9
120      PRINT N$(K), P(K)
130 NEXT K
140 END
150 REM
200 SWAP N$(J), N$(J + 1)
210 SWAP P(J), P(J + 1)
220 RETURN
230 REM
300 DATA "Michele", 5702, "Kristen", 3586, "James", 5122, "Sue", 5000
310 DATA "Ken", 5257, "Turner", 4088, "Kimberly", 4858, "Mike", 7015
320 DATA "Kenny", 9771
```

Conclusion

This section presented a technique for sorting string variables, and a useful function called SWAP. Test your skills in the following Section Review.

8.3 Section Review

1. State what would be displayed if Program 8.21 were executed.

Program 8.21

```
10 IF "A" > "B" THEN PRINT "First statement."
20 IF "AC" < "AB" THEN PRINT "Second statement."
30 IF "ADAM" < "EVE" THEN PRINT "Third statement."
```

2. Explain how relational string statements can be compared in BASIC.
3. State the major difference between a numerical and a string sorting program.
4. If the following data were entered into a string sorting program that sorted in descending order, in what order would the sorted data be displayed?

```
Transistor   35   Capacitor   100
```

5. Explain the reason for the result of the string sort in Problem 4.
6. State what Program 8.22 would output to the screen when executed.

Program 8.22

```
10 L$ = "Left"
20 R$ = "Right"
30 FOR X = 1 TO 3
40      SWAP L$, R$
50      PRINT L$, R$
60 NEXT X
```

7. Explain how the SWAP statement works.

8.4 String Applications

We conclude our study of string variables with a look at four simple applications that make use of many of the string functions presented in the first three sections.

Displaying Your Name

Programs 8.23 and 8.24 use the LEN and MID$ functions to display all characters of an input string one at a time in different formats. Program 8.23 contains nested FOR loops that are used to display the user's last name as a large block of text.

Program 8.23

```
10 INPUT "Enter your last name "; A$
20 PRINT
30 FOR N = 1 TO LEN(A$)
40      FOR M = 1 TO 10
50            PRINT MID$(A$, N, 1); " ";
60      NEXT M
70      PRINT
80 NEXT N
90 PRINT
```

A sample execution of Program 8.23 is as follows:

```
Enter your last name ? Author
A A A A A A A A A A
u u u u u u u u u u
t t t t t t t t t t
h h h h h h h h h h
o o o o o o o o o o
r r r r r r r r r r
```

The width of the block of text is controlled by the number of inner FOR loops.

Program 8.24 displays the user's last name on a single line, with dots in between each letter.

Program 8.24

```
10 INPUT "Enter your last name "; A$
20 PRINT
30 FOR N = 1 TO LEN(A$) - 1
40      PRINT MID$(A$, N, 1); "...";
50 NEXT N
60 PRINT MID$(A$, LEN(A$), 1)
```

Program 8.24's execution looks like this:

```
Enter your last name ? Author
A...u...t...h...o...r
```

Based on the PRINT statement in line 40, you might expect to see three more dots following the last letter in the name. But if you look at the FOR statement in line 30 you will see that one less than the length of the input string is used to set the number of passes. So, the last letter is not printed in the FOR loop. This makes line 60 necessary.

Converting Letters into Uppercase

It is often necessary to convert a string input from the user into uppercase. For example, if the user answers "yes," the string is converted into "YES." Having everything in uppercase makes doing comparisons easier, as in

```
1000 IF IN$ = "YES" THEN GOSUB 5000
```

If the user were allowed to enter any combination of uppercase or lowercase letters Y, E, and S, the IF-THEN statement would have to look for *eight* different YES strings. For this reason, we may want to convert all lowercase letters into uppercase. This is accomplished by knowing a little more about the structure of the ASCII code. An uppercase "A" has a code of 65, whereas a lowercase "a" has a code of 97. The difference between these two codes is 32. So, a lowercase letter can be converted into an uppercase letter by subtracting 32 from its ASCII code. This is what Program 8.25 does.

Program 8.25

```
10 C$ = ""
20 PRINT "Enter a complete sentence..."
30 INPUT A$
40 FOR I = 1 TO LEN(A$)
```

```
50      B$ = MID$(A$, I, 1)
60      IF B$ >= "a" AND B$ <= "z" THEN GOSUB 200
70      C$ = C$ + B$
80 NEXT I
90 PRINT
100 PRINT "The new sentence is..."
110 PRINT C$
120 END
200 A = ASC(B$)
210 B$ = CHR$(A - 32)
220 RETURN
```

Program 8.25 takes an entire sentence as input from the user and examines it one character at a time. An IF-THEN statement is used to determine if the current character is a lowercase letter. If so, the ASC and CHR$ functions are used to convert the letter into uppercase. Examine lines 200 and 210 to see how this is done.

When Program 8.25 is executed, the results are as follows:

```
Enter a complete sentence...
Hello, How are you?

The new sentence is...
HELLO, HOW ARE YOU?
```

The IF-THEN statement is necessary to prevent incorrect conversions of characters that are not lowercase letters.

Counting Vowels

Programs that work with text, such as data encryption/compression programs and word processing programs, often require statistical information about the block of text they are working with. For instance, a compression technique called **Huffman coding** must know how many As there are, as well as Bs, Cs, and so on. In order to determine this kind of information, the input text must be scanned. In Program 8.26, the sentence of text entered by the user is scanned for vowels.

Program 8.26

```
10 PRINT "Enter a complete sentence..."
20 INPUT A$
30 FOR N = 1 TO LEN(A$)
40      P$ = MID$(A$, N, 1)
50      IF P$ = "A" OR P$ = "a" THEN V = V + 1
60      IF P$ = "E" OR P$ = "e" THEN V = V + 1
70      IF P$ = "I" OR P$ = "i" THEN V = V + 1
80      IF P$ = "O" OR P$ = "o" THEN V = V + 1
90      IF P$ = "U" OR P$ = "u" THEN V = V + 1
100 NEXT N
110 PRINT
120 PRINT "That sentence contains "; V; " vowels."
```

In this case, all that the program will determine is the total number of vowels in the sentence. The OR operation is required in the five IF-THEN statements to ensure that both uppercase and lowercase letters are examined.

A sample execution of Program 8.26 is as follows:

```
Enter a complete sentence...
How many VOWELS here?

That sentence contains 6 vowels.
```

A similar technique can be used to count individual words in a sentence. That is left for you to think about.

Conclusion

The short string applications presented in this section showed how many of the string operations can be used to perform useful work with string data. We also saw how to convert letters from lowercase into uppercase. Test your understanding of this section with the following Section Review.

8.4 Section Review

1. How does MID$ pick a single character out of the input strings?
2. Why is line 60 needed in Program 8.24?
3. Explain how to convert from uppercase into lowercase.
4. Why is it improper to convert a character such as "7" into uppercase or lowercase?
5. Can the five IF-THEN statements be replaced by a single IF-THEN statement in Program 8.26?

8.5 The Waveform Viewer Project

As a courtesy to the user of the Waveform Viewer program, the program eliminates the need for the user to enter the ".WAV" extension on the WAV file name. This is a nice convenience, especially when many different WAV file names must be entered. The user will appreciate the time and effort spared. One simple statement is all it takes to tack the extension onto the end of the WAV file name supplied by the user:

```
1240 INPUT "Enter WAV file to display --> "; F$
1250 F$ = F$ + ".WAV"
1260 OPEN F$ FOR RANDOM AS #1 LEN = 1
```

Statement 1250 adds the extension string onto the end of the WAV file name stored in F$. The new string is used to open the file in statement 1260.

Conclusion

Check your knowledge of this material by trying the following Section Review.

8.5 Section Review

1. What happens if the user enters "ECHO.WAV"?
2. Explain how a sequence of WAV files may be displayed using information stored in a two-dimensional string array.

8.6 Troubleshooting Techniques

Working with strings presents many challenges to the BASIC programmer. One of these challenges is encountered when sorting strings that contain both uppercase and lowercase characters. Remember that uppercase letters and lowercase letters are treated differently because they map to different ASCII codes. The character "A" has an ASCII character code of 65 and the character "a" has an ASCII code of 97, 32 more than the uppercase letter. When sorting strings, it may be convenient to convert all string characters to the uppercase equivalent so that no matter what combination of uppercase and lowercase characters are in the string, they are treated equally and sorted properly into the correct order.

Conclusion

Test your understanding of this material by trying the following Section Review.

8.6 Section Review

1. Why are uppercase letters and lowercase letters treated differently?
2. Is it necessary to convert lowercase letters to uppercase when sorting strings?

Interactive Exercises

DIRECTIONS

These exercises require that you have access to a computer that supports BASIC. They are provided here to give you valuable experience and, most importantly, immediate feedback on the concepts and functions introduced in this chapter.

Exercises

1. What happens when you enter a string while executing the following program line?

```
10 INPUT "Give me something ==>";V
```

2. What happens when you enter a number while executing the following program line?

```
10 INPUT "Give me something ==>";V$
```

3. See how your computer responds to Program 8.27 when executed.

Program 8.27

```
10 REM Computer surprise
20 FOR N = 0 TO 255
30    PRINT N; " = "; CHR$(N); " ";
40 NEXT N
```

4. How does your computer system respond to Program 8.28, a modification of Program 8.27?

Program 8.28

```
10 REM Computer surprise
20 FOR N = 0 TO 300
30    PRINT N; " = "; CHR$(N); " ";
40 NEXT N
```

5. An interesting demonstration of the LEFT$ function follows. See if you can predict what will happen before you execute Program 8.29.

Program 8.29

```
10 REM LEFT$ demonstration
20 W$ = "TECHNOLOGY"
30 FOR N = 1 TO 15
40    PRINT LEFT$(W$, N)
50 NEXT N
```

6. See if you can predict what the RIGHT$ function in Program 8.30 will do.

Program 8.30

```
10 REM RIGHT$ demonstration
20 W$ = "TECHNOLOGY"
30 FOR N = 1 TO 15
40    PRINT RIGHT$(W$, N)
50 NEXT N
```

7. See what combining the two functions will do in Program 8.31.

Program 8.31

```
10 REM RIGHT$ and LEFT$ demonstration
20 W$ = "TECHNOLOGY"
30 FOR N = 1 TO 15
40    PRINT RIGHT$(W$, N) + LEFT$(W$, N)
50 NEXT N
```

8. Program 8.32 uses the MID$ function. See if you can predict what it will do before executing the program.

Program 8.32

```
10 REM MID$ demonstration
20 W$ = "TECHNOLOGY"
30 FOR N = 5 TO 1 STEP -1
40    P$ = MID$(W$, N, 2)
50    PRINT P$
60 NEXT N
```

9. Notice how the INKEY$ variable is used in Program 8.33. This is a useful technique to know.

Program 8.33

```
10 REM INKEY$ demonstration
20 CLS
30 PRINT "Press any key to continue..."
40 KY$ = ""
50 WHILE KY$ = ""
60    KY$ = INKEY$
70 WEND
80 PRINT "Program continues..."
```

10. Program 8.34 presents a simple way to find the ASCII code of an input character. See what happens when you enter a string of characters or a number greater than 9.

Program 8.34

```
10 REM ASC demonstration
20 INPUT "Give me something ==> "; W$
30 PRINT ASC(W$)
```

11. Program 8.35 is supposed to center any string you enter on your monitor. You may have to make adjustments according to your system. Try the program and see.

Program 8.35

```
10 REM Auto-center
20 INPUT "Give me a string to center ==>"; S$
30 V = LEN(S$)
40 H = 40 - V / 2
50 PRINT TAB(H); S$
```

Self-Test

DIRECTIONS

Program 8.36 was developed for electronics technology. It is a component inventory program that does alphabetical and numerical sorting. The program is only partially completed. Answer the following questions by referring to Program 8.36.

Program 8.36

```
100 REM Component Inventory Program
110 REM
120 REM This program will allow the user to
130 REM input the value, type, and supplier of
140 REM electronic components or other items.
150 REM
160 REM The program will then sort the input
170 REM according to the type or supplier.
180 REM
190 REM Variables used:
200 REM
500 REM Main program block
510 GOSUB 1000: REM Explain program to user
520 GOSUB 2000: REM Get data from user
```

```
530 GOSUB 3000: REM Select type of sort
540 GOSUB 4000: REM Perform selected sort
550 GOSUB 5000: REM Display output
560 GOSUB 6000: REM Ask for program repeat
570 END
580 REM
1000 REM Explain program to user
1010 RETURN
2000 REM Get data from user
2010 N = 1
2020 WHILE (E$ <> "N") AND (E$ <> "n")
2030    PRINT
2040    INPUT "Component type ==> "; T$(N)
2050    INPUT "Value ==> "; V$(N)
2060    INPUT "Quantity ==> "; Q(N)
2070    INPUT "Supplier ==> "; M$(N)
2080    PRINT
2090    INPUT "Another entry? (Y/N) ==> "; E$
2100    N = N + 1
2110 WEND
2120 REM End of loop
2130 RETURN
2140 REM
3000 REM Select type of sort
3010 S$ = STRING$(20, "*")
3020 PRINT S$ + S$
3030 PRINT "Select one of the following:"
3040 PRINT S$ + S$
3050 PRINT "1] Component 2] Supplier"
3060 PRINT S$ + S$
3070 INPUT "Your selection ==> "; S
3080 RETURN
3090 REM
4000 REM Perform selected sort
4010 ON S GOSUB 11000, 12000
4020 RETURN
4030 REM
5000 REM Display output
5010 CLS : REM Clear the screen
5020 PRINT
5030 PRINT S$ + S$ + S$
5040 PRINT "Component  Value  Quantity  Supplier"
5050 PRINT S$ + S$ + S$
5060 L$ = STRING$(60, 95)
5070 REM
5080 REM Beginning of output loop
5090 FOR V = 1 TO N
5100    H = LEN(T$(V))
5110    D = INT(10 - H / 2)
5120    PRINT TAB(D); T$(V); TAB(20); V$(V); TAB(35); Q(V); TAB(45); M$(V)
5130    PRINT L$
5140 NEXT V
5150 REM End of output loop
5160 RETURN
```

```
5170 REM
6000 REM Ask for program repeat
6010 RETURN
6020 REM
11000 REM Begin sort by component loop
11010 SWITCH = TRUE:     REM Set switch flag true
11020 WHILE SWITCH
11030    SWITCH = FALSE
11040    FOR V = 1 TO N
11050         IF T(V) < T(V + 1) THEN GOSUB 11500
11060    NEXT V: REM Continue through the list
11070 WEND
11080 REM End of sort
11090 RETURN
11100 REM
11500 REM Swap entry
11510 SWAP T(V), T(V + 1)
11520 SWAP V$(V), V$(V + 1)
11530 SWAP Q(V), Q(V + 1)
11540 SWAP M$(V), M$(V + 1)
11550 SWITCH = TRUE
11560 RETURN
11570 REM
12000 REM Sort by supplier loop
12010 RETURN
```

Questions

1. How many string variables are used in Program 8.36? How many numerical variables?
2. What kind of input will cause the Get data from user loop block to repeat?
3. State the purpose of line 3010.
4. Show what lines 3020 and 3040 cause to be displayed.
5. State the purpose of line 5060.
6. Indicate the program line that determines if component strings are to be exchanged for sorting. What kind of sort is this?
7. State which variable is used to indicate that the list sorting is complete. What causes this variable to change? What is this type of variable usually called? Why is it called this?
8. State the purpose of lines 5100 and 5110.
9. Write a program line that will cause the name of the supplier to be centered under the Supplier column. Be sure to change any necessary TAB commands.

Study Questions

Program Design

For each program you are assigned, document your design process and hand it in with your program. This process should include the design outline, process on the input, and required output as well as the program algorithm. Be sure to include all of the documentation in your final program.

1. Create a structured BASIC program that will find the sum of numbers entered by the user when each entry begins with a dollar sign ($). ***Hint:*** Your program must get the input as a string, remove the dollar sign, and convert the remaining string to a number.

2. Develop a structured BASIC program that will find the length of the words entered by the user. Each word is entered separately (followed by ENTER). When the program user is finished entering each word, the words are alphabetized and displayed along with each word's length.
3. Write a structured BASIC program that will allow a user to input the value of any resistor using metric prefixes (k or M). The program must then convert the input to a number (Example: Convert 12 k to 12000).
4. Create a structured BASIC program that will create a border around the monitor screen consisting of a repetition of any single character input by the user.
5. Develop a structured BASIC program that will alphabetize a list of agricultural products.
6. An insurance company requires a structured BASIC program that will present an alphabetized list of patients. The user will be entering the name of each patient (last name only) along with the amount of the total hospital bill. The program will display the alphabetized list of names, along with the amount owed by each, and the average amount owed by all patients.
7. Create an inventory program that will monitor program user input and ask for a special identification code if any inventory is entered that contains the string "nuclear."
8. Develop a structured BASIC program that will allow the user to input a name, address, ZIP code, and phone number for the creation of a mailing list. The program is to sort the input according to the ZIP code.
9. A computer science class requires a structured BASIC program that will convert a hexadecimal number to a decimal number. The size of the hexadecimal number is limited to three hexadecimal places.
10. Expand the electronics program of Study Question 3 so that it will do the same for the additional metric prefixes: μ = micro, m = milli.
11. Create a structured BASIC program that will display a list of architectural items input by the user. The list must be displayed under these three columns:

```
Windows      Doors      Other Items
```

    Any strings containing the character sequence "window" (such as bay window, kitchen window) must appear under the "Windows" column, while any strings containing the character sequence "door" (such as front door, screen door) must appear under the "Doors" column. All other items are to be displayed under the "Other Items" column.
12. Develop a structured BASIC program that will take a list of items entered by the user and list under a separate column called "Dairy Products" any entered item that is a dairy product (such as milk, butter, or cream). User may input strings such as "sour cream."
13. Create a sorting program that will sort patient information by illness, age, gender, or last name.
14. Develop a sorting program in structured BASIC that enables a manufacturing company to sort parts according to their quantity, name, price, or supplier.
15. Develop a sorting program that will sort the accounts of bank customers according to amount, name of account holder, city of residence, or date of last withdrawal.
16. Write a BASIC program that will ask the user to enter a number in scientific notation (e.g., 2.5e3) and check the number for validity. If valid, convert the number into the appropriate value.
17. Write a BASIC program that allows the user to enter ten sentences. Then scan the ten sentences for any of the following words:

one	two	three	four	five	six
seven	eight	nine	ten	help	see
saw	boy	girl	fast	slow	up
down	left	right	top	go	stop

18. Write a BASIC program that scans the two-dimensional tic-tac-toe matrix TICTAC(3,3) for three Xs in any row, column, or diagonal.
19. Write a BASIC program that determines if an input string is a **palindrome.** A palindrome is a string that reads the same forwards *and* backwards, such as RADAR, MOM, and 110011.
20. Write a BASIC program that checks a user-supplied binary string to determine if it is of the form WW, where W is any binary string. For example, 110110 is accepted, because W is 110; 10111011 is also accepted, because W must be 1011. However, 100001 is not accepted, because 100 does not match 001.
21. Develop a subroutine that inserts the numeric value stored in the variable AMT into the following string:

    "The amount %f is acceptable."

    The value of AMT replaces the "%f" sequence.
22. Write a BASIC program that accepts 8 strings from the user, sorts them, and displays the longest string. Strings with more than one word are rejected.

9 Computer Graphics

Don, the senior technician, arrived at Ken Koder's office after receiving an excited phone call from Ken.

"What's going on, Ken?" he asked as he entered.

Ken stepped back from his computer and let Don see what was being displayed on the monitor. It was the output of the Waveform Viewer program.

"Use the arrow keys to move the start/stop cursors, Don," Ken instructed. "Then press ENTER."

Don fiddled around with the program for a few minutes, happily zooming in and out. Then he shook Ken's hand and said, "Excellent job, Ken. Let's go to lunch so you can tell me how it works."

Objectives

This chapter gives you an opportunity to learn

1. How computer screens are used to represent graphical displays.
2. What aspects of computer graphics are common to all microcomputers.
3. How pixels are manipulated.
4. How to cause lines to be drawn on the graphics screen.
5. How to plot trigonometric functions using the graphics screen.
6. How to use the graphics screen of any microcomputer to represent technical data.
7. The fundamental concepts of using color in both text and graphics.

Introduction

This chapter introduces you to the exciting world of computer graphics. For many, the first introduction to computers has been through graphics—in games or simulation models.

Graphics are used extensively in the analysis and display of all kinds of technical data, from simple bar graphs to three-dimensional models that demonstrate complex technical data and relationships. Creating graphics hardware and software is one of the fastest-growing areas of the computer field.

This chapter presents the main ideas behind all computer graphics; if you understand them, you will have a solid foundation to build upon no matter what graphics system you may work with. You also have the opportunity to learn the fundamentals of the exciting dimension of color. If you have access to a system with color, a whole new world of computer programming will be open to you.

9.1 Basic Concepts of Graphics

The most common coordinate system used to display technical data is the Cartesian coordinate system, named in honor of the French philosopher and mathematician René Descartes (1596–1650). Examples of the use of the Cartesian coordinate system are shown in Figure 9.1.

The coordinate system can be used to graphically display the relationship of voltage and current (Ohm's law), a mathematical expression, or the total sales for different months. In all cases, each graph is referenced to two perpendicular lines, one horizontal, the other vertical. The relationship between two quantities can be quickly and easily seen in these graphs. For example, the relationship of voltage and current for a given circuit can be predicted before the circuit is constructed, as shown in Figure 9.2.

The value of the circuit current for a given value resistor depends upon the value of the voltage. Hence, in this case, the voltage can be thought of as the **independent variable** and the current as the **dependent variable.**

The same is true of the sales graph. To find the amount of sales for a given month, the technique shown in Figure 9.3 is used. The value of the sales depends upon which month is selected. Since you independently select the month you want and the amount of sales depends upon this selection, the month is the independent variable and the amount of sales is the dependent variable.

Developing Coordinates

It's important to note that in each case, the horizontal line represented the independent variable and the vertical line the dependent variable. In the Cartesian coordinate system, the two perpendicular lines are called **axes;** the horizontal line is called the ***X*-axis** while the vertical line is called the ***Y*-axis.** Where these lines intersect is called the **origin.** Both of the axes are divided into values that can represent either positive or negative numbers. Being able to represent negative as well as positive numbers gives the Cartesian coordinate system tremendous power in the display of technical data.

A generalized Cartesian coordinate system is shown in Figure 9.4. Note that positive values are measured from the origin toward the right on the *X*-axis and from the origin toward the top on the *Y*-axis. Negative values are measured from the origin toward the left on the *X*-axis and from the origin toward the bottom on the *Y*-axis.

Points of data can easily be represented by the following notation:

$$(X, Y)$$

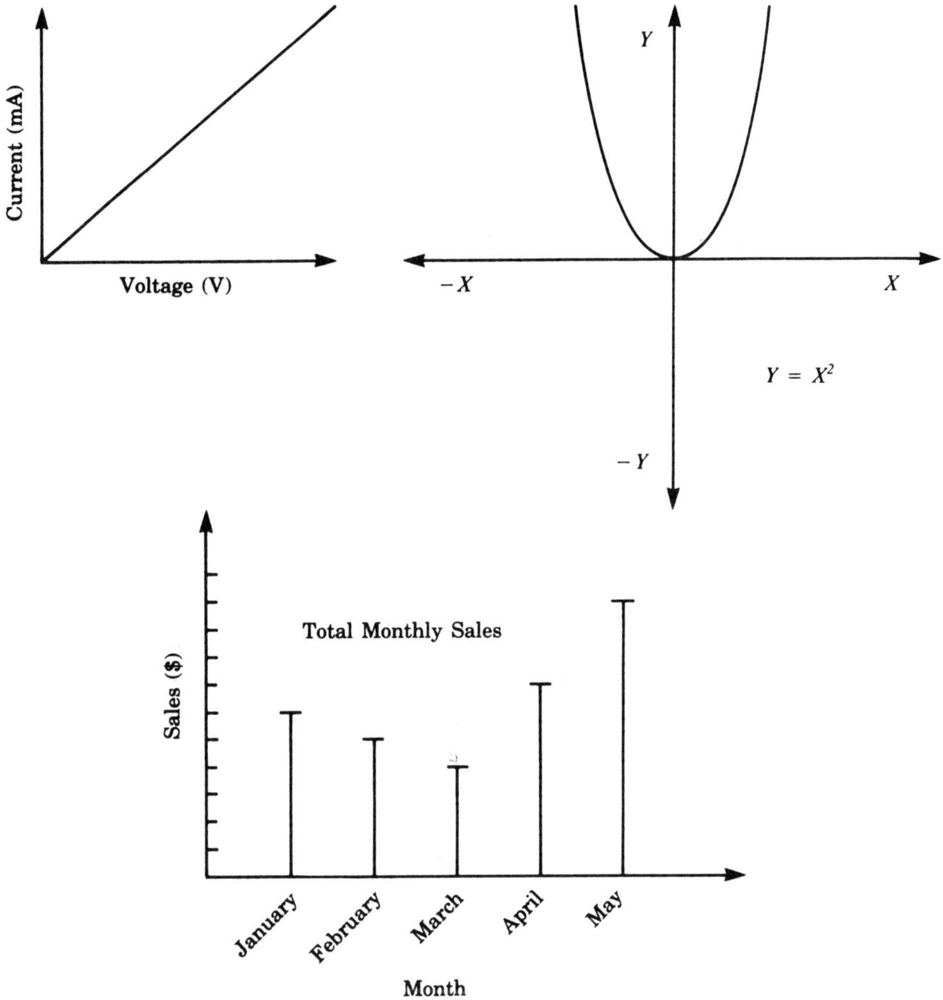

Figure 9.1 Examples of Using Cartesian Coordinates

where X = value of the X-axis
Y = value of the Y-axis

The use of this notation is illustrated in Figure 9.5.

This powerful system automatically divides itself into four major sections called **quadrants,** shown in Figure 9.6.

The following observations can be made from Figure 9.6:

1. The **first quadrant** contains only positive X and positive Y values (X,Y).
2. The **second quadrant** contains only negative X and positive Y values $(-X,Y)$.
3. The **third quadrant** contains only negative X and negative Y values $(-X,-Y)$.
4. The **fourth quadrant** contains only positive X and negative Y values $(X,-Y)$.

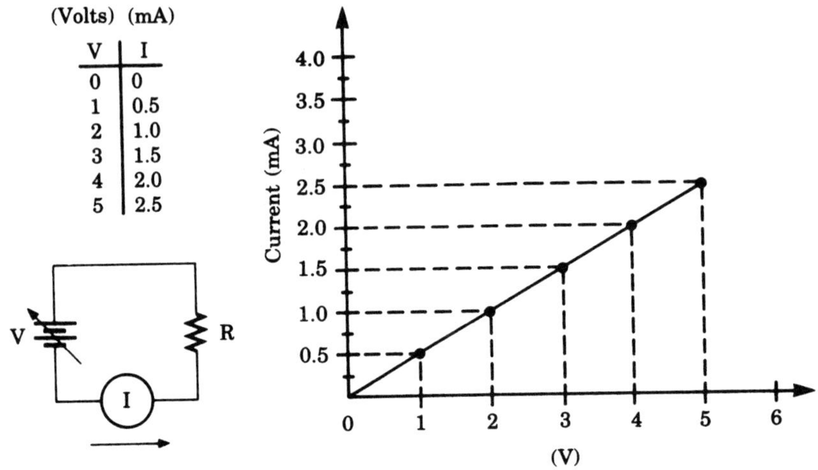

Figure 9.2 Finding the Value of Current for a Given Voltage

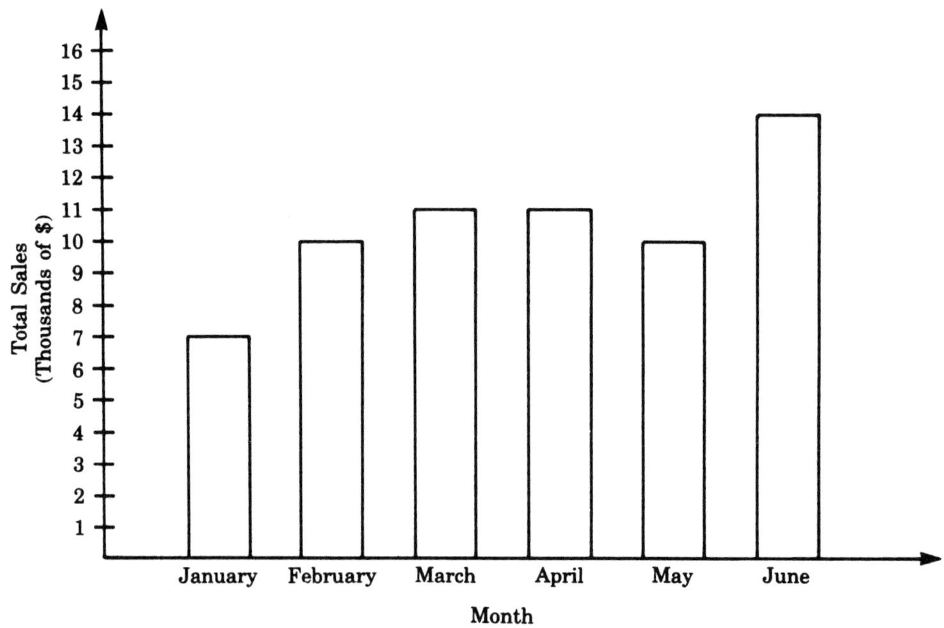

Figure 9.3 Finding the Amount of Sales for a Given Month

Conclusion

The concept of quadrants is very important in developing computer graphics for the display of technical information because of the limited display space available on the computer monitor. For example, if the information you want to display is positive only, you

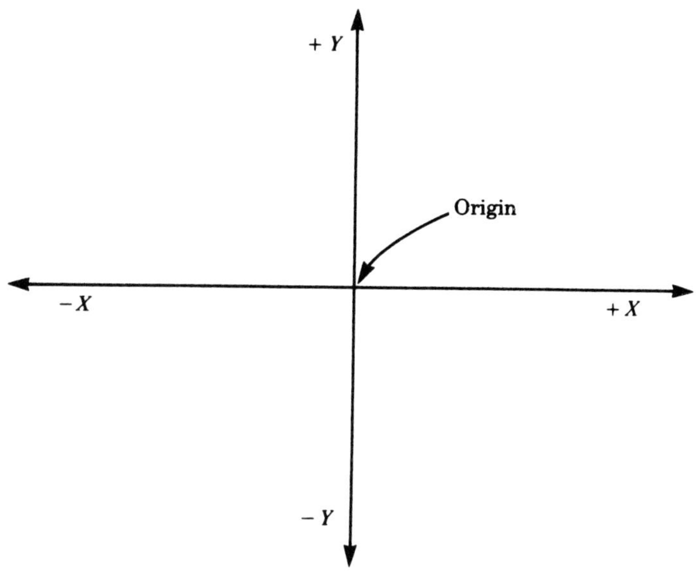

Figure 9.4 Generalized Cartesian Coordinate System

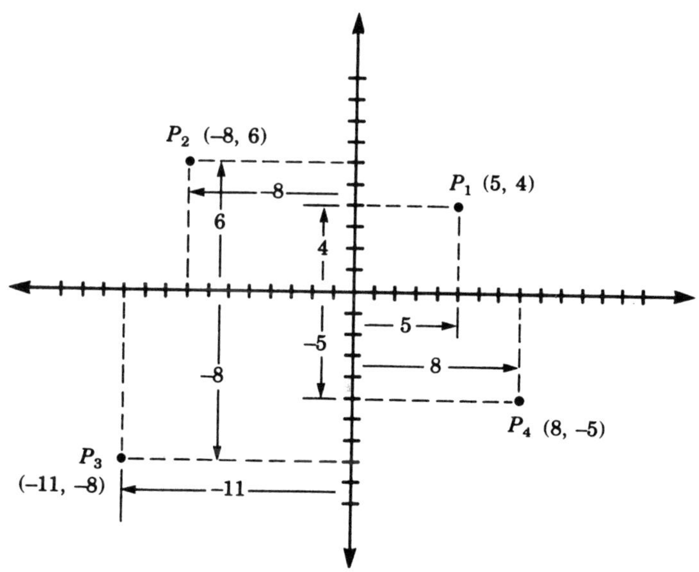

Figure 9.5 Representing Points on the Cartesian System

only need to use the first quadrant of the Cartesian system. However, if the display of more complex technical relations is necessary, all four quadrants may be required. Now, before going on, try the following Section Review.

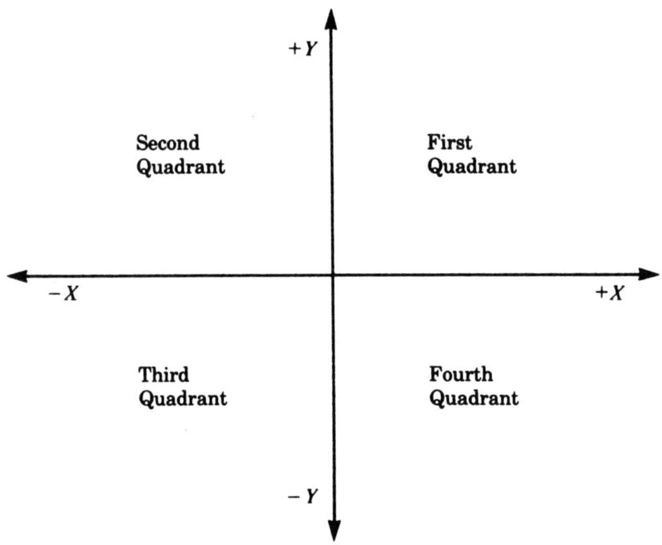

Figure 9.6 Four Quadrants of the Cartesian System

9.1 Section Review

1. Give the name of the most common coordinate system used to display technical data.
2. State the names and purposes of the two axes used in this coordinate system.
3. What are the four regions of this coordinate system called? What are the values of each axis in these regions?

9.2 Computer Graphics

The Computer Screen

Think of the computer screen as a flat surface that is part of a Cartesian coordinate system, with one slight difference. Most computer manufacturers use the upper left-hand corner of the computer screen to represent the origin, where the X-axis and Y-axis meet.

Observe in Figure 9.7 that for computer graphics, the Y-axis going down is positive. This is the opposite of the coordinate system commonly used where the Y-axis going down is treated as a negative value. However, in spite of this one difference, locating a point on the computer screen is a very easy thing to do.

Pixels

The word **pixel** means "picture element." Think of the computer screen as being broken up into tiny dots that can be turned on or off by a simple BASIC command.

The command used to turn a picture element on is

```
PSET (X,Y)
```

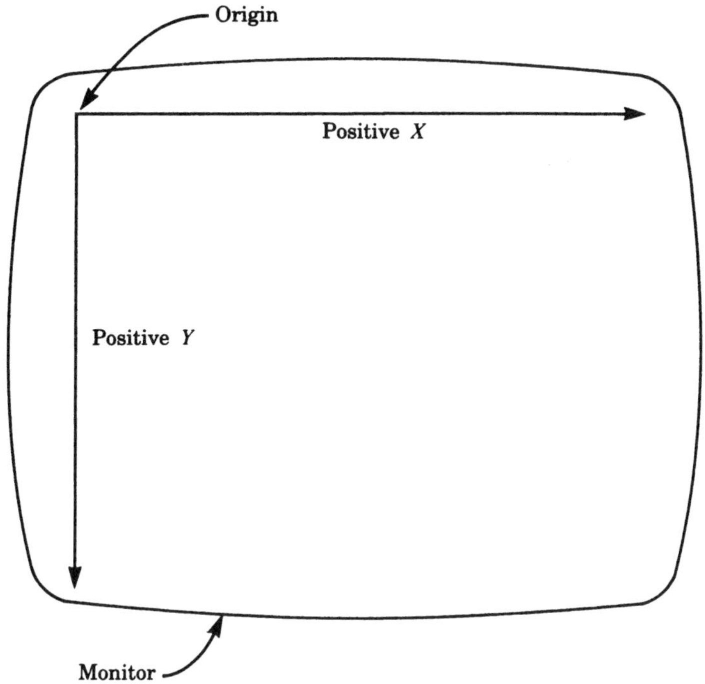

Figure 9.7 Computer Coordinate System

where `X,Y` = integers representing the location of the pixel to be set (turned on)

The *X* direction of the picture element is located first, followed by the *Y* direction.

Size of Graphics Screen

The number of pixels that can be displayed on the computer screen is referred to as the **resolution.** The more pixels, the greater the resolution.

The number of pixels available is not the same for all microcomputer manufacturers. The size of a graphic screen really means how many pixels there are horizontally and vertically that are available to be turned on or off. In this text, a graphics screen of 640 pixels horizontally (the *X*-axis) and 200 pixels vertically (the *Y*-axis) will be used. The computer system you are using may be different. This is discussed in the interactive exercises section of this chapter.

The number of pixels in the *X* direction is thus greater than those in the *Y* direction. This is true of all computer graphics screens and is due to the **aspect ratio** of the monitor. The aspect ratio is defined as the ratio of the display screen width to the display screen height. Program 9.1 turns on a pixel at each corner of the graphics screen. It makes no difference in what order the graphic commands are given. The resulting display when correct graphic commands are used is shown in Figure 9.8.

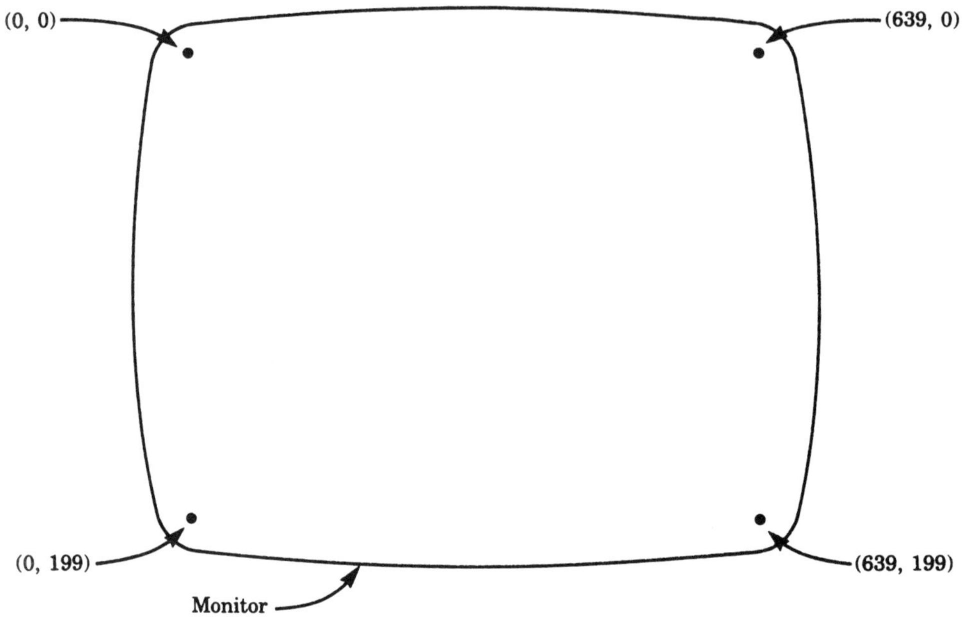

Figure 9.8 Four Corners of the Graphics Screen

Program 9.1

```
100 SCREEN 2
110 REM Plot point in upper left-hand corner
120 PSET (0, 0)
130 REM plot point in upper right-hand corner
140 PSET (639, 0)
150 REM plot point in lower left-hand corner
160 PSET (0, 199)
170 REM plot point in lower right-hand corner
180 PSET (630, 199)
```

The Graphics Screen

When a microcomputer is first turned on, it will automatically display a **text screen.** This means it's ready to show symbols from the keyboard.

You must give a command, which varies from system to system, that will cause the computer to display the **graphics screen;** only then can you use graphic commands to cause pixels to turn on and become visible.

The graphics command is

SCREEN N, M

where N = 0 : selects the text screen
N = 1 : selects medium-resolution graphics
N = 2 : selects high-resolution graphics
[In text mode]
M = 0 : color is OFF (default)

M = 1 : color is ON
[In graphics mode]
M = 0 : color is ON (default)
M = 1 : color is OFF

The screen command is used to select the text or graphics screen and enable or disable color. Later sections in this chapter will give more details about this command.

This command first switches from the text screen to the graphics screen; the graphics screen is then displayed on the monitor. The monitor actually displays the contents of a memory location that differs from that used to display text. That is, the text screen is stored in one section of computer memory, and the graphics screen in another, different section. For example, Program 9.2, when executed, will cause the computer to switch from the text screen to the graphics screen. The resultant graphic display is illustrated in Figure 9.9.

Program 9.2

```
10 CLS
20 SCREEN 1
30 PSET (20, 20)
40 PSET (10, 40)
50 PSET (40, 40)
```

Conclusion

In this section you learned the most fundamental concepts about computer graphics in regard to pixels (picture elements). These concepts can now be applied to any computer system that is capable of using graphics. In the following sections you will see that all graphic displays (lines, rectangles, or areas) can be thought of as causing specific pixels to be displayed on the screen. Test your understanding of this section with the following Section Review.

9.2 Section Review

1. State the purpose of computer graphics.
2. Describe the arrangement of the *X*- and *Y*-axes on most computer graphics screens.
3. Define the word *pixel* as used in computer graphics.

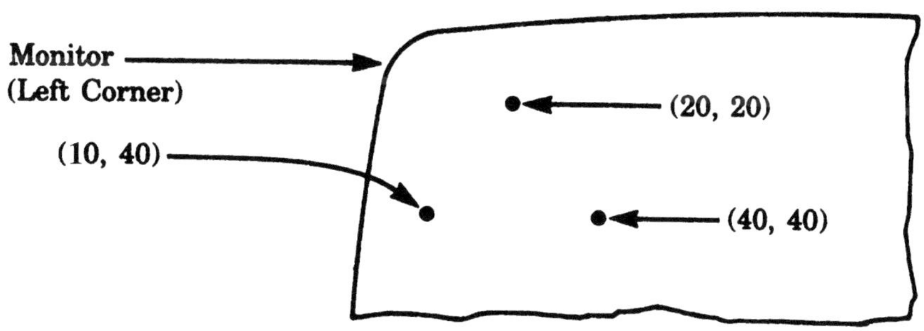

Figure 9.9 Graphics Display Resulting from Program 9.2

9.3 Technical Graphics

Technical graphics requires the manipulation of pixels to be extended into **lines, planes,** and **mathematical functions.** In this section, you will see the basic concepts behind the graphing of lines and planes. You will also be introduced to the important trigonometric and logarithmic functions, as well as the color graphics used in technical work. Armed with this knowledge, you will be ready to understand technical graphics.

Creating a Line

Most forms of BASIC have a command for drawing a line on the graphics screen. For example,

$$\text{LINE } (X_1, Y_1)-(X_2, Y_2)$$

will cause a line to be drawn on the IBM screen from point X_1, Y_1 to point X_2, Y_2. Programs 9.3 and 9.4 will both draw the line shown in Figure 9.10.

Program 9.3

```
10 REM Using PSET(X,Y)
20 SCREEN 2
30 FOR X = 0 TO 300
40    PSET (X, 100)
50 NEXT X
```

Program 9.4

```
10 REM Using LINE(X1, Y1)-(X2, Y2)
20 SCREEN 2
30 LINE (0, 100)-(300, 100)
```

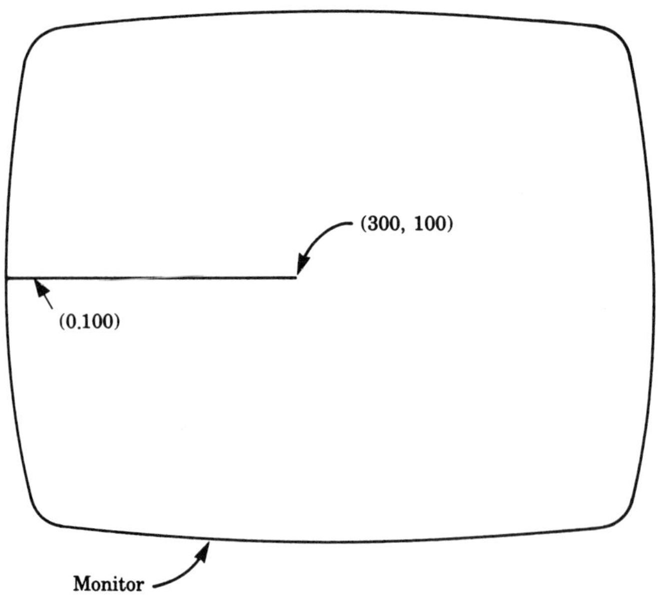

Figure 9.10 Line Created by Two Different Programs

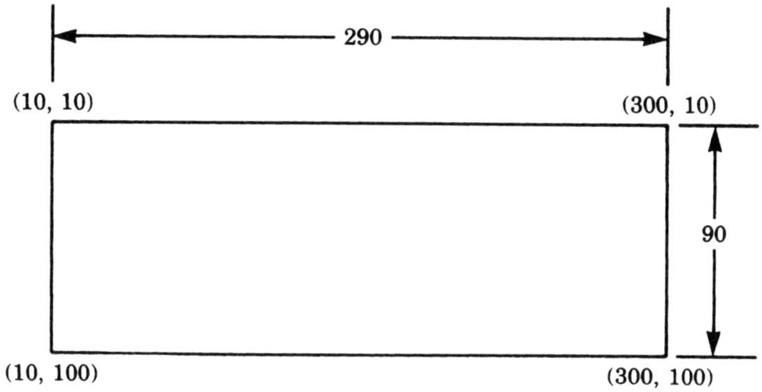

Figure 9.11 Sketching the Coordinates of a Rectangle

Comparing Programs 9.3 and 9.4, the **LINE statement** obviously takes fewer programming lines; however, it isn't necessary to use the LINE command because the **PSET statement** can still be used in a FOR-NEXT loop. It is still good programming practice to use LINE commands, because time is saved when the graph is generated, and it makes the program easier to understand.

Creating Rectangles

Once you know how to generate lines on the graphics screen, it's an easy next step to generate a rectangle. Essentially, four LINE commands are used.

One way to develop a program to generate a rectangle is to first sketch the rectangle you want to have appear on the graphics screen and then write the coordinate values, as illustrated in Figure 9.11.

Program 9.5 will create the rectangle illustrated in Figure 9.11. You could have used the PSET *(X,Y)* command to generate each line (inside FOR-NEXT loops). This would have required many more program lines and taken more time for the rectangle to be generated on the graphics screen.

Program 9.5

```
10 REM Draw a rectangle
20 SCREEN 2
30 REM Top line
40 LINE (10, 10)-(300, 10)
50 REM Right side
60 LINE (300, 10)-(300, 100)
70 REM Bottom line
80 LINE (10, 100)-(300, 100)
90 REM Left side
100 LINE (10, 10)-(10, 100)
```

Filling Areas

There are times when you may want to turn on all of the pixels within a given rectangle, as for a **bar graph.**

Program 9.6 will produce a **filled-in rectangle** by using FOR-NEXT loops with the PSET (*X,Y*) command. Figure 9.12 shows the resulting filled-in rectangle.

Program 9.6

```
10 REM Fill in a rectangle
20 SCREEN 2
30 REM
40 FOR Y = 10 TO 100
50       FOR X = 10 TO 300
60              PSET (X, Y)
70       NEXT X
80 NEXT Y
90 REM
```

Using the PSET command to create an **area-filled** rectangle is time-consuming, not only because the programming takes longer, but also because it takes a long time to generate the graphic. This is because the program must access the interpreter each time the PSET command is used. A more efficient way of generating an area-filled rectangle is shown in Program 9.7, which produces the same kind of graph as shown in Figure 9.12, but does it about twice as fast because only one FOR-NEXT loop is required.

Program 9.7

```
10 REM Filling-in again
20 SCREEN 2
30 FOR Y = 10 TO 100
40    LINE (10, Y)-(300, Y)
50 NEXT Y
```

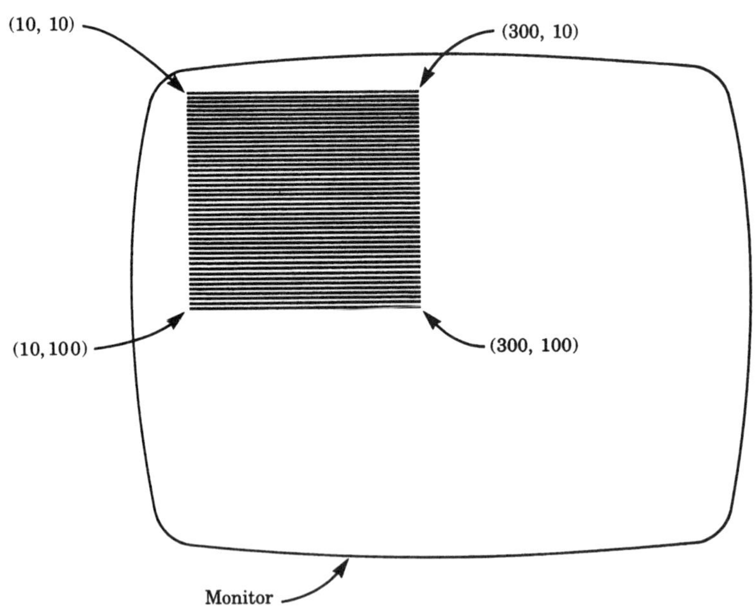

Figure 9.12 Graphic Display Resulting from Program 9.6

Some forms of BASIC have a statement that will fill a specified area of the graphics screen. This statement is presented in the last section of this chapter under color graphics.

Conclusion

There are many variations available in computer graphic programming. In this section, you saw some of the most fundamental ways of creating lines, rectangles, and filling areas. It's important that you understand the main concepts in order to be able to move on to more complex displays.

Test your understanding of this section by trying the following Section Review.

9.3 Section Review

1. Name two ways of creating a line on the graphics screen.
2. State how you would create a rectangle on the graphics screen.
3. Give two ways of creating an area-filled rectangle.

9.4 Application Program

This section contains an application program that will generate a bar graph display for the program user. Bar graphs find wide use in displaying various kinds of technical data. The details you learn here can be applied to more expansive bar graph–generating programs.

One-Bar Program

Program 9.8 will generate a single bar across the top of the monitor screen. The length of the bar is determined by the user.

Program 9.8

```
100 REM One-bar Display Program
110 REM
120 REM This program will display a single bar
130 REM across the top of the monitor screen.  The
140 REM user may select the length of the bar
150 REM within the limitations of the graphics
160 REM system.
170 REM
180 REM Variables used:
190 REM X2 = Ending X coordinate
200 REM A$ = Dummy variable
210 REM
220 REM Constants used:
230 W = 639:    REM Maximum screen width
240 Y2 = 30:    REM Thickness of the bar
250 REM
500 REM Main program loop
510 WHILE GO$ <> "N"
520    GOSUB 1000: REM Explain program to user
```

```
530    GOSUB 2000: REM Get values from user
540    GOSUB 3000: REM Display graphic
550    GOSUB 4000: REM Ask for program repeat
560 WEND
570 END
580 REM
1000 REM Explain program to user
1010 PRINT
1020 PRINT "This program will display a single bar"
1030 PRINT "across the top of the computer screen."
1040 PRINT "You only need select the length of the"
1050 PRINT "bar within the limitations of your"
1060 PRINT "computer system."
1070 PRINT
1080 INPUT "Press ENTER to continue . . . "; A$
1090 CLS : REM Clear the screen
1100 RETURN
1110 REM
2000 REM Get values from user
2010 PRINT
2020 PRINT "Maximum value of bar is "; W
2030 INPUT "Width of bar ==> "; X2
2040 RETURN
2050 END
2060 REM
3000 REM Display graphic
3010 SCREEN 2, 0
3020 REM Display single bar
3030 LINE (1, 1)-(X2, 1): REM Top line of bar
3040 LINE (1, Y2)-(X2, Y2): REM Bottom line of bar
3050 LINE (X2, 1)-(X2, Y2): REM End line of bar
3060 REM
3070 INPUT "Press -ENTER- to continue."; A$
3080 RETURN
3090 REM
4000 REM Ask for program repeat
4010 SCREEN 0, 1: REM Return to text screen
4020 INPUT "Do you want to repeat program? (Y/N) ==> "; GO$
4030 RETURN
4040 REM
```

Figure 9.13 shows the resultant display if the user selects to have the single bar graph displayed halfway across the screen.

Observe from Program 9.8 that the actual display of the graphic takes place in program block 3000. Note that program lines 3030, 3040, and 3050 draw a partial rectangle (the left side is left open). The value of *X*2 is selected by the user, while the value of *Y*2 is fixed by the program. Figure 9.14 shows the effects of the values of *X*2 and *Y*2 on the size of the displayed bar.

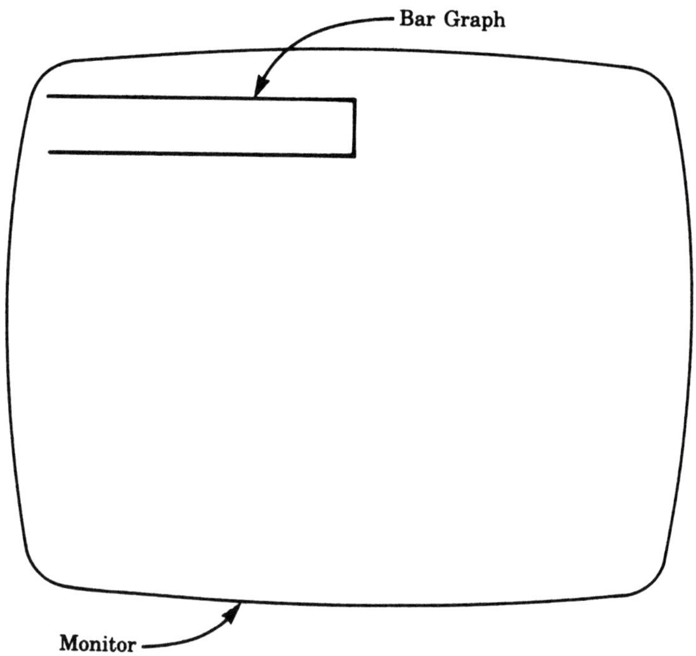

Figure 9.13 Single Bar Graph Display

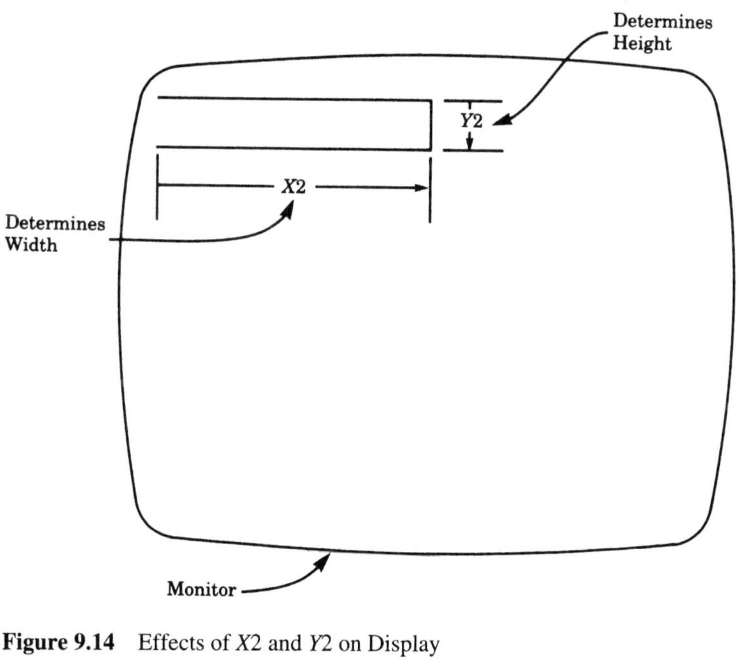

Figure 9.14 Effects of *X*2 and *Y*2 on Display

The value of *Y2* is set as a constant in program line 240, in order to make it easy for the programmer to change the width of the bar. If the value of *Y2* were put into program lines 3040 and 3050, the programmer would have to make changes in two places, rather than in just one.

The setting of the maximum value of the screen width is also done the same way, in line 230. If this program is to be written for a system that has a different screen width, only one program line needs to be changed.

Four-Bar Program

Program 9.8 can be modified to present more than one bar in a bar graph display. The following program changes will allow the program user to select the width of four separate bars in a single graphic display.

Program 9.9

```
2000 REM Get values from user
2010 PRINT
2020 PRINT "Maximum value of bar is "; W
2030 REM Get values for each bar
2040 FOR C = 1 TO 4
2050    PRINT "Value for bar "; C; " = ";
2060    INPUT X2(C)
2070 NEXT C
```

As shown in Program 9.9, the first modification is in the Get values from user block; a dimensioned variable *X2*(C) is introduced in a program loop. The maximum values of each of the four bar graphs will now be represented by the values *X2*(1), *X2*(2), *X2*(3), and *X2*(4). These four values will then be used in the Display graphic program block shown in Program 9.10.

Program 9.10

```
3000 REM Display graphic
3010 SCREEN 2:  REM Select graphic mode
3020 REM
3030 FOR C = 1 TO 4: REM Display 4 bars
3040    GOSUB 10000: REM Select vertical dimensions
3050    LINE (1, Y1)-(X2(C), Y1): REM Top line of bar
3060    LINE (1, Y2)-(X2(C), Y2): REM Bottom line
3070    LINE (X2(C), Y1)-(X2(C), Y2): REM Side line
3080 NEXT C
3090 RETURN
4000 REM
10000 REM Select vertical dimensions
10010 REM Case C of
10020 IF C = 1 THEN Y1 = 1: Y2 = 20
10030 IF C = 2 THEN Y1 = 25: Y2 = 45
10040 IF C = 3 THEN Y1 = 50: Y2 = 70
10050 IF C = 4 THEN Y1 = 75: Y2 = 96
10060 REM End case
10070 RETURN
10080 REM
```

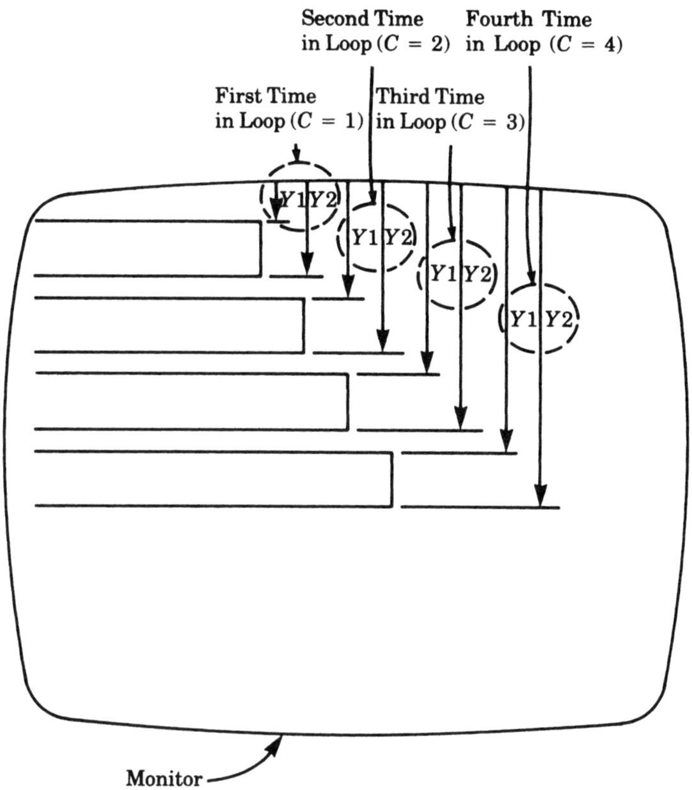

Figure 9.15 Effects of *Y*1 and *Y*2 on Bar Graph Display

The program modification in Program 9.10 uses a FOR-NEXT loop starting on line 3030. Note the use of a subroutine (program line 3040) used to select the value of vertical coordinates *Y*1 and *Y*2. Figure 9.15 shows the effect of these coordinates on each of the four displayed bars.

The CASE statement in program block 10000 of Program 9.10 causes the thickness of each bar to be 20 pixels and the distance between each bar to be 5 pixels. Other methods could have been used to determine the thickness of each bar and the distance between them. This method was used here because it is the most effective in demonstrating the concept of the bar graph program.

Conclusion

This section presented a simple bar graph–generation program that could be used to graphically represent technical data. The next section presents a methodology of representing the graphs of more complex technical data. Test your understanding of this section by trying the following Section Review.

9.4 Section Review

1. In the one-bar display program (Program 9.8), what is the purpose of the two constants in the programmer's block?
2. Explain why constants were used in Program 9.8.
3. State what modifications would be needed to increase the four-bar program to display five bars.

9.5 Practical Graphics

There are times when a method of adjusting the value of a function is necessary in order to plot it on a standard graphics screen. This section gives you the two major building blocks necessary—**scaling** and **transformation.**

Fundamental Concepts

Scaling is the process of using numerical methods to ensure that all the required data appears on the graphics screen and utilizes the full pixel capability. Remember that for any computer system, the number of pixels is limited. For the system used in this text, there are only 640 horizontally and 200 vertically.

To understand how to apply scaling to produce practical graphics, consider the graph shown in Figure 9.16, which uses three of the four quadrants of the Cartesian coordinate system. Suppose you needed to develop a computer program that would display such a graph, and wanted the full graphics screen to be used in the display. This means that the actual values used to plot the graph would not be the values used in the equation.

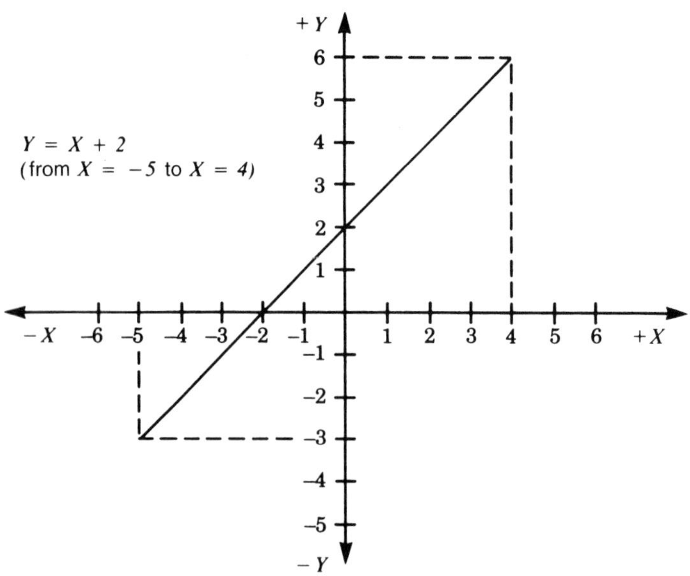

Figure 9.16 Graph for Scaling Example

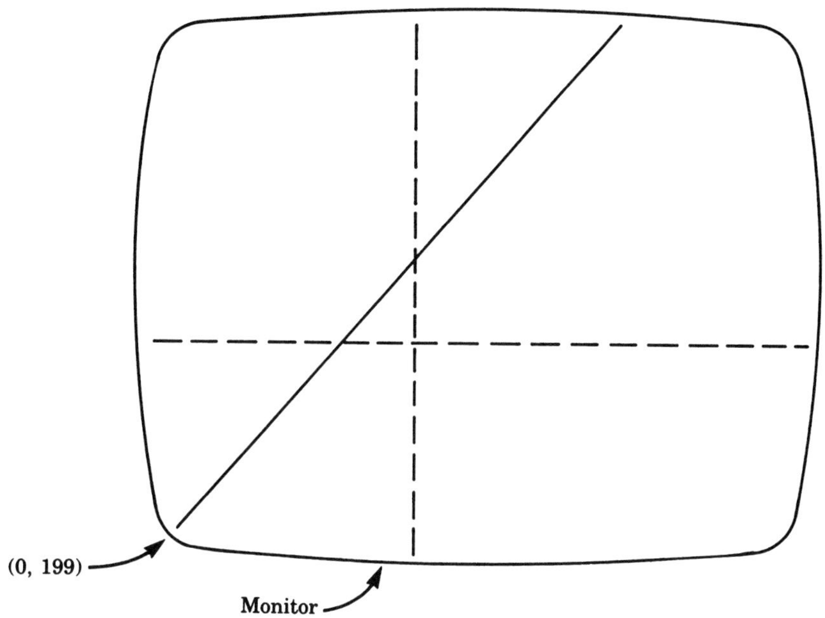

Figure 9.17 Actual Plotting Values for Graphical Display

Figure 9.17 illustrates this important point. Observe that the extreme left of the graph (the point that represents $X = -5$ and $Y = -3$) must actually have the plotted values of $X_P = 0$ and $Y_P = 199$ (the P subscript is used to denote the actual plotted values). The process used to achieve this transformation is called scaling. Also note that the origin of the coordinate system is not placed in the exact center of the screen, in order to make practical use of the full size of the monitor. Both scaling and also **coordinate transformation** have been used. Both processes are explained below.

Scaling

The **horizontal scale factor** can be expressed mathematically as

$$HS = \frac{P_H}{|X_2 - X_1|}$$

where HS = the horizontal scale factor
P_H = number of pixels in the horizontal direction
X_1 = minimum value of X
X_2 = maximum value of X

The **vertical scale factor** can be expressed mathematically as

$$VS = \frac{P_V}{|Y_2 - Y_1|}$$

where VS = the vertical scale factor
P_v = number of pixels in the vertical direction
Y_1 = minimum value of Y
Y_2 = maximum value of Y

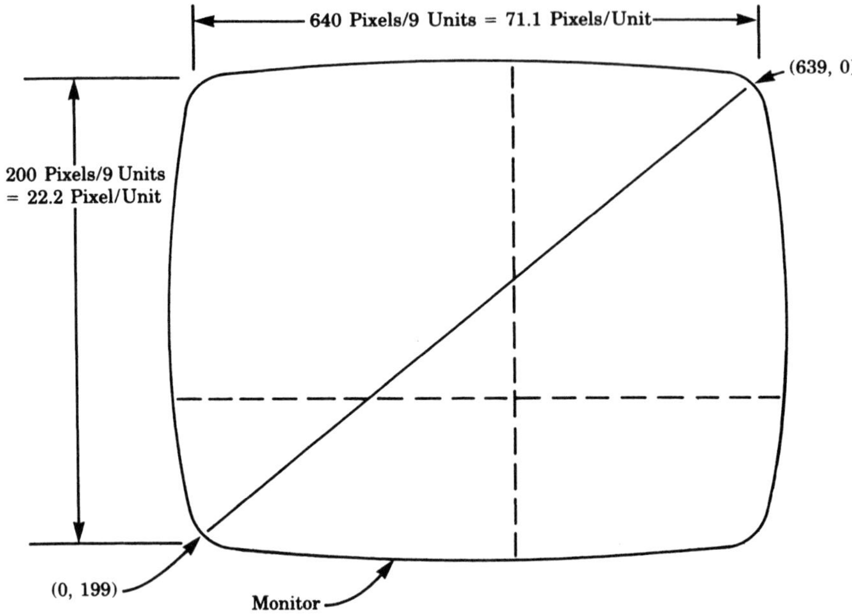

Figure 9.18 Minimum and Maximum Values of Scaling Example

Calculate the horizontal scale factor for the graph of Figure 9.18.

$$\begin{aligned} HS &= \frac{P_H}{|X_2 - X_1|} \\ &= 640/(4 - (-5)) \\ &= 640/(4 + 5) \\ &= 640/9 \\ &= 71.1 \end{aligned}$$

Calculate the vertical scale factor next.

$$\begin{aligned} VS &= \frac{P_V}{|Y_2 - Y_1|} \\ &= 200/(6 - (-3)) \\ &= 200/(6 + 3) \\ &= 200/9 \\ &= 22.2 \end{aligned}$$

These calculations mean that every major division along the X-axis will be 71 pixels and every major division along the Y-axis will be 22 pixels. Doing this will use the full capabilities of the graphics screen, as shown in Figure 9.19.

Coordinate Transformation

Note that in Figure 9.19 the origin of the coordinate system used to display the example graph is not in the exact center of the graphics screen. This was intentionally done to display the full range of required data utilizing the full graphics screen. Accomplishing this display required the use of coordinate transformation, the process of using numerical methods to cause the origin of the coordinate system to appear at any desired place on the graphics screen.

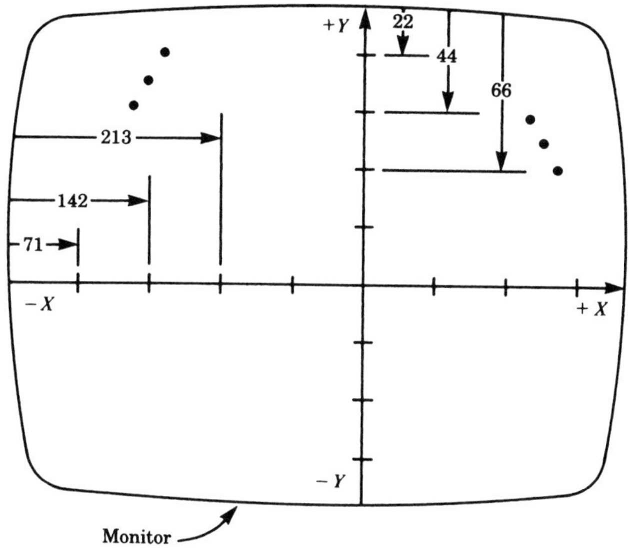

Figure 9.19 Meaning of Scaling for Example Graph

The process of transforming coordinates can be expressed mathematically as follows

Horizontal Transformation

$$XT = |(HS)(X_1)|$$

where XT = horizontal transformation
HS = horizontal scaling factor
X_1 = minimum value of X

Vertical Transformation

$$YT = |(VS)(Y_2)|$$

where YT = vertical transformation
VS = vertical scaling factor
Y_2 = maximum value of Y

For the example in Figure 9.19, this becomes

Horizontal Transformation

$$\begin{aligned} XT &= |(HS)(X_1)| \\ &= |(71.1)(-5)| \\ &= |-355| \\ &= 355 \end{aligned}$$

Vertical Transformation

$$\begin{aligned} YT &= |(VS)(Y_2)| \\ &= |(22.2)(6)| \\ &= |133| \\ &= 133 \end{aligned}$$

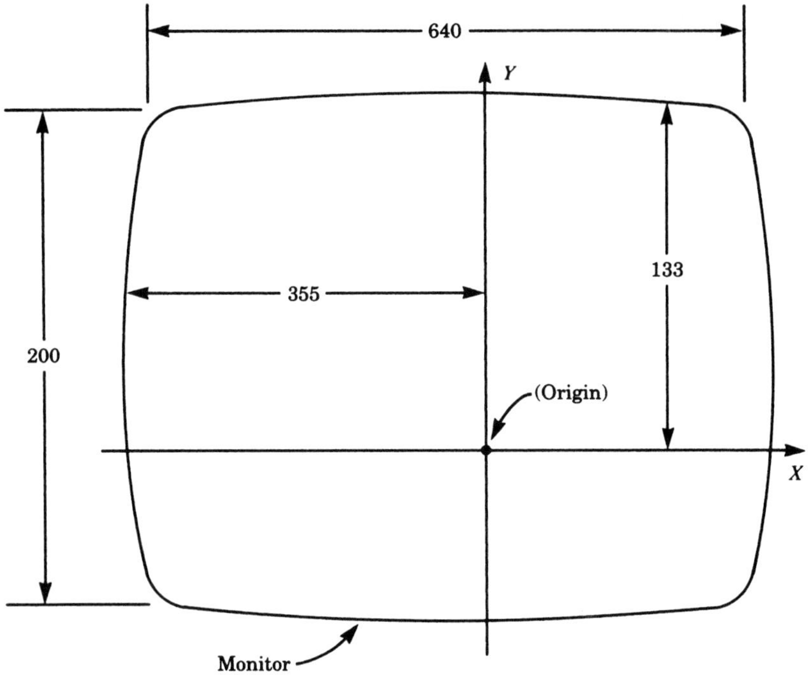

Figure 9.20 Actual Location of Origin for Example Graph

These calculations mean that the origin of the coordinate system will be at the location of $X_0 = 355$ and $Y_0 = 133$, as illustrated in Figure 9.20.

Now, we only need to develop equations that can be used to display the data on the graphics screen.

Putting It Together

To display the graph of any continuous function related by two variables when scaling and coordinate transformations are used, the following equations are necessary.

Horizontal Value of Graph

$$\text{XG} = \text{XT} - (X)(\text{HS})$$

where XG = graphical X value
XT = horizontal transformation
HS = horizontal scaling factor

Vertical Value of Graph

$$\text{YG} = \text{YT} - (Y)(\text{VS})$$

where YG = graphical Y value
YT = vertical transformation
VS = vertical scaling factor

A program that would cause ten points on the line of the example graph to be plotted is given in Program 9.11.

Program 9.11

```
10 REM Graph a line
20 REM Y = X + 2
30 SCREEN 2
40 REM Set values of constants
50 XT = 355
60 YT = 133
70 HS = 71.1
80 VS = 22.22
90 REM Draw coordinate system
100 REM X axis
110 LINE (0, YT)-(640, YT)
120 REM Y axis
130 LINE (XT, 0)-(XT, 200)
140 REM Plot graph
150 FOR X = -5 TO 4
160    Y = X + 2
170    XG = XT + X * HS
180    YG = YT - Y * VS
190    PSET (XG, YG)
200 NEXT X
```

The resulting graph is shown in Figure 9.21. Note that the **relative values** of the actual equation and the **absolute values** used for actually displaying the graph take on the values shown in Table 9.1.

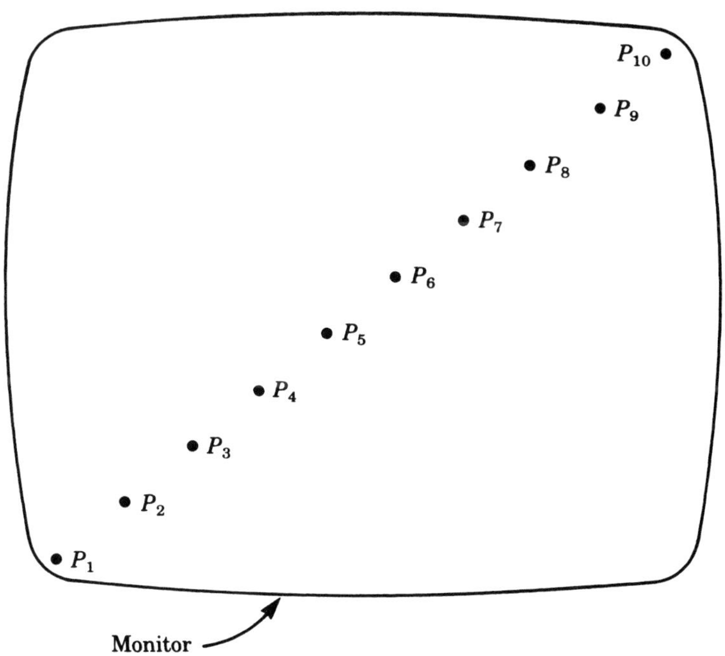

Figure 9.21 Ten-Point Plot Resulting from Program 9.11

Table 9.1 Relative and Absolute Values of Sample Graph

Relative Values $Y = X + 2$		Absolute Values After Scaling and Transformation	
X	Y	X_0	Y_0
–5	–3	0	199
–4	–2	70	177
–3	–1	141	155
–2	0	212	133
–1	1	283	111
0	2	355	89
1	3	426	67
2	4	497	45
3	5	568	23
4	6	639	1

More Detail

Program 9.11 plotted only ten points. To increase the number of points plotted on the graphics screen, add the STEP function to the FOR-NEXT instruction on line 150.

```
150 FOR X = -5 TO 4 STEP .1
```

This modification will now cause 100 pixels to be activated representing the graph of the equation.

Conclusion

This section introduced you to the practical requirements for displaying technical data. In the next section, you will be introduced to some important computational tools available with BASIC. Understanding these tools will broaden your capability to create graphical displays of complex technical data. Test your understanding of this section by trying the following Section Review.

9.5 **Section Review**

1. Define *scaling* as it applies to computer graphics.
2. Define *coordinate transformation* as it applies to computer graphics.
3. State the factors that determine the values of the scaling factors.
4. State the factors that determine the values of the coordinate transformation values.

9.6 Useful Functions

BASIC offers some useful mathematical functions with a wide range of applications, including computer graphics. This section will introduce these functions and show you some practical applications.

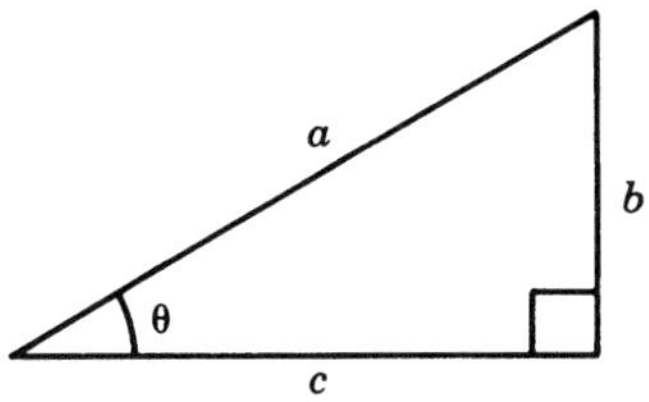

$$\text{SIN}\,\theta = \frac{b}{a}$$

$$\text{COS}\,\theta = \frac{c}{a}$$

$$\text{TAN}\,\theta = \frac{b}{c}$$

Figure 9.22 Three Basic Trigonometric Relations

Trigonometric Functions

Trigonometric functions find a wide range of applications in many fields of technology. Not only electronics, but also drafting, manufacturing technology, and agriculture make important use of the trigonometric functions.

The trigonometric functions used in BASIC are

SIN(expression)
COS(expression)
TAN(expression)
ATN(expression)

where SIN = sine of the angle (ratio of the opposite side and the hypotenuse)
COS = cosine of the angle (ratio of the adjacent side and the hypotenuse)
TAN = tangent of the angle (ratio of the opposite side and the adjacent side)
ATN = arctangent, in radians (angle whose tangent is given by the value of (expression))
expression = any valid arithmetic expression expressed in radians

The three basic trigonometric relations are shown in Figure 9.22. In addition you may find BASIC's LOG, EXP, and RND functions useful in graphics applications.

Example Program

Program 9.12 will compute the selected trigonometric function. After the program user selects the desired trigonometric function (line 130), the program will then ask for the number of radians (line 140). Line 150 then causes a branch to the appropriate subroutine. Program 9.12 needs some better structure (such as defining the variables). It does serve to illustrate a direct application of the three trigonometric functions.

Program 9.12

```
100 REM Compute a trig function
110 PRINT "Select the function by number:"
120 PRINT "1] Sine  2] Cosine  3] Tangent"
130 INPUT "Enter your selection ==> "; S
140 INPUT "Number of radians ==> "; R
150 ON S GOSUB 1000, 2000, 3000
160 REM
170 REM Display the answer
180 PRINT "The "; F$; " of "; R; " radians is "; A
```

```
190 END
200 REM
1000 REM Compute sine function
1010 A = SIN(R)
1020 F$ = "SIN"
1030 RETURN
1040 REM
2000 REM Compute cosine function
2010 A = COS(R)
2020 F$ = "COS"
2030 RETURN
2040 REM
3000 REM Compute tangent function
3010 A = TAN(R)
3020 F$ = "TAN"
3030 RETURN
3040 REM
```

Conversion Between Radians and Degrees

It often is useful to compute the function of an angle directly from degrees rather than radians. The conversion from radians to degrees is

Degrees = (180/pi) (radians)
Radians = (pi/180) (degrees)

where pi = The constant pi (3.14159 . . .)

In Program 9.12, the user could have entered the number of degrees rather than the number of radians. The input would then have to be converted to radians before any of the trigonometric functions could be used. The following statement will convert from degrees (D) to radians (R).

```
R = (3.14159/180) * D
```

Applying Graphics

The sine function is useful in many different fields, including electronics technology. The sine function can represent any type of **periodic event** (an event that repeats itself). The action of a pendulum, the pistons of a car engine, the rotation of a turbojet engine, and the action of alternating current (AC) can all be represented by the sine function.

Being able to construct a graph of the sine function using computer graphics gives you the power to illustrate the action of these useful periodic functions.

The fundamental concept of graphically displaying the sine function is shown in Program 9.13.

Program 9.13

```
10 C = 3.14159
20 SCREEN 2
30 FOR D = 0 TO 360
40    R = D * C / 180
50    Y = SIN(R)
60    PSET (D, Y)
70 NEXT D
```

Line 10 simply sets the constant C equal to π.

Line 20 is the statement that causes the computer to display its graphic commands by invoking the graphics screen.

Line 30 is the beginning of a FOR-NEXT loop that will cause the sine function to be computed for every degree of 360 degrees along the *X*-axis.

Line 40 converts the angle from degrees to radians.

Line 50 computes the value of the sine function at each angle. The variable *Y* will contain the amplitude of the sine function for each angle.

Line 60 contains the command for plotting a point on the screen. The value of *D* represents the number of degrees on the *X*-axis. The value of *Y* represents the amplitude of the sine function along the *Y*-axis.

Line 70 is the command needed to complete the FOR-NEXT loop.

Program 9.13 contains all the essentials necessary to generate a computer display of a sine wave. However, the program isn't practical. One reason is that the sine function produces negative as well as positive values for the *Y*-axis. The graphics screen of the generic computer doesn't have a negative *Y*-axis; it has only a positive *Y*-axis along the left side of the graphics screen. Negative values of *Y* will not be displayed. In addition, the maximum value of a pure sine function goes only from 0 to 1, to 0 to –1. For the graphics screen, this represents an amplitude change of only one pixel; you couldn't even see the sine wave.

A Practical Program

The graphics program for displaying a sine wave needs two major modifications. The first is to move the *X*-axis to the center of the screen. This will allow negative values of the sine wave to be displayed. The second is to give the sine wave enough amplitude so its changes can be seen.

Program 9.14 accommodates both these changes. It allows the user to specify the peak value of the sine wave to be displayed.

Program 9.14

```
10 C = 3.14159
20 SCREEN 2
30 PRINT "Peak value (100 maximum)"
40 INPUT P
50 FOR D = 0 TO 360
60     R = D * C / 180
70     Y = P * SIN(R)
80     PSET (D, (100 - Y))
90 NEXT D
```

The result of Program 9.14 for a value of $P = 50$ is shown in Figure 9.23.

The two computational changes are in lines 70 and 80 of Program 9.14. Line 70 causes the value of the sine function to be multiplied by the number *P*. If $P = 50$, then the value of *Y* will now go from 0 to 50, to 0 to –50. This will give enough vertical change to see the sine wave clearly on the graphics screen.

Line 80 has the modification $(100 - Y)$, which effectively brings the *X*-axis to the center of the graphics screen, allowing both negative and positive values of *Y* to be displayed.

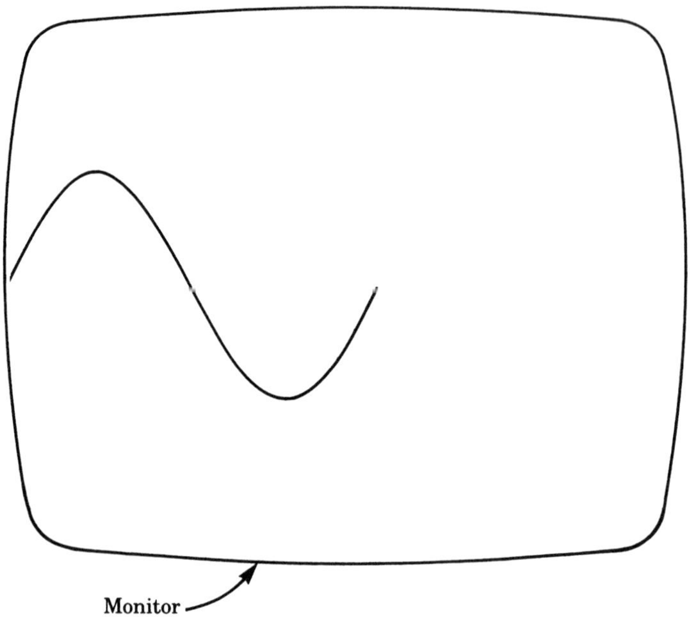

Figure 9.23 Graph of Program 9.14

The Complete Sine Function

Program 9.14 will display one **cycle** of the sine function. (When displayed this way, it is sometimes referred to as a **sine wave.**) Cycle comes from the word circle. So one cycle of a sine wave is all of its values before it starts to repeat itself.

To display something other than one cycle of the sine function, use

$$A = P * SIN(R * N + T)$$

where A = amplitude of the sine function
P = peak value of the sine function
R = angle in radians
N = number of cycles to be displayed
T = phase of the sine wave

The meaning of the preceding terms is illustrated in Figure 9.24.

Conclusion

In this section, you learned how to display a sine wave on the computer graphics screen. You also gained the ability to change the characteristics of a sine wave by mathematically manipulating the sine function. In the next section, you will have an introduction to the exciting world of color graphics.

Test your understanding of this section by trying the following Section Review.

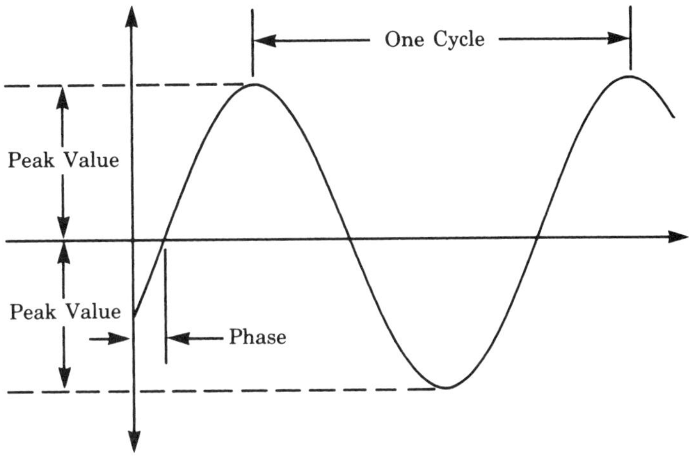

Figure 9.24 Sine Wave Terminology

9.6 Section Review

1. Name the trigonometric functions found in BASIC.
2. Does BASIC compute the trigonometric functions in degrees or radians? Show how to convert from one to the other.
3. Describe the kind of graphic display you would expect from Program 9.13. Explain.
4. State how you could change the graphic display of the sine function concerning
   a. Amplitude.
   b. Phase.
   c. Number of cycles displayed.

9.7 Color Graphics

The use of **color** provides the technical programmer with an extra dimension in computer graphics. Technical graphics in color gives an added impact and demands more attention than the simple on/off display of monochrome (one-color) graphics.

Think of a program to display information from an assembly line or to monitor a power plant. Graphic displays could use green to mean that items are in normal operation. Yellow or orange could be used to alert the operator that a particular condition is not in specification, or that a failure is anticipated. Red could be used to alert the operator of a situation that demands immediate attention. Thus, a new and useful dimension of information is available with the aid of color.

What Is Needed

To display color graphics with your computer system, two major items are required: a color monitor and the necessary hardware inside your computer.

The monitor for your system displays information by using a coat of **phosphor** on the inside of the picture tube. A **monochrome** (single-color) monitor has only one kind of phosphor. When this phosphor is excited by an electrical current, light is emitted and may be amber, green, or any other single color, depending upon the type of phosphor used.

A **color monitor** is coated on the inside of the picture tube with three different kinds of phosphor. Each phosphor will produce a unique color when electrically excited: one phosphor produces red, the other green, and the third blue. The combination of these three colors emitted by the three different phosphors gives the various kinds of color. White is seen when the red, green, and blue phosphors are electrically intensified to a precise degree.

Some computer systems require extra hardware to display color graphics. Check with your system manual to see what is necessary.

Basic Concepts of Color

There are two different items that can be in color: the screen **background** and the **foreground,** the information being displayed on the screen (text or graph). Figure 9.25 illustrates the basic idea of background and foreground.

Most computers have three modes of display.

1. Text mode for displaying text.
2. Medium-resolution graphics used to get a wide selection of colors, but some loss of detail.
3. High-resolution graphics, giving good detail but limiting the colors that can be displayed to just black and white.

Each of these display modes will be discussed in this section.

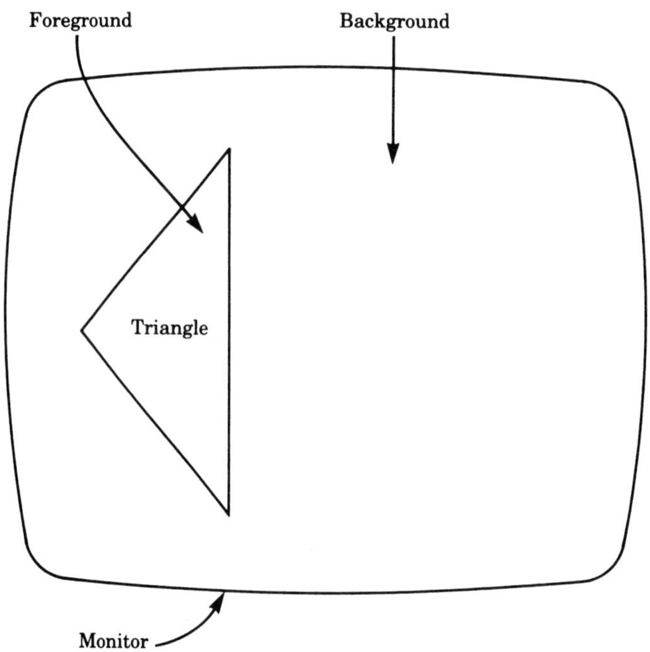

Figure 9.25 Basic Idea of Color Graphics

On the PC the command for selecting the different modes is

```
SCREEN N, M
```

where `N` = 0 : the text screen
`N` = 1 : medium-resolution graphics
`N` = 2 : high-resolution graphics
(In text mode)
`M` = 0 : color is OFF (default)
`M` = 1 : color is ON
(In graphics mode)
`M` = 0 : color is ON (default)
`M` = 1 : color is OFF

Text Color Mode

Some computer systems such as the PC allow the use of color in the text mode. The command is

```
COLOR A, B, C
```

where `A` = foreground color
`B` = background color
`C` = color of the border

Figure 9.26 shows the concept of the **border** on the IBM text screen.

The ranges of colors are

Foreground = 1 of 16 colors
Background = 1 of 8 colors
Border = 1 of 16 colors

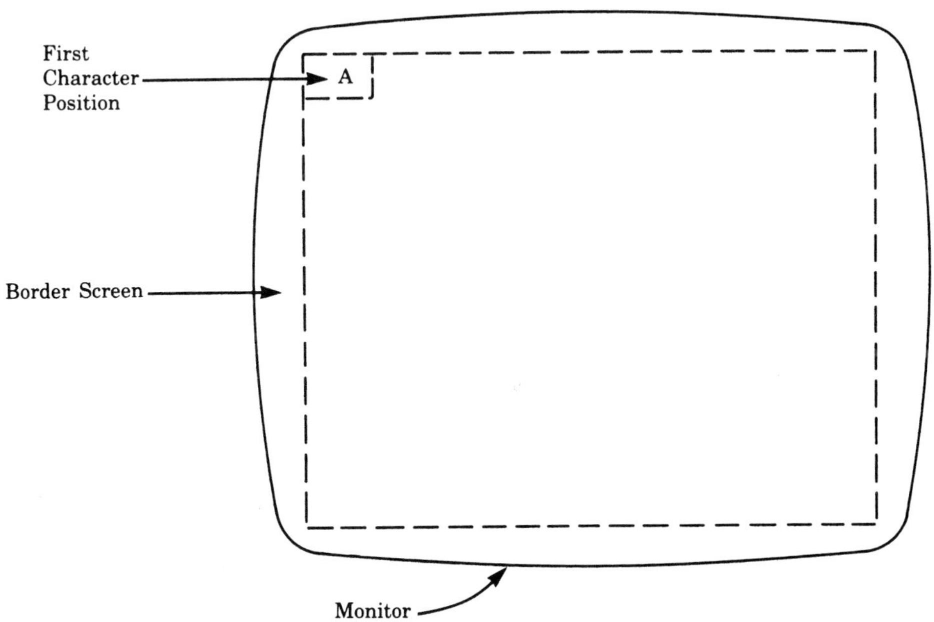

Figure 9.26 Concept of the Border in IBM Text Screen

Table 9.2 Colors for the PC

Number	Color*	Number	Color*
0	Black	8	Gray
1	Blue	9	Light Blue
2	Green	10	Light Green
3	Cyan	11	Light Cyan
4	Red	12	Light Red
5	Magenta	13	Light Magenta
6	Brown	14	Yellow
7	White	15	Intense White

*Blinking colors add 16 to the number. For example, 1 + 16 = 17 produces a blinking blue.

The available colors for the PC are given in Table 9.2.

You can make the foreground blink by adding 16 to any of the foreground color values.

The amount of text displayed on the PC can be varied between 80 characters and 40 characters across the width of the screen. The command for doing this is

```
WIDTH N
```

where `N` = 40 : gives 40 characters across the screen
`N` = 80 : gives 80 characters across the screen

No matter which WIDTH statement is selected, there are twenty-five horizontal lines of text available. The first twenty-four lines of text will **scroll up** as new text is added, while the twenty-fifth line will not (it is usually used as a **prompt line**).

Figure 9.27 summarizes the different variables available in the text mode for the PC.

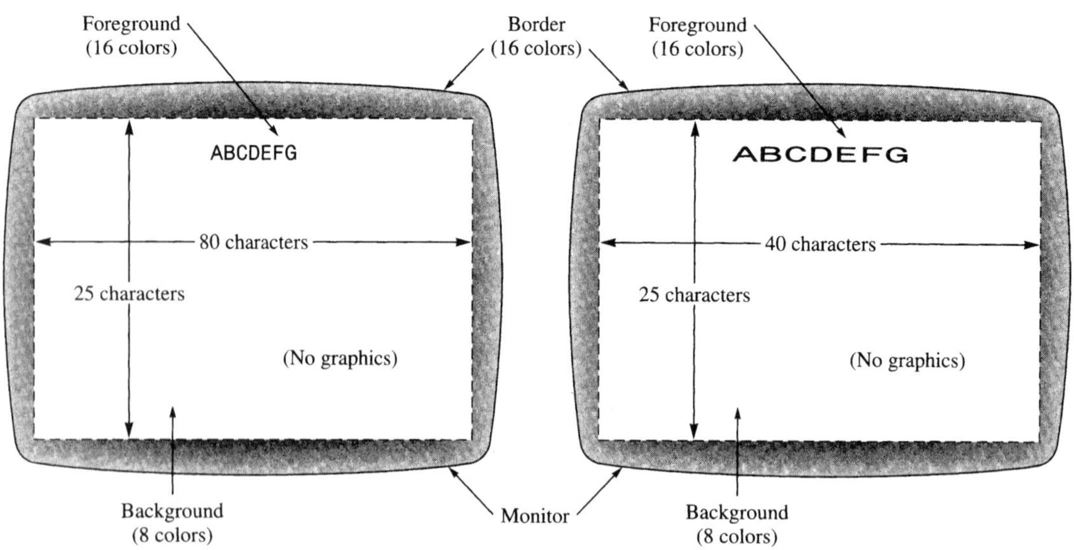

Figure 9.27 Summary of Text Mode

Sample Text Color Program

Program 9.15 demonstrates all the color combinations available in the PC text screen. The 40-character-wide screen is used to make the colors of the text more obvious (text color may be difficult to see on some monitors if the small 80-column text is used).

Program 9.15

```
100 REM Text Color Demo
110 REM
120 REM This program will generate all the different color
130 REM combinations possible with the IBM PC text color mode.
140 REM
150 REM Variables used:
160 REM BK = Background color
170 REM FG = Foreground color
180 REM BD = Border color
190 REM A$ = Dummy variable
200 REM T = Text counting variable
210 REM
220 REM Main programming block
230 REM Explain program to user
240 GOSUB 1000
250 WHILE GO$ <> "N"
260    REM Show display
270    GOSUB 2000
280    REM Program repeat
290    GOSUB 3000
300 WEND
310 END
1000 REM Explain program to user
1010 REM Text mode, color off
1020 SCREEN 0, 0
1030 REM 80 X 25 text
1040 WIDTH 80
1050 PRINT
1060 PRINT "This program will display all of the possible color"
1070 PRINT "combinations available on the IBM PC in text mode."
1080 PRINT
1090 INPUT "Press -ENTER- to start demo."; A$
1100 RETURN
2000 REM Show display
2010 REM Text mode, color on
2020 SCREEN 0, 1
2030 REM 40 X 25 text (easier to see color)
2040 WIDTH 40
2050 REM Start background color loop
2060 REM 8 colors available
2070 FOR BK = 0 TO 7
2080    REM Start border color loop
2090    REM 16 colors
2100    FOR BD = 0 TO 15
```

```
2110          REM Start foreground color loop
2120          REM 16 colors
2130          FOR F = 0 TO 15
2140             REM Color command
2150             COLOR F, BK, BD
2160             REM Clear the screen
2170             CLS
2180             PRINT "FGND="; F; "BKG="; BK; "BDR="; BD
2190             REM Start text display loop
2200             FOR T = 1 TO 960
2210               PRINT "*";
2220             NEXT T
2230             REM End text display loop
2240          NEXT F
2250          REM End foreground color loop
2260       NEXT BD
2270       REM End border color loop
2280 NEXT BK
2290 REM End background color loop
2300 RETURN
3000 REM Program repeat
3010 REM Text mode, color off
3020 SCREEN 0, 0
3030 REM 80 X 25 text
3040 WIDTH 80
3050 PRINT
3060 PRINT "Do you wish to repeat the program?"
3070 INPUT "Enter Y or N and press -ENTER-"; GO$
3080 RETURN
```

Explanation of Text Color Demo

Program 9.15 shows many examples of color usage in the text mode. These important concepts are summarized for each program block.

In **Program Block 1000,** line 1020 makes sure the computer is in the text mode and turns the color off. The reason for turning the color off is to make it easier to read 80-column text. If the color is turned ON, the 80-column text usually appears "smeared" with color and makes it more difficult to read. Line 1040 makes sure the computer is in the 80-column text mode.

In **Program Block 2000,** all of the text display work is done. The first line, 2020, sets the computer to text with the color ON. This is necessary in order to get color displays.

Line 2040 sets the computer to the 40-column text mode. This is done to make it easier to see the foreground color of the text changing.

There are actually four loops in this block. The first, starting at line 2070, causes all eight of the background colors to be displayed. The second, starting at line 2100, causes all sixteen of the border colors to be displayed. The third loop, starting at line 2130, ensures that all sixteen of the foreground colors are displayed. The last loop, starting at line 2200, causes a display of asterisks (*) across the screen. In this 40×25 text mode, there is room for $40 \times 24 = 960$ characters. (Only 960 can be scrolled—recall that the twenty-fifth line is not scrolled.) The loop thus goes from 1 to 960.

In **Program Block 3000,** line 3020 sets text with color OFF. Line 3040 produces the 80-column width. The remainder of the block asks the user if the display is to be repeated.

Medium-Resolution Graphics

The **medium-resolution graphics mode** for the IBM PC produces 320 horizontal and 200 vertical points and allows a maximum of four different colors at any one time. The command for selecting this mode is

```
SCREEN 1
```

Text characters can still be printed in the medium-resolution graphics mode, but now there will be 40 characters across the screen rather than the standard 80 characters.

When you are in medium-resolution graphics, there is a very important change in the COLOR command, taking on a different meaning. In the medium-resolution graphics mode, the color command means

```
COLOR A, B
```

where A = a number from 0 to 15 that represents the background color (the same colors as in Table 9.2 for text mode)
B = an odd or even number that determines the palette color

Palette colors are shown in Table 9.3.

The **palette** colors do not take effect until something is actually drawn on the graphics screen.

Program 9.16 will cause the screen to be cleared to blue with an even palette. This will cause all text that is normally white to appear as brown.

Program 9.16

```
100 REM Color demonstration
110 SCREEN 1:   REM Select medium resolution
120 COLOR 1, 2: REM Blue background
130 CLS :       REM Clear the screen
```

To draw graphs in color, use

```
PSET(X, Y), COLOR
```

where X, Y = graphic coordinates
COLOR = a number from 0 to 3

This command will plot a point on the graphics screen with a color that is determined by the initial choice of the palette with the SCREEN command and the color number.

Table 9.3 Palette Colors

Color Number	Palette (Even)	Palette (Odd)
1	Green	Cyan
2	Red	Magenta
3	Brown	White

Program 9.17 causes a point to appear in the middle of the graphics screen. The color of the point is green, because line 140 set an even palette and the color number selected by PSET was 1 (Table 9.3).

Program 9.17

```
100 REM Color demo again
110 REM Select medium resolution
120 SCREEN 1
130 REM Blue background
140 COLOR 1, 2
150 REM Clear the screen to background color
160 CLS
170 PSET (160, 100), 1
```

Observe the modifications in Program 9.18; because of the change in line 120, the palette will now be odd. This will display a point in the same location of the graphics screen, but now the color will be cyan.

Program 9.18

```
100 REM Another color demonstration
110 SCREEN 1:    REM Select medium resolution
120 COLOR 1, 3: REM Blue background, odd palette
130 CLS :        REM Clear screen to background color
140 PSET (160, 100), 1
```

The foreground is handled by two different palettes, each containing three different colors. There can thus be a maximum of four colors displayed on the IBM medium-resolution graphics screen at a time: one background color and three different foreground colors, selected from one of the two palettes. Both palettes cannot be active at the same time on the medium-resolution graphics screen.

A summary of medium-resolution graphics is illustrated in Figure 9.28.

High-Resolution Graphics

The command

```
SCREEN 2
```

will cause the PC to go into **high-resolution graphics.** Here, the maximum horizontal resolution is 640 points and the vertical is 200 points. High-resolution graphics has only two colors on the PC: black and white. Black is always a 0 and white is always a 1. Text characters can be displayed on the high-resolution graphics screen as the standard 80 characters per line. But, unlike the text screen, characters displayed on the high-resolution graphics screen can only be white on black.

A summary of high-resolution graphics is illustrated in Figure 9.29.

Color Summary

A summary of the different color modes available on the PC is given in Table 9.4.

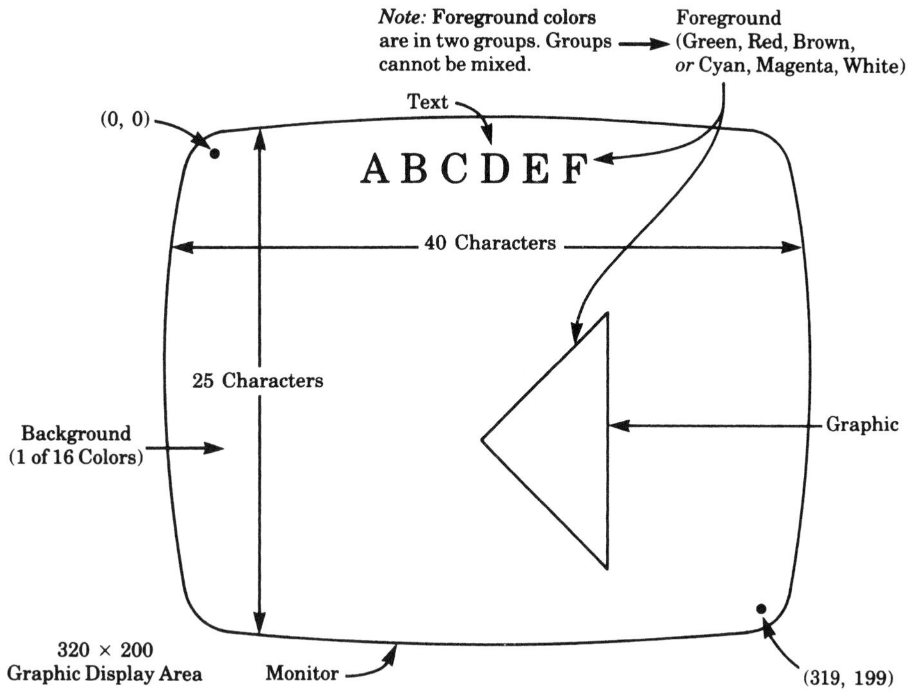

Figure 9.28 Summary of Medium-Resolution Graphics

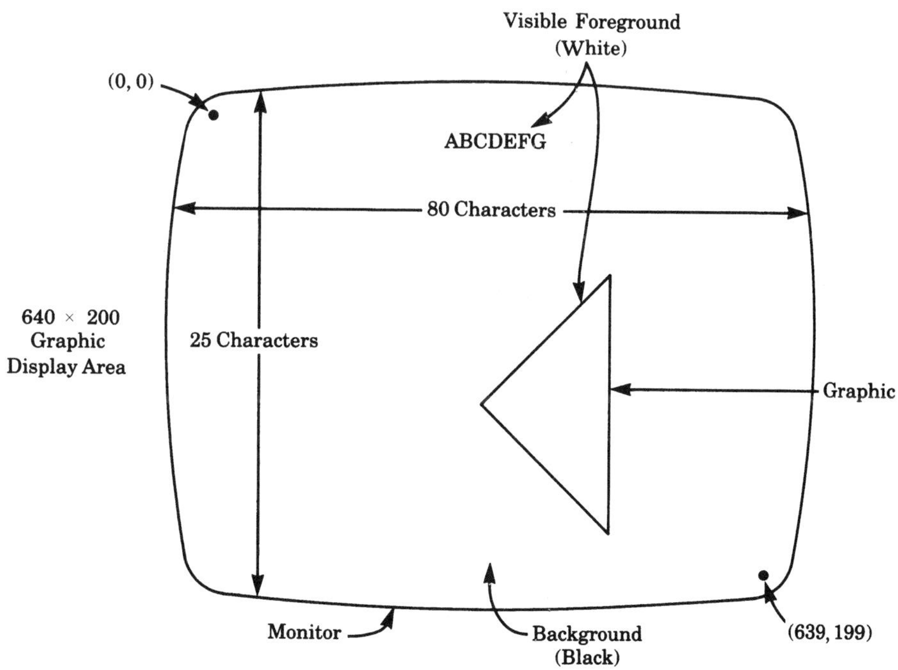

Figure 9.29 Summary of High-Resolution Graphics

Table 9.4 Display Modes

Mode	Display Area	Color Capabilities	Command
Text (80 wide)	80 × 25 characters No graphics	16 foreground 8 background 16 border	SCREEN 0,1 WIDTH 80
Text (40 wide)	40 × 25 characters No graphics	16 foreground 8 background 16 border	SCREEN 0,1 WIDTH 40
Medium Res.	40 × 25 characters 320 × 200 graphics	6 foreground 16 background	SCREEN 1,0
High Res.	80 × 25 characters 640 × 200 graphics	White foreground Black background No border	SCREEN 2

Sample Color Program

Program 9.19 is similar to the first graphics program, Program 9.8. It generates a horizontal bar graph, but this time the user can select not only the length of each graph but also its color and the color of the background. Medium-resolution graphics is used, and since no more than four colors can be displayed at a time in this mode, only three bar graphs are generated.

Program 9.19

```
100 REM Color Graphics Demo
110 REM
120 REM This program will generate three horizontal color bars.
130 REM The user may select the color of each bar and the
140 REM background color as well as the length of each bar.
150 REM
160 REM Variables used:
170 REM C(N) = Color of each bar
180 REM X(N) = Width of each bar
190 REM Y1, Y2 = Y coordinate of bar
200 REM PT = Palette choice
210 REM A$ = Dummy variable
220 REM BC = Background color
230 REM
240 REM Main programming block
250 REM Explain program to user
260 GOSUB 1000
270 WHILE GO$ <> "N"
280    REM Get values from user
290    GOSUB 2000
300    REM Display bar graph
310    GOSUB 3000
320    REM Program repeat
330    GOSUB 4000
340 WEND
350 END
```

```
1000 REM Explain program to user
1010 REM Text mode, color off
1020 SCREEN 0, 0
1030 REM 40 X 25 text
1040 WIDTH 40
1050 PRINT
1060 PRINT "This program will display a bar graph"
1070 PRINT "consisting of three different horizontal"
1080 PRINT "bars. You may select the color of the"
1090 PRINT "background and the color of the bar."
1100 PRINT
1110 INPUT "Press -ENTER- to continue..."; A$
1120 RETURN
2000 REM Get values from user
2010 REM Clear the screen
2020 CLS
2030 PRINT
2040 INPUT "Background color (number from 0 to 15) = "; BC
2050 PRINT
2060 PRINT "Select one of the following palettes:"
2070 PRINT "1] Palette 1: Cyan, Magenta, White"
2080 PRINT "2] Palette 2: Green, Red, Brown"
2090 INPUT "Your selection (enter 1 or 2) = "; PT
2100 PRINT
2110 REM Colors for palette 1
2120 IF PT = 1 THEN GOSUB 10000
2130 REM Colors for palette 2
2140 IF PT = 2 THEN GOSUB 11000
2150 REM Information for 3 bars
2160 FOR N = 1 TO 3
2170    PRINT "Bar "; N;
2180    INPUT "Color (enter 1, 2, or 3) = "; C(N)
2190    INPUT "Width (maximum of 320) = "; X(N)
2200 NEXT N
2230 RETURN
3000 REM Display bar graphs
3010 REM Low resolution graphics color ON
3020 SCREEN 1, 0
3030 REM Set background color and palette
3040 COLOR BC, PT
3050 REM Display three bars
3060 FOR N = 1 TO 3
3070    REM Set Y dimension subroutine
3080    GOSUB 12000
3090    REM Draw it
3100    LINE (1, Y1)-(X(N), Y2), C(N), BF
3110 NEXT N
3120 RETURN
4000 REM Program repeat
4010 REM Hold the graphic screen for user
4020 WHILE HOLD$ = ""
4030    HOLD$ = INKEY$
4040 WEND
```

```
4050 REM Go to text screen when any key is pressed
4060 SCREEN 0
4070 PRINT "Do you want to repeat the program?"
4080 INPUT "Enter Y or N and press -ENTER- ..."; GO$
4090 RETURN
10000 REM Colors for palette 1
10010 PRINT "Colors are:"
10020 PRINT "1] Cyan  2] Magenta  3] White"
10030 RETURN
11000 REM Colors for palette 2
11010 PRINT "Colors are:"
11020 PRINT "1] Green  2] Red  3] Brown"
11030 RETURN
12000 REM Set Y dimension subroutine
12010 REM Case N of
12020 IF N <> 1 THEN 12060
12030    Y1 = 1
12040    Y2 = 20
12050    RETURN
12060 IF N <> 2 THEN 12100
12070    Y1 = 25
12080    Y2 = 45
12090    RETURN
12100 IF N <> 3 THEN 12130
12110    Y1 = 50
12120    Y2 = 70
12140    RETURN
```

The program makes use of the "box-fill" command

```
LINE (X1, Y1)-(X2, Y2), N, BF
```

where `(X1, Y1)` and `(X2, Y2)` = opposite coordinates of the rectangle to be drawn
`N` = 0 to 3 : 0 = background color. 1 to 3 is color from selected color palette
`BF` = box fill in given color

Conclusion

This section introduced the fundamentals of computer graphics. Test your understanding of this section by trying the following Section Review.

9.7 Section Review

1. State the two major requirements to produce color on a computer system.
2. Explain the difference between a color and monochrome monitor.
3. Name the three basic modes for displaying information on the PC.
4. List the three different items that can display color in the text mode. How many different colors can each display?
5. State how much text can be displayed on the screen.
6. Explain how foreground colors are selected in the medium-resolution graphics mode for the PC. What is the maximum number of different colors that can appear on the graphics screen at the same time?
7. How many colors are available on the PC in the high-resolution graphics mode?

9.8 The Waveform Viewer Project

Before writing any statements associated with the graphics required by the Waveform Viewer, it would be useful to make a list of the types of things that must be drawn.

1. The horizontal and vertical axes.
2. The waveform samples.
3. The zoom arrows.

Now, to add some detail, the horizontal and vertical axes should have a number of tick marks drawn on them to aid in interpretation and zooming. The waveform samples will be scaled vertically by a factor of 0.5, so that only 128 display lines (out of 200) are required for amplitude display. The zoom arrows are drawn and erased by several calls to PSET and PRESET. The waveform display area must be vertically offset from the zoom pointer area so that samples are not overwritten as the pointers are moved.

Figure 9.30 shows a sample execution of the Waveform Viewer processing the BOING.WAV file.

Examine Program 9.20, the complete Waveform Viewer program, to see how these graphic requirements are implemented.

Program 9.20

```
100 DIM WAVBUFF (8300)
110 GOSUB 1210:         REM Open WAV file
120 SCREEN 2
130 A$ = "Y"
140 WHILE A$ = "Y"
150     GOSUB 360:      REM Draw axis
160     GOSUB 720:      REM Draw waveform
170     GOSUB 200:      REM Move pointers
```

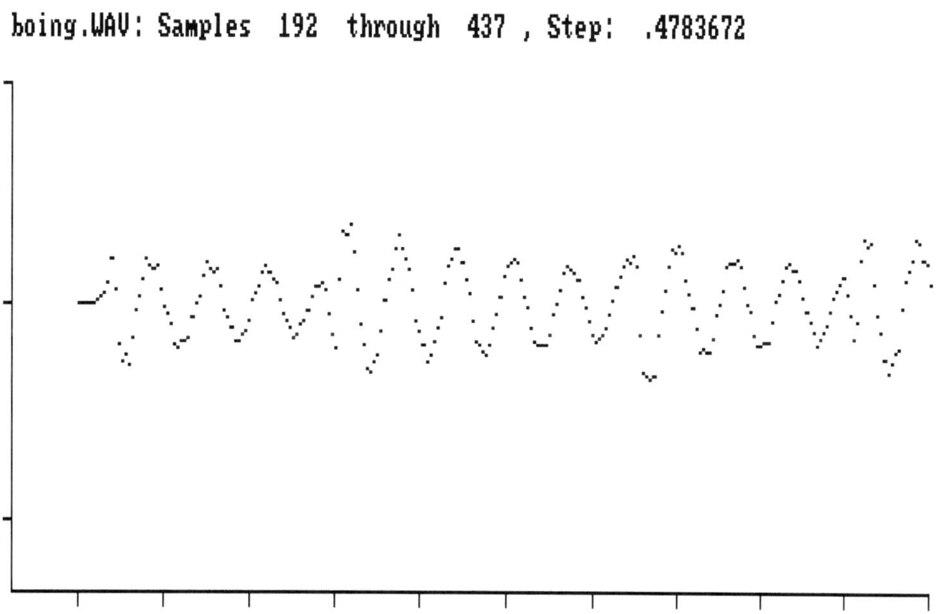

Figure 9.30 Sample Waveform Viewer Output

```
180 WEND
190 END
200 REM Move pointers or quit
210 A$ = INKEY$
220 WHILE A$ = ""
230     A$ = INKEY$
240 WEND
250 IF A$ = "Q" OR A$ = "q" THEN RETURN
260 X = 88
270 GOSUB 840:          REM Change starting point
280 SAVEWST = WAVSTART + (X - 88) * WAVSTEP
290 X = 599
300 GOSUB 840:          REM Change ending point
310 WAVEND = WAVEND - (599 - X) * WAVSTEP
320 WAVSTEP = (WAVEND - SAVEWST) / 512
330 WAVESTART = SAVEWST
340 A$ = "Y"
350 RETURN
360 REM Display waveform stats and draw axis
370 CLS
380 PRINT "         "; F$; ": Samples "; INT(WAVSTART - 44);
390 PRINT " through "; INT(WAVEND - 44);
400 PRINT ", Step: "; WAVSTEP
410 FOR Y = 20 TO 167:          REM Draw vertical axis
420     PSET (48, Y)
430 NEXT Y
440 FOR X = 48 TO 599:          REM Draw horizontal axis
450     PSET (X, 168)
460 NEXT X
470 SAVEWST = WAVSTART
480 FOR I = 88 TO 599 STEP 51.2:        REM Draw horizontal ticks
490 X = INT(I)
500     GOSUB 620
510 NEXT I
520 X = 599:            REM Last horizontal tick
530 GOSUB 620
540 Y = 20:             REM Draw vertical tick
550 GOSUB 670
560 Y = 84
570 GOSUB 670
580 Y = 147
590 GOSUB 670
600 WAVSTART = SAVEWST
610 RETURN
620 REM Draw horizontal axis ticks
630 FOR Y = 169 To 172
640     PSET (X, Y)
650 NEXT Y
660 RETURN
670 REM Draw vertical axis tick
```

```
680 FOR X = 43 TO 47
690     PSET (X, Y)
700 NEXT X
710 RETURN
720 REM Draw waveform
730 K = 88
740 SAVEWST = WAVSTART
750 WHILE K <= 600
760     D = 255 - WAVBUFF(WAVSTART)
770     D = INT(.5 + D / 2)
780     PSET (K, 20 + D)
790     K = K + 1
800     WAVSTART = WAVSTART + WAVSTEP
810 WEND
820 WAVSTART = SAVEWST
830 RETURN
840 REM Move arrow
850 MOVINGS$ = "Y"
860 WHILE MOVING$ = "Y"
870     GOSUB 1140
880     A$ = INKEY$
890     WHILE A$ = ""
900             A$ = INKEY$
910     WEND
920     IF A$ = "L" OR A$ = "l" THEN GOSUB 970
930     IF A$ = "R" OR A$ = "r" THEN GOSUB 1020
940     IF A$ = "" THEN MOVING$ = "N"
950 WEND
960 RETURN
970 REM Move arrow left
980 GOSUB 1070
990 X = X - 1
1000 IF X < 88 THEN X = 88
1010 RETURN
1020 REM Move arrow right
1030 GOSUB 1070
1040 X = X + 1
1050 IF X > 599 THEN X = 599
1060 RETURN
1070 REM Erase arrow
1080 FOR Y = 155 TO 159
1090    PRESET (X, Y)
1100 NEXT Y
1110 PRESET (X - 1, 156)
1120 PRESET (X + 1, 156)
1130 RETURN
1140 REM Draw arrow
1150 FOR Y = 155 TO 159
1160     PSET (X, Y)
1170 NEXT Y
```

```
1180 PSET (X - 1, 156)
1190 PSET (X + 1, 156)
1200 RETURN
1210 REM Load WAV data
1220 WAVSTART = 44
1230 MAXLEN = 8192 + WAVSTART
1240 INPUT "Enter WAV file to display --> "; F$
1250 F$ = F$ + ".WAV"
1260 OPEN F$ FOR RANDOM AS #1 LEN = 1
1270 FIELD #1, 1 AS W$
1280 WAVLEN = 0
1290 WHILE (WAVLEN < MAXLEN) AND NOT EOF(1)
1300    GET #1
1310    WAVBUFF(WAVLEN) = ASC(W$)
1320    WAVLEN = WAVLEN + 1
1330 WEND
1340 CLOSE #1
1350 WAVEND = WAVLEN
1360 WAVLEN = WAVLEN - WAVSTART
1370 WAVSTEP = WAVLEN / 512
1380 RETURN
```

Notice how the program is structured, especially the hierarchy of the graphics routines. For example, GOSUB 360 causes calls to subroutines at lines 620 and 670. It may be worthwhile to make a diagram of the program structure, with subroutines and their functions grouped in their hierarchical positions.

Conclusion

Check your knowledge of this material by trying the following Section Review.

9.8 Section Review

1. How are the horizontal and vertical tick marks drawn?
2. Which lines are responsible for drawing the arrowhead?
3. Explain what happens when an arrow is moved to the right or the left.
4. Which lines are responsible for drawing the entire waveform?

9.9 Troubleshooting Techniques

Troubleshooting a problem in a graphical application can be very tricky. Here is a short list of things that often go wrong:

1. The screen goes blank and the computer locks up.
2. The screen is a meaningless jumble of graphics.
3. The colors are wrong.
4. An image slants to the left or the right.
5. The proportions of the display are incorrect.

Finding the cause behind any of these problems requires patience and careful examination of every statement. In graphical applications the calculations that generate coordinates (such as those for the end points of a line) must be checked with all possible combinations of input values. If an input requires an angle, you must be sure the trigonometry operations of the angle give the proper results for all quadrants.

It is often useful to print out the results of individual calculations as the program executes. Unfortunately, the information printed shows up on the graphics screen and interferes with the real graphical work being done.

One way to fix this problem is to leave the print statements in the program but *redirect* the output to a data file. This generates a permanent record of what went on during the program's execution. Chapter 10 will show the details of file creation. Any data printed during execution will be placed into the data file, which can then be viewed with a text editor or printed.

Having a permanent record of the results is much more useful than trying to read the results off the graphical screen before they are overwritten by other graphics.

Conclusion

Check your understanding of this material by trying the following Section Review.

9.9 Section Review

1. Why are PRINT statements useful when troubleshooting a graphical application?
2. What is *output redirection?*

Interactive Exercises

DIRECTIONS

Because the commands used for graphics differ so much among computers, the exercises presented here are in a question rather than an exercise format, to encourage you to explore the graphic capabilities of your computer system.

1. Computer systems have different graphics modes. Depending on the system, these can be divided into low-resolution, medium-resolution, and high-resolution graphics. Generally speaking, the low-resolution offers the fewest picture elements, and the high-resolution the greatest number of picture elements. How many graphics modes does your system possess? How many horizontal and vertical picture elements are available in each of these modes?
2. Many computer systems offer different **text formats.** This means that the number of characters that can be presented on the screen can be different. The choices usually are a **larger text,** easier to read, or a **smaller text,** offering more information per screen. How many text formats does your computer system possess? For each of these text formats, how many characters can be presented horizontally and vertically?
3. There are computer systems that allow text to be displayed at the same time as graphics. Some systems will only display text on a separate portion of the screen, not just anywhere on the graphics screen. See what mixing of text and graphics your system allows. Do you have the option of placing text anywhere on the graphics screen? Explain.

4. Most computer systems have the capability to display color. A color monitor and proper system hardware are required for color graphics. Does your system have color graphics capabilities? Is this color capability available in text mode as well as graphics mode?
5. For systems with color capabilities, the number of colors available usually depends on the graphics mode. As an example, all of the system's colors are available in low-resolution graphics and a limited number of colors are available in the high-resolution graphics mode. For each graphics mode of your system, how many colors are available?
6. What statement is used by your system to get in and out of the various graphics and text modes?
7. For your system, determine the commands for
   a. Drawing a point at a specific screen location.
   b. Selecting a color.
   c. Erasing a point at a specific screen location.
   d. Drawing a line.
   e. Changing the background color.
8. Some forms of BASIC have an abundance of graphics commands. For the BASIC used with your system, determine the commands, if any, for
   a. Drawing a rectangle.
   b. Drawing a circle.
   c. Filling in an area.
   d. Moving an image on the screen.
9. For the graphics screen used in your system, where is the physical location on the monitor screen of the origin? Does your system have the capability of changing the origin location? If it does, what command is used to do this? Give an example.
10. Some computer systems use a **mouse** along with a special **help screen** to simplify graphics. Is such a system available to you? Have you tried it? If you have tried it, what are some of the advantages/disadvantages compared to using BASIC commands?

Self-Test

DIRECTIONS

The following program was developed for electronics technology. It displays various sine waves on the graphics screen.

Answer the questions by referring to Program 9.21.

Program 9.21

```
100 REM A Sine Wave Display Program
110 REM
120 REM This program will display a sine wave.
130 REM The user must enter the number of cycles,
140 REM amplitude, and phase of the wave to be
150 REM displayed.
160 REM
170 REM Variables used:
180 REM R = Angle in radians
190 REM D = Angle in degrees
200 REM A = Amplitude
210 REM P = Peak value
```

```
220 REM N = Number of cycles
230 REM T = Phase
240 REM A$ = Dummy variable
250 REM
260 REM Constants used:
270 PI = 3.14159: REM PI
280 REM
500 REM Main program block
510 GO$ = "Y"
520 WHILE GO$ = "Y"
530     GOSUB 2000: REM Get values from user
540     GOSUB 3000: REM Display sine wave
550     GOSUB 4000: REM Ask for program repeat
560 WEND
570 END
580 REM
2000 REM Get values from user
2010 PRINT
2020 INPUT "Peak value (100 units maximum)==> "; P
2030 INPUT "Number of cycles ==> "; N
2040 INPUT "Phase angle ==> "; T
2050 RETURN
2060 REM
3000 REM Display sine wave
3010 SCREEN 2, 1
3020 REM
3030 REM Start loop
3040 FOR D = 0 TO 639
3050    R = (PI / 180 * D) * .5625
3060    A = P * SIN(R * N + T)
3070    PSET (D, (100 - A))
3080 NEXT D
3090 RETURN
3100 REM
4000 REM Ask for program repeat
4010 INPUT "Do you want to repeat the program? (Y/N) ==> "; GO$
4020 RETURN
4030 REM
```

Questions

1. What will happen if the user enters a value of less than 1 for the number of cycles? Explain.
2. Are the phase angles entered in degrees or radians?
3. Explain what effect entering different values of phase angles has on the output display.
4. State what purpose is served by the number .5625 being multiplied by the sine function in program line 3050.
5. Give the purpose of "100–A" in the PSET command of program line 3070.
6. State the number of vertical and horizontal pixels that are assumed in this program. How did you arrive at this?
7. State what program changes you would make to
   a. Always display an amplitude that is half of the user-input value.
   b. Have all sine waves start with a phase shift of 180 degrees.
   c. Make twice the number of sine waves appear as input by the user.

Study Questions

Note: If your system has color graphics or color text available, include it where possible in the following programs.

1. Create a structured BASIC program that will display a line graph of the amount of money spent for the current month as shown in Figure 9.31.
2. Develop a structured BASIC program that will place either a vertical or a horizontal line anywhere on the graphics screen.
3. Your chief engineer needs a structured BASIC program that will show the relationship of the inductive reactance of an inductor with frequency. Select the *X*-axis to represent frequency in hertz and the *Y*-axis to represent the inductive reactance in ohms. The program limits are

   Inductive reactance from 0 to 1000 ohms

   Frequency from 0 to 1000 Hz

   The formula for inductive reactance is

$$X_L = 2\pi f L$$

4. Design a structured BASIC program that will allow the user to select the dimensions of a rectangle and have it appear on the graphics screen. The maximum size of the rectangle is limited to the size of the graphics screen in your computer system.
5. Develop a structured BASIC program that displays the land defined by four posts. The user may enter the coordinates of each post and the program returns with a display of lines connecting each of the posts. The boundaries of the coordinates must be limited to the size of the graphics screen in your computer system.

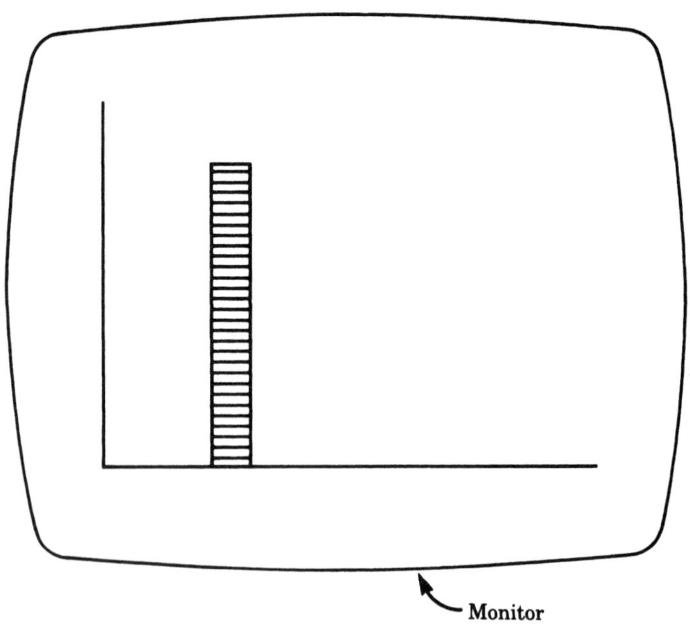

Figure 9.31 Graph for Study Question 1

6. The department head needs a structured BASIC program that will display a graph of a patient's temperature reading, taken four times a day. The *X*-axis represents the temperature reading and the *Y*-axis represents the value of the temperature in degrees Fahrenheit. The user is to enter four temperature values and the program will return with a graph of the four readings joined by lines.
7. A machine shop requires a structured BASIC program that will display the number of parts used each day over a five-day work week. The *X*-axis is to represent the day of the week, while the *Y*-axis represents the number of parts used. Assume the maximum number of parts that can be used for any one day is 100.
8. Expand the program from Study Question 1 so the amount of sales for the year may be graphically displayed. The *X*-axis will represent the months of the year and the *Y*-axis will represent the amount of money. Assume that the maximum earnings for any one month will not be more than $10,000.
9. Develop a structured BASIC program that will allow the user to display a Cartesian coordinate system anywhere on the graphics screen. The maximum positive and negative values of the system are to be determined by the user.
10. The Deep Space Communications Department hires you to create a structured BASIC program that will display the frequency response of a series resonant circuit. The *X*-axis is to represent frequency and the *Y*-axis impedance. Assume the frequency range to be from 1000 to 2000 Hz, and the impedance from 0 to 1000 ohms. The formula for the impedance of a series resonant circuit is

$$Z = X_L - X_C$$

where $X_L = 2\pi fL$
$X_C = 1/(2\pi fC)$

The user is to enter the value of the capacitor in farads and the value of the inductor in henrys.
11. Modify Study Question 4 so the user can select the location on the graphics screen for the rectangle to appear.
12. Expand the program in Study Question 5 so that the user may enter up to a maximum of ten posts. The graphics screen will show lines defining the land by connecting each post with a line, in the order the locations of the posts were entered by the program user.
13. Modify the program in Study Question 6 so the patient's blood pressure is displayed along with the temperature. If text is available on your graphics screen, be sure to label both axes. The *Y*-axis will now represent the value of the temperature as well as the blood pressure.
14. Create a structured BASIC program that will display a bar graph of the production output of ten factory workers for a given month. The *Y*-axis is to represent each individual factory worker, and the *X*-axis the amount of production output (assume 100 units maximum). The user is to enter the production output for each of the ten workers. If text is available with graphics on your system, have the name of each worker (as assigned by the program user) appear on the *Y*-axis, and scale the *X*-axis to indicate the number of units.
15. Modify the program in Study Question 8 so that it automatically scales itself. This will mean that the user can enter any maximum value of money to represent earnings along the *X*-axis.
16. Create a structured BASIC program that will display a three-dimensional wire model of a rectangle. The size of the rectangle is to be entered by the user. The graphics display is to be with the face and back flat and the sides at a 30-degree angle.
17. The design department needs a structured BASIC program that will simulate an oscilloscope. The user is to enter the frequency and amplitude of the waveform to be displayed as well as the settings of the period of the horizontal sweep and the gain of the vertical amplifier. The range of the horizontal sweep is from 1 ms to 1 micros per centimeter and the vertical gain range is from

1 mV to 1 V per centimeter. Assume that the scope to be simulated has a vertical display height of 10 cm and a horizontal time display of 10 cm. Time is displayed horizontally starting at 0. Voltage is displayed vertically with the center of the graphics screen representing 0 volts.

18. Write a BASIC program that simulates a moving starfield on the graphics screen by constantly shifting a preset pattern of dots (representing stars) to the left.
19. Repeat Study Question 18, except have the stars follow their own individual straight-line paths from a central viewpoint, as if you were flying a spacecraft.
20. Write a BASIC program that turns each pixel on the graphics screen red, one at a time. How long does it take?
21. Design a BASIC program that generates a kaleidoscope image on the display that constantly changes. Whatever pixels are displayed in quadrant 1 are mirrored in the other three quadrants.
22. Generate the appropriate graphics patterns to stimulate a digital clock on the screen.

10 Using Files

Ken Koder called Don, the senior technician, into his office.

"Don, look at this," he said, and pointed to the waveform viewer display on his computer monitor.

Don looked at the monitor and then back at Ken. "Looks the same as it did last time, Ken."

Ken nodded and smiled. "It is, Don, except for one important change. All the data used to generate the waveform is now stored in a separate data file from the Waveform Viewer program."

"Really?" Don asked. "That's great! Now you can change the waveform by supplying a different data file."

Don thought for a moment. "How did you get the data into the file?"

Ken's answer was simple enough. "I used an editor to strip off the headers in the DATA statements of the original program and saved the results to the data file. Then I added a subroutine to read data from the file."

Objectives

This chapter gives you an opportunity to learn

1. The characteristics of three common file types.
2. How to read from a data file.
3. How to write to a data file.
4. What to do if a data file is missing.
5. How to catch and recover from file errors.

Introduction

This chapter demonstrates the use of files for performing input to and output from a running BASIC program. These files are stored on the hard disk or floppy disk. You will see that using files for input/output operations greatly enhances the type of applications you can create using BASIC.

10.1 What Is a File?

In this section we will examine the different types of files, their purposes and default extensions, and advantages of using one type or another.

Types of Files

In Chapters 1 and 2 you saw how to use the hard disk or floppy disk to store your own BASIC programs. Each BASIC program is stored on disk as a DOS *file*. Specifically, your BASIC programs (and all of the programs included on the companion disk for this textbook) are referred to as *source* files. Recall that these files have a .BAS extension. They are the "source" of BASIC statements for the interpreter. Source files usually contain only text characters, and may be displayed on the screen or printed. So, even though a BASIC source file may contain a valid set of BASIC statements, the file itself is not executable because it is composed of only text characters. Executable files, which have the DOS extensions .COM and .EXE, may or may not contain text characters but always contain special binary codes that represent instructions for the processor inside the computer. These types of files are also called *binary* files. Accidentally printing a binary file results in pages of generally unintelligible nonsense.

A third type of file is called a *data* file. As indicated by its name, a data file stores data for use by a program or the results of a program execution (or both). An extension of .DAT is commonly used for data files, although you may use any extension you want.

An input data file might contain the names and test grades for all students in a programming course. An output data file might then contain the name and average for each student. A different data file might contain opening moves for several classic chess games and a set of strategy rules.

Data files may be stored as text or binary information. The advantage to using only text in a data file is that the file may be displayed or printed. The advantage to using a binary format in a data file is that binary data usually requires less storage space than text data. For instance, suppose that the following test scores are saved as text characters:

```
86,91,78,87,95
```

A total of fourteen character codes must be stored: ten for the numerals and four for the commas. The same data may be stored in binary as just five numerical codes.

Table 10.1 summarizes the characteristics of the different file types.

Why Use a Data File?

Up to this point, we have used two methods of entering data into a running program. The first method utilized an INPUT statement to read in a number or string, as in

```
100 INPUT NAME$, GRADE
```

Table 10.1 File Characteristics

File Type	Extension	Contains Text	Contains Binary	File Is Printable
Source	.BAS	Yes	No	Yes
Executable	.COM .EXE	Maybe	Yes	No
Data	.DAT	May contain text or binary or both		Only if pure text

The user is required to enter information from the keyboard, such as

```
James, 95
```

The user input is then written into the storage locations for the INPUT variables.

The second method required the data to be placed *within* the program, in the form of DATA statements. The READ statement was used to extract information from the DATA statements, like this:

```
100 READ NAME$, GRADE
.
.
.
500 DATA "James", 95
```

In this method, the user does not have to do any typing while the program executes.

Let us consider the disadvantages of both methods. The first method is acceptable when a small amount of data must be entered. But what if a class of thirty students must be entered? This will surely take the user a long time to do. And what if a mistake is made when entering the data, but it is not noticed until after the program has executed? The unfortunate user will have to enter all the data a second time. It is much better to enter the data *once* into a data file. If a mistake is found, the data file can be edited and corrected. Another execution of the program will then give the proper results without the user having to enter all the information again.

The second method requires the user to add DATA statements to the program. This requires the same amount of typing as a data file would, but has the disadvantage of causing the program to give the same results each time it is executed, unless all the DATA statements are changed. If the program were to use a data file for input, the output would change to reflect the different sets of data being sent into the program. In addition, no changes need to be made to the program to use a new set of data. Only a new data file must be supplied. The user does not have to know anything about line numbers or DATA statements either.

Conclusion

In the next section we will see how a data file is actually used. For now, test your understanding of file types with the following Section Review.

10.1 Section Review

1. Is a BASIC source file executable by itself?
2. What are the two extensions reserved by DOS for executable files?
3. Can DATA.BAS be used as a name for a data file?
4. Name one advantage of using a data file.
5. What are some differences between the binary and text formats?

10.2 Working with Data Files

Using a text editor or word processor, it is very easy to enter a small text-based data file. This can be done with the EDIT program that is supplied with DOS. Let us assume that the following lines of text are stored in the data file called SCORES.DAT:

```
Debbie, 88, 100, 94
James, 90, 85, 92
Ken, 97, 91, 89
```

This data file stores grades for three students in a class.

Opening a Data File

Program 10.1 shows how SCORES.DAT is accessed through BASIC.

Program 10.1

```
10 OPEN "SCORES.DAT" FOR INPUT AS #1
20 INPUT #1, N$, A, B, C
30 PRINT N$, A, B, C
40 INPUT #1, N$, A, B, C
50 PRINT N$, A, B, C
60 INPUT #1, N$, A, B, C
70 PRINT N$, A, B, C
80 CLOSE #1
```

The first statement that must be used to work with a data file is the OPEN statement. The OPEN statement has the following format:

```
OPEN <filename> FOR <mode> AS <filenumber>
```

where `<filename>` is a valid DOS file name (including drive and path if necessary)
`<mode>` is either INPUT, OUTPUT, or APPEND
`<filenumber>` is a number used to represent the file for future accesses

Opening a file for INPUT indicates to BASIC that you are going to read data from the file. An error is generated if the input file does not exist.

Opening a file for OUTPUT indicates that you will be writing data to the file. If the file does not exist, it is created. If the file does exist, the current contents of the file are lost. To preserve the contents and add new data to the end of the file, use APPEND instead.

The OPEN statement in Program 10.1 is written as

```
10 OPEN "SCORES.DAT" FOR INPUT AS #1
```

which indicates that "SCORES.DAT" is an input file identified by the number 1 during execution. This statement may also be written in the following ways:

```
10 OPEN "SCORES.DAT" FOR INPUT AS 1
```

or

```
10 OPEN "SCORES.DAT" AS 1
```

Note that when no mode is specified in the OPEN statement, BASIC will allow both read *and* write operations on the data file.

Reading from a Data File

To actually read from a data file after it is opened, the file number must be included in the INPUT statement, as indicated in lines 20, 40, and 60 in Program 10.1. We have

```
20 INPUT #1, N$, A, B, C
```

The #1 parameter directs BASIC to input data from file number 1, not the keyboard. As indicated, a string variable and three numeric variables will be read from the data file.

When Program 10.1 executes, the following is displayed:

```
Debbie   88   100   94
James    90   85    92
Ken      97   91    89
```

which is the information stored in SCORES.DAT.

Closing a Data File

The last statement in Program 10.1 is

```
80 CLOSE #1
```

The CLOSE statement allows DOS to perform any required housekeeping on the file (such as updating the file size). If CLOSE is left out, BASIC will automatically close any open files before exiting. It is, however, good programming practice to always use a matching CLOSE statement for all of your OPEN statements.

Creating a Data File

Program 10.2 shows how to use BASIC to create the SCORES.DAT data file.

Program 10.2

```
10 OPEN "SCORES.DAT" FOR OUTPUT AS #1
20 PRINT #1, "Debbie, 88, 100, 94"
30 PRINT #1, "James, 90, 85, 92"
40 PRINT #1, "Ken, 97, 91, 89"
50 CLOSE #1
```

The OPEN statement now uses the OUTPUT mode to indicate that data will be written to the data file. Notice that only string data is written to SCORES.DAT. There are no actual numbers present, just characters. Numerals "0" through "9" are converted back into their numerical form when processed by an INPUT statement.

Program 10.3 uses the numbers read from SCORES.DAT to compute the average for each student.

Program 10.3

```
10 OPEN "SCORES.DAT" FOR INPUT AS #1
20 GOSUB 70
30 GOSUB 70
40 GOSUB 70
50 CLOSE #1
60 END
70 INPUT #1, N$, A, B, C
80 PRINT N$, A, B, C
90 AVE = (A + B + C) / 3
100 PRINT "Average: ", AVE
110 PRINT
120 RETURN
```

To avoid repetition, a GOSUB is used to do all the work. Program 10.3, when executed, looks like this:

```
Debbie         88          100         94
Average:       94

James          90          85          92
Average:       89

Ken            97          91          89
Average:       92.33333
```

Clearly, the characters "0" through "9" read from SCORES.DAT were converted into actual numbers, or the AVE calculation would not have been correct.

The format of the data in SCORES.DAT may be changed without altering the execution of Program 10.3. Examine Program 10.4, which uses separate PRINT statements to write data into SCORES.DAT.

Program 10.4

```
10 OPEN "SCORES.DAT" FOR OUTPUT AS #1
20 PRINT #1, "Debbie"
30 PRINT #1, 88, 100, 94
40 PRINT #1, "James"
50 PRINT #1, 90, 85, 92
60 PRINT #1, "Ken"
70 PRINT #1, 97, 91, 89
80 CLOSE #1
```

The first PRINT statement writes a student's name string into SCORES.DAT and the second PRINT statement writes the three scores for the student. After Program 10.4 executes, SCORES.DAT looks like this:

```
Debbie
88          100          94
James
90          85           92
Ken
97          91           89
```

Compare this format with that of the original SCORES.DAT:

```
Debbie, 88, 100, 94
James, 90, 85, 92
Ken, 97, 91, 89
```

There are no commas in the new version and twice as many lines. This does not matter to the INPUT statement. When BASIC processes

```
INPUT N$, A, B, C
```

it knows that four items must be read. BASIC will search through the input file until it finds valid data to read, even if it has to skip to the next line in the file. The reason that the commas are required in the first version of SCORES.DAT is because we are mixing string data with numerical data. The commas are not needed in the new version of SCORES.DAT, since the string is on a separate line. How you structure your data is simply a matter of style and readability.

Using WRITE Instead of PRINT

To automatically generate the commas and string quotes in a data file, a different statement is used. Instead of

```
PRINT #1,"Debbie, 88, 100, 94"
```

use

```
WRITE #1, "Debbie", 88, 100, 94
```

This new statement is shown in Program 10.5.

Program 10.5

```
10 OPEN "SCORES.DAT" FOR OUTPUT AS #1
20 WRITE #1, "Debbie", 88, 100, 94
30 WRITE #1, "James", 90, 85, 92
40 WRITE #1, "Ken", 97, 91, 89
50 CLOSE #1
```

After execution, the contents of SCORES.DAT are as follows:

```
"Debbie", 88, 100, 94
"James", 90, 85, 92
"Ken", 97, 91, 89
```

This data file is also acceptable to Programs 10.1 and 10.3.

Variables may be used in PRINT and WRITE statements as well. Program 10.6 shows how a table of squares may be saved in an output file called SQUARES.DAT.

Program 10.6

```
10 OPEN "SQUARES.DAT" FOR OUTPUT AS #1
20 PRINT #1, "N", "N ^ 2"
30 PRINT #1, ""
40 FOR N = 1 TO 10
50      PRINT #1, N, N ^ 2
60 NEXT N
70 CLOSE #1
80 END
```

The statement

```
50      PRINT #1, N, N ^ 2
```

causes the value of variable N and the value of N-squared to be written to the output file. The execution produces the following results, which can be seen with the DOS command TYPE SQUARES.DAT:

```
N   N ^ 2
1   1
2   4
3   9
4   16
5   25
6   36
7   49
8   64
9   81
10  100
```

It is interesting to note that if the #1 parameter is left out of the PRINT statement, the output on the screen looks identical to the output file. This is not the case with the WRITE statement, which will automatically write a comma between each number output to the data file. If WRITE statements are used in Program 10.6 instead of PRINT statements, the resulting output file becomes:

```
"N","N ^ 2"
""
1,1
2,4
3,9
4,16
5,25
6,36
7,49
8,64
9,81
10,100
```

This format is acceptable for reading but does not look like a table very much. Keep this difference in mind when you create your own output files.

Conclusion

In this section we examined the different methods used to access data files. Test your understanding of this section with the following Section Review.

10.2 **Section Review**

1. Show the OPEN statement needed to open the file "NAMES.LST" for output.
2. What happens if the CLOSE statement is left out of a program?
3. What does the following statement do?

```
50 INPUT #1, A, B
```

4. What are the contents of the data file after the following statements execute?

```
10 OPEN "NUMS.DAT" FOR OUTPUT AS #1
20 PRINT #1, "A", 7
30 WRITE #1, "A", 7
40 CLOSE #1
```

10.3 General File Operations

The programming examples presented in the previous section were limited for at least two reasons. First, the name of the data file used by the program was set to SCORES.DAT and cannot be changed without editing the program. So, every user must know in advance to name his/her data file SCORES.DAT. This is not very practical. The user should be allowed to specify the name of the data file.

The second limitation is that the length of the data file is fixed. Three groups of data (called **records**) are always present in SCORES.DAT, and only three groups are ever read. Once again, this is not very practical. The program should be able to determine where the end of the data is, so that data files of varying sizes may be used with the same program.

Let us see how to improve our file operations.

Specifying a File Name

Program 10.7 shows how to allow the user to specify the file name.

Program 10.7

```
10 INPUT "Enter the file name ==>"; FILE$
20 OPEN FILE$ FOR OUTPUT AS #1
30 PRINT #1, "Here is the new output file."
40 CLOSE #1
```

The string variable FILE$ is set equal to the user's file name. The OPEN statement in line 20 uses FILE$ instead of a specific file name. This allows the user to enter his/her own file name during execution. Suppose that the user enters the following when Program 10.7 is executed:

```
Enter the file name ==>? MYFILE.TXT
```

It is easy to verify that the file MYFILE.TXT is created. Just use the DIR command, or display the data file with TYPE MYFILE.TXT.

Any legal string variable can be used in the OPEN statement.

Finding the End of the File

Let us take another look at the SCORES.DAT data file. We have three sets of data:

```
"Debbie", 88, 100, 94
"James", 90, 85, 92
"Ken", 97, 91, 89
```

Program 10.8 attempts to read and display this data.

Program 10.8

```
10 OPEN "SCORES.DAT" FOR INPUT AS #1
20 FOR N = 1 TO 5
30      INPUT #1, N$, A, B, C
40      PRINT N$, A, B, C
50 NEXT N
60 CLOSE #1
```

During execution of Program 10.8, the three sets of data are in fact read and displayed. Unfortunately, since the FOR-NEXT loop is set up for five passes, an error message is generated when line 30 attempts to read data from SCORES.DAT a fourth time. There is no more data to be read because the end of the data file has been reached. BASIC is able to determine when this happens. BASIC keeps track of a file **pointer** when reading or writing a data file and knows when the pointer has reached the end of the file. The function

```
EOF(file number)
```

is used to report the end-of-file status for a particular file. If the end of the file has been reached, EOF returns a true (non-zero) value. Otherwise, EOF returns a false value (zero). Program 10.9 makes use of the EOF function in a WHILE-WEND loop.

Program 10.9

```
10 OPEN "SCORES.DAT" FOR INPUT AS #1
20 WHILE NOT EOF(1)
30      INPUT #1, N$, A, B, C
40      PRINT N$, A, B, C
50 WEND
60 CLOSE #1
```

When Program 10.9 is executed, the three sets of data are read and displayed, and the WHILE-WEND loop terminates before the fourth pass is made.

Adding More Data to a File

Suppose that we want to add a few more students to the SCORES.DAT data file. This can be done by opening the data file for an APPEND operation. APPEND is similar to OUTPUT, with one major difference. Opening a file for OUTPUT positions the file pointer at the beginning of the data file. Opening the data file for APPEND positions the file pointer at the end of the file. This allows new data to be written to the end of the file, where it belongs. Otherwise, we might write over data that already exists. Program 10.10 shows how we can add more students to SCORES.DAT by appending new data to it.

Program 10.10

```
10 OPEN "SCORES.DAT" FOR APPEND AS #1
20 N$ = "OK"
30 WHILE 0 <> LEN(N$)
```

```
40      INPUT "Enter student name (or ENTER to exit) ==>"; N$
50      IF 0 <> LEN(N$) THEN GOSUB 100
60 WEND
70 CLOSE #1
80 END
100 INPUT "Enter all three grades ==>", A, B, C
110 WRITE #1, N$, A, B, C
120 PRINT "Student added."
130 RETURN
```

The WHILE-WEND loop in Program 10.10 tests the N$ variable at the beginning of each pass. The N$ variable can only have the length of 0 if the user enters an empty name string. So, the user may enter as many names as needed (assuming that there is room on the disk for the updated data file).

Let us look at two executions of Program 10.10. In the first execution only one student is added:

```
Enter student name (or ENTER to exit) ==>? Jane
Enter all three grades ==>? 76, 88, 91
Student added.
Enter student name (or ENTER to exit) ==>?
```

Examination of SCORES.DAT indicates the new student has been added:

```
"Debbie", 88, 100, 94
"James", 90, 85, 92
"Ken", 97, 91, 89
"Jane", 76, 88, 91
```

During the second execution two new students are added:

```
Enter student name (or ENTER to exit) ==>? Bob
Enter all three grades ==>? 100, 96, 97
Student added.
Enter student name (or ENTER to exit) ==>? Jeff
Enter all three grades ==>? 86, 96, 100
Student added.
Enter student name (or ENTER to exit) ==>?
```

Now there are six students in the data file SCORES.DAT:

```
"Debbie", 88, 100, 94
"James", 90, 85, 92
"Ken", 97, 91, 89
"Jane", 76, 88, 91
"Bob", 100, 96, 97
"Jeff", 86, 96, 100
```

To compute the averages of all six students it is necessary to rewrite Program 10.3, which only works for three students. Program 10.11 uses the EOF function in a WHILE-WEND loop to control how many students are processed.

Program 10.11

```
10 OPEN "SCORES.DAT" FOR INPUT AS #1
20 WHILE NOT EOF(1)
30      GOSUB 70
40 WEND
50 CLOSE #1
60 END
70 INPUT #1, N$, A, B, C
80 PRINT N$, A, B, C
90 AVE = (A + B + C) / 3
100 PRINT "Average: ", AVE
110 PRINT
120 RETURN
```

When Program 10.11 is executed, we get the following results:

```
Debbie      88          100         94
Average:    94

James       90          85          92
Average:    89

Ken         97          91          89
Average:    92.33333

Jane        76          88          91
Average:    85

Bob         100         96          97
Average:    97.66667

Jeff        86          96          100
Average:    94
```

It is obvious that the EOF function did its job correctly, or we would have seen fewer students displayed, or gotten an error message when the program tried to read the seventh set of data.

Handling File Errors

It has been mentioned several times that an error will occur if an attempt is made to read past the end of a data file. This is just one of many error conditions that may occur during a file operation. Suppose we try to open a file for input, and the file does not exist? How can BASIC read data from a nonexistent file? What if we try to write to a file and there is no more room on the disk? Fortunately, BASIC provides a mechanism to catch these kinds of errors (and many more) and allow the programmer to decide what to do if one occurs. Let us look at a simple example.

Program 10.12

```
10 ON ERROR GOTO 50
20 OPEN "NOTTHERE.DAT" FOR INPUT AS #1
30 CLOSE #1
40 END
50 PRINT "File is not there!"
60 RESUME NEXT
```

Table 10.2 Common Error Codes for ERR

Error Code	Meaning
1	NEXT without FOR
2	Syntax error
3	RETURN without GOSUB
4	Out of data
5	Illegal function call
6	Overflow
9	Subscript out of range
11	Division by 0
26	FOR without NEXT
53	File not found
55	File is already open
58	File already exists
61	Disk is full
62	Input past end of file
70	Disk is write-protected
71	Disk is not ready

Program 10.12 uses an ON ERROR statement in line 10 to tell the BASIC interpreter to catch any errors that occur. The ON ERROR statement specifies a line number to go to when an error occurs. Suppose that the file NOTTHERE.DAT does not exist. The OPEN statement in line 20 will generate an error when it tries to open NOTTHERE.DAT. Instead of the program exiting with an error message, the ON ERROR statement allows execution to switch to line 50 when the error occurs in line 20. The programmer-supplied error message "File is not there!" will be displayed. The RESUME NEXT statement in line 60 tells the interpreter to go back to the next line after the line that just generated the error. Since line 20 generated the error, the RESUME NEXT statement resumes execution at line 30. The CLOSE statement has nothing to do because the file was never opened, so the program exits.

Now, when there are many file operations in a program, we will need a way to determine what type of error has occurred. Once again, BASIC provides a mechanism to identify the error condition. It does so through a set of error variables. The variables are defined as follows:

`ERR` Error code for the last error that occurred
`ERL` The line number where the error was generated

Table 10.2 lists some of the more common error codes that the programmer should look for. Program 10.13 checks for two of these errors.

Program 10.13

```
10 ON ERROR GOTO 50
20 OPEN "A:\NOTTHERE.DAT" FOR INPUT AS #1
30 CLOSE #1
40 END
50 IF ERR = 53 THEN PRINT "File is not there!"
```

```
60 IF ERR = 71 THEN PRINT "Disk is not ready!"
70 IF ERR <> 71 THEN RESUME NEXT
80 INPUT "Make the disk ready and press ENTER..."; A$
90 RESUME 20
```

Program 10.13 makes use of two error codes from Table 10.2. Error codes 53 (File not found) and 71 (Disk is not ready), if they occur, will cause special messages to be output to indicate what is wrong. To test the operation of the error codes, do the following:

1. Make sure drive A: is empty.
2. Execute Program 10.13. You should get the "Disk is not ready!" message.
3. Place a working disk into drive A:. Make sure the file NOTTHERE.DAT is not on the disk.
4. Press ENTER to allow the program to continue. You should now get the "File is not there!" error message.

It is important to examine the error code to determine if the error may be corrected in some way. In Program 10.13, if ERR is equal to 71 the user is given time to fix the problem with the disk drive and try to open the file again. The RESUME 20 statement on line 90 instructs the interpreter to continue execution at line 20 (where the OPEN statement originally generated the error). Thus, the OPEN statement will get executed again.

If ERR equals 53 the file NOTTHERE.DAT is not on disk, so there is no reason to try opening it again while the program is running. The IF statement on line 70 will process the RESUME NEXT statement in this case, which takes the interpreter back to line 30.

Conclusion

Together, the flexibility of the OPEN statement and the use of error codes greatly increases your control over data files. Test your understanding of the operations presented in this section with the following Section Review.

10.3 Section Review

1. Show how the string variable V$ can be used to open an output file.
2. What does the following WHILE-WEND loop do?

```
50 WHILE NOT EOF(1)
60     INPUT #1, N
70     PRINT #2, N
80 WEND
```

3. What OPEN statement is needed to open the data file TEST.DAT on drive B: in order to add additional information to it?
4. What is required to catch errors that occur during execution of a program?
5. What is the difference between RESUME NEXT and RESUME 20 in Program 10.13?

10.4 File Applications

We continue our examination of file operations by looking at four additional applications. The purpose of each application is to show useful and practical file techniques.

A Simple Telephone Directory

Program 10.14 is used to read, display, and search a short list of names and phone numbers read from a data file.

Program 10.14

```
10 REM Telephone directory
20 DIM NAMES$(25), NUMS(2, 25)
30 ON ERROR GOTO 200
40 OPEN "PHONES.DAT" FOR INPUT AS #1
50 K = 0
60 WHILE NOT EOF(1)
70      INPUT #1, NAMES$(K + 1), NUMS(1, K + 1), NUMS(2, K + 1)
80      K = K + 1
90 WEND
100 CLOSE #1
110 PRINT "There are "; K; " names in the phone directory."
120 C$ = ""
130 WHILE C$ <> "Q"
140      INPUT "Enter choice: S (search), L (list), or Q (quit) ==>"; C$
150      IF C$ = "S" THEN GOSUB 300
160      IF C$ = "L" THEN GOSUB 400
170      IF C$ <> "S" AND C$ <> "L" AND C$ <> "Q" THEN PRINT "Invalid choice."
180 WEND
190 END
200 IF ERR = 53 THEN PRINT "PHONES.DAT does not exist."
210 RESUME 190
300 INPUT "Enter name to search for ==>"; N$
310 J = K
320 M = 0
330 WHILE J > 0
340      IF N$ = NAMES$(J) THEN PRINT NAMES$(J), NUMS(1, J); " - "; NUMS(2, J)
350      IF N$ = NAMES$(J) THEN M = M + 1
360      J = J - 1
370 WEND
380 PRINT "There were "; M; " matches."
390 RETURN
400 FOR J = 1 TO K
410     PRINT NAMES$(J), NUMS(1, J); " - "; NUMS(2, J)
420 NEXT J
430 RETURN
```

The data file PHONES.DAT is read by Program 10.14 (assuming that the file exists). This is where the names and phone numbers are stored. A sample PHONES.DAT file looks like this:

```
Alan, 555, 8901
Charlie, 555, 8989
James, 555, 1234
Ken, 555, 5678
Ken, 555, 5679
Sharon, 555, 4985
```

The structure of the data may be edited (all numbers aligned in the same column, for example) without changing the execution of Program 10.14. The first WHILE-WEND loop reads all the information from PHONES.DAT, counting the number of entries as it goes. The variable K represents the number of names in the phone directory. As you can see by examining the PHONES.DAT listing, duplicate names (Ken) are allowed.

The second WHILE-WEND loop in Program 10.14 is the command loop. The user may enter uppercase L, S, or Q only. Command L means list all the names and numbers in the directory. Command S is used to search the directory for a specific name supplied by the user. This search technique is performed in the third WHILE-WEND loop.

The last command Q is for quitting the program. Look over the following sample execution:

```
There are 6 names in the phone directory.
Enter choice: S (search), L (list), or Q (quit) ==>? L
Alan        555 - 8901
Charlie     555 - 8989
James       555 - 1234
Ken         555 - 5678
Ken         555 - 5679
Sharon      555 - 4985
Enter choice: S (search), L (list), or Q (quit) ==>? S
Enter name to search for ==>? Ken
Ken         555 - 5679
Ken         555 - 5678
There were  2  matches.
Enter choice: S (search), L (list), or Q (quit) ==>? S
Enter name to search for ==>? Charlie
Charlie     555 - 8989
There were  1  matches.
Enter choice: S (search), L (list), or Q (quit) ==>? S
Enter name to search for ==>? Ed
There were  0  matches.
Enter choice: S (search), L (list), or Q (quit) ==>? Q
```

You may agree that having only six names in our phone directory would hardly require a program to look up a number. If, however, the phone directory contains hundreds of names, Program 10.14 can be quite useful.

Displaying Text Files

Program 10.15 reads and displays one line at a time from a user-specified text file.

Program 10.15

```
10 REM Text file display
20 INPUT "Enter the name of a text file ==>"; T$
30 OPEN T$ FOR INPUT AS #1
40 LNUM = 1
50 WHILE NOT EOF(1)
60      LINE INPUT #1, FDATA$
70      PRINT "Line "; LNUM; ": "; FDATA$
80      IF 0 = (LNUM MOD 22) THEN GOSUB 200
```

```
90      LNUM = LNUM + 1
100 WEND
110 CLOSE #1
120 END
200 PRINT
210 INPUT "Press ENTER for more..."; E$
220 PRINT
230 RETURN
```

No error trapping is included to detect if a requested file does not exist. If the file does exist, it is displayed one line at a time, with a running counter keeping track of the number of lines. A new statement is used to read an entire line (up to the carriage return) from a data file. It is

```
LINE INPUT #1, FDATA$
```

Normally, string input terminates when a comma is encountered in the input data. In the case of LINE INPUT, the comma is just another character to be read.

During the following sample execution, a data file named PARTS.TXT is displayed:

```
Enter the name of a text file ==>? parts.txt
Line 1 : Parts List: LED Flasher Project
Line 2 :
Line 3 : One 555 Timer
Line 4 : One 8-pin wire-wrap socket
Line 5 : Two 100K-ohm resistors
Line 6 : One 150-ohm resistor
Line 7 : One 0.1 µF capacitor
Line 8 : One Light-Emitting Diode (LED)
Line 9 :
Line 10 : Assemble the flasher circuit according to the schematics
Line 11 : provided. If the circuit works properly, the LED will
Line 12 : flash approximately five times per second.
Line 13 :
Line 14 : Good luck!!!
Line 15 :
```

Only 15 lines of text were stored in the PARTS.TXT file.

Suppose that there were 300 lines of text in a data file. It would not be very useful to have all of them fly past the screen in half a second. It would be better to display a portion of the file, maybe 22 lines, and then pause while the user is allowed to view what is on the screen. The next group of 22 lines can be seen by pressing ENTER. Program 10.15 uses a test in line 80 to determine if 22 lines have been displayed. The subroutine at line 200 waits for the user to press ENTER.

Try creating a long text file by redirecting the output of the DIR command to a file. A typical DOS command to do this is

```
DIR > DIRLIST.TXT
```

Use Program 10.15 to display the DIRLIST.TXT file. The output will look something like this:

```
.
.
.
Line  21 : MEM       EXE 32,502 05-31-94  6:22a
Line  22 : NLSFUNC   EXE  7,036 05-31-94  6:22a
Press ENTER for more...?
Line  23 : README    TXT 60,646 05-31-94  6:22a
Line  24 : NETWORKS  TXT 17,465 05-31-94  6:22a
.
.
.
```

Program 10.15 is similar to the MORE facility provided with DOS.

Encrypting a Text File

Often, for purposes of security, it is necessary to convert a data file into an encoded or encrypted format so that the meaning cannot be determined. For example, the short message

```
KU,
THIS IS A SECRET MESSAGE.
THE ANSWERS TO THE HOMEWORK ARE IN THE FILE CABINET.
JU
```

is converted into the following encrypted text:

```
PZ,
YMNX NX F XJHWJY RJXXFLJ.
YMJ FSXBJWX YT YMJ MTRJBTWP FWJ NS YMJ KNQJ HFGNSJY.
OZ
```

The technique used to do the encryption is called a *Caesar-shift*. All the letters in the original message are shifted forward in the alphabet a certain number of positions (five in this case). Thus, an A becomes an F, a B becomes a G, and so on. Letters near the end of the alphabet cause a wraparound to the beginning of the alphabet.

Program 10.16 implements a Caesar-shift.

Program 10.16

```
10 REM Text file encryption
20 INPUT "Enter the name of a text file to encrypt ==>"; T$
30 OPEN T$ FOR INPUT AS #1
40 OPEN "CRYPT.OUT" FOR OUTPUT AS #2
50 WHILE NOT EOF(1)
60      LINE INPUT #1, FDATA$
70      CDATA$ = ""
80      FOR J = 1 TO LEN(FDATA$)
90             C$ = MID$(FDATA$, J, 1)
100            IF C$ >= "A" AND C$ <= "Z" THEN GOSUB 200
110            CDATA$ = CDATA$ + C$
120     NEXT J
130     PRINT #2, CDATA$
140 WEND
150 CLOSE #1
```

```
160 CLOSE #2
170 END
200 C = ASC(C$) + 5
210 IF C > 90 THEN C = C - 26
220 C$ = CHR$(C)
230 RETURN
```

The encryption is only performed on uppercase letters, which are identified by the test in line 100. The subroutine beginning at line 200 does the actual shifting and wraparound testing.

The user must supply the name of an existing text file. After encryption, the results are written to the file CRYPT.OUT. How do you think decryption might be performed?

Using a Random-Access File

A random-access file is a file that may be read in any order, instead of from beginning to end. This is very useful, since we may want to go directly to the 500th record of a file right away, without having to read the first 499 records. Program 10.17 demonstrates how to perform random reads from a data file.

Program 10.17

```
10 REM Random-access demonstration
20 OPEN "CODES.LST" FOR RANDOM AS #1 LEN = 17
30 FIELD #1, 8 AS CLR$, 4 AS NUM$, 3 AS ABR$
40 RECS = 0
50 GET #1
60 WHILE NOT EOF(1)
70      RECS = RECS + 1
80      GET #1
90 WEND
100 PRINT "There are "; RECS; " records in the data file."
110 RN = 1
120 WHILE RN <> 0
130      INPUT "Enter a record number (or 0 to quit) ==>"; RN
140      IF RN <> 0 THEN GET #1, RN
150      IF RN <> 0 THEN PRINT CLR$, NUM$, ABR$
160 WEND
170 CLOSE #1
180 END
```

In order to allow random access to the CODES.LST data file, the OPEN statement in line 20 uses the keyword RANDOM. The length of the records (which all have an identical format) is specified as 17 characters. This requires the use of the FIELD statement in line 30, which describes the format of the records that will be read from the data file. As indicated, the first eight positions in the record are set aside for CLR$. The next four positions are for NUM$ and the last three for ABR$. The FIELD statement allocates 15 of the 17 character positions specified by the LEN parameter. The last two positions are needed to read the carriage return and line feed codes from the data file.

In order to read a record from the data file, the GET statement is used. There are two forms of the GET statement used in Program 10.17. In the first WHILE-WEND loop, the GET statement merely specifies the file number to get a record from. In the second WHILE-WEND loop, the GET statement includes a record number to read.

Recall that BASIC maintains a file pointer when accessing files. When GET is used without a record number, the record at the position of the file pointer is read, and the pointer is advanced to the next record position. When a record number is used with GET, the pointer is first advanced to the position of the specified record, and then the data is read.

The CODES.LST data file contains the following information:

```
Black   0   BLA
Brown   1   BRO
Red     2   RED
Orange 3    ORA
Yellow 4    YEL
Green   5   GRE
Blue    6   BLU
Violet 7    VIO
Gray    8   GRA
White   9   WHI
```

It is necessary to format the data the same way it is defined in the FIELD statement, with eight characters for the first column, four characters for the second, and three for the third.

A sample execution of Program 10.17 is as follows:

```
There are 10 records in the data file.
Enter a record number (or 0 to quit) ==>? 1
Black          0              BLA
Enter a record number (or 0 to quit) ==>? 5
Yellow         4              YEL
Enter a record number (or 0 to quit) ==>? 10
White          9              WHI
Enter a record number (or 0 to quit) ==>? 12

Enter a record number (or 0 to quit) ==>? 0
```

Record numbers that are larger than the actual number of records in the data file are ignored by GET. This is why nothing is displayed when the record number 12 was used. Also, records are numbered beginning with record 1, which is why the user may enter 0 to exit the program.

Along with the GET statement, BASIC provides the PUT statement to write data into a random file record. The record fields must be loaded with data before PUT is used. Two other functions, LSET and RSET, are used to load data into the record fields. The following statements will replace the contents of the third record in the CODES.LST file:

```
162 LSET COLOR$ = "NewRED"
164 LSET NUM$ = "2"
166 LSET ABR$ = "Rd."
168 PUT #1, 3
```

LSET and RSET are used to left- and right-justify string data when it is written.

Together, GET and PUT provide the means to fully manipulate random-access files. You are encouraged to experiment with their use on your own.

Conclusion

The sample applications presented in this section provide a brief look at how file operations can be used in practical ways. Test your understanding of the concepts presented in this section with the following Section Review.

10.4 Section Review

1. What is the difference between INPUT #1, A$ and LINE INPUT #1, A$?
2. How does Program 10.15 determine when twenty-two lines have been displayed?
3. Why are the ASC and CHR$ functions used in Program 10.16?
4. What are the contents of C and C$ after the subroutine in Program 10.16 executes, if the initial value of C$ equals "X"?
5. Why is the first GET statement (line 50) needed in Program 10.17?
6. Why does the LEN parameter need to be 17 in Program 10.17?

10.5 The Waveform Viewer Project

The WAV file used to create the waveform is read once, the first 8192 samples being stored in the WAVBUFF array. Samples are read out of the WAV file as ASCII characters and converted into the corresponding decimal value with the use of the ASC function. Thus, values from 0 to 255 are possible.

The first 44 items read from the WAV file are not waveform samples. Instead, they are the parameters stored in the WAV file's *header*. The actual parameters, and their offset within the header, are shown in Table 10.3.

The Waveform Viewer specification states that only 8-bit, mono-channel, PCM-encoded WAV files should be displayed. It is necessary to examine the header parameters

Table 10.3 WAV File Header Format

Offset	Header Parameter
0	"RIFF"
4	<File length - 8>
8	"WAVE"
12	"fmt "
16	<Length of the fmt data>
20	<WAVE File Encoding Tag>
22	<Channels>
24	<Sample rate>
28	<bytes/second>
32	<block align>
34	<bits/sample>
36	"data"
40	<Number of samples>
44	<First sample>

to determine if the WAV file meets the program's requirements. This part of the Waveform Viewer is left for you to design and code. In addition, here are some other features that may be useful:

- Sliding window zooming
- Automatic amplitude scaling
- Zoom-out
- Waveform editing, such as cut, copy, paste, and reverse
- Waveform save during zoom
- Overlay two or more waveforms (using different colors)

With a little effort, the Waveform Viewer can be a sophisticated WAV file analysis tool. Test your programming skills by creating a better version.

Conclusion

Check your knowledge of this material by trying the following Section Review.

10.5 Section Review

1. Are all parameters in the header four locations wide?
2. What is the first array element that contains a sample?
3. Identify three additional features that can be added to the Waveform Viewer.

10.6 Troubleshooting Techniques

Always make sure the operation was successful. This statement really sums up the best course of action to take when using file operations. When you attempt to open a file, make sure it is opened. When you write data to a file, make sure the data was written completely. The values returned by the file functions must be examined to determine whether the operation was successful. In general, it is a good programming habit to include code to handle every case that might be encountered during a file operation.

Know your data. It is also important to keep in mind that data is interpreted differently depending on the mode of a file. For example, the byte values 13 (ASCII carriage return) and 10 (ASCII line feed) from a file opened in text mode may be interpreted as a single *newline* character. The same two values are treated as individual bytes if the file is opened as a binary file. Some word processors use CTRL-Z (26) to denote the end of a file. If this value happens to occur in a data file, it might incorrectly be interpreted as the end-of-file character. To be safe, always check the description of the file function being used, and open the file in the proper mode. This will help keep the data flowing smoothly between the disk and your program.

Conclusion

Check your understanding of this material by trying the following Section Review.

10.6 Section Review

1. List the error codes associated with file operations. Why are these values important?
2. Name one difference between a text file and a binary file.

Interactive Exercises

DIRECTIONS

These exercises require that you have access to a computer that supports BASIC. They are provided here to give you valuable experience and, most importantly, immediate feedback on the concepts introduced in this chapter.

Exercises

1. Predict the contents of the file created by Program 10.18. Then execute the program and display the output file.

Program 10.18

```
10 OPEN "TEST.DAT" FOR OUTPUT AS #1
20 PRINT #1, "abcde", 12345
30 WRITE #1, "abcde", 12345
40 CLOSE #1
50 END
```

2. What are the final contents of the COUNT.NUM data file created by Program 10.19?

Program 10.19

```
10 FOR K = 1 TO 5
20       OPEN "COUNT.NUM" FOR OUTPUT AS #1
30       WRITE #1, K
40       CLOSE #1
50       OPEN "COUNT.NUM" FOR INPUT AS #1
60       INPUT #1, NUMBER
70       PRINT "The count is "; NUMBER
80       CLOSE #1
90 NEXT K
100 END
```

3. Program 10.20 has a different OPEN statement than the one used in Program 10.19. What does COUNT.NUM look like after Program 10.20 executes?

Program 10.20

```
10 FOR K = 1 TO 5
20       OPEN "COUNT.NUM" FOR APPEND AS #1
30       WRITE #1, K
40       CLOSE #1
50       OPEN "COUNT.NUM" FOR INPUT AS #1
60       INPUT #1, NUMBER
70       PRINT "The count is "; NUMBER
80       CLOSE #1
90 NEXT K
100 END
```

4. What does Program 10.21 do?

Program 10.21

```
10 ON ERROR GOTO 100
20 F$ = "SCORES"
30 F$ = F$ + "."
40 F$ = F$ + "DAT"
50 OPEN F$ FOR RANDOM AS #1
60 CLOSE #1
70 END
100 PRINT "File error."
110 RESUME NEXT
```

Try Program 10.21 with and without the data file (delete it if it already exists).

5. What is printed out by Program 10.22?

Program 10.22

```
10 REM Do you see this?
20 OPEN "P10-22.BAS" FOR INPUT AS #1
30 LINE INPUT #1, T$
40 PRINT T$
50 CLOSE #1
60 END
```

Self-Test

DIRECTIONS

Answer the following questions by referring to Program 10.14 and its sample execution.

Questions

1. How many names may be stored in PHONES.DAT?
2. Explain what happens if the PHONES.DAT file does not exist.
3. How does the search subroutine work? In which direction are the names compared?
4. Is the variable M incremented with each pass through the WHILE-WEND loop at line 330?
5. Are the phone numbers stored as characters or numbers in the data file?
6. Are the phone numbers stored in memory as characters or numbers while the program is running?

Study Questions

1. Write a program that allows the student data in SCORES.DAT to be edited. The user should be able to change the name or any of the numbers for any student.
2. Modify Program 10.6 so that a table of squares, cubes, and square roots are written to the data file.
3. Develop a program that uses the ON ERROR statement to trap a write-protected disk error.
4. Change Program 10.14 as necessary to allow the user to enter or delete names in the telephone directory.
5. Rewrite Program 10.16 to include lowercase characters and symbols in the encryption. Suggested symbols to encrypt are .,!? and $.

6. Write a program to decrypt a Caesar-shift data file.
7. Write a program that counts the individual letters in a text file. Write the histogram of the letter frequencies to an output file.
8. Develop a program that merges two text files into a single file. For example, the input files

```
File 1      File 2

James       123
Ken         456
```

cause the following output file to be created:

```
James, 123
Ken, 456
```

9. Create a program that simulates the operation of a savings account. Suggested operations are
   1. Open account (with initial balance)
   2. Deposit
   3. Withdraw
   4. Get balance
   5. Apply interest

   The account information should be stored in the file ACCOUNT.SAV.
10. Write a program that estimates how many pages a text file will use when printed. Assume that fifty-five lines from the text file constitute one printed page.
11. Develop a program that maintains a simple database of parts. The name, cost, and quantity of each part should be stored in a data file. The program should be able to compute the total cost of any part, or of all the parts in the inventory.
12. Write a program that reads a set of names from a data file, sorts them, and writes the results back to the same file.
13. Create a program that counts all of the different words in a text file. Display the words and their counts.
14. Develop a program that searches a text file for a specified substring. Display the entire line (with a line number) for every occurrence of the substring.
15. Write a program that reads the integer stored on the last line of the file COUNTER.BIN, adds one to it, and writes the new count into the file.
16. Write a program that allows the user to enter the contents of a text file. Provide line numbers for reference when writing each line to the output file.
17. Create a program that reads an equation from a data file, such as

```
X = 5 + 4 * 3 - 2
```

and calculates and displays the result, as in

```
The value of X is 15
```

18. Develop a program that reads the numbers in a data file called BOWL.ING and computes the score in a bowling game. The file should contain two numbers per frame and ten frames of data. The tenth frame must store three numbers, in case there is a strike on the first throw.
19. Write a program that converts all lowercase text found in an input file into uppercase. Write the results to a new file.
20. Write a program that creates a working BASIC program (in the form of a text file that can be read by the interpreter). For example, write the following to the file NEW.BAS:

```
100 FOR I = 1 TO 10
110     PRINT I,
120 NEXT I
130 END
```

Answers

Answers to Section Reviews—Chapter 1

1.2 Section Review

1. The major parts of a computer system are the monitor, keyboard, disk drive, printer, and the computer itself, which consists of the processor and memory (RAM and ROM).
2. Hardware is the computer and all physical things attached to it. Software is a list of instructions, called a program, that the computer processor will perform.
3. Some examples of a peripheral device are the printer, disk drive, monitor, and keyboard. (There are also others, such as game paddles and joysticks.)
4. The purpose of applications software is to make the computer act as a word processor, accounting spreadsheet, game, or some other specialized system.
5. RAM is memory that can store instructions entered by the computer user or a peripheral device. These instructions will be lost when the computer is turned off. ROM is memory that has been programmed at the factory and it will be retained even when power is not applied to the computer.
6. The purpose of a disk operating system is to have a program that will give instructions to the computer about how to operate the computer's disk drive system.
7. The purposes of a disk operating system are to:
   1. Format (initialize) a disk.
   2. Copy information from memory to the disk.
   3. Copy information from the disk to memory.
   4. Copy information from one disk to another.
   5. Display information from the disk on the monitor.
   6. Copy information from a disk to the printer.

1.3 Section Review

1. A computer language is a set of characters used to form symbols and the rules for combining these symbols into meaningful communications between the programmer and the computer.

2. The two things computers "understand" are ON and OFF or 1 and 0.
3. The computer language used by the microprocessor in your computer is machine language.
4. Language levels refer to how close the symbolism and structure of the computer language is to the everyday common language of the user, contrasted with how close the computer language is to the ON and OFF instructions understood by the microprocessor.
5. An interpreter is a program stored in the computer that converts (interprets) the symbolism of a higher level language into the ON and OFF code understood by the microprocessor.
6. A BASIC interpreter is a program in the computer that converts the symbolism of BASIC into the ON and OFF symbolism understood by the microprocessor.
7. The computer must have an interpreter before it can use any high-level language.
8. Some of the most commonly used high-level languages are FORTRAN, used for solving mathematical formulas; BASIC, which is easy to learn; Pascal, which teaches good programming habits; and C/C++, used to easily control the computer.
9. An interpreter is needed each time the program executes; a compiler is needed only one time.

1.4 Section Review

1. One measure of a good program is that it can be understood by anyone, even if he or she doesn't know the programming language.
2. Structured BASIC is a method of programming in BASIC with small groups of instructions that are easy to understand, well defined, and consistent in structure.
3. Structured BASIC is written with two purposes in mind: program operation and programming legibility. Unstructured BASIC is written for one purpose: program operation.
4. Unstructured BASIC takes up less memory and, for short programs, it is easier to program.
5. Structured BASIC takes longer to program for short programs. Also, it is hard for experienced unstructured BASIC programmers to change to a more structured approach to BASIC.

1.5 Section Review

1. Two input devices for the computer are the keyboard and the disk drive.
2. Two output devices for the computer are the monitor and the disk drive.
3. The main difference between a hard drive and a floppy disk drive is that the disk of the hard drive is not user removable, whereas the disk for a floppy disk drive is.
4. The names of the drives for a computer with a hard drive and two floppy drives are A: and B: for the two floppy disk drives and C: for the hard disk drive.
5. The 3½-inch disk can usually hold more information than the 5¼-inch floppy disk.

1.6 Section Review

1. The main difference between MS-DOS and PC-DOS is that MS-DOS is manufactured by Microsoft Corporation, while PC-DOS is manufactured by IBM.
2. User-specific answer (hopefully DOS 6.2 or above).
3. The term *booting* originates from the concept of pulling yourself up by your bootstraps.
4. The term *booting* refers to turning on your computer and having DOS automatically loaded into it from a disk drive.
5. DOS normally gets into the computer from a hard drive. If there is no hard drive, DOS gets loaded from the floppy drive.

1.7 Section Review

1. The purpose of the DOS DATE command is to allow you to input a date into the computer.
2. The purpose of the DOS TIME command is to allow you to input a time into the computer.
3. The DOS prompt A> means that the A: drive is the active drive and the computer is ready to receive input from you.

4. The two methods of resetting the computer are called a *cold boot* and a *warm boot.* A cold boot is accomplished by turning the computer off and then on again. A warm boot is accomplished by depressing the CTRL, ALT, and DEL keys at the same time.
5. You can make your formatted disk bootable by using the /S extension with the DOS FORMAT command:

   FORMAT/S [ENTER]

1.8 Section Review

1. As a new BASIC programmer one of the most important things you can do for yourself is to learn how to make backups of all important files.
2. The best course of action to take when a floppy disk cannot be read is to try the disk in another computer. This might work because the alignment of the read/write heads in each disk drive may be different.

Answers to Self-Test—Chapter 1

1. The program computes the volume of a room.
2. First, it explains the program to the user, then it gets the values from the program user, does the computations, and displays the answer.
3. L = Length of room.
   W = Width of room.
   H = Height of room.
   V = Volume of room.
4. The answer is displayed by line number 720.
5. The difference between the INPUT statements is that Program 1.1 does printing as well as inputting with one statement.

Answers to Section Reviews—Chapter 2

2.1 Section Review

1. It is necessary to make backup copies of a disk in case the original gets lost, stolen, or damaged.
2. An internal DOS command has already been loaded into the computer memory when the system is booted. An external DOS command has not been loaded into computer memory and must therefore be copied from the disk that contains the DOS programs.
3. A DOS file is a set of data stored on a disk that has a unique name.
4. A DOS file name must contain from one to eight characters, starting with a number or any letter of the alphabet and then any letter or number including the symbols ~{ }_-!#%^&.
5. A DOS file extension may contain up to three characters and numbers.
6. A DOS directory is a listing of the contents of the disk.
7. The DOS command DIR is used to list files on a disk.

2.2 Section Review

1. The four main areas involved in the BASIC programming process are: Beginning a new program. Using the program. Modifying an existing program. Saving the program.

2. Your floppy disk label should contain the following information:

   BASIC DATA DISK [1]
   [YOUR NAME]
   [INSTRUCTOR'S NAME]
   [DATE OF LABEL]

3. The steps you must go through before beginning a new BASIC program are: Have a formatted floppy disk ready. Turn on the computer, making sure DOS is loaded into it. Load BASIC into the computer.
4. User-specific answer (hopefully QBASIC).

2.3 Section Review

1. A BASIC statement is an instruction to the computer to perform some action.
2. Each BASIC statement must have a line number. (Optional in QBASIC.)
3. The maximum number of characters that may appear in a single BASIC statement is 255.
4. The purpose of the REM statement is to display comments or notes for the programmer's information. The statement by itself performs no action during program execution.
5. A screen editor is used to create and edit BASIC programs using the arrow keys or mouse to position the cursor on the screen. QBASIC includes a screen editor.
6. The PRINT statement displays information on the monitor screen during program execution, whereas the INPUT statement is designed to get information from the program user during execution.

2.4 Section Review

1. A BASIC statement is contained within the BASIC program for action when the program is executed. A BASIC command is an action performed in immediate mode and usually affects the BASIC environment.
2. An example of a BASIC instruction that may be used as a command or a statement is CLS (clear the screen).
3. A BASIC program is executed by the command RUN.
4. SYNTAX ERROR means that there is a mistake in the programming syntax somewhere in the program.
5. All errors in a BASIC program will not be caught and given a SYNTAX ERROR. For example, if there is an error in the text you want to display to the monitor screen (by a PRINT), it will not cause a SYNTAX ERROR.
6. To view the entire BASIC program, use the LIST command.
7. You cause a BASIC program to be copied to your floppy disk by entering the SAVE command.
8. To see the names of the files on your floppy disk when programming a BASIC program, use the BASIC command FILES.
9. The purpose of the BASIC command NEW is to clear the BASIC program from memory. This command is normally used when starting a new BASIC program.
10. QBASIC contains a screen editor, pull-down menu items, and a check to make sure all programs have been saved before exiting.

2.5 Section Review

1. You use the BASIC LOAD "filename" command to copy a BASIC program from your floppy disk into memory.
2. The action taken by the BASIC command LOAD"B:MYBASIC.1" is to copy the file on the disk in the B: drive named MYBASIC.1 to memory.
3. To add one or more characters to an existing BASIC statement, use the arrow keys to move the cursor to the desired location on the monitor screen. Press the INS key, then enter the required character(s).

4. To give an existing program line a new line number, use the arrow keys to get to the beginning of the line number of the existing program line. Then enter the new line number (overwriting the old one). Now LIST the program. There will be two identical program lines, the one with the original line number and the one with the new line number. Delete the program line with the original line number.
5. To remove a given program line from an existing BASIC program, simply type the line number and press the ENTER key.
6. The statements must be selected before the Edit menu can be used.
7. The BASIC command RENUM renumbers all existing program lines of the program currently in memory, from 10 on up, in increments of 10, starting with the lowest line number of the existing program.

2.6 Section Review

1. When you save another BASIC program on the same disk with the same file name as an existing file, the old existing file will be written over.
2. The command KILL"MYSTUFF.05" causes the file on the disk in the active drive named MYSTUFF.05 to be erased.
3. No. DOS must be used to delete a file.
4. You can get into DOS from the BASIC editor without losing the BASIC program in memory with the BASIC SHELL command. To get back into BASIC from DOS, type EXIT.
5. To permanently leave BASIC, use the command SYSTEM.

2.7 Section Review

1. BASIC does not report every type of error condition. A typographical error may be accepted by the system, causing the program to work improperly.
2. It is important to become familiar with both the system and software because it can help a programmer to locate errors and solve problems quickly.
3. Program errors can be located and solved quickly by becoming familiar with both the system and the software.

Answers to Self-Test—Chapter 2

1. No, REM statements are never displayed during program execution.
2. The variable L receives its value in line 420. The variable W receives its value in line 450, whereas H receives its value in line 480. Variable V receives its value in line 610.
3. The different BASIC commands are
   REM PRINT INPUT LET END
4. The PRINT statement on line 320 causes the display to skip a space between the displayed text.
5. Line 420 causes the program to pause for the user to enter a number and press the ENTER key.

Answers to Section Reviews—Chapter 3

3.1 Section Review

1. No, a BASIC interpreter does not require structured programming. Structured programming is used to make the program more readable and understandable for people.
2. Block structure means the program will be constructed so that there are a few groups of instructions rather than one continuous listing of instructions.

3. Each program block must begin with a REM statement that explains what the block is to do.
4. Program blocks are separated using block separators. The block separators used in this text are similar to the following:

```
180    REM    End of last block
190    REM
200    REM    This is a new block
```

5. The body of a program block is highlighted by the use of a comment.
6. The three types of blocks are the action block, loop block, and branch block.
7. The programmer's block gives necessary information about the structured BASIC program. It starts at the beginning and contains the following information.

   Name of program.
   Programmer's name.
   Description of the program, including constants and variables used.
8. An action block is a straight sequence of action statements. A loop block can cause statements to be repeated. A branch block allows only certain statements to execute.

3.2 Section Review

1. Bottom-up design is the process of developing a program entering program code as the first part of the program design process.
2. Top-down design is a method of designing a computer program that consists of stating the program in the most generalized and complete terms. Program coding is done as the last step in the process.
3. The three steps used in top-down design are
   1. Start with the most generalized idea of what the program is to do. Write this down in outline form.
   2. Assign blocks of BASIC line numbers to each major heading of the completed outline. Enter these using no more than REM or LET statements.
   3. Develop and test each of the separate major program headings by entering program code.
4. The five major sections were
   1. Programmer's block.
   2. Explain program to user block.
   3. Get values from user block.
   4. Computations block.
   5. Display answer(s) block.
5. Program stubs are program blocks that indicate what will take place in the program when the coding is entered.
6. Some of the advantages of using program stubs are:
   1. Creates a quick overview of the program.
   2. Enables the design of program structure without having to worry about program code.
   3. Helps prevent the program from being modified while program code is being developed.
   4. Allows program blocks to be assigned to others so that a large program can be assigned to more than one person.

3.3 Section Review

1. The purpose of the main programming block is to show how the program is structured. In doing this, it controls the sequencing of the structured program.
2. The GOSUB command causes the program to jump to the (line number) following the GOSUB (line number) command.
3. A target line is the program line reached by a GOSUB command.
4. A companion remark is the REMark statement immediately following a GOSUB command. It should contain the same information as the target line.

5. The target line is a REMark statement that describes the purpose of the program block.
6. The RETURN command causes the program to RETURN to the program line following the GOSUB command that caused the branch to the program block that has the RETURN command.
7. Each main programming block must have an END statement as its last program line to prevent the program from falling through and going directly to the first program block when the program should be ENDing.

3.4 Section Review

1. Flowcharting is primarily used to explain or present an already completed program.
2. The flowchart symbols are Subroutine, Process Operation, Decision Logic, and Input/Output.
3. A process block is a part of an action block. An example could be

```
100 REM Do calculations
110 LET S = R1 + R2
120 RETURN
```

4. A decision logic block flowchart symbol is used to represent a branch or a loop block.
5. The input/output block flowchart symbol represents data that is received (input) from or outputted to an external device. An example is the keyboard as an input device.
6. The purpose of a terminal point in flowcharting is to mark the start or END of a program. It is also used to mark the RETURN statement.

3.5 Section Review

1. A program loop is that part of the program that can repeat itself.
2. The WHILE is used at the beginning of the program section to be repeated, and the WEND is used at the end of the part of the program to be repeated.
3. In the WHILE-WEND structure, if the condition statement following the WHILE part is true, then the loop will be repeated. A false condition will allow the program to continue on beyond the WEND part of the structure.
4. As long as the string variable SELECTION$ is A, the loop will continue from program lines 110 to 150 and back again to 110. When the string variable SELECTION$ is no longer equal to A, then the program will continue on past the WEND and to the END statement in line 160. The loop as written will not execute even once.

3.6 Section Review

1. The purpose of a specification is to completely describe the programming application that is required.
2. The information left out of a specification involves the implementation details.
3. Only the first 8192 samples will be examined.

3.7 Section Review

1. A loop variable must be initialized to ensure that the loop executes the correct number of times.
2. The GOSUB statement executes four times.

Answers to Self-Test—Chapter 3

1. The main program block begins at 500. It contains six lines.
2. There are six blocks in the program:

   Programmer's block
   Main program block

Explain program to user block
Get values from user block
Compute future value block
Display results block

3. The program may be rewritten using a loop structure to display the accumulated interest at the end of each year.
4. The value of INTEREST is 1.06.
5. A WHILE-WEND loop can be added to the program to allow the user to choose if the program should be repeated.
6. Execution of the program will begin to change after what appeared to be a normal execution. Because the END statement is missing the program falls through into the explain program to user block. The program ends with an error because there is no GOSUB statement to return to when the program encounters the RETURN statement at the end of the block.

Answers to Section Reviews—Chapter 4

4.1 Section Review

1. The computer can be used the same as a calculator. This may or may not be an advantage depending on the number of repeated operations to be done.
2. Use `PRINT` $N_1 + N_2 + N_3$
3. An example could be

```
3 - 5 = -2
-4 - 6 = -10
-2 * 4 = -8
-6/2 = -3
```

4. To calculate 4^2, use `PRINT 4 ^ 2`.
5. 40000 in BASIC would be represented as 4E4. Entering a number with commas, such as 45,000, would not be accepted by BASIC.
6. The order of operations specify that mathematical operations are performed in a strict order. See Figure 4.1.
7. The result is 51.

4.2 Section Review

1. The two types of constants are numeric and string.
2. The value 5 is stored in a memory location identified as R.
3. Q = 15; W = 5; Z = 15
4. A string can be composed of alphabetic, numeric, or special characters—or a combination of two or all three—enclosed in quotation marks.
5. `LET W$ = "Hello"`
6. PRINT K will output the numeric value of memory location K. PRINT K$ will output the string beginning at memory location K$.
7. A BASIC variable
   - Begins with a letter of the English alphabet.
   - May use letters, numbers, and periods after the first letter.
   - Is always converted to uppercase.
   - Recognizes the first 40 characters.

- Cannot be a BASIC reserved word.
- Cannot begin with the letters FN.

8. 24SKIDOO is not a legal BASIC variable name because it starts with a number. FN.ME is not a legal BASIC variable because it starts with the letters FN, which is reserved to indicate a BASIC function.

4.3 Section Review

1. Screen formatting means the method used to design your program to appear on the monitor screen.
2. The first program would display

   `Your name`

   `?` (Waits for input on next line.)

   The second program would display

   `Your name?` (Waits for input on same line.)

3. The comma can be used to suppress the ? when used with an INPUT statement. It can be used to automatically tab information on the screen. It can also be used for inputting the values of more than one variable for the same INPUT statement.
4. Enter the price of each part separated by commas.

   ```
   25,12,8
   ```

5. The displayed output would be formatted according to the settings of the preset tabs on your computer system. For example, when the line is executed it could appear as

   ```
   Area of Circle      Volume of Sphere      Totals
   ```

6. The TAB(N) function causes printed output to be displayed N spaces to the right of the left margin of the monitor screen.
7. When executed, the TAB(20) will cause the following to be displayed:

   ```
   Acres         Crops
   ```

8. When the program is executed, the output is

   ```
   This is the number T
   This is the number 55
   ```

4.4 Section Review

1. The four arithmetic operations available in BASIC are addition, subtraction, multiplication, and division.
2. The three built-in functions presented in this section are square root, absolute value, and integer.
3. Order of operations means the order in which arithmetic operations are performed.
4. The answers are
   a. 3 + 8 * 2 = 19
   b. 3 * (4 + 2) = 18
   c. 5 + ABS(–5) = 10
5. Operations are done within the innermost parentheses first.
6. The correct order is
   1. (), INT
   2. ^

3. *, /
4. +, −

7. When the program is executed, the result is

```
7
```

4.5 Section Review

1. The IF-THEN statement is

```
IF (arithmetic expression) THEN (BASIC statements)
```

where `(arithmetic expression)` = any numeric expression
`(BASIC statement)` = one or more BASIC statements

If the expression is true, then the BASIC statement is executed.

2. The PRINT statement will be displayed when the arithmetic expression (X = 3 + 5) is true. This will happen when X = 8.
3. When executed, the program will display

```
Statement two.
Third statement.
```

4. Relational operators are symbols that are used in arithmetic or character relation to show the comparison to be performed between the terms in the relation.
5. The meanings are
   a. = (Equal)
   b. <> or >< (Not equal)
   c. => (Greater than or equal)
   d. <= (Less than or equal)
6. ASCII is the acronym for American Standard Code for Information Interchange.
7. The ASCII code represents

   Upper- and lowercase letters of the English alphabet.
   All numbers.
   Punctuation symbols.
   Various assignments depending upon the system.

8. ASCII codes for letters of the alphabet are in numerical order to simplify alphabetizing by computer.
9. A numeric code, such as the ASCII code, is necessary because the computer can only store and interpret numbers.
10. When the program is executed, it displays

```
First statement.
```

This is because the ASCII value of C is greater than the ASCII value of A.

4.6 Section Review

1. A logical operation has only two conditions: true or false.
2. The AND operation is true only when both logical operations separated by it are true.
3. The OR operation is true any time either or both logical quantities on either side of it are true.
4. An example is

```
10 IF (X = 3) AND (Y = 5) THEN PRINT "Pass inspection."
```

5. An example is

```
10 IF (W$ = "YES") OR (A$ = "NO") THEN PRINT "OK"
```

6. The NOT operation will change the logic condition of the expression following it.
7. An example is

```
10 IF NOT ((A = 1) AND (B = 2)) THEN PRINT "No pass."
```

8. When executed, the program would display

```
First statement.
Number two.
This is three.
```

4.7 Section Review

1. The value of SAVEWST is 120. The value with parentheses removed is –690.
2. The L and R character keys cause the arrow to move by incrementing or decrementing the arrow's *X* coordinate, and erasing/redrawing the arrow with each keystroke.

4.8 Section Review

1. Case sensitivity means uppercase and lowercase letters are treated differently.
2. The order of operations specifies the correct way to determine the result of an arithmetic expression.

Answers to Self-Test—Chapter 4

1. It computes the total hospital bill for three patients. It also determines which patient had the largest bill.
2. The purposes of lines 430, 450, and 470 are to get the name of the patient (a string variable) and the total days spent in the hospital (a numeric variable). The comma is there to separate the two variables and allow the program user to input their values, separated by a comma.
3. The purpose of the comma before the variable is to remove the ? that normally appears with an INPUT statement.
4. There are sixteen different variables used in the program: P1$, P2$, P3$, D1, D2, D3, N1, N2, N3, E1, E2, E3, T1, T2, T3, T.
5. The sequence of operations is

   Explain program to user.
   Get information from user.
   Get information about additional expenses.
   Compute total cost for each patient.
   Compute total hospital bill.
   Display who has the largest bill.
   End the program.

6. A suggested program addition is

```
900 REM Display who has stayed longer than a week.
910 IF N1 > 7 THEN PRINT P1$;" longer than a week."
920 IF N2 > 7 THEN PRINT P2$;" longer than a week."
930 IF N3 > 7 THEN PRINT P3$;" longer than a week."
```

7. A suggested modification is

```
620 REM Compute total cost for each patient.
630 Let T1 = 1.06*(D1 * N1 + E1)
```

```
640 Let T2 = 1.06*(D2 * N2 + E2)
650 Let T3 = 1.06*(D3 * N3 + E3)
```

8. The purpose of the commas between the variables is to take advantage of the automatic screen formatting available in the computer.
9. Suggested changes

```
800 REM Display who has the smallest bill.
810 IF (T1<T2)AND(T1<T3) THEN PRINT P1$" has smallest"
820 IF (T2<T1)AND(T2<T3) THEN PRINT P2$" has smallest"
830 IF (T3<T1)AND(T3<T2) THEN PRINT P3$" has smallest"
840 REM End this block
```

Answers to Section Reviews—Chapter 5

5.1 Section Review

1. A program branch has a TRUE or FALSE test condition that will determine the outcome of the program.
2. An *open branch* contains only one option in the branch.
3. The different types of program branches are the *open branch* and the *closed branch.*
4. Yes, an *open branch* can have an option activated on a FALSE condition.
5. The difference between an open branch and a closed branch is the number of options available. An open branch has one option and the closed branch has two or more options available.

5.2 Section Review

1. A *closed branch* contains two separate choices based upon the TRUE or FALSE results of a *condition* statement.
2. You may use CTRL-J to create a new line in the BASIC editor without having to add a new line number.
3. The limitations are a total of 255 characters and spaces.
4. Yes, you can have more than one BASIC statement for a given program line. This is done by using the colon (:) to separate BASIC statements on the same program line.
5. The advantage of using a GOSUB in a program branch is that you can preserve program structure while increasing the amount of program code for each condition.

5.3 Section Review

1. a. When A = 8: `This program will continue.`
   b. When A > 8: `Value is larger than 8.`
   `This program will continue.`
2. A case structure presents a choice between alternatives and one of the alternatives must be selected. An example would be

```
100 REM Case of N
110    IF N = 1 THEN PRINT "Resistor"
120    IF N = 2 THEN PRINT "Capacitor"
130    IF N = 3 THEN PRINT "Inductor"
140 REM End case
```

3. The ON-GOSUB statement will GOSUB to 100, 200, 300, 400 if the value of K is 1, 2, 3, or 4, repectively.
4. No. One of the rules of block structure is that each program block must be entered from the top and exited from the bottom. This is done to preserve program structure.

5. The intended results of a case statement may not be achieved if a condition is not tested by any of the IF statements used in the case statement. To avoid this problem, the programmer must provide a check for every possible condition.

5.4 Section Review

1. The GOSUB statement in line 3060 will be executed when V1 is less than 30.
2. The purpose of the logical AND in line 3080 is to get all values of V1 between and including 30 and 35.
3. The ON S GOSUB . . . in line 11050 causes the program to branch to a different subroutine depending upon the value of the variable S.
4. Yes, the three IF statements can be rewritten as one nested IF statement.

5.5 Section Review

1. Keys other than "Q," "L," "R," or Space are ignored.
2. No. The single If statement calls the subroutines at 1020 for all inputs that are not "L" or "l," not just "R" or "r" inputs.

5.6 Section Review

1. No special coding is required when writing branch blocks, although it is important to use comments and structured programming techniques.
2. It might be necessary to use a GOSUB statement inside an IF-THEN-ELSE statement when several statements need to be executed, and the programmer does not want to put them inside the IF statement because it detracts from the program's readability.
3. It is important for conditional statments to be structured properly so that they can be identified easily by a programmer.

Answers to Self-Test—Chapter 5

1. Program 5.10 computes the area of a square, rectangle, triangle, or a circle.
2. The program uses ten variables: ANSWER$, ITEM, AREA, ITEM$, SLENGTH, RLENGTH, RWIDTH, TBASE, THEIGHT, CRADIUS.
3. The sequence of operations used in the program are
   a. User selects type of area to compute.
   b. Use of ON-GOSUB command to call correct subroutine depending on user response.
   c. Get values from the user for the selected structure.
   d. Compute area of the selected structure.
   e. Print the result.
   f. Ask for program repeat.
4. If the user enters 1.4, the program will run as if the user entered 1. If the user enters an invalid choice, the ON-GOSUB statement will either produce an error or display an area of 0 units.
5. The program contains five program blocks:

   Get choice from user.
   Area of a square.
   Area of a rectangle.
   Area of a triangle.
   Area of a circle.

6. The ON-GOSUB statement calls the appropriate subroutine to compute the area of the structure selected by the user.

Answers to Section Reviews—Chapter 6

6.1 Section Review

1. The three kinds of programming blocks are action blocks, branch blocks, and loop blocks.
2. The more values of T to be computed, the more programming lines are required.
3. A loop block has the potential of going back and repeating a process over again.
4. A loop block will cause the program to go back and repeat a process; a branch block is a choice that will cause the program to move forward.

6.2 Section Review

1. This line adds 2 to the number located at the memory location indicated by the variable V.
2. A loop block must have a beginning value, an ending value, an increment value, and problem statements to be repeated.
3. ```
   100  REM A WHILE-WEND loop program
   110  COUNT = 8
   120  WHILE COUNT >= 0
   130      PRINT COUNT
   140      COUNT = COUNT - 2
   150  WEND
   ```
4. ```
   100  REM A loop program
   110  FOR N = 10 TO 18 STEP .5
   120      PRINT N
   130  NEXT N
   140  REM
   ```

6.3 Section Review

1. The purpose of the STEP part of the FOR-NEXT statement is to determine the increment of the loop.
3. The output would be

   ```
   1
   1.5
   2
   ```

3. The program output would be

   ```
   2
   1.5
   1
   ```

4. The default STEP value is 1.
5. The missing program line is one that would determine the value of X. As an example

   ```
   5 INPUT "What are the loop increments ==>"; X
   ```

6.4 Section Review

1. A nested loop is one loop contained inside another.
2. The program will output

   ```
   2    3    4
   3    4    5
   4    5    6
   ```

3. The suggested structure for the program includes REM statements to explain the program and tabs to indent and highlight the program structure.
4. Line 110 executes 10,000 times.

5. The loops are crossing.
6. More than one loop may be nested. This must be done without having any of the loops crossing each other. From a program structure standpoint, each loop should be indented with its FOR aligned vertically with the NEXT part of the same loop.
7. The output of the program would be:

```
X = 0
Y = 1   Y = 2   Y = 3   Y = 4   X = 1
X = 2
```

6.5 Section Review

1. The length of the waveform is maintained by adding 1 to WAVLEN each time a character is read from the WAV file.
2. Two exits from the WHILE-WEND loop are necessary because two conditions can occur while reading data from the file: the array limit is reached or the end of the file condition is encountered.

6.6 Section Review

1. Statement 220 executes seven times (1 plus 11 minus 5).
2. The innermost statement of a nested loop executes many times because, in general, we use the product of the number of passes through each loop.

Answers to Self-Test—Chapter 6

1. The resonant frequency is 851.1505 Hz.
2. A new program statement can be added to check if the current frequency is equal to the resonant frequency. If so, the RESONANCE! message can be printed.

```
4235 IF FR = F THEN PRINT "RESONANCE!"
```

3. Lines 4070 and 4090 could be modified directly by the programmer to change the range or the user can be prompted to enter the appropriate range of values to display.
4. Yes, the FOR-NEXT loop is nested within a WHILE-WEND loop.
5. No. The default STEP is 1. This would alter the output of the program significantly.

Answers to Section Reviews—Chapter 7

7.1 Section Review

1. The word *array* means "arrangement."
2. A subscript could be used to select one of many different prices stored in an array of grocery store items.
3. Using subscripts is an easy way of making a distinction between otherwise similar objects (such as patients in a hospital or items in a grocery list).
4. BASIC uses subscript notation in arrays.
5. (0,0)

7.2 Section Review

1.
```
10 READ A
20 DATA 3
```
This is equivalent to `10 LET A = 3`.

2. The DATA statement that occurs first number will be READ first.
3. Yes, you can have a DATA statement without a READ statement, but none of the data will be read.
4. A READ statement without a DATA statement will cause a run-time error and the program will terminate.
5. Use a FOR-NEXT loop to step an index variable through all eight elements.

7.3 Section Review

1. The RESTORE statement causes the pointer of READ and DATA statements to return to the first piece of data. This is sometimes called initializing the pointer.
2. Running out of data in READ DATA statements causes display of an error message and termination of the program.
3. A data terminator causes the program to leave a READ loop without evoking a run-time error.
4. Although it is possible to use a data terminator with a FOR-NEXT statement, it is not recommended. Use a WHILE-WEND instead.
5. An IF statement must be used to check if the current item contains the value of the data terminator. If so, do not print the value.

7.4 Section Review

1. BASIC saves 11 memory locations for arrays.
2. A DIMension statement reserves memory locations for arrays.
3. An out-of-range error means that not enough memory locations were reserved for the arrayed variable.
4. The contents of each array element is automatically initialized to 0.

7.5 Section Review

1. It is necessary to set HIGHEST equal to N(1) since we do not want to make any assumptions about the magnitude of the data. Assuming N(1) is the highest at the beginning is an acceptable starting point.
2. Generally N – 1 passes are required to sort N numbers using the bubble sort technique. For 25 numbers, 24 passes are required.
3. The TEMP variable is used to temporarily hold one of the numbers being swapped. (The extra memory location is required so that neither number is overwritten while being swapped.)
4. The standard deviation is 1.67.
5. A histogram is used to count the number of identical objects sampled from a large group of objects.

7.6 Section Review

1. An array is required in the Waveform Viewer so that the waveform samples may be accessed more than once. Translating the file directly to the screen would require accessing the file each time the waveform is zoomed. This could be very time consuming.
2. If the value read out of WAVBUFF is 0, the PSET coordinate is 148. If the value is 255, the PSET coordinate is 20.

7.7 Section Review

1. Bounds checking is the process of enforcing the proper index values at runtime.
2. If an illegal index value is used during runtime, the data pointed to by the index variables will not be valid.
3. Bounds checking can be performed on a two-dimensional array defined as:

```
10 DIM POINTS (4,7)
```

by

```
IF (((J > 0) AND (J < 5)) AND ((K > 0) AND (K < 8)))
     ACCESS TO POINTS(J, K)
```

Answers to Self-Test—Chapter 7

1. The sum of all rows, columns, and diagonals is 15.
2. The sequence of ROW and COL value is [0][1], [2][0], [1][2], [2][2], [1][1], [0][0], [1][0], [0][2], [2][1].
3. Line 160 checks the ROW subscript.
4. Line 180 is necessary to check the current position in the magic square to make sure it is 0. If it is not 0, the statements within the GOSUB determine the next location in the magic square to fill. Otherwise the current count of K is stored in the empty location.
5. The sums are all 65.
6. The sums are all 260. Yes, the PRINT statement should be modified to print each ROW using one line.
7. Additional statements can be added to the program to check if the number is even. A suggested method is

```
20 ODD = 0
40 WHILE NOT ODD
60   INPUT "Enter the size of the magic square ===> "; N
80   IF N / 2 = N \ 2 THEN ODD = 0 ELSE ODD = 1
90   IF NOT ODD THEN PRINT "PLEASE ENTER AN ODD NUMBER..."
100 WEND
```

8. The program does not produce magic squares for EVEN numbers.

Answers to Section Reviews—Chapter 8

8.1 Section Review

1. A string is any connected sequence of characters, words, or other elements.
2. User-specific answer.
3. The alphabetical order of the alphabet is preserved by the numerical order of the ASCII code.
4. The last four letters of the alphabet, ZYXW, will be displayed.
5. LEFT$(W$, N) causes the leftmost characters starting at N to be returned, while RIGHT$ (W$, N) causes the rightmost characters starting at N to be returned.
6. The display will be `nicalcations`.
7. Use either `10 PRINT STRING$(10,"+")`
   or `10 PRINT STRING$(10,43)`

8.2 Section Review

1. The complement of CHR$(N) is ASC(W$). It returns a numerical value that is the ASCII code for the first character of the string W$.
2. The value `6` will be displayed on the screen.
3. The number `6` will be displayed.

4. The display will be `6`.
5. The display will show the string `2020`.
6. Program 1 will return the number `23`. Program 2 will return the number `0`.

8.3 Section Review

1. `"Third statement"` would be displayed.
2. All string characters are represented by a number assigned by the ASCII code; it is these numbers that are compared in relational statements.
3. The string sorting program uses string variables and the numerical sorting program does not.
4. The sorted string data would be: 100, 35, Capacitor, Transistor.
5. The data treated as a string variable and are sorted by the ASCII code value, not the indicated numerical value. The ASCII code for a string of number characters is smaller than a string of alphabetical characters.
6. ```
   RightLeft
   LeftRight
   RightLeft
   ```
7. The SWAP statement is used to swap two variable values in memory without the need to have a TEMP variable.

8.4 Section Review

1. MID$ picks a single character by identifying the position in the string and then specifying a length of 1. For example,

   ```
   MID$("TEST",3,1) will return the "S".
   ```
2. Line 60 is needed to PRINT the last character of the last name.
3. Uppercase can be converted to lowercase by adding 32 to the ASCII code.
4. The numbers 0–9 each have unique representations; therefore, we cannot speak of numbers in terms of uppercase or lowercase. If 32 is added or subtracted from a number's ASCII code, the results no longer represent the original numeric values 0 through 9.
5. Yes, the IF statements can be combined, although the readability of the program will suffer as a result. Keep statements as simple as possible.

8.5 Section Review

1. If the user enters "ECHO.WAV", the resulting F$ will be "ECHO.WAV.WAV".
2. A sequence of WAV files may be displayed using information stored in a two-dimensional string array by loading one string at a time into F$ and calling the display subroutine.

8.6 Section Review

1. Uppercase letters and lowercase letters are treated differently because each character has a unique ASCII code.
2. If lowercase letters are converted to uppercase when sorting strings, all data is sorted into alphabetical order regardless of the case of the characters.

Answers to Self-Test—Chapter 8

1. There are six string variables: T$, V$, M$, S$, L$, and E$. There are seven numeric variables: N, Q, S, H, D, V, and FL.
2. Any input other than an N or n will cause the loop block to repeat.
   ```

3. The purpose of line 3010 is to assign a string of 20 *s to the string variable S$.
4. Lines 3020 and 3040 cause 40 *s to be displayed.
5. Line 5060 assigns 60 string characters whose ASCII code is 95 (the "_").
6. Line 11050 determines whether strings are to be exchanged. This is a bubble sort.
7. The switch variable FL is used to indicate if the sorting is complete. If a switch occurs, FL is set to 1; it is reset every time a pass through the list is completed. FL is called a flag, and it has only two conditions: 0 or 1, which can be thought of as a flag being either down or up.
8. Line 5100 assigns a value to the variable H that is equal to the length of string T$(V). From this value, the distance D is computed on line 5110 so that the component type will appear centered in its column. This is accomplished in conjunction with the TAB(D) of line 5120.
9. Suggested program lines are

```
5112 H = LEN(M$(V))
5114 A = INT(50-H/2)
```

The required TAB change is

```
5120 PRINT TAB(D); T$(V)........TAB(A);M$(V)
```

Answers to Section Reviews—Chapter 9

9.1 Section Review

1. The most common coordinate system is the Cartesian coordinate system.
2. The *X*-axis is used as the independent variable, and the *Y*-axis is used as the dependent variable.
3. The four regions of this system are called quadrants. The first quadrant: *X* and *Y* positive. The second quadrant: *X* negative, *Y* positive. The third quadrant: *X* and *Y* negative. The fourth quadrant: *X* positive, *Y* negative.

9.2 Section Review

1. Computer graphics are used to display pictures, graphs, and other information, usually not in the form of text or numbers.
2. The origin is at the upper left-hand corner. The *X*-axis is positive going to the right horizontally, while the *Y*-axis is positive going down vertically.
3. A pixel is a picture element, the smallest area that can be controlled on a given graphics screen.

9.3 Section Review

1. You can create a line with the PSET *(X,Y)* command in a FOR-NEXT loop, or with the LINE $(X_1, Y_1) - (X_2, Y_2)$ command.
2. You can create a rectangle by using four line commands, one for each side of the rectangle.
3. You can create an area-filled rectangle by using two FOR-NEXT loops with a PSET *(X,Y)* command, or by using one FOR-NEXT loop with a LINE command.

9.4 Section Review

1. The two constants set the value of the maximum screen width and the thickness of the bar.
2. Constants were used to make modification of the program easier.
3. The input and output loops would need to loop five times, and the CASE statement would need one more program line to set the values of *Y*1 and *Y*2 for the fifth bar.

9.5 Section Review

1. Scaling is a process that uses numerical methods to ensure that all of the required data appears on the graphics screen and utilizes the full pixel capability.
2. Coordinate transformation is the process of using numerical methods to cause the origin of the coordinate system to appear at any desired place on the graphics screen.
3. The values of the scaling factors are determined by the number of horizontal and vertical pixels, and the minimum and maximum values of *X* and *Y*.
4. The coordinate transformation values are determined by the horizontal and vertical scaling factors, and the minimum value of *X* and the maximum value of *Y*.

9.6 Section Review

1. The trigonometric functions in BASIC are the sine, cosine, tangent, and arctangent.
2. BASIC computes the trigonometric functions in radians. To convert, use
   Degrees = (180/pi) (radians)
   Radians = (pi/180) (degrees)
3. Program 9.13 would produce a horizontal line 360 pixels long displayed across the top of the graphics screen. The value of the sine function goes from 0 to 1 to 0 to –1. Since negative numbers cannot be displayed directly on the graphics screen, this represents a change of only one pixel.
4. Use A = P * SIN(2 * R * N + T), where P = maximum peak value (amplitude), R = radians, N = number of cycles displayed, and T = the phase.

9.7 Section Review

1. The two major requirements are a color monitor and the required hardware.
2. A color monitor has three different phosphors which make it capable of producing a wide variety of colors; a monochrome monitor has only one phosphor, which allows it to produce only one color.
3. The three basic modes are text, medium-resolution graphics, and high-resolution graphics.
4. The text, background, and border can display color in the text mode. The text and border have one of sixteen different colors, while the background has one of eight.
5. There are two text modes: 80 × 25 and 40 × 25. The last text line does not scroll up.
6. Foreground colors are selected by first specifying one of two palettes with the COLOR command. Thereafter, one of three colors may be selected by a graphic command that causes a display. One background and three different foreground colors can appear at the same time.
7. Only two colors, black and white, are available for high-resolution graphics.

9.8 Section Review

1. The horizontal and vertical tick marks are drawn by turning four or five pixels on in the same row or column, at regular intervals on the axis.
2. The arrowhead is drawn by lines 1180 and 1190, which turn on two pixels near the top of the arrow.
3. When an arrow is moved to the right or the left it is first erased, then redrawn at the *X* coordinate specified by the user.
4. The entire waveform is drawn by lines 720 through 830.

9.9 Section Review

1. PRINT statements are useful when troubleshooting a graphical application because they can report on the progress of the calculations (coordinates, slopes, pixel values).
2. Output redirection is a process that diverts data from the display to a file.

Answers to Self-Test—Chapter 9

1. Less than one cycle would appear. Program line 3060 has no restrictions on the value of N.
2. The phase angles are entered in radians.
3. Different values of phase angles wil! cause the sine wave display to begin at the indicated phase shift.
4. The scaling factor is used to cause one cycle to appear when 640 pixels are used.
5. This moves the *X*-axis to the center of the graphic screen (assuming there are 200 pixels in the vertical direction).
6. Horizontal = 640, vertical = 200. These can be assumed from program line 3040, and from program line 3070 (100 – A).
7. a. `3060 A = .5 * P * SIN(R * N + T)`
   b. `3060 A = P * SIN(R * N + PI + T)`
   c. `3060 A = P * SIN(2 * R * N + T)`

Answers to Section Reviews—Chapter 10

10.1 Section Review

1. No, the BASIC source code must be read by the interpreter to be executed.
2. The .EXE and .COM extensions are reserved for executable files.
3. Yes, DATA.BAS can be used as a name for a data file although it is not recommended because it does not describe what the file contains.
4. A data file can be changed without changing the BASIC source code.
5. Some differences between binary and text formats are
   a. A text format is printable, a binary format is not.
   b. Numbers are stored efficiently in binary. Numbers are stored as ASCII characters in text format.

10.2 Section Review

1. `100 OPEN "NAMES.LST" FOR OUTPUT AS #1`
2. BASIC will automatically close files at the end of execution. It is recommended that the programmer always close any files opened during the execution.
3. The statement will retrieve data from file #1 and store the contents in variables A and B.
4. The file "NUMS.DAT" will contain

```
A   7
"A",7
```

10.3 Section Review

1. The string variable V$ can be used to open an output file by the following statements:

```
100 INPUT "Enter the file name ==>"; V$
110 OPEN V$ FOR OUTPUT AS #1
```

2. The WHILE-WEND loop inputs data file #1 and then prints it to file #2 until the end of file #1 is reached.
3. To open the data file TEST.DAT on drive B: and add additional information to it requires a statement similar to the following:

```
100 OPEN "B:\TEST.DAT" FOR APPEND AS FILE #1
```

4. The ON-ERROR statement is used to catch errors that occur during execution of a program.
5. The difference between RESUME NEXT and RESUME 20 in Program 10.13 is the location at which the program will resume after an error. The RESUME NEXT causes execution to begin on the next statement, whereas the RESUME 20 will cause the program to begin on line 20.

10.4 Section Review

1. The difference between INPUT #1, A$ and LINE INPUT #1, A$ is that the LINE keyword allows an entire line of text, up to the carriage return, to be read, including commas. The plain INPUT statement only reads string data up to the first comma encountered.
2. Program 10.15 determines when 22 lines have been displayed by the use of the MOD function.
3. The ASC and CHR$ functions are used in Program 10.16 because it is necessary to modify the numerical ASCII code of a character being encrypted.
4. If the initial value of C$ equals "X", the contents of C and C$ after the subroutine in Program 10.16 executes are C = 67 and C$ = "C".
5. The first GET statement (line 50) is needed in Program 10.17 to initialize the EOF value to indicate if data exists in the file before executing the WHILE-WEND loop.
6. The LEN parameter needs to be 17 in Program 10.17 to accommodate the carriage return and line feed codes located at the end of each record.

10.5 Section Review

1. No, parameters are two or four locations wide.
2. The first array element that contains a sample is WAVBUFF(44).
3. Answer depends on user preference.

10.6 Section Review

1. The error codes associated with file operations (from Table 10.2) are 53, 55, 58, 61, 62, 70, and 71. These values are important because, without them, we have no way of determining that a file operation was successful.
2. One difference between a text file and a binary file is the way in which the contents of the files are interpreted.

Answers to Self-Test—Chapter 10

1. Twenty-five names and numbers may be stored in PHONES.DAT.
2. If the PHONES.DAT file does not exist, a warning message is displayed and the program exits because it resumes on the END statement.
3. The search subroutine works by using a WHILE-WEND loop to cycle through the names in the string array, comparing each one to N$. The names are compared in a bottom-up (last name first) direction.
4. No, the variable M is only incremented when a name match occurs.
5. The phone numbers are stored as characters in the data file.
6. The phone numbers are stored in memory as numbers while the program is running.

APPENDIX A: ASCII Character Set

Character*	Code	Character	Code	Character	Code	Character	Code
NUL	0	blank	32	@	64	‘	96
SOH	1	!	33	A	65	a	97
STX	2	“	34	B	66	b	98
ETX	3	#	35	C	67	c	99
EOT	4	$	36	D	68	d	100
ENQ	5	%	37	E	69	e	101
ACK	6	&	38	F	70	f	102
BEL	7	‘	39	G	71	g	103
BS	8	(	40	H	72	h	104
HT	9	)	41	I	73	i	105
LF	10	*	42	J	74	j	106
VT	11	+	43	K	75	k	107
FF	12	,	44	L	76	l	108
CR	13	–	45	M	77	m	109
SO	14	.	46	N	78	n	110
SI	15	/	47	O	79	o	111
DLE	16	0	48	P	80	p	112
DC1	17	1	49	Q	81	q	113
DC2	18	2	50	R	82	r	114
DC3	19	3	51	S	83	s	115
DC4	20	4	52	T	84	t	116
NAK	21	5	53	U	85	u	117
SYN	22	6	54	V	86	v	118
ETB	23	7	55	W	87	w	119
CAN	24	8	56	X	88	x	120
EM	25	9	57	Y	89	y	121
SUB	26	:	58	Z	90	z	122
ESC	27	;	59	[	91	{	123
FS	28	<	60	\	92	|	124
GS	29	=	61	]	93	}	125
RS	30	>	62	↑	94	-	126
US	31	?	63	_	95	DEL	127

*These 32 characters (code numbers 0 through 31) are known as **control characters.**

APPENDIX B: An Introduction to Visual BASIC

What Is Visual BASIC?

Visual BASIC is Microsoft's version of the BASIC programming language adapted for use in the Windows environment. Like Visual C/C++, Visual BASIC is also an object-oriented programming language. This requires a change in thinking about how a program is structured, as well as a change in how a program is written.

Procedural Versus Event-Driven

In a procedural programming environment, such as QBASIC, the main program calls subroutines in a particular order and determines when the user is allowed to enter data or commands. In an event-driven environment, subroutines are called as needed to handle events that occur during execution, such as the user clicking on a "Convert" button to perform a conversion.

Event-driven programs utilize objects, such as the display window shown during execution (the user interface). The programmer adjusts the properties of the object as needed by the application. For example, some of the properties associated with a window are the name displayed in the title bar, the number and type of menu options, the font style used to display text, and its color.

After setting the properties, the code associated with the object is written.

In summary, the steps in writing a Visual BASIC program are as follows:

1. Design the user interface.
2. Set all properties.
3. Write the event-handling code.

Designing the User Interface

A Visual BASIC application typically uses one or more forms to provide the graphical interface to the user. A form is a fancy name for a window displayed during execution. Figure B.1 shows a simple form in development. The form contains a number of controls, predefined objects that add functionality to the form.

The three controls in Figure B.1 called Text1, Text2, and Command1. In reality, these three names refer to the objects associated with each control.

Setting Properties

The properties of the controls placed on a form (and the form's own properties), must be adjusted as part of the programming process. In Figure B.1 some of the Form1 properties

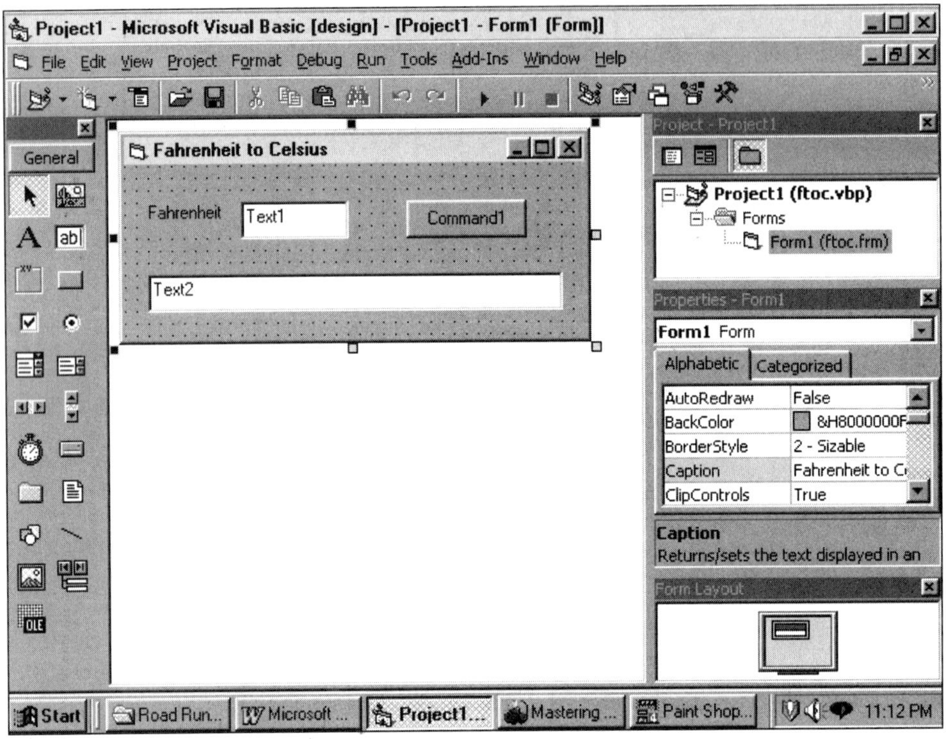

Figure B.1 Visual BASIC form under development

are shown. Note in particular the "Caption" property. This is where the name in the title bar is entered.

Double-clicking on a control brings up the property list associated with its object. As shown in Figure B.2, the label on the Command1 button has been set to "Convert." Each control must have its properties adjusted before continuing.

Writing the Code

Each control placed on the form may have one or more subroutines associated with it, depending on the features desired by the programmer. For example, a button control may have event-handling subroutines for mouse-click and mouse-over events.

When a control is placed onto a form, a stub procedure is created for it whose name is based on the type of event specified. For example, clicking the "Convert" button will activate its Command1_Click() procedure. The Visual BASIC code shown here uses the Command1_Click() procedure to convert the Fahrenheit input temperature (Text1.Text) into Celsius.

```
Private Sub Command1_Click()
  Dim Cel As Single
  On Error GoTo Notnum
  Cel = (Text1.Text - 32) * 5 / 9
```

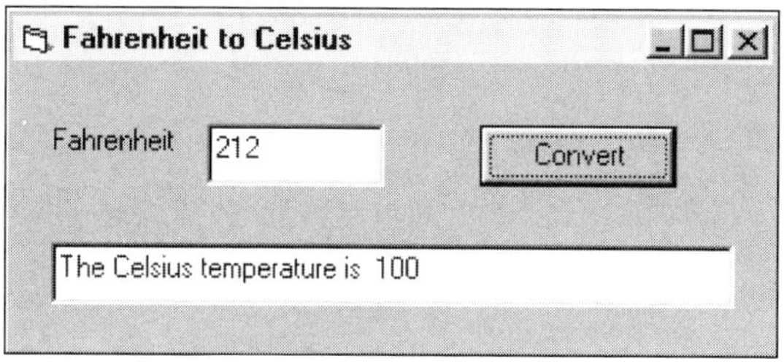

Figure B.2 Sample execution

```
  Text2.Text = "The Celsius temperature is " + Str(Cel)
  Exit Sub
Notnum:
  If Err.Number = 13 Then
    Text2.Text = "Cannot convert!"
  End If
End Sub
```

Notice that Text2.Text is assigned the value of the result. This causes the output to appear in the Text2 box. Also note that error handling is provided to guarantee that the user enters a valid number in the Text1 box.

The only way that Command1_Click() gets called is if the user clicks on the "Convert" button. This is the essence of event-driven programming.

Creating an Executable File

The Make option under the File menu is used to make an executable file from your Visual BASIC project. A sample execution of the temperature conversion application (FTOC.EXE on the companion disk) is shown in Figure B.2.

The user enters a Fahrenheit temperature in the Text1 box (a default value of 212 is placed in the box at startup). After clicking "Convert," the result, or an error message, is displayed in the Text2 box.

Summary

As you can see, programming in Visual BASIC is significantly different from the procedural environment. Even so, once you have learned simple methods of inputting and outputting data and handling errors, it should be possible to translate a working program from QBASIC into Visual BASIC with a minimum of difficulty.

Index